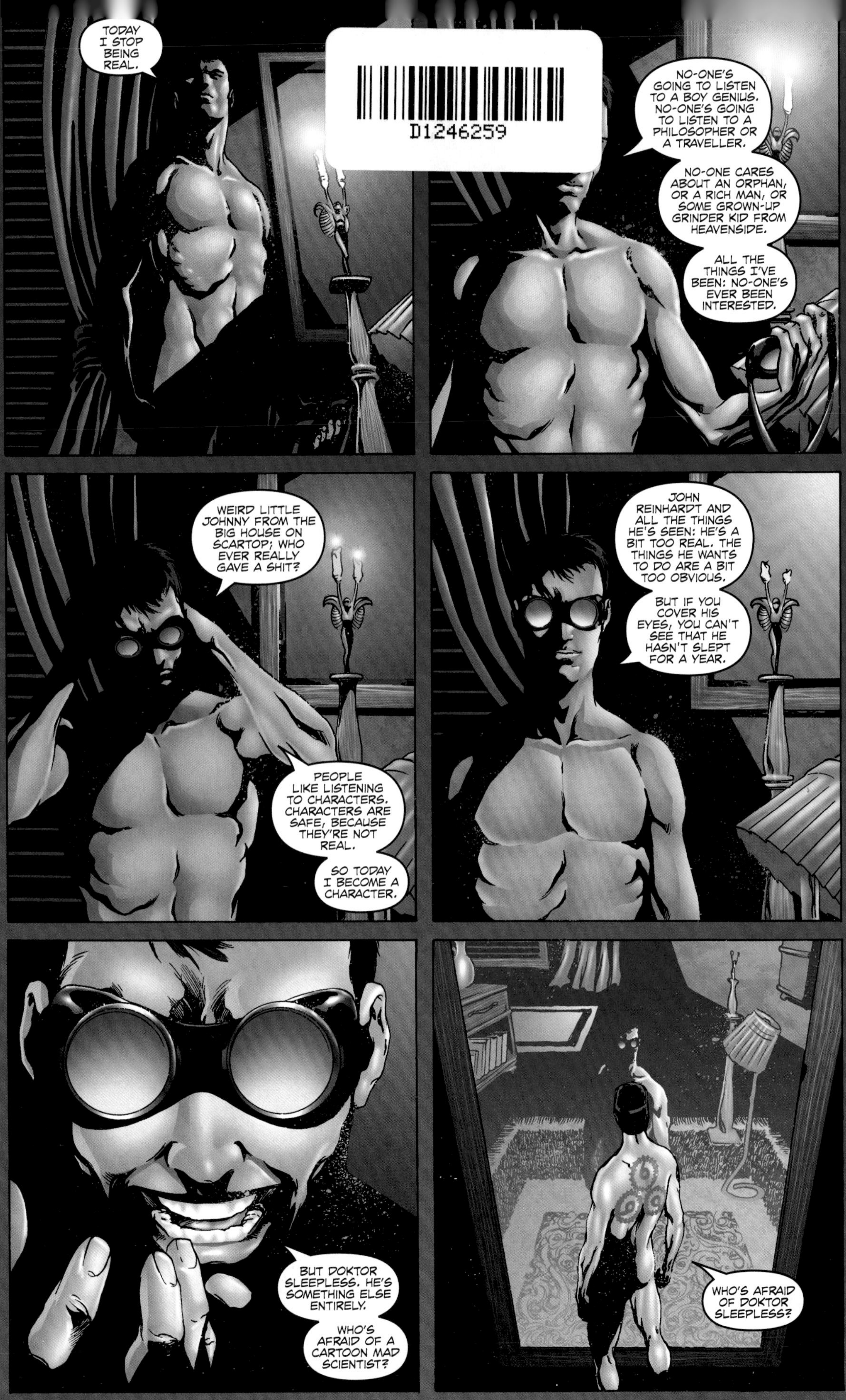
TODAY I STOP BEING REAL.
NO-ONE'S GOING TO LISTEN TO A BOY GENIUS. NO-ONE'S GOING TO LISTEN TO A PHILOSOPHER OR A TRAVELLER.
NO-ONE CARES ABOUT AN ORPHAN, OR A RICH MAN, OR SOME GROWN-UP GRINDER KID FROM HEAVENSIDE.
ALL THE THINGS I'VE BEEN: NO-ONE'S EVER BEEN INTERESTED.
WEIRD LITTLE JOHNNY FROM THE BIG HOUSE ON SCARTOP; WHO EVER REALLY GAVE A SHIT?
PEOPLE LIKE LISTENING TO CHARACTERS. CHARACTERS ARE SAFE, BECAUSE THEY'RE NOT REAL.
SO TODAY I BECOME A CHARACTER.
JOHN REINHARDT AND ALL THE THINGS HE'S SEEN: HE'S A BIT TOO REAL. THE THINGS HE WANTS TO DO ARE A BIT TOO OBVIOUS.
BUT IF YOU COVER HIS EYES, YOU CAN'T SEE THAT HE HASN'T SLEPT FOR A YEAR.
BUT DOKTOR SLEEPLESS. HE'S SOMETHING ELSE ENTIRELY.
WHO'S AFRAID OF A CARTOON MAD SCIENTIST?
WHO'S AFRAID OF DOKTOR SLEEPLESS?

THAT'S MUSLIMGAUZE REMIXED BY JAPANESE RAPE DIVISION, AND I'VE GOT ABOUT HALF A GIG MORE OF THAT TO PLAY ON MY RADIO SHOW TOMORROW NIGHT.

HEAVEN'S PIRATES, 98.3FM-- THE COPS HAVEN'T SHUT ME DOWN YET!

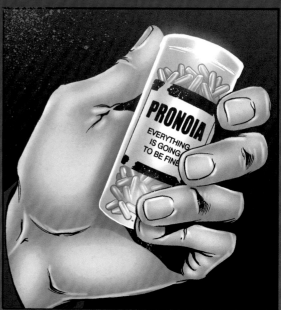

PRONOIA

EVERYTHING IS GOING TO BE FINE

YOU MOVE AROUND A LOT.

PART ONE

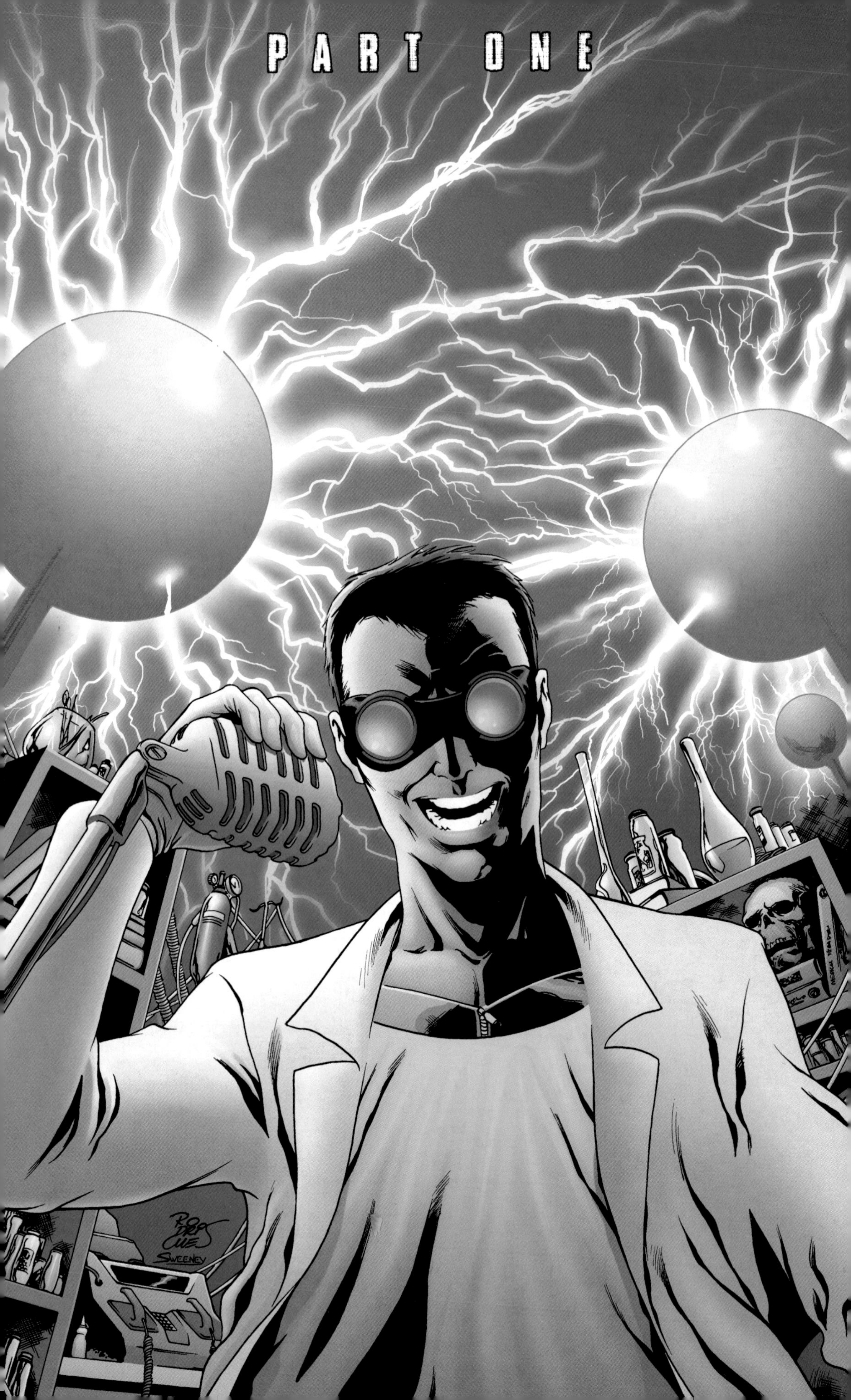
SWEENEY

WARREN ELLIS
story

IVAN RODRIGUEZ
artwork

GREG WALLER
parts 1,4-8, cover
color

ANDREW DALHOUSE
parts 2,3, cover gallery
color

MARK SWEENEY
chapter breaks,
cover gallery
color

FELIPE MASSAFERA
backmatter art

IVAN RODRIGUEZ
JACEN BURROWS
JUAN JOSE RYP
RAULO CACERES
cover gallery art

WILLIAM CHRISTENSEN
editor-in-chief

MARK SEIFERT
creative director

ARIANA OSBORNE
chief mechanic

DAVID MARKS
marketing director

DOKTOR SLEEPLESS VOLUME ONE: ENGINES OF DESIRE. Sept 2008.
Published by Avatar Press, Inc., 515 N. Century Blvd. Rantoul, IL
61866. ©2008 Avatar Press, Inc. Doktor Sleepless and all related
properties TM & ©2008 Warren Ellis. All characters as depicted in
this story are over the age of 18. The stories, characters, and
institutions mentioned in this magazine are entirely fictional.

www.doktorsleepless.com
www.avatarpress.com

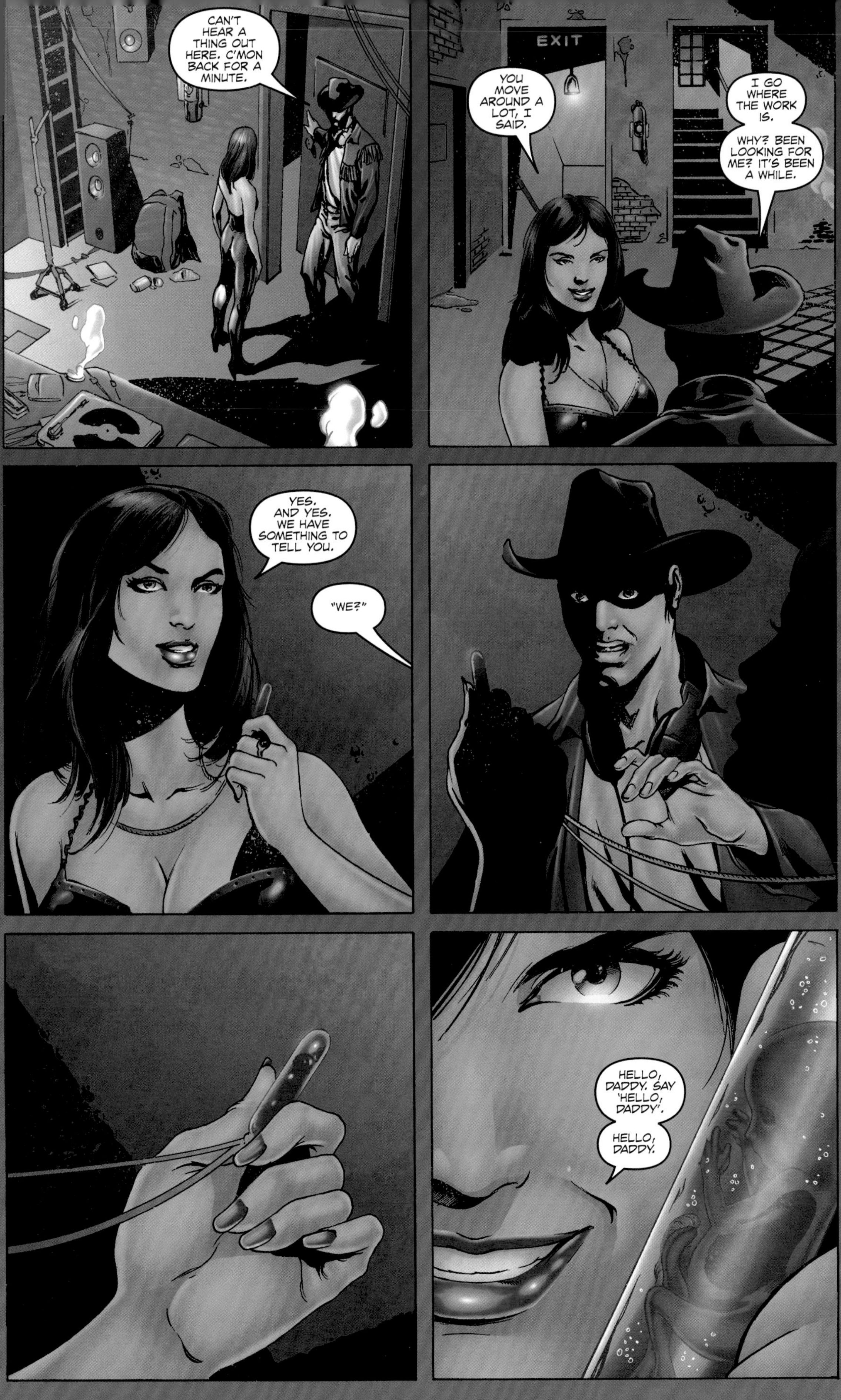
CAN'T HEAR A THING OUT HERE. C'MON BACK FOR A MINUTE.
EXIT
YOU MOVE AROUND A LOT, I SAID.
I GO WHERE THE WORK IS.
WHY? BEEN LOOKING FOR ME? IT'S BEEN A WHILE.
YES. AND YES. WE HAVE SOMETHING TO TELL YOU.
"WE?"
HELLO, DADDY. SAY 'HELLO, DADDY'.
HELLO, DADDY.

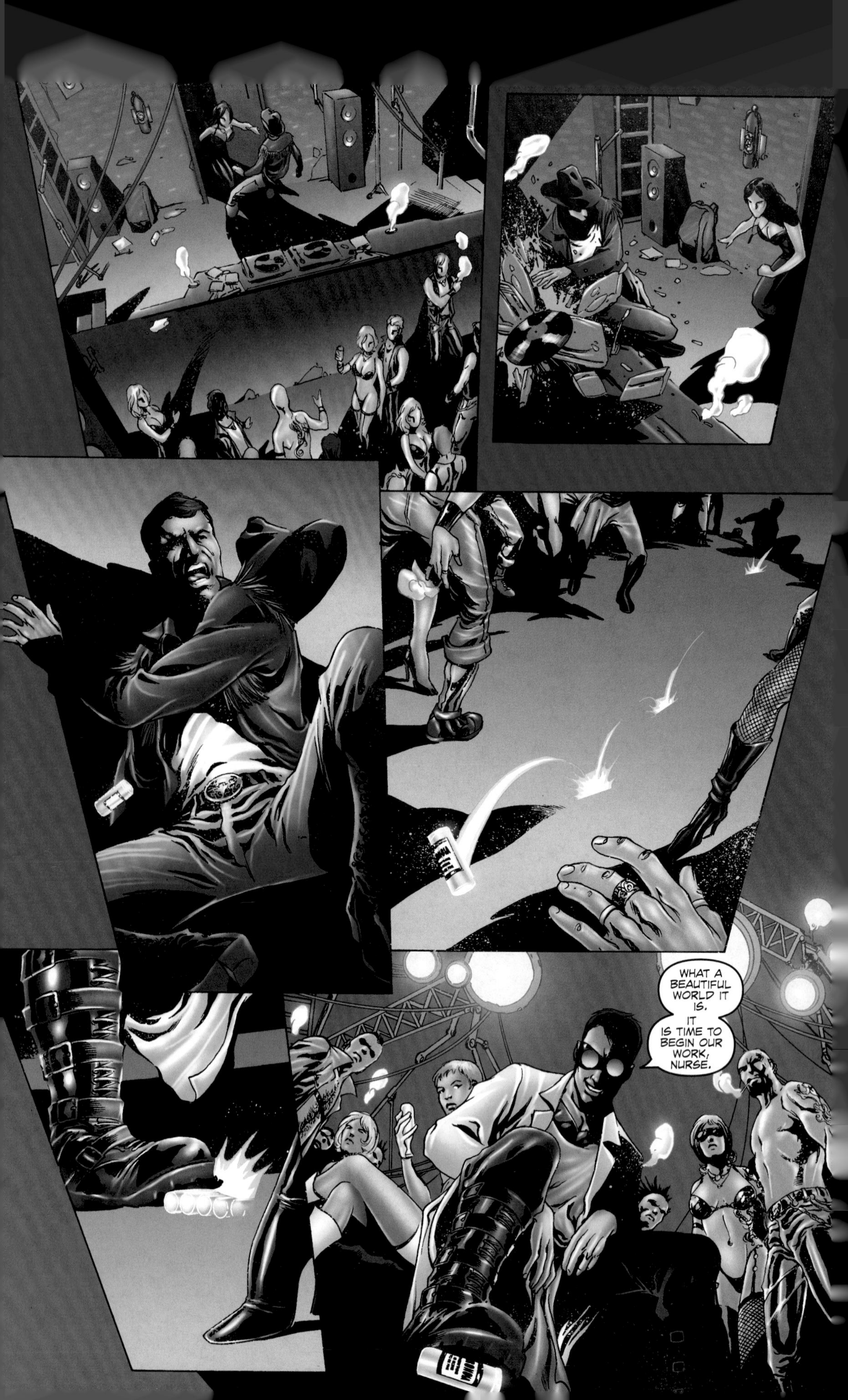
WHAT A BEAUTIFUL WORLD IT IS.
IT IS TIME TO BEGIN OUR WORK, NURSE.

DOKTOR SLEEPLESS

And THE RETURN TO SCARTOP MOUNTAIN

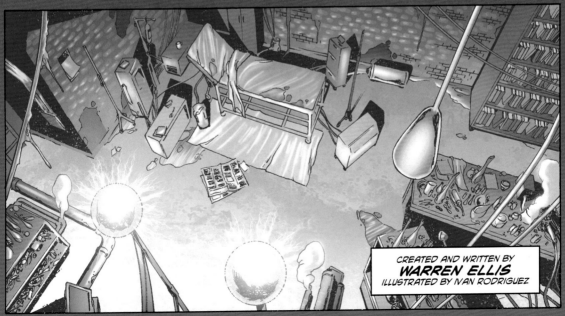

CREATED AND WRITTEN BY
WARREN ELLIS
ILLUSTRATED BY IVAN RODRIGUEZ

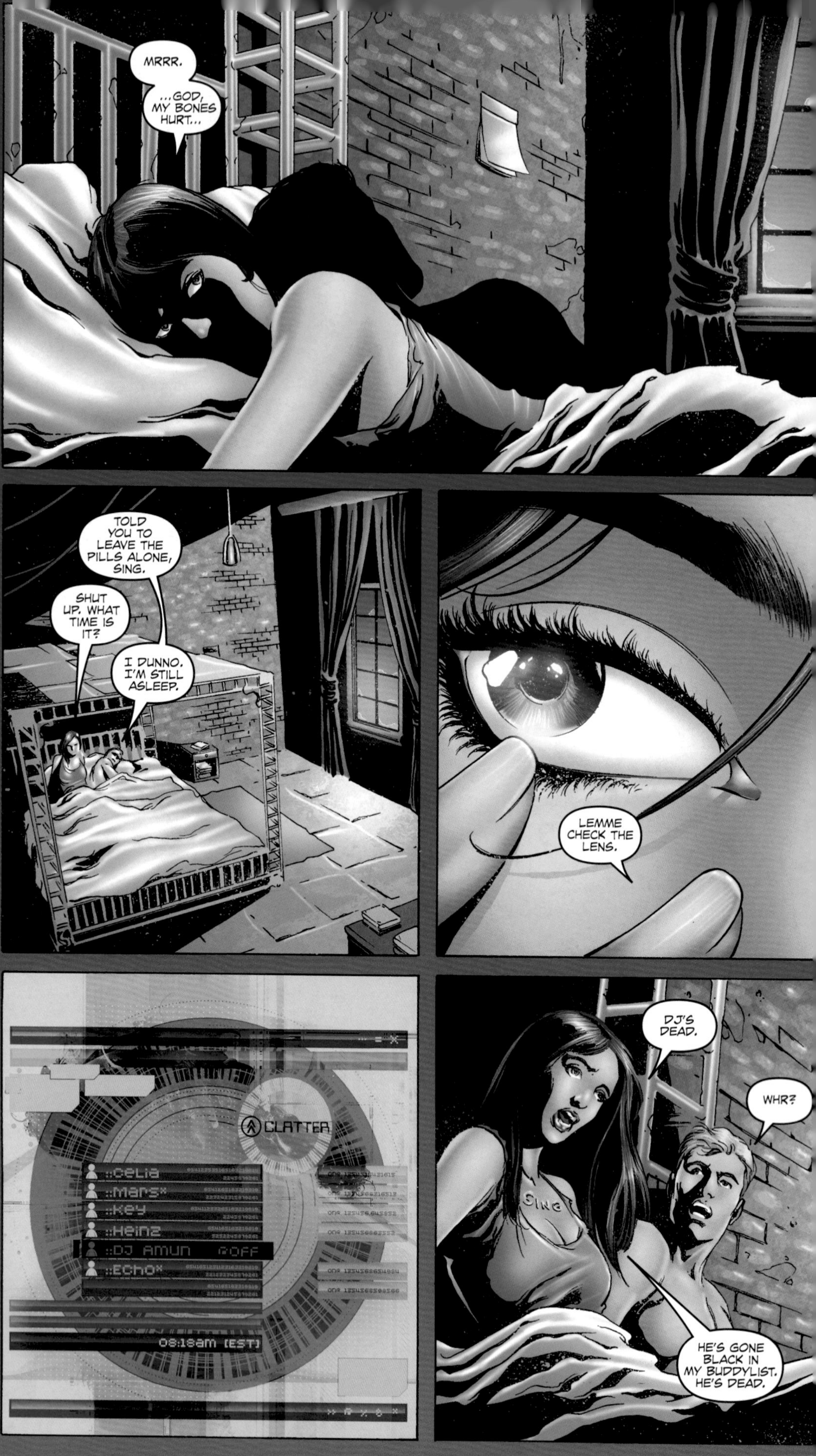
MRRR.
...GOD, MY BONES HURT...
TOLD YOU TO LEAVE THE PILLS ALONE, SING.
SHUT UP. WHAT TIME IS IT?
I DUNNO. I'M STILL ASLEEP.
LEMME CHECK THE LENS.
CLATTER
::Celia
::Mars×
::Key
::Heinz
::DJ Amun
OFF
::Echo×
08:18am [EST]
DJ'S DEAD.
WHR?
SING
HE'S GONE BLACK IN MY BUDDYLIST. HE'S DEAD.

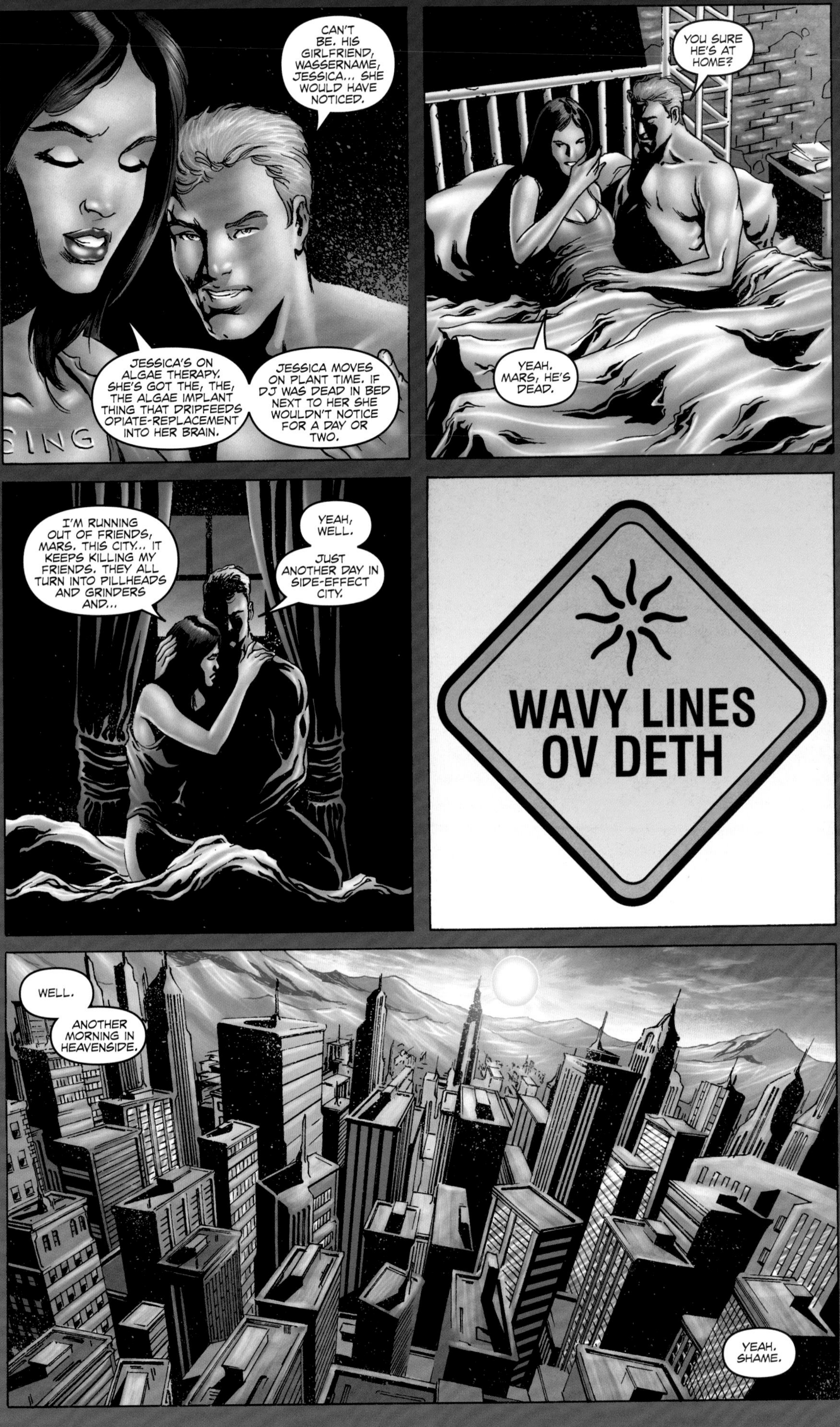
CAN'T BE. HIS GIRLFRIEND, WASSERNAME, JESSICA... SHE WOULD HAVE NOTICED.
JESSICA'S ON ALGAE THERAPY. SHE'S GOT THE, THE, THE ALGAE IMPLANT THING THAT DRIPFEEDS OPIATE-REPLACEMENT INTO HER BRAIN.
JESSICA MOVES ON PLANT TIME. IF DJ WAS DEAD IN BED NEXT TO HER SHE WOULDN'T NOTICE FOR A DAY OR TWO.
YOU SURE HE'S AT HOME?
YEAH. MARS, HE'S DEAD.
I'M RUNNING OUT OF FRIENDS, MARS. THIS CITY... IT KEEPS KILLING MY FRIENDS. THEY ALL TURN INTO PILLHEADS AND GRINDERS AND...
YEAH, WELL.
JUST ANOTHER DAY IN SIDE-EFFECT CITY.
WAVY LINES OV DETH
WELL.
ANOTHER MORNING IN HEAVENSIDE.
YEAH. SHAME.

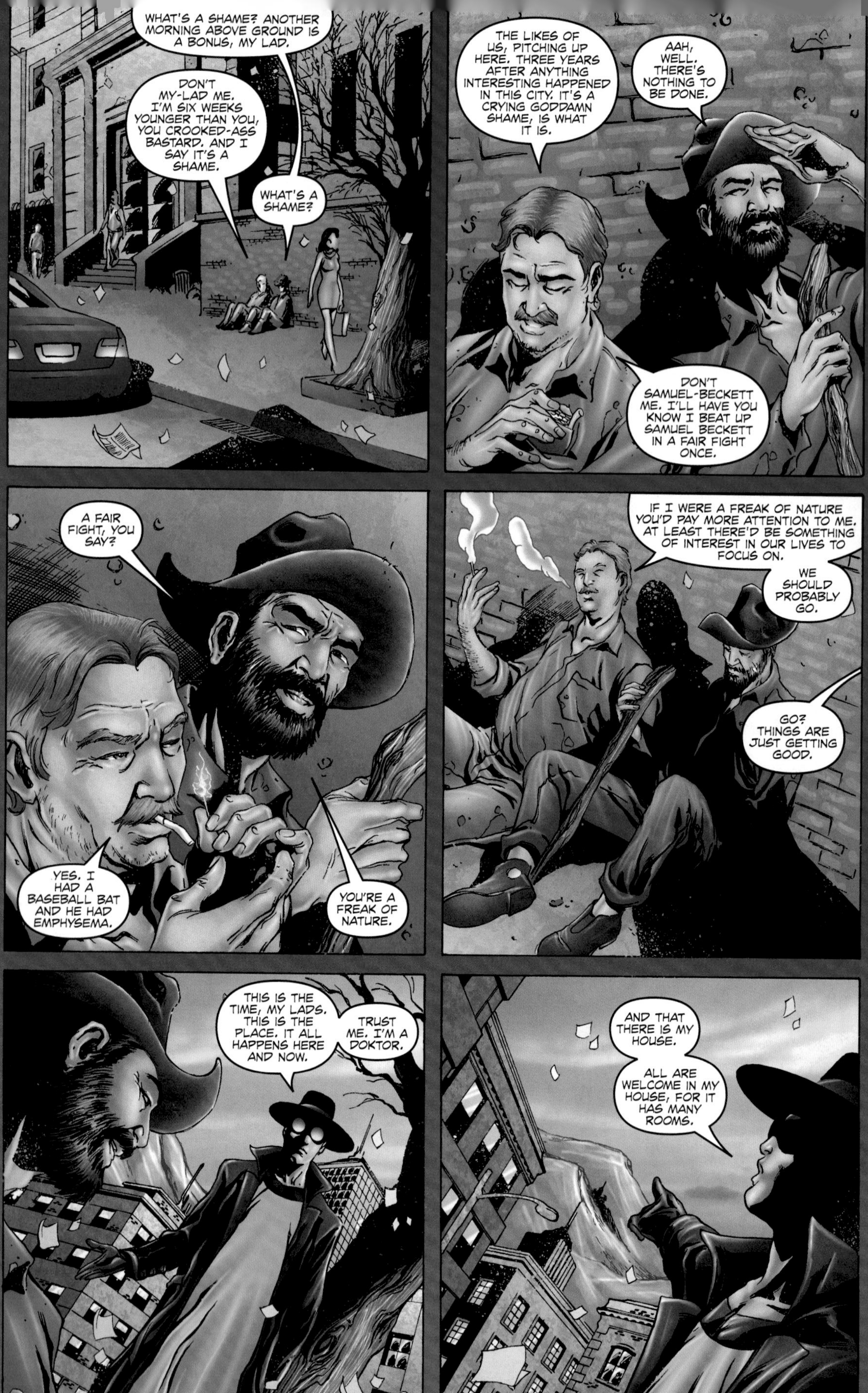
WHAT'S A SHAME? ANOTHER MORNING ABOVE GROUND IS A BONUS, MY LAD.
DON'T MY-LAD ME. I'M SIX WEEKS YOUNGER THAN YOU, YOU CROOKED-ASS BASTARD. AND I SAY IT'S A SHAME.
WHAT'S A SHAME?
THE LIKES OF US, PITCHING UP HERE. THREE YEARS AFTER ANYTHING INTERESTING HAPPENED IN THIS CITY. IT'S A CRYING GODDAMN SHAME, IS WHAT IT IS.
AAH, WELL. THERE'S NOTHING TO BE DONE.
DON'T SAMUEL-BECKETT ME. I'LL HAVE YOU KNOW I BEAT UP SAMUEL BECKETT IN A FAIR FIGHT ONCE.
A FAIR FIGHT, YOU SAY?
YES. I HAD A BASEBALL BAT AND HE HAD EMPHYSEMA.
YOU'RE A FREAK OF NATURE.
IF I WERE A FREAK OF NATURE YOU'D PAY MORE ATTENTION TO ME. AT LEAST THERE'D BE SOMETHING OF INTEREST IN OUR LIVES TO FOCUS ON.
WE SHOULD PROBABLY GO.
GO? THINGS ARE JUST GETTING GOOD.
THIS IS THE TIME, MY LADS. THIS IS THE PLACE. IT ALL HAPPENS HERE AND NOW.
TRUST ME. I'M A DOKTOR.
AND THAT THERE IS MY HOUSE.
ALL ARE WELCOME IN MY HOUSE, FOR IT HAS MANY ROOMS.

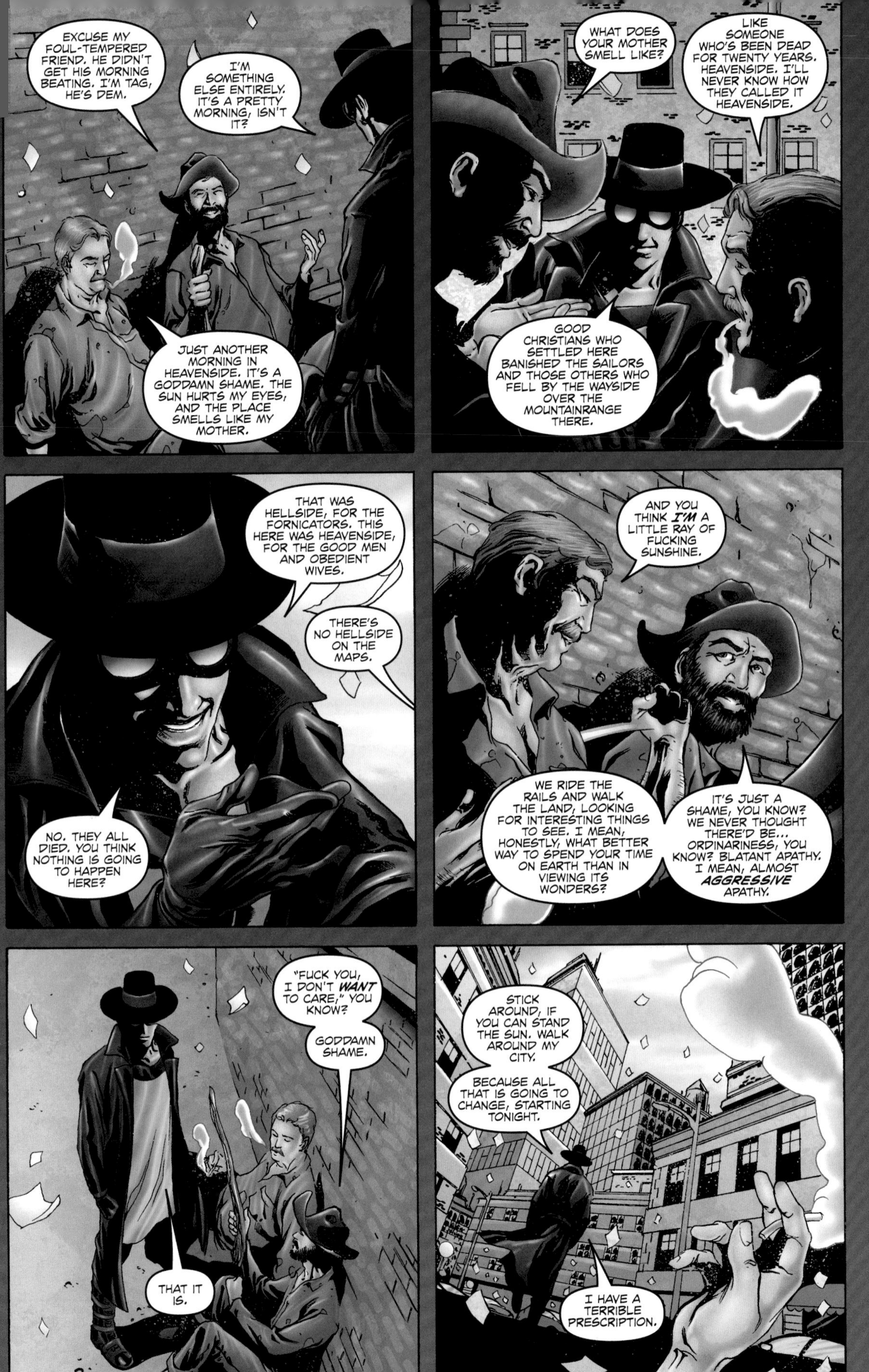
EXCUSE MY FOUL-TEMPERED FRIEND. HE DIDN'T GET HIS MORNING BEATING. I'M TAG, HE'S DEM.
I'M SOMETHING ELSE ENTIRELY. IT'S A PRETTY MORNING, ISN'T IT?
JUST ANOTHER MORNING IN HEAVENSIDE. IT'S A GODDAMN SHAME. THE SUN HURTS MY EYES, AND THE PLACE SMELLS LIKE MY MOTHER.
WHAT DOES YOUR MOTHER SMELL LIKE?
LIKE SOMEONE WHO'S BEEN DEAD FOR TWENTY YEARS. HEAVENSIDE. I'LL NEVER KNOW HOW THEY CALLED IT HEAVENSIDE.
GOOD CHRISTIANS WHO SETTLED HERE BANISHED THE SAILORS AND THOSE OTHERS WHO FELL BY THE WAYSIDE OVER THE MOUNTAINRANGE THERE.
THAT WAS HELLSIDE, FOR THE FORNICATORS. THIS HERE WAS HEAVENSIDE, FOR THE GOOD MEN AND OBEDIENT WIVES.
THERE'S NO HELLSIDE ON THE MAPS.
NO. THEY ALL DIED. YOU THINK NOTHING IS GOING TO HAPPEN HERE?
AND YOU THINK *I'M* A LITTLE RAY OF FUCKING SUNSHINE.
WE RIDE THE RAILS AND WALK THE LAND, LOOKING FOR INTERESTING THINGS TO SEE. I MEAN, HONESTLY, WHAT BETTER WAY TO SPEND YOUR TIME ON EARTH THAN IN VIEWING ITS WONDERS?
IT'S JUST A SHAME, YOU KNOW? WE NEVER THOUGHT THERE'D BE... ORDINARINESS, YOU KNOW? BLATANT APATHY. I MEAN, ALMOST ***AGGRESSIVE*** APATHY.
"FUCK YOU, I DON'T ***WANT*** TO CARE," YOU KNOW?
GODDAMN SHAME.
THAT IT IS.
STICK AROUND, IF YOU CAN STAND THE SUN. WALK AROUND MY CITY.
BECAUSE ALL THAT IS GOING TO CHANGE, STARTING TONIGHT.
I HAVE A TERRIBLE PRESCRIPTION.

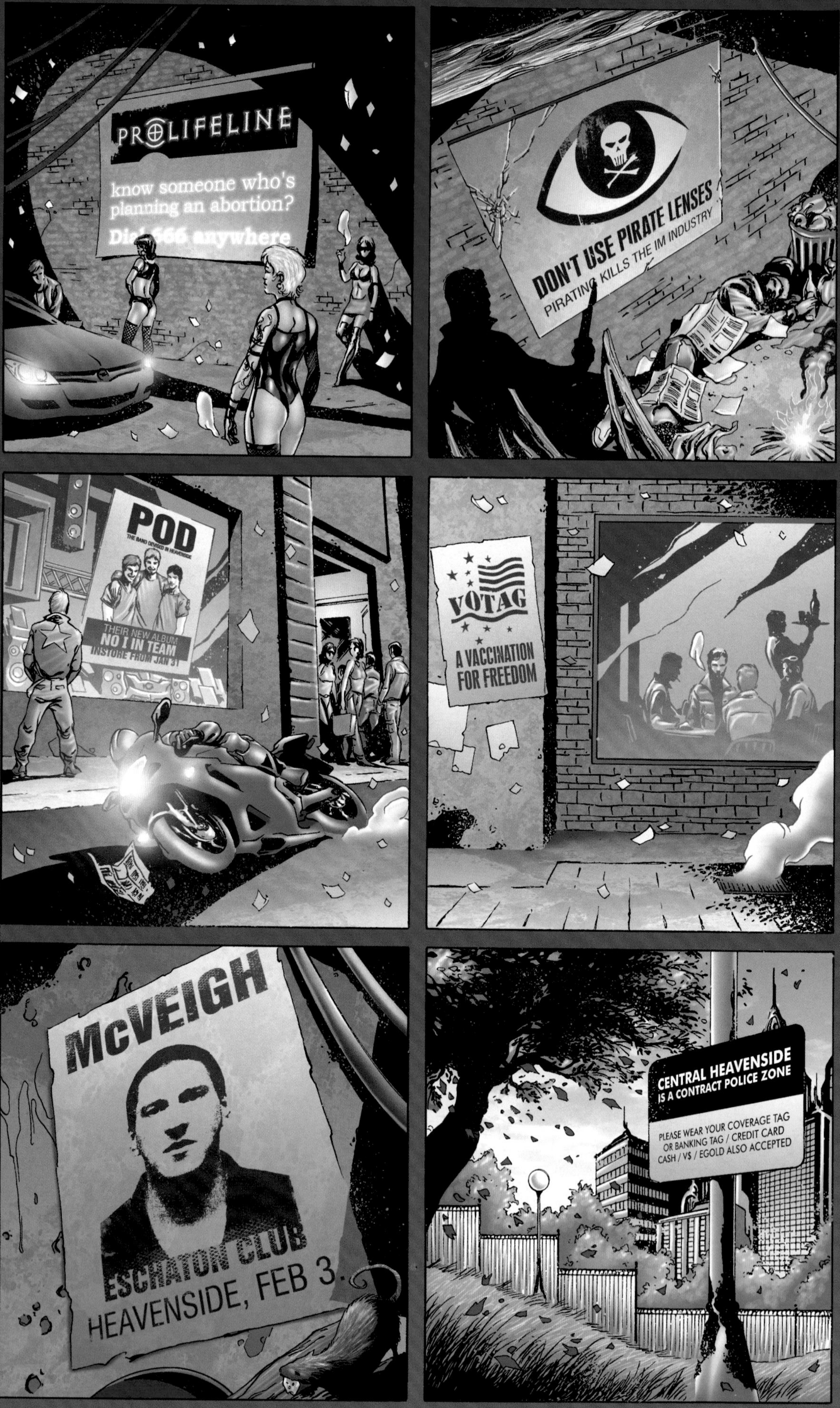
PROLIFELINE
know someone who's planning an abortion?
anywhere
DON'T USE PIRATE LENSES
PIRATING KILLS THE IM INDUSTRY
POD
THE BAND DEVISED IN HEAVENSIDE
THEIR NEW ALBUM
NO I IN TEAM
INSTORE FROM JAN 31
VOTAG
A VACCINATION FOR FREEDOM
McVEIGH
ESCHATON CLUB
HEAVENSIDE, FEB 3
CENTRAL HEAVENSIDE IS A CONTRACT POLICE ZONE
PLEASE WEAR YOUR COVERAGE TAG OR BANKING TAG / CREDIT CARD
CASH / V$ / EGOLD ALSO ACCEPTED

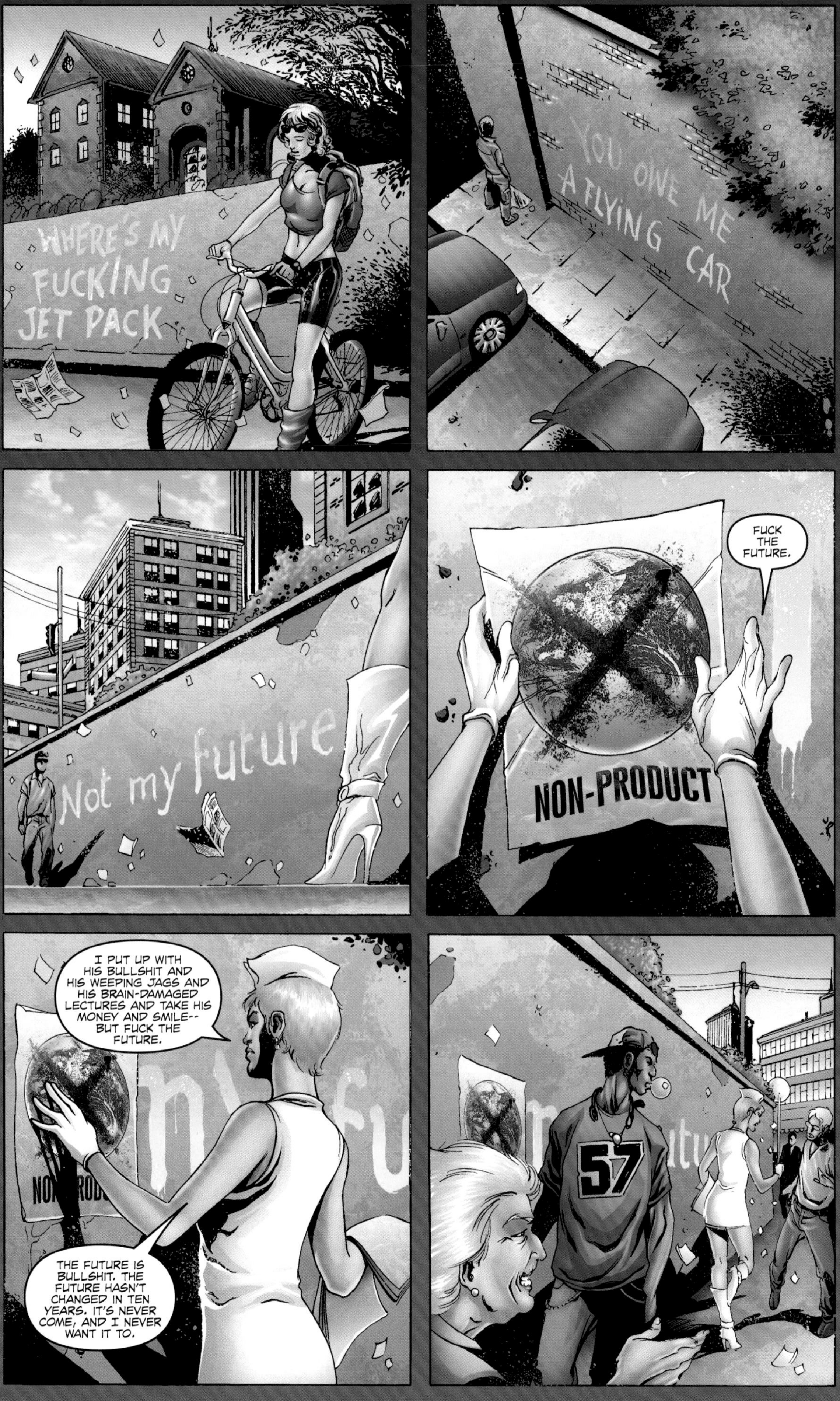
WHERE'S MY FUCKING JET PACK
YOU OWE ME A FLYING CAR
Not my future
FUCK THE FUTURE.
NON-PRODUCT
I PUT UP WITH HIS BULLSHIT AND HIS WEEPING JAGS AND HIS BRAIN-DAMAGED LECTURES AND TAKE HIS MONEY AND SMILE-- BUT FUCK THE FUTURE.
THE FUTURE IS BULLSHIT. THE FUTURE HASN'T CHANGED IN TEN YEARS. IT'S NEVER COME, AND I NEVER WANT IT TO.
57

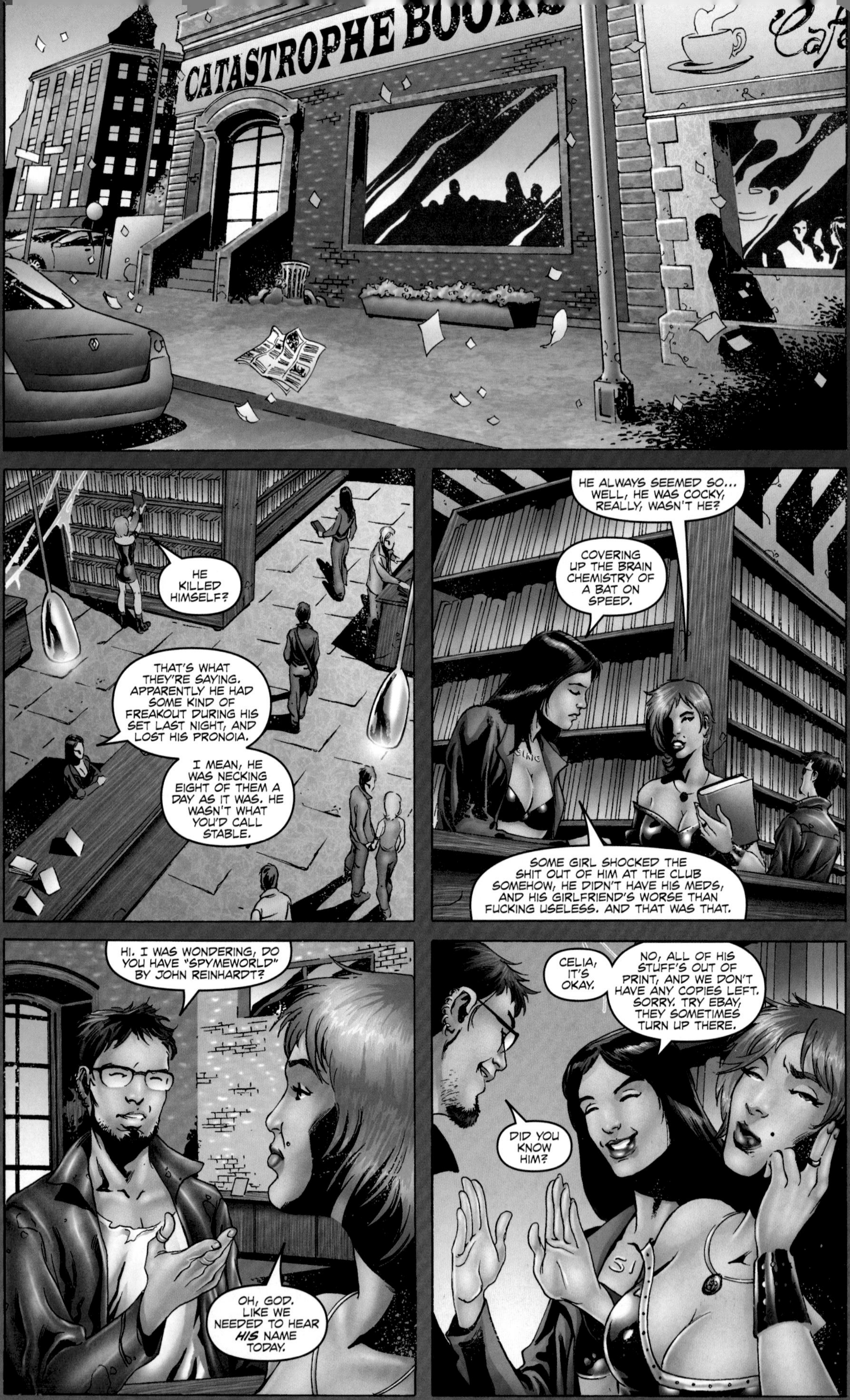
CATASTROPHE BOOKS
Café
HE KILLED HIMSELF?
THAT'S WHAT THEY'RE SAYING. APPARENTLY HE HAD SOME KIND OF FREAKOUT DURING HIS SET LAST NIGHT, AND LOST HIS PRONOIA.
I MEAN, HE WAS NECKING EIGHT OF THEM A DAY AS IT WAS. HE WASN'T WHAT YOU'D CALL STABLE.
HE ALWAYS SEEMED SO... WELL, HE WAS COCKY, REALLY, WASN'T HE?
COVERING UP THE BRAIN CHEMISTRY OF A BAT ON SPEED.
SOME GIRL SHOCKED THE SHIT OUT OF HIM AT THE CLUB SOMEHOW, HE DIDN'T HAVE HIS MEDS, AND HIS GIRLFRIEND'S WORSE THAN FUCKING USELESS. AND THAT WAS THAT.
HI. I WAS WONDERING, DO YOU HAVE "SPYMEWORLD" BY JOHN REINHARDT?
OH, GOD. LIKE WE NEEDED TO HEAR *HIS* NAME TODAY.
CELIA, IT'S OKAY.
NO, ALL OF HIS STUFF'S OUT OF PRINT, AND WE DON'T HAVE ANY COPIES LEFT. SORRY. TRY EBAY, THEY SOMETIMES TURN UP THERE.
DID YOU KNOW HIM?

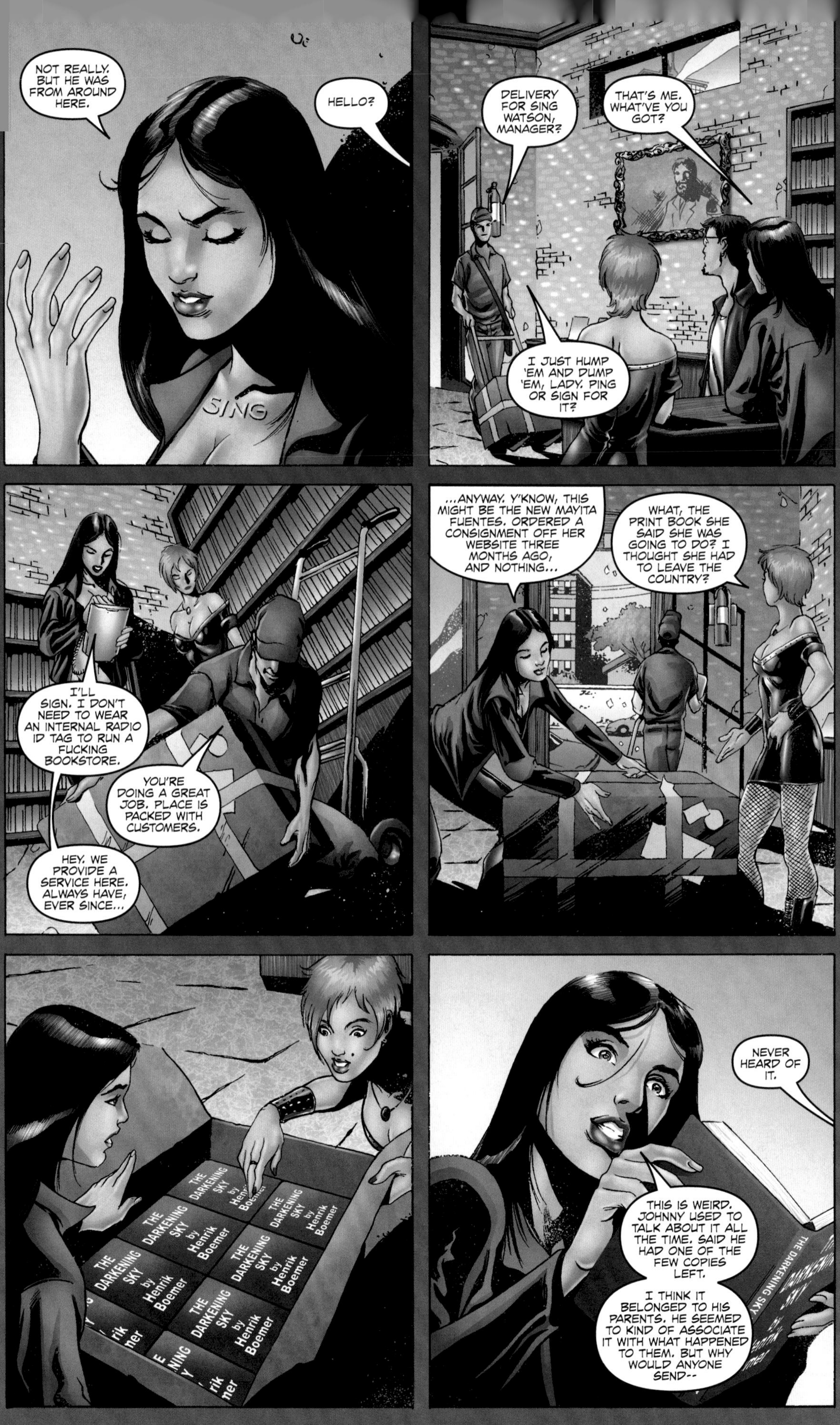

NOT REALLY. BUT HE WAS FROM AROUND HERE.
SING
HELLO?
DELIVERY FOR SING WATSON, MANAGER?
THAT'S ME. WHAT'VE YOU GOT?
I JUST HUMP 'EM AND DUMP 'EM, LADY. PING OR SIGN FOR IT?
I'LL SIGN. I DON'T NEED TO WEAR AN INTERNAL RADIO ID TAG TO RUN A FUCKING BOOKSTORE.
YOU'RE DOING A GREAT JOB. PLACE IS PACKED WITH CUSTOMERS.
HEY. WE PROVIDE A SERVICE HERE. ALWAYS HAVE, EVER SINCE...
...ANYWAY. Y'KNOW, THIS MIGHT BE THE NEW MAYITA FUENTES. ORDERED A CONSIGNMENT OFF HER WEBSITE THREE MONTHS AGO, AND NOTHING...
WHAT, THE PRINT BOOK SHE SAID SHE WAS GOING TO DO? I THOUGHT SHE HAD TO LEAVE THE COUNTRY?
THE DARKENING SKY by Henrik Boemer
NEVER HEARD OF IT.
THIS IS WEIRD. JOHNNY USED TO TALK ABOUT IT ALL THE TIME. SAID HE HAD ONE OF THE FEW COPIES LEFT.
I THINK IT BELONGED TO HIS PARENTS. HE SEEMED TO KIND OF ASSOCIATE IT WITH WHAT HAPPENED TO THEM. BUT WHY WOULD ANYONE SEND--
THE DARKENING SKY

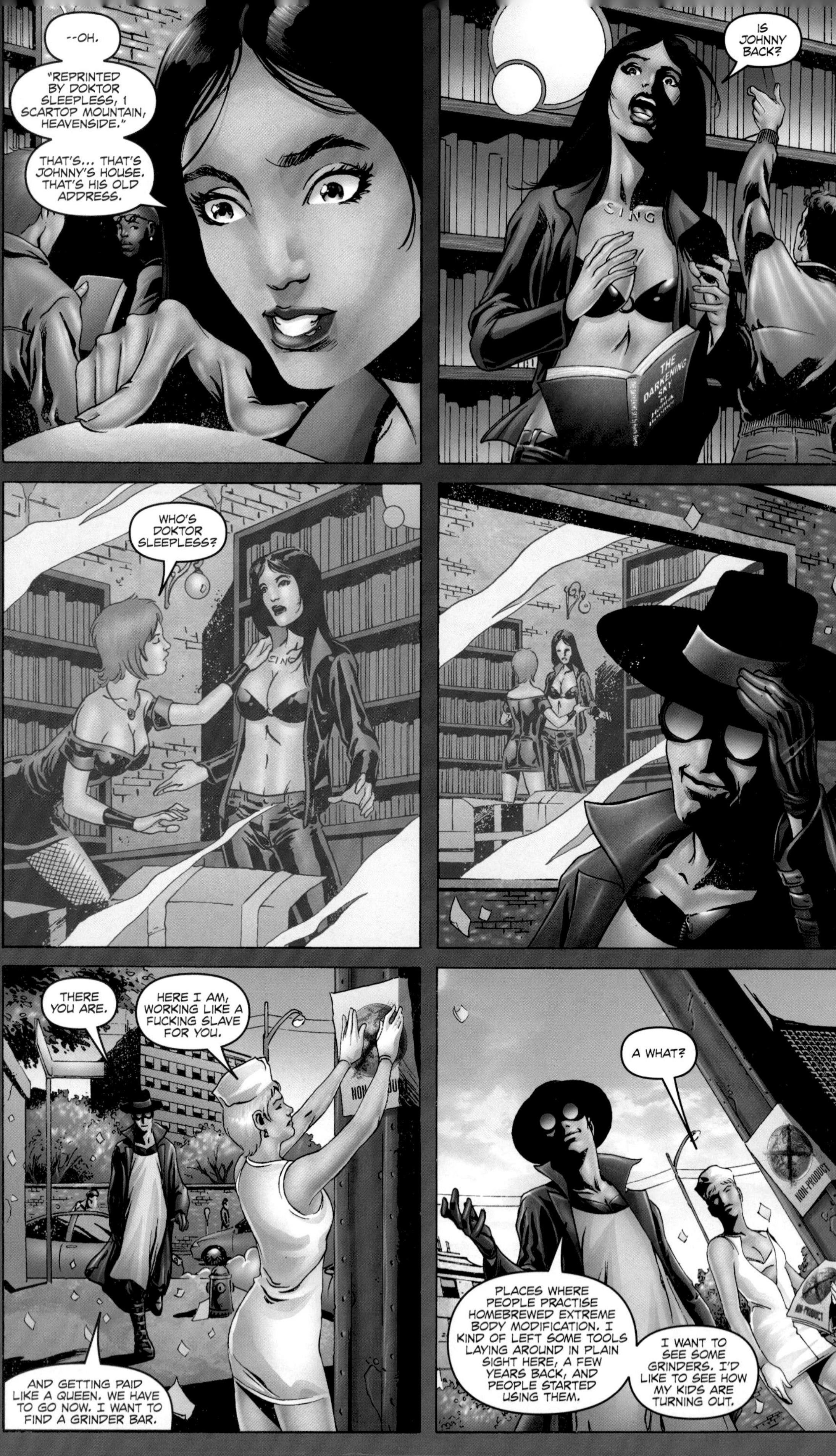
--OH.
"REPRINTED BY DOKTOR SLEEPLESS, 1 SCARTOP MOUNTAIN, HEAVENSIDE."
THAT'S... THAT'S JOHNNY'S HOUSE. THAT'S HIS OLD ADDRESS.
IS JOHNNY BACK?
THE DARKENING SKY
WHO'S DOKTOR SLEEPLESS?
THERE YOU ARE.
HERE I AM, WORKING LIKE A FUCKING SLAVE FOR YOU.
AND GETTING PAID LIKE A QUEEN. WE HAVE TO GO NOW. I WANT TO FIND A GRINDER BAR.
A WHAT?
NON-PRODUCT
PLACES WHERE PEOPLE PRACTISE HOMEBREWED EXTREME BODY MODIFICATION. I KIND OF LEFT SOME TOOLS LAYING AROUND IN PLAIN SIGHT HERE, A FEW YEARS BACK, AND PEOPLE STARTED USING THEM.
I WANT TO SEE SOME GRINDERS. I'D LIKE TO SEE HOW MY KIDS ARE TURNING OUT.

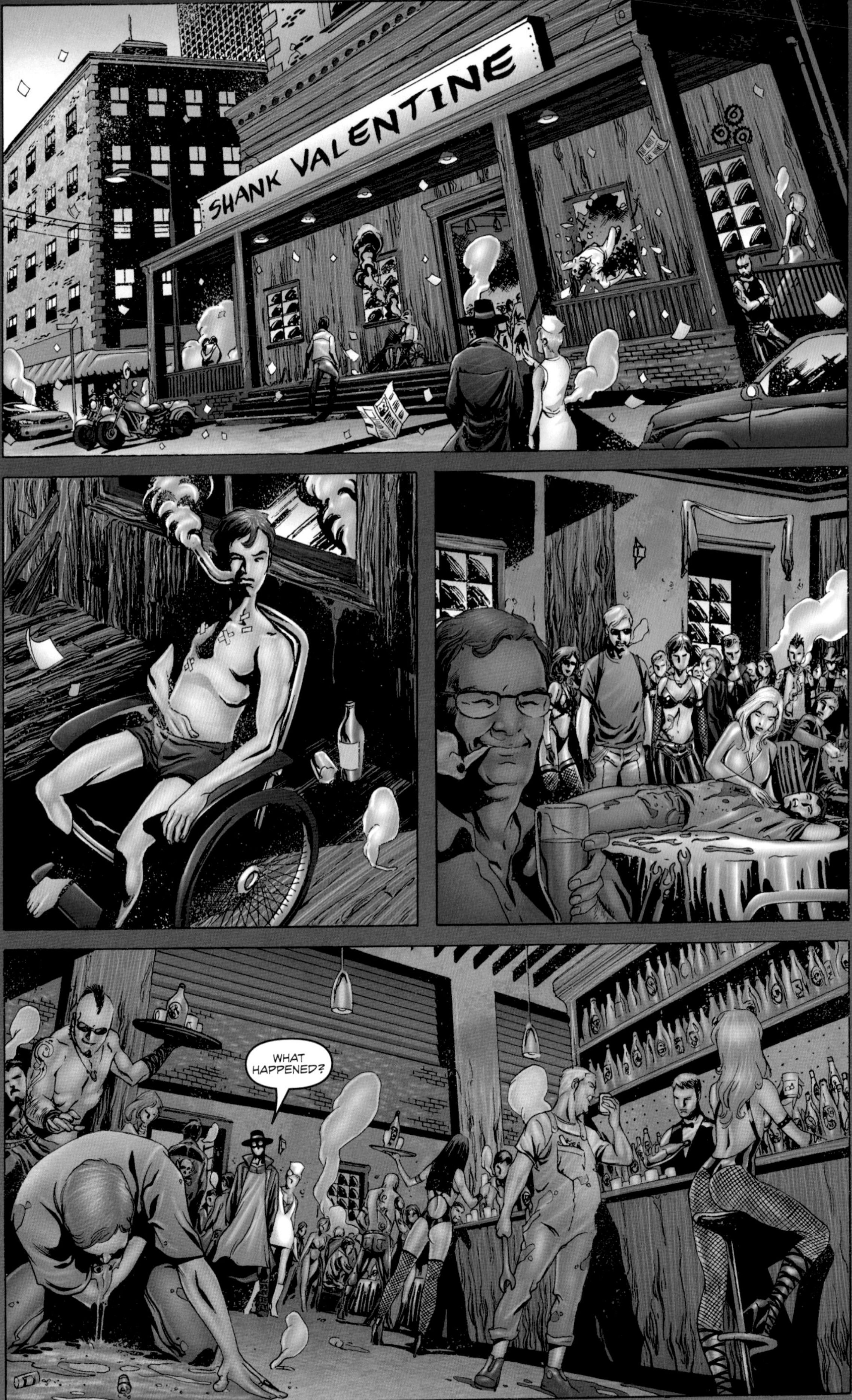
SHANK VALENTINE
WHAT HAPPENED?

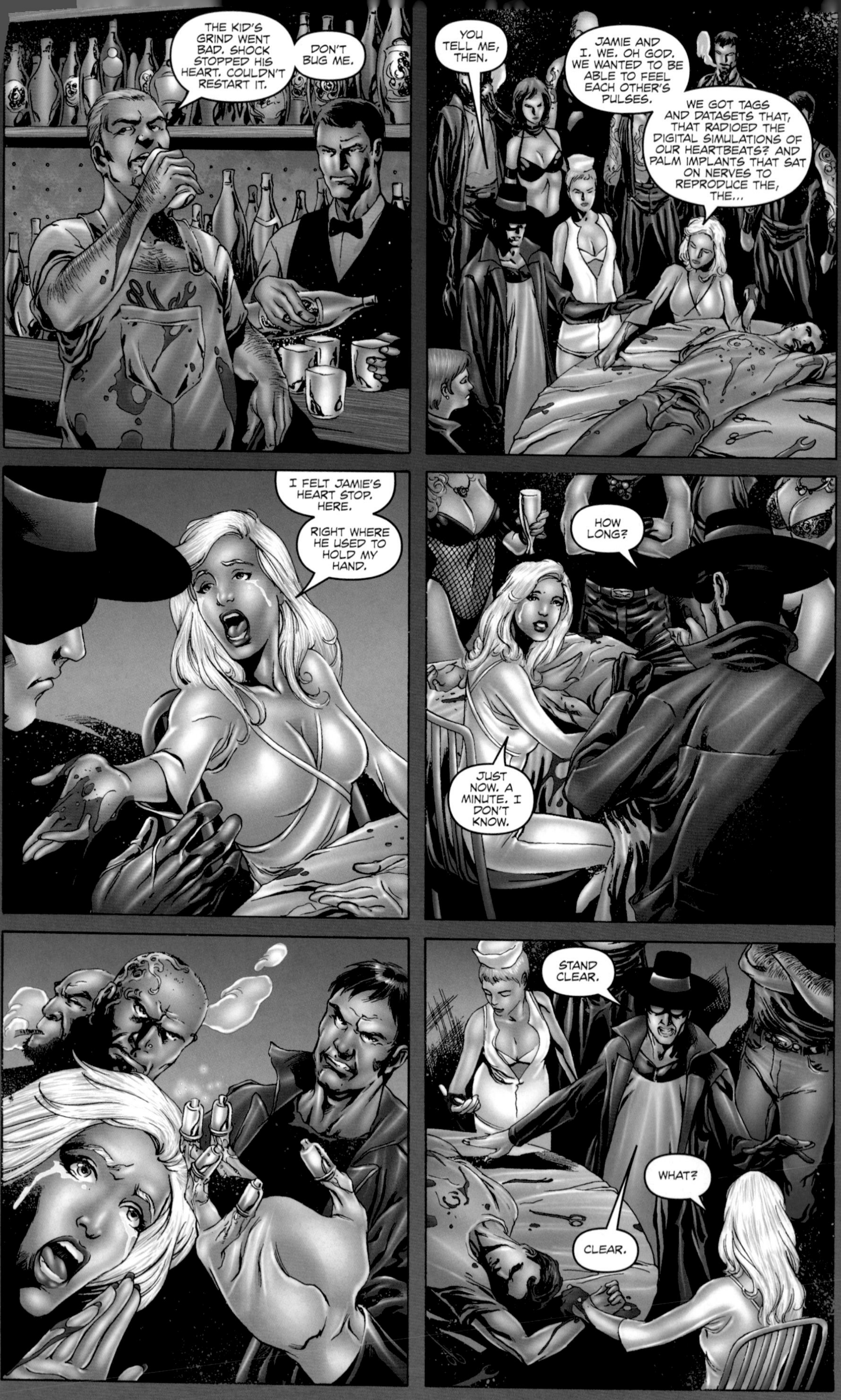
THE KID'S GRIND WENT BAD. SHOCK STOPPED HIS HEART. COULDN'T RESTART IT.
DON'T BUG ME.
YOU TELL ME, THEN.
JAMIE AND I. WE. OH GOD. WE WANTED TO BE ABLE TO FEEL EACH OTHER'S PULSES.
WE GOT TAGS AND DATASETS THAT, THAT RADIOED THE DIGITAL SIMULATIONS OF OUR HEARTBEATS? AND PALM IMPLANTS THAT SAT ON NERVES TO REPRODUCE THE, THE...
I FELT JAMIE'S HEART STOP. HERE.
RIGHT WHERE HE USED TO HOLD MY HAND.
HOW LONG?
JUST NOW. A MINUTE. I DON'T KNOW.
STAND CLEAR.
WHAT?
CLEAR.

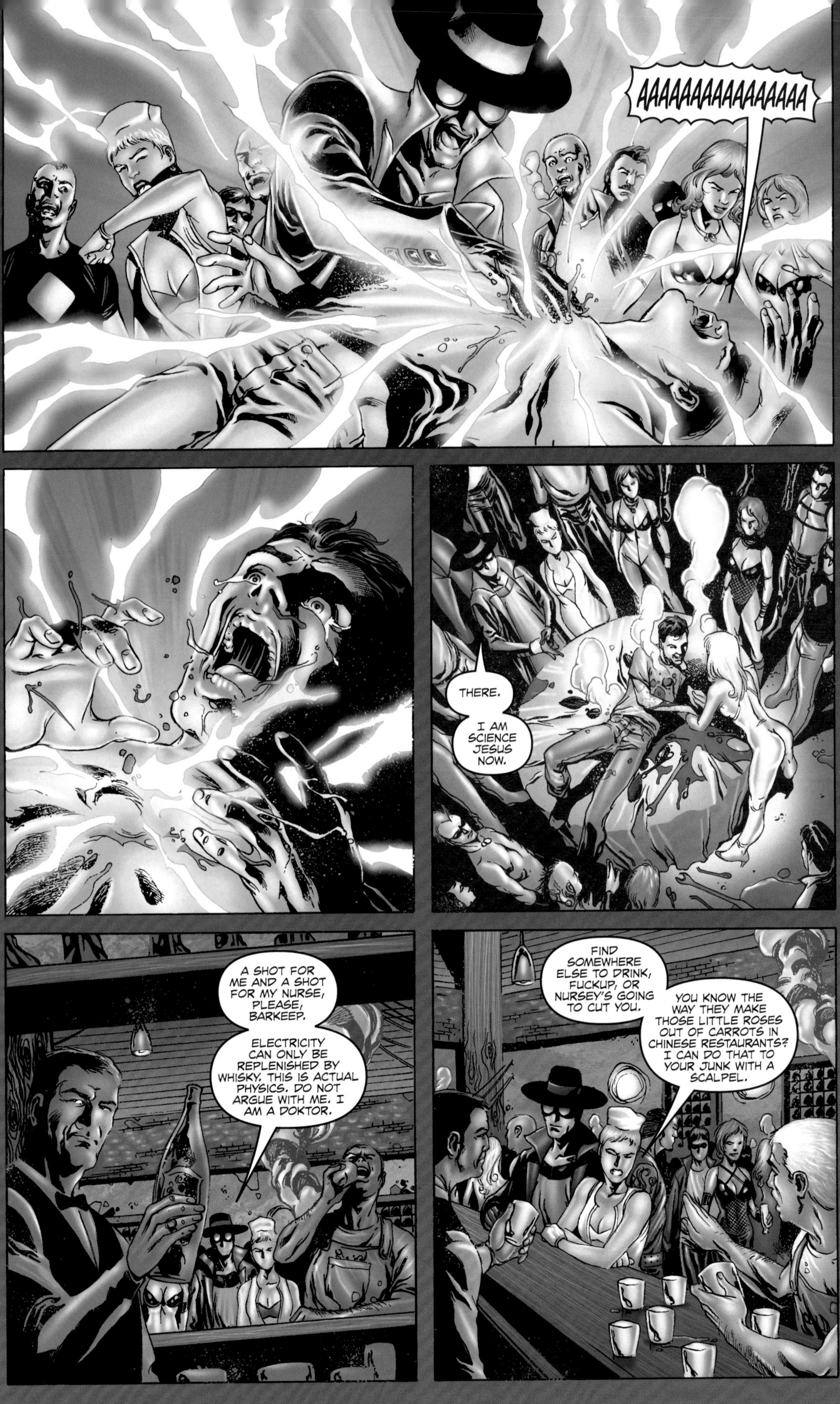
AAAAAAAAAAAAAAAA
THERE.
I AM SCIENCE JESUS NOW.
A SHOT FOR ME AND A SHOT FOR MY NURSE, PLEASE, BARKEEP.
ELECTRICITY CAN ONLY BE REPLENISHED BY WHISKY. THIS IS ACTUAL PHYSICS. DO NOT ARGUE WITH ME. I AM A DOKTOR.
FIND SOMEWHERE ELSE TO DRINK, FUCKUP, OR NURSEY'S GOING TO CUT YOU.
YOU KNOW THE WAY THEY MAKE THOSE LITTLE ROSES OUT OF CARROTS IN CHINESE RESTAURANTS? I CAN DO THAT TO YOUR JUNK WITH A SCALPEL.

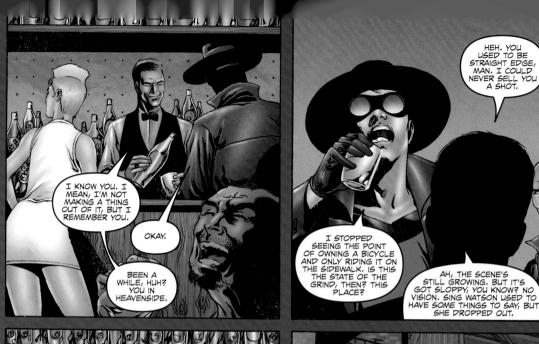

I KNOW YOU. I MEAN, I'M NOT MAKING A THING OUT OF IT, BUT I REMEMBER YOU.

OKAY.

BEEN A WHILE, HUH? YOU IN HEAVENSIDE.

HEH. YOU USED TO BE STRAIGHT EDGE, MAN. I COULD NEVER SELL YOU A SHOT.

I STOPPED SEEING THE POINT OF OWNING A BICYCLE AND ONLY RIDING IT ON THE SIDEWALK. IS THIS THE STATE OF THE GRIND, THEN? THIS PLACE?

AH, THE SCENE'S STILL GROWING. BUT IT'S GOT SLOPPY, YOU KNOW? NO VISION. SING WATSON USED TO HAVE SOME THINGS TO SAY, BUT SHE DROPPED OUT.

HEH. WOULD YOU LOOK AT THAT.

YEAH, YOU GOT QUITE A VIEW OF YOUR OLD PLACE FROM HERE.

HOME SWEET HOME.

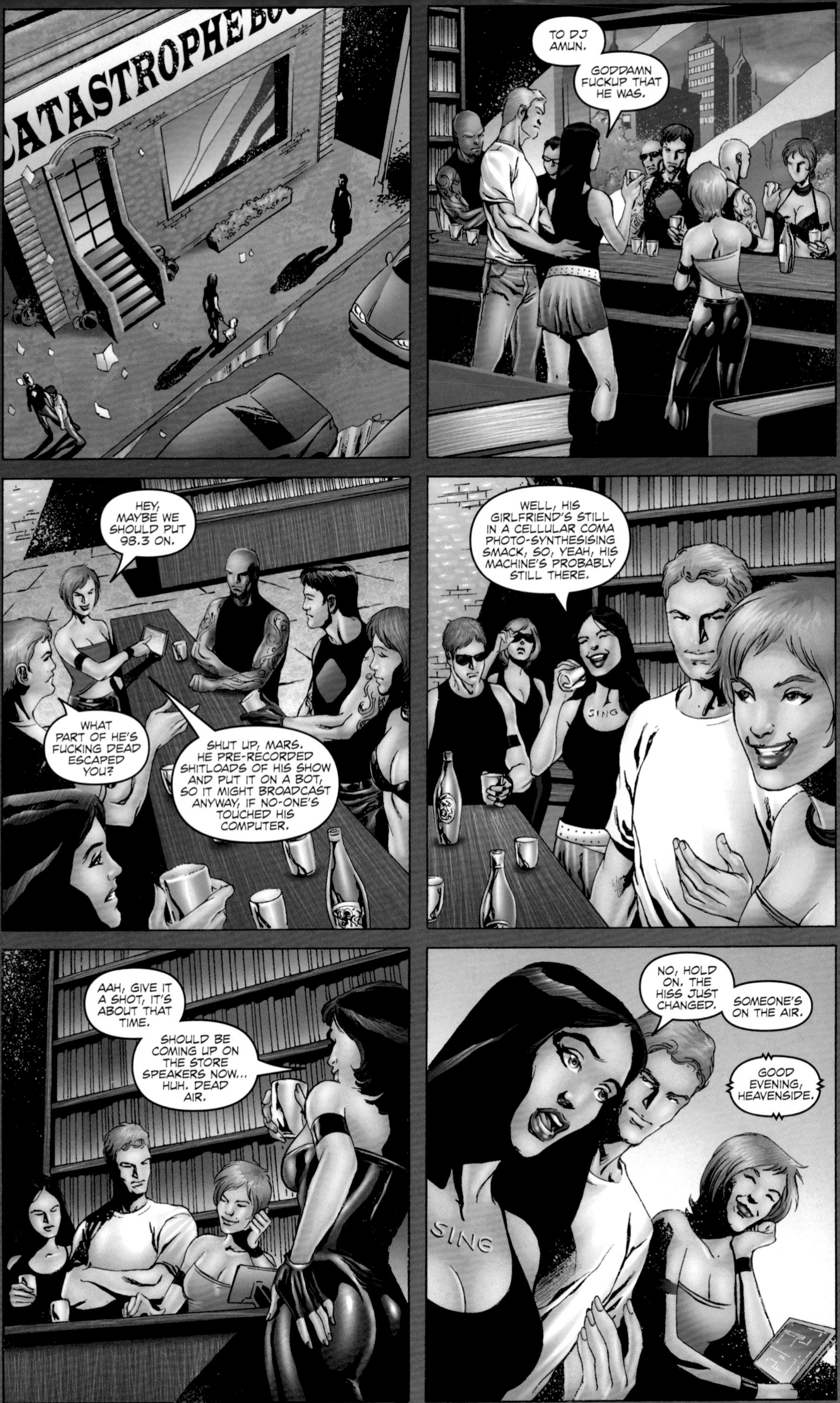
CATASTROPHE BO
TO DJ AMUN.
GODDAMN FUCKUP THAT HE WAS.
HEY, MAYBE WE SHOULD PUT 98.3 ON.
WHAT PART OF HE'S FUCKING DEAD ESCAPED YOU?
SHUT UP, MARS. HE PRE-RECORDED SHITLOADS OF HIS SHOW AND PUT IT ON A BOT, SO IT MIGHT BROADCAST ANYWAY, IF NO-ONE'S TOUCHED HIS COMPUTER.
WELL, HIS GIRLFRIEND'S STILL IN A CELLULAR COMA PHOTO-SYNTHESISING SMACK, SO, YEAH, HIS MACHINE'S PROBABLY STILL THERE.
SING
AAH, GIVE IT A SHOT, IT'S ABOUT THAT TIME.
SHOULD BE COMING UP ON THE STORE SPEAKERS NOW... HUH. DEAD AIR.
NO, HOLD ON. THE HISS JUST CHANGED.
SOMEONE'S ON THE AIR.
GOOD EVENING, HEAVENSIDE.
SING

THIS IS THE FREQUENCY PREVIOUSLY HELD BY DJ AMUN OF THESE STREETS.

DJ AMUN WAS A FRAGGLE WHO SPENT HIS DAYS DOPED TO THE NIPPLES ON PRONOIA AND SCREWING ANYTHING THAT LOOKED LIKE IT MIGHT BE ON HIS HALF OF THE EVOLUTIONARY LADDER.

HE KILLED HIMSELF AFTER DISCOVERING THAT ONE OF HIS CONQUESTS HAD BOTTLED HIS ABORTION AND TURNED IT INTO JEWELRY.

THEREFORE, DEAR OLD DJ AMUN IS NO LONGER USING THIS FREQUENCY, HAVING SAWED OFF HIS OWN COCK DURING THE NIGHT AND BLED OUT BEFORE BREAKFAST.

OH DEAR. HOW SAD. NEVER MIND. I'M NOT TO TALK ABOUT THAT. HERE TO TALK ABOUT

EVERYWHERE I GO, I HEAR THE SAME THING:

WHERE'S MY FUCKING JET PACK? WHERE'S MY FLYING CAR?

YOU'RE THINKING IT RIGHT NOW. WHERE'S MY VACATION ON THE MOON? WHERE'S MY ROBOT LOVER? WHERE'S MY ALIEN DANCING GIRLS?

OKAY, THAT BIT MIGHT JUST BE ME. BUT STILL.

WHERE'S THE FUTURE WE WERE PROMISED? THAT'S WHAT I HEAR YOU SAY. WHO CHEATED ME OUT OF MY SPACESHIP AND MY RAY GUN?

OH MY GOD.

I KNOW THAT VOICE.

STOP LOOKING FOR SOMETHING THAT ISN'T THERE.

YOU LIVE IN THE FUTURE AND YOU DON'T KNOW IT.

HALF OF YOU KNOW WHERE YOUR FRIENDS ARE BY LOOKING INSIDE YOUR OWN EYEBALL, FOR GOD'S SAKE.

IT'S NOT SO LONG AGO THAT A LETTER OR A PHOTO TOOK MONTHS TO CROSS THE WORLD.

YOU CAN TELL PEOPLE WHERE YOU ARE TODAY AND WHAT IT LOOKS LIKE IN SECONDS, NO MATTER WHERE THEY ARE.

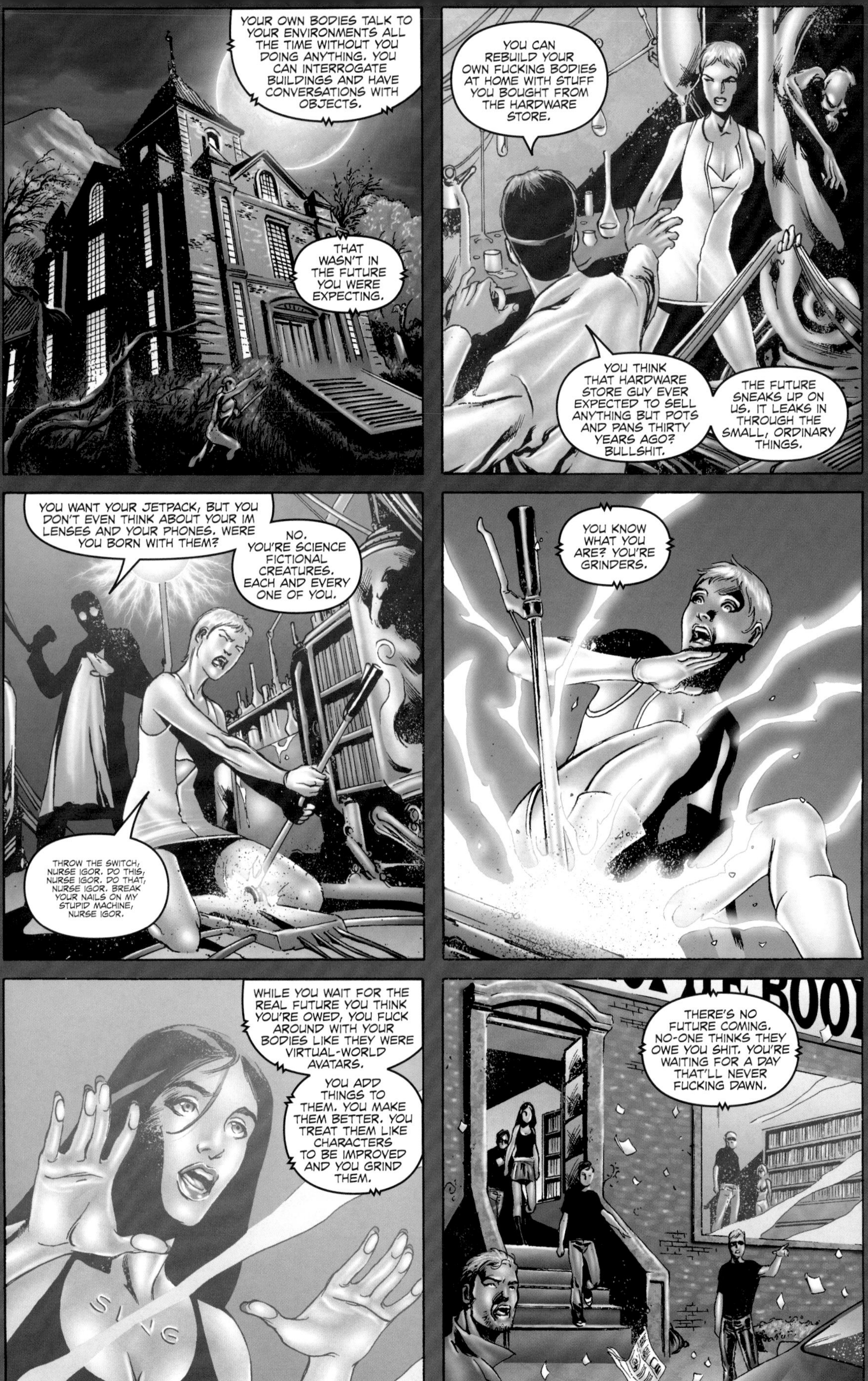

YOUR OWN BODIES TALK TO YOUR ENVIRONMENTS ALL THE TIME WITHOUT YOU DOING ANYTHING. YOU CAN INTERROGATE BUILDINGS AND HAVE CONVERSATIONS WITH OBJECTS.
THAT WASN'T IN THE FUTURE YOU WERE EXPECTING.
YOU CAN REBUILD YOUR OWN FUCKING BODIES AT HOME WITH STUFF YOU BOUGHT FROM THE HARDWARE STORE.
YOU THINK THAT HARDWARE STORE GUY EVER EXPECTED TO SELL ANYTHING BUT POTS AND PANS THIRTY YEARS AGO? BULLSHIT.
THE FUTURE SNEAKS UP ON US. IT LEAKS IN THROUGH THE SMALL, ORDINARY THINGS.
YOU WANT YOUR JETPACK, BUT YOU DON'T EVEN THINK ABOUT YOUR IM LENSES AND YOUR PHONES. WERE YOU BORN WITH THEM?
NO. YOU'RE SCIENCE FICTIONAL CREATURES. EACH AND EVERY ONE OF YOU.
THROW THE SWITCH, NURSE IGOR. DO THIS, NURSE IGOR. DO THAT, NURSE IGOR. BREAK YOUR NAILS ON MY STUPID MACHINE, NURSE IGOR.
YOU KNOW WHAT YOU ARE? YOU'RE GRINDERS.
WHILE YOU WAIT FOR THE REAL FUTURE YOU THINK YOU'RE OWED, YOU FUCK AROUND WITH YOUR BODIES LIKE THEY WERE VIRTUAL-WORLD AVATARS.
YOU ADD THINGS TO THEM. YOU MAKE THEM BETTER. YOU TREAT THEM LIKE CHARACTERS TO BE IMPROVED AND YOU GRIND THEM.
THERE'S NO FUTURE COMING. NO-ONE THINKS THEY OWE YOU SHIT. YOU'RE WAITING FOR A DAY THAT'LL NEVER FUCKING DAWN.

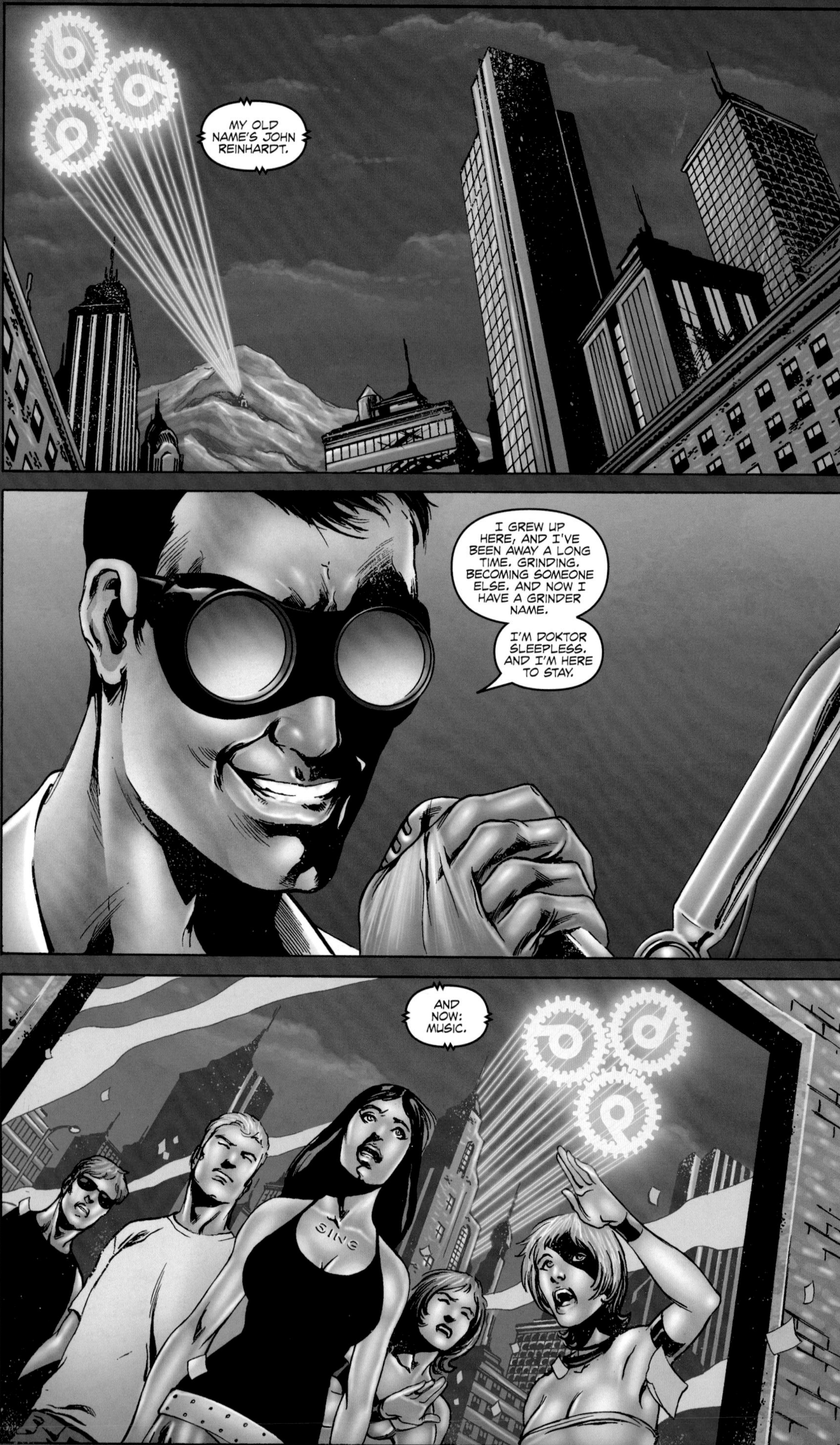

MY OLD NAME'S JOHN REINHARDT.
I GREW UP HERE, AND I'VE BEEN AWAY A LONG TIME. GRINDING. BECOMING SOMEONE ELSE. AND NOW I HAVE A GRINDER NAME.
I'M DOKTOR SLEEPLESS. AND I'M HERE TO STAY.
AND NOW: MUSIC.
SING

PART TWO

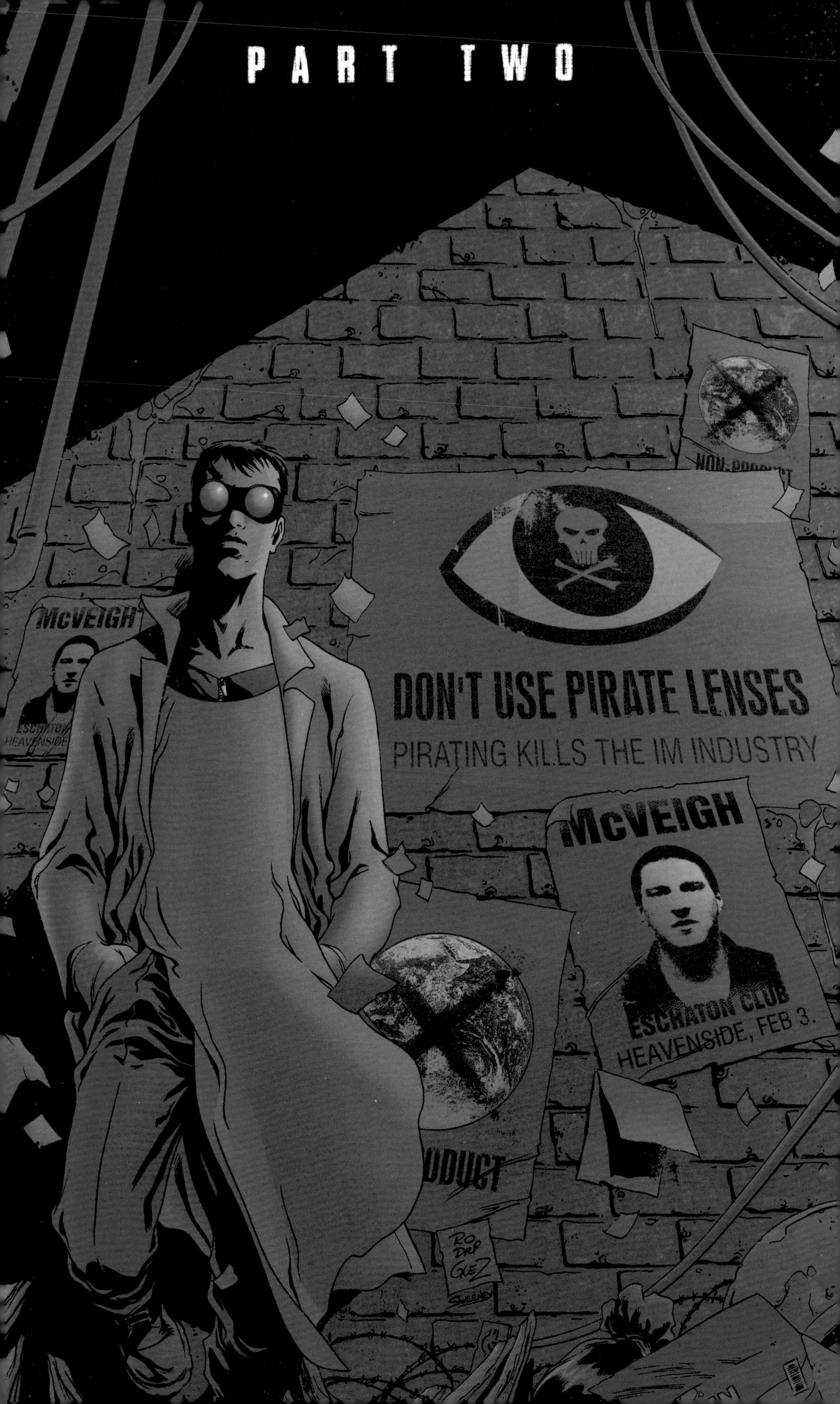

McVEIGH
ESCHATON
HEAVENSIDE
DON'T USE PIRATE LENSES
PIRATING KILLS THE IM INDUSTRY
McVEIGH
ESCHATON CLUB
HEAVENSIDE, FEB 3.
SWEENEY

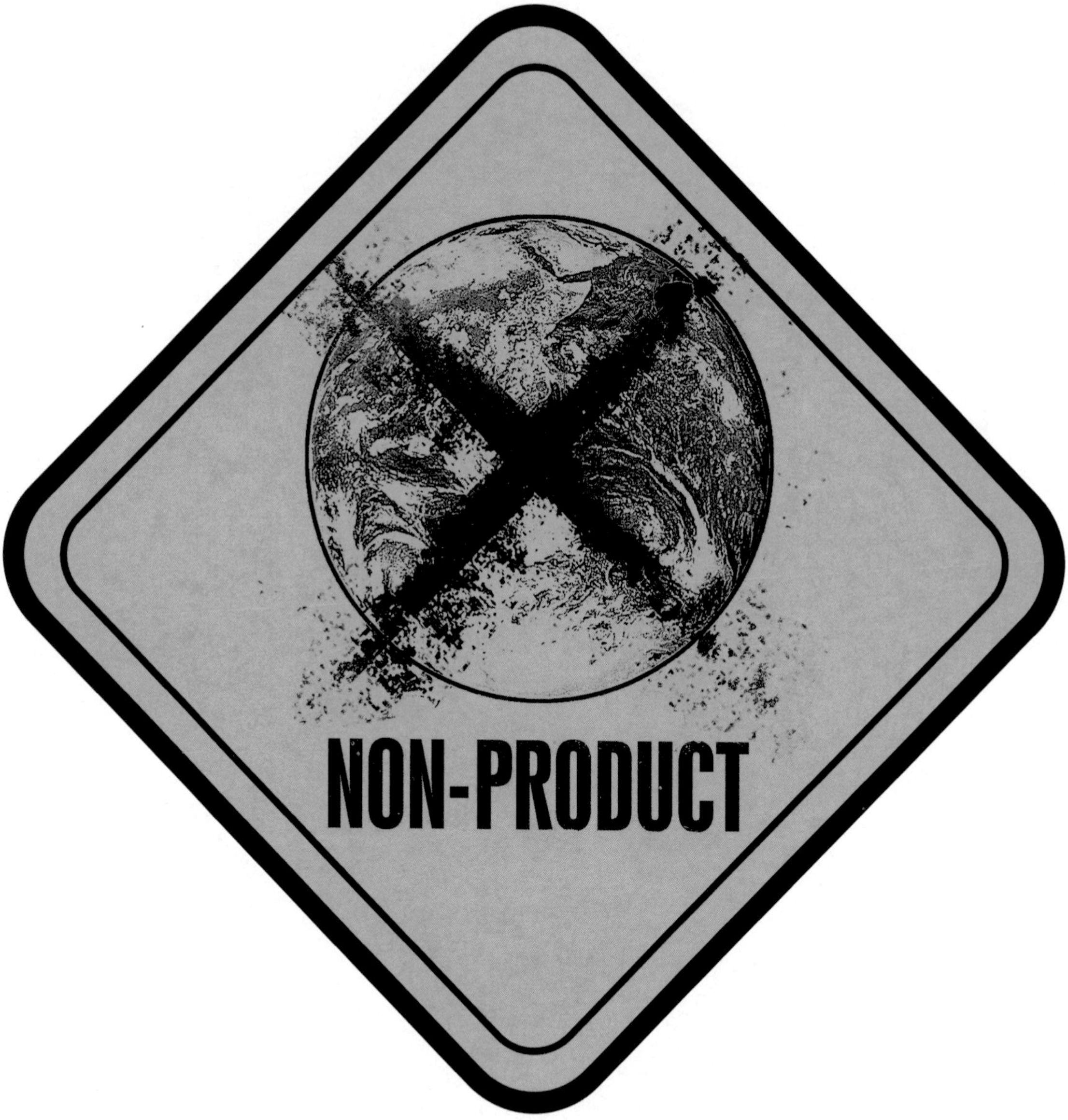
NON-PRODUCT

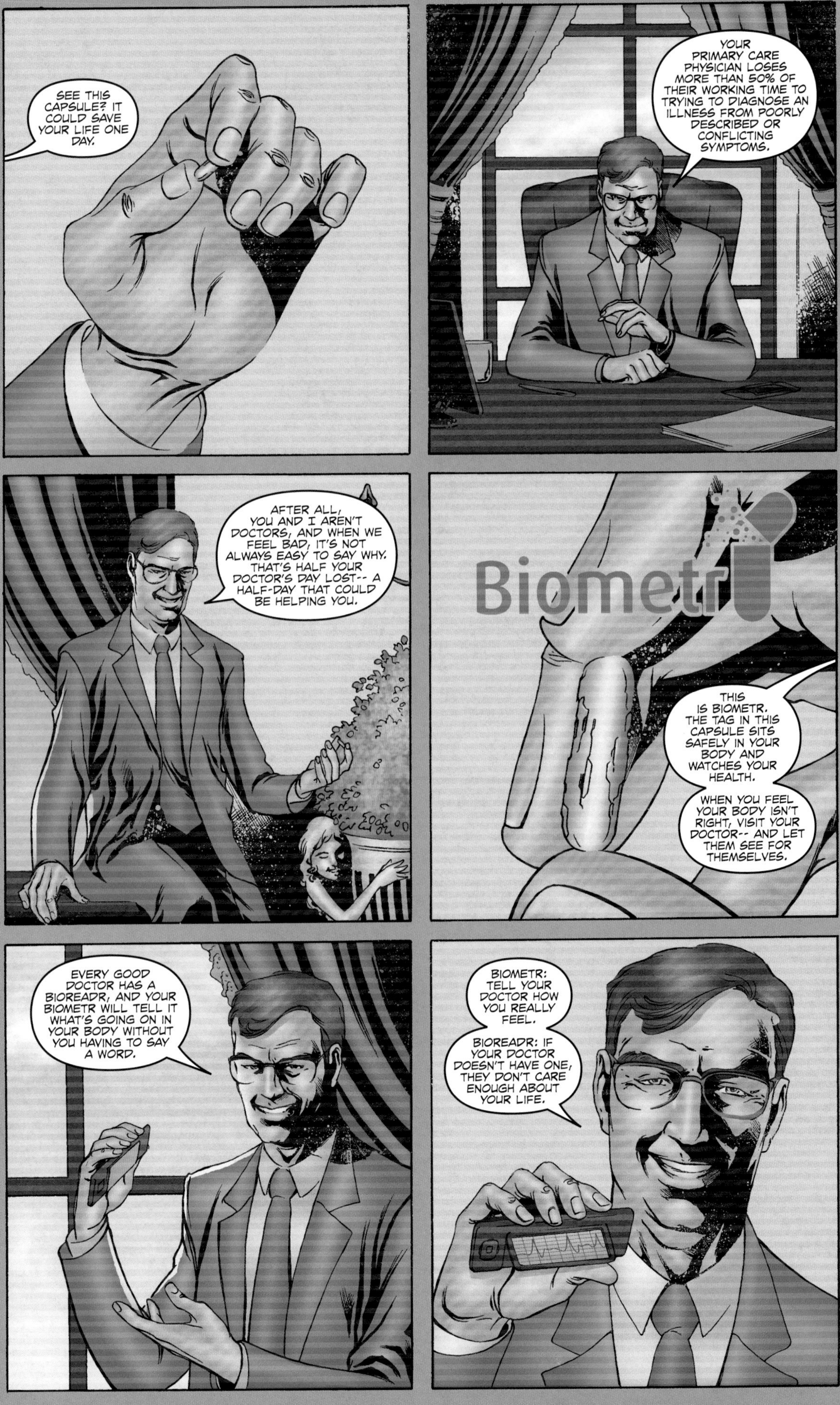

SEE THIS CAPSULE? IT COULD SAVE YOUR LIFE ONE DAY.
YOUR PRIMARY CARE PHYSICIAN LOSES MORE THAN 50% OF THEIR WORKING TIME TO TRYING TO DIAGNOSE AN ILLNESS FROM POORLY DESCRIBED OR CONFLICTING SYMPTOMS.
AFTER ALL, YOU AND I AREN'T DOCTORS, AND WHEN WE FEEL BAD, IT'S NOT ALWAYS EASY TO SAY WHY. THAT'S HALF YOUR DOCTOR'S DAY LOST-- A HALF-DAY THAT COULD BE HELPING YOU.
Biometr
THIS IS BIOMETR. THE TAG IN THIS CAPSULE SITS SAFELY IN YOUR BODY AND WATCHES YOUR HEALTH.
WHEN YOU FEEL YOUR BODY ISN'T RIGHT, VISIT YOUR DOCTOR-- AND LET THEM SEE FOR THEMSELVES.
EVERY GOOD DOCTOR HAS A BIOREADR, AND YOUR BIOMETR WILL TELL IT WHAT'S GOING ON IN YOUR BODY WITHOUT YOU HAVING TO SAY A WORD.
BIOMETR: TELL YOUR DOCTOR HOW YOU REALLY FEEL.
BIOREADR: IF YOUR DOCTOR DOESN'T HAVE ONE, THEY DON'T CARE ENOUGH ABOUT YOUR LIFE.

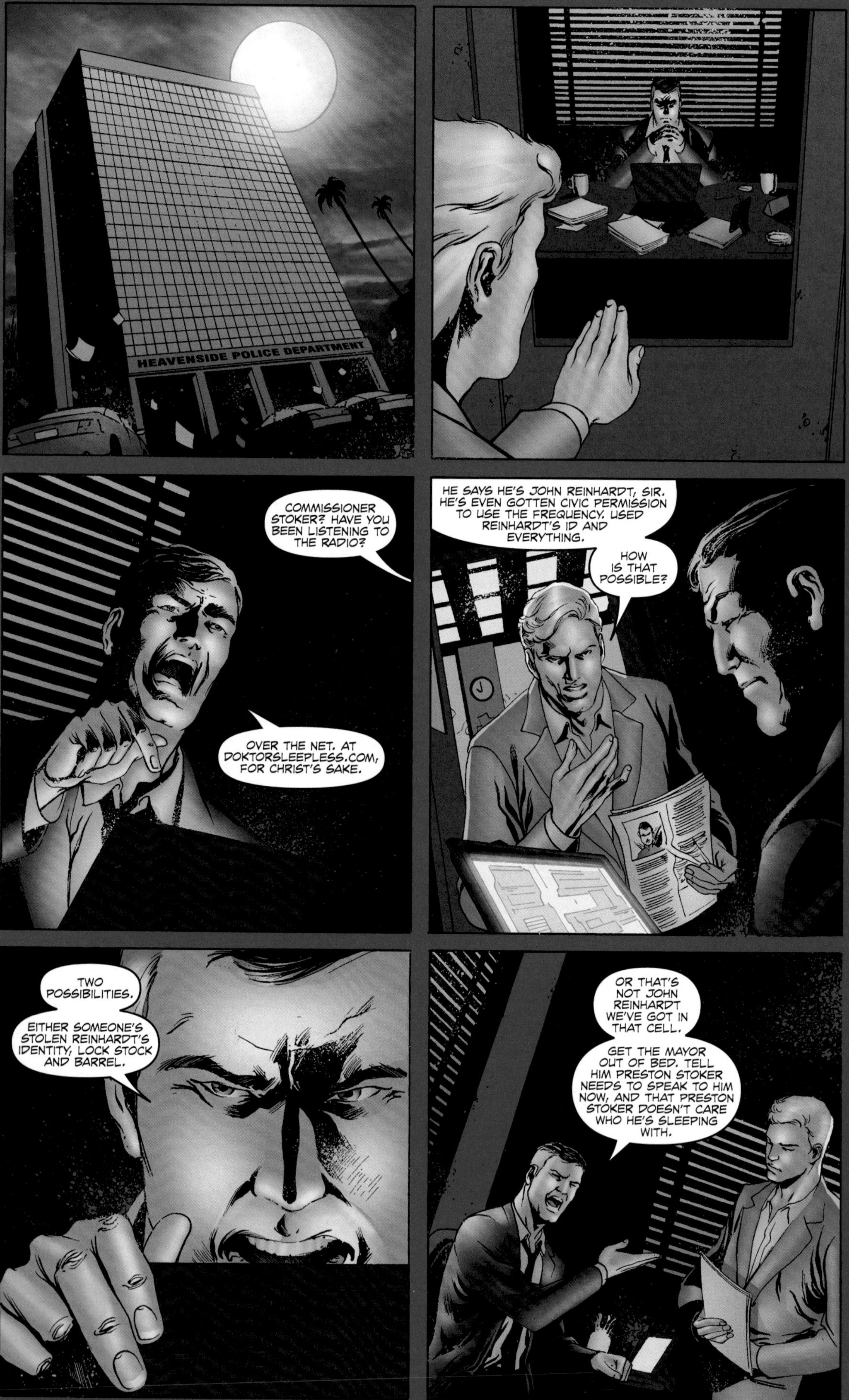
HEAVENSIDE POLICE DEPARTMENT
COMMISSIONER STOKER? HAVE YOU BEEN LISTENING TO THE RADIO?
OVER THE NET. AT DOKTORSLEEPLESS.COM, FOR CHRIST'S SAKE.
HE SAYS HE'S JOHN REINHARDT, SIR. HE'S EVEN GOTTEN CIVIC PERMISSION TO USE THE FREQUENCY. USED REINHARDT'S ID AND EVERYTHING.
HOW IS THAT POSSIBLE?
TWO POSSIBILITIES.
EITHER SOMEONE'S STOLEN REINHARDT'S IDENTITY, LOCK STOCK AND BARREL.
OR THAT'S NOT JOHN REINHARDT WE'VE GOT IN THAT CELL.
GET THE MAYOR OUT OF BED. TELL HIM PRESTON STOKER NEEDS TO SPEAK TO HIM NOW, AND THAT PRESTON STOKER DOESN'T CARE WHO HE'S SLEEPING WITH.

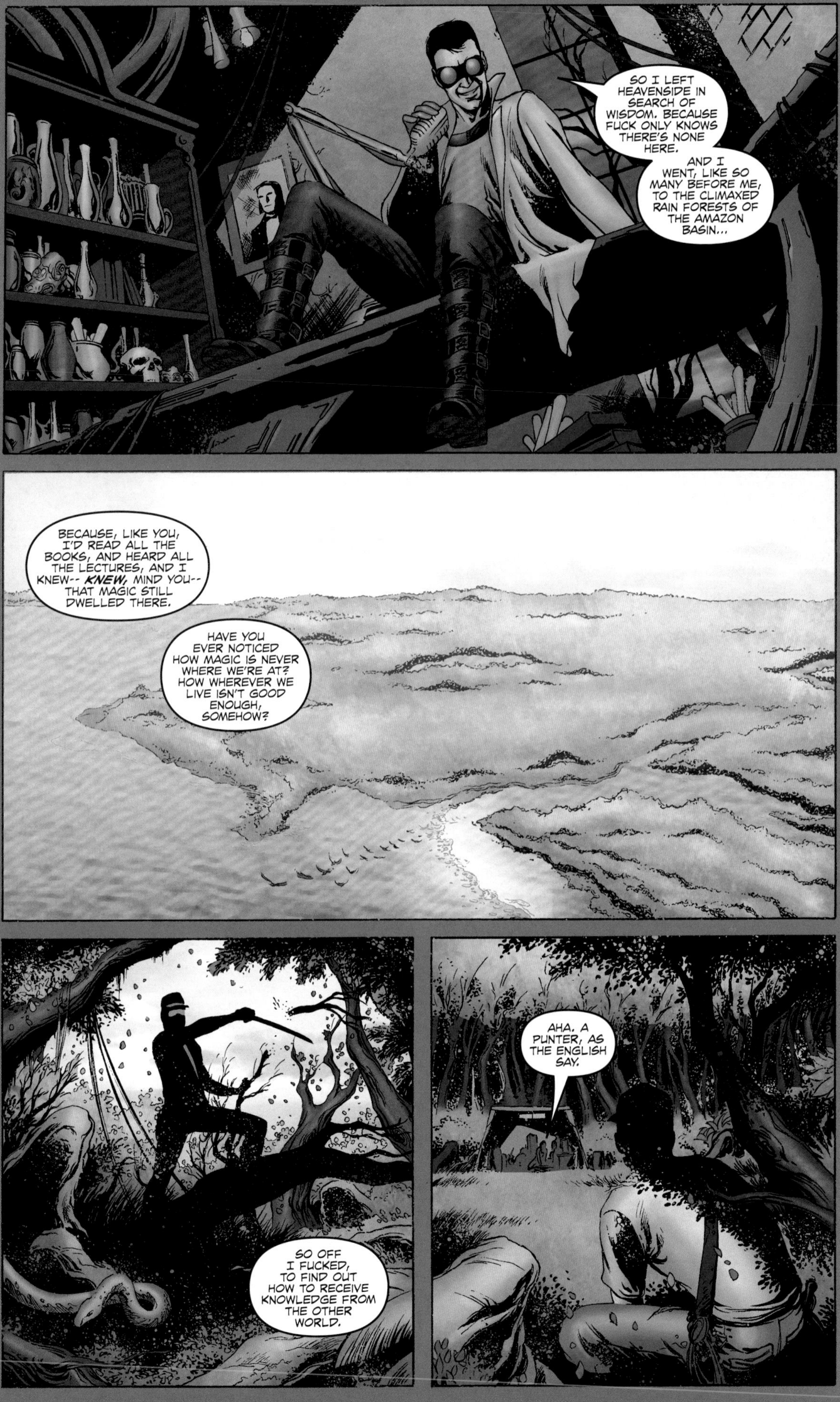
SO I LEFT HEAVENSIDE IN SEARCH OF WISDOM. BECAUSE FUCK ONLY KNOWS THERE'S NONE HERE.
AND I WENT, LIKE SO MANY BEFORE ME, TO THE CLIMAXED RAIN FORESTS OF THE AMAZON BASIN...
BECAUSE, LIKE YOU, I'D READ ALL THE BOOKS, AND HEARD ALL THE LECTURES, AND I KNEW-- *KNEW,* MIND YOU-- THAT MAGIC STILL DWELLED THERE.
HAVE YOU EVER NOTICED HOW MAGIC IS NEVER WHERE WE'RE AT? HOW WHEREVER WE LIVE ISN'T GOOD ENOUGH, SOMEHOW?
SO OFF I FUCKED, TO FIND OUT HOW TO RECEIVE KNOWLEDGE FROM THE OTHER WORLD.
AHA. A PUNTER, AS THE ENGLISH SAY.

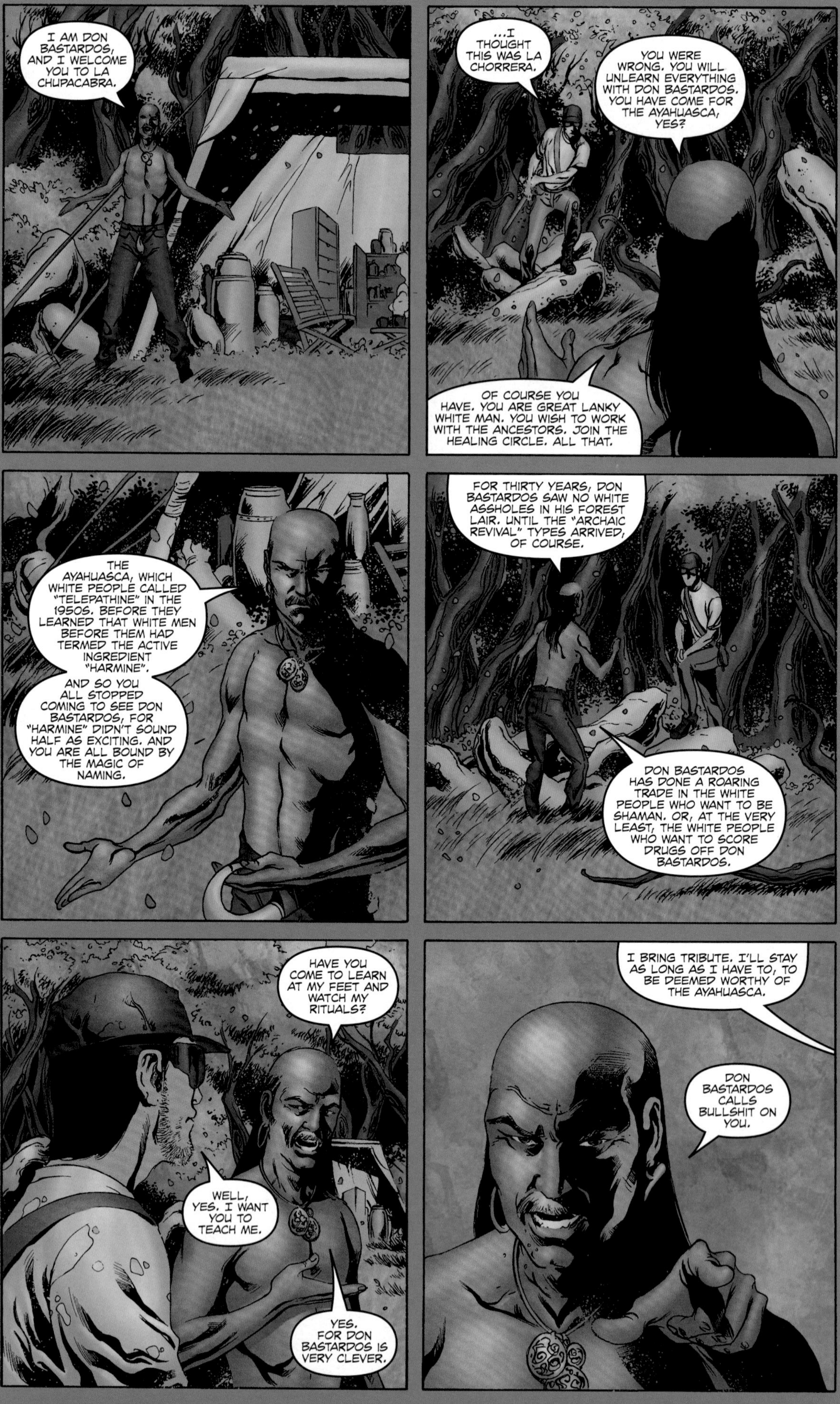
I AM DON BASTARDOS, AND I WELCOME YOU TO LA CHUPACABRA.
...I THOUGHT THIS WAS LA CHORRERA.
YOU WERE WRONG. YOU WILL UNLEARN EVERYTHING WITH DON BASTARDOS. YOU HAVE COME FOR THE AYAHUASCA, YES?
OF COURSE YOU HAVE. YOU ARE GREAT LANKY WHITE MAN. YOU WISH TO WORK WITH THE ANCESTORS. JOIN THE HEALING CIRCLE. ALL THAT.
THE AYAHUASCA, WHICH WHITE PEOPLE CALLED "TELEPATHINE" IN THE 1950S. BEFORE THEY LEARNED THAT WHITE MEN BEFORE THEM HAD TERMED THE ACTIVE INGREDIENT "HARMINE".
AND SO YOU ALL STOPPED COMING TO SEE DON BASTARDOS, FOR "HARMINE" DIDN'T SOUND HALF AS EXCITING. AND YOU ARE ALL BOUND BY THE MAGIC OF NAMING.
FOR THIRTY YEARS, DON BASTARDOS SAW NO WHITE ASSHOLES IN HIS FOREST LAIR. UNTIL THE "ARCHAIC REVIVAL" TYPES ARRIVED, OF COURSE.
DON BASTARDOS HAS DONE A ROARING TRADE IN THE WHITE PEOPLE WHO WANT TO BE SHAMAN. OR, AT THE VERY LEAST, THE WHITE PEOPLE WHO WANT TO SCORE DRUGS OFF DON BASTARDOS.
HAVE YOU COME TO LEARN AT MY FEET AND WATCH MY RITUALS?
WELL, YES. I WANT YOU TO TEACH ME.
YES. FOR DON BASTARDOS IS VERY CLEVER.
I BRING TRIBUTE. I'LL STAY AS LONG AS I HAVE TO, TO BE DEEMED WORTHY OF THE AYAHUASCA.
DON BASTARDOS CALLS BULLSHIT ON YOU.

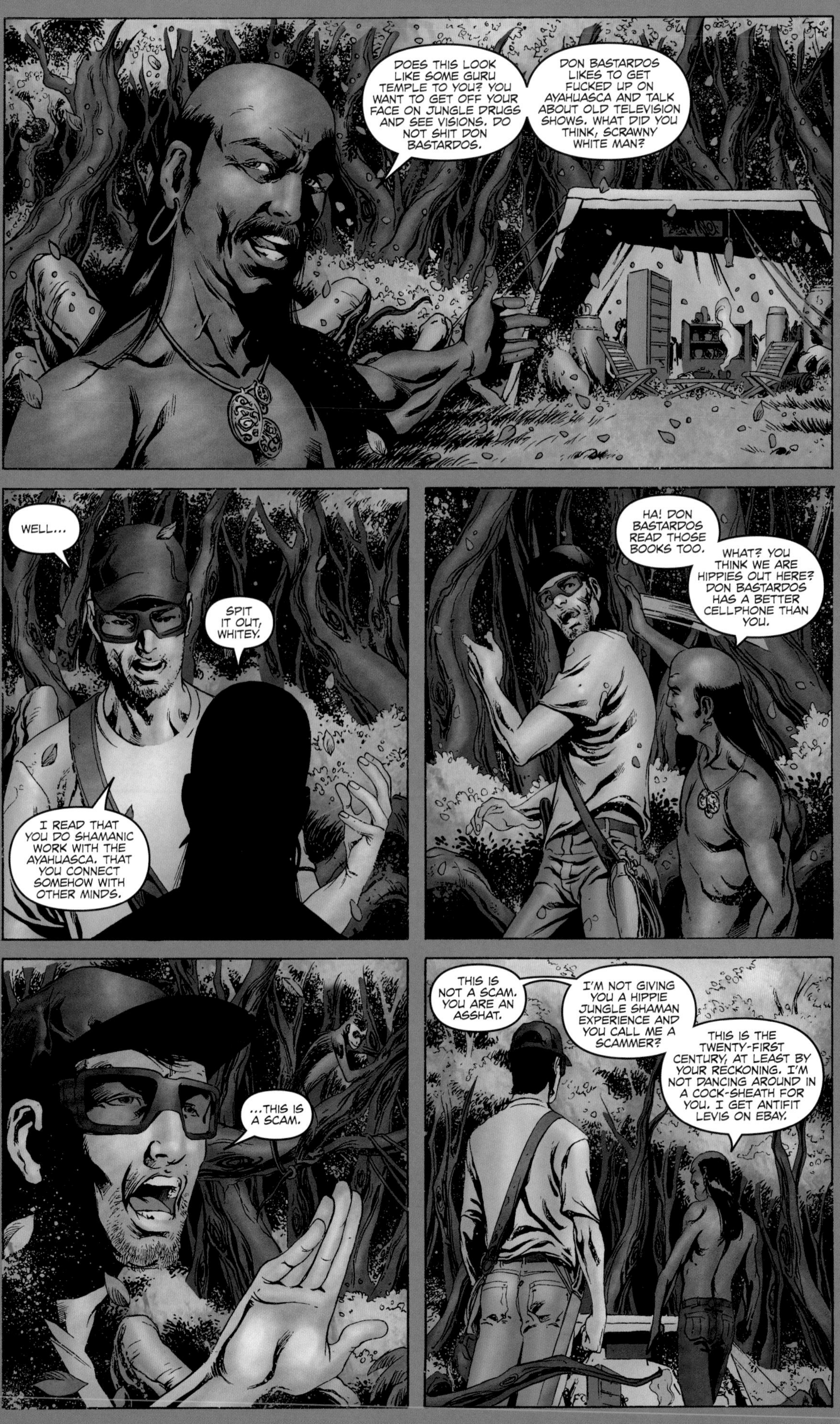
DOES THIS LOOK LIKE SOME GURU TEMPLE TO YOU? YOU WANT TO GET OFF YOUR FACE ON JUNGLE DRUGS AND SEE VISIONS. DO NOT SHIT DON BASTARDOS.
DON BASTARDOS LIKES TO GET FUCKED UP ON AYAHUASCA AND TALK ABOUT OLD TELEVISION SHOWS. WHAT DID YOU THINK, SCRAWNY WHITE MAN?
WELL...
SPIT IT OUT, WHITEY.
I READ THAT YOU DO SHAMANIC WORK WITH THE AYAHUASCA. THAT YOU CONNECT SOMEHOW WITH OTHER MINDS.
HA! DON BASTARDOS READ THOSE BOOKS TOO.
WHAT? YOU THINK WE ARE HIPPIES OUT HERE? DON BASTARDOS HAS A BETTER CELLPHONE THAN YOU.
...THIS IS A SCAM.
THIS IS NOT A SCAM. YOU ARE AN ASSHAT.
I'M NOT GIVING YOU A HIPPIE JUNGLE SHAMAN EXPERIENCE AND YOU CALL ME A SCAMMER?
THIS IS THE TWENTY-FIRST CENTURY, AT LEAST BY YOUR RECKONING. I'M NOT DANCING AROUND IN A COCK-SHEATH FOR YOU. I GET ANTIFIT LEVIS ON EBAY.

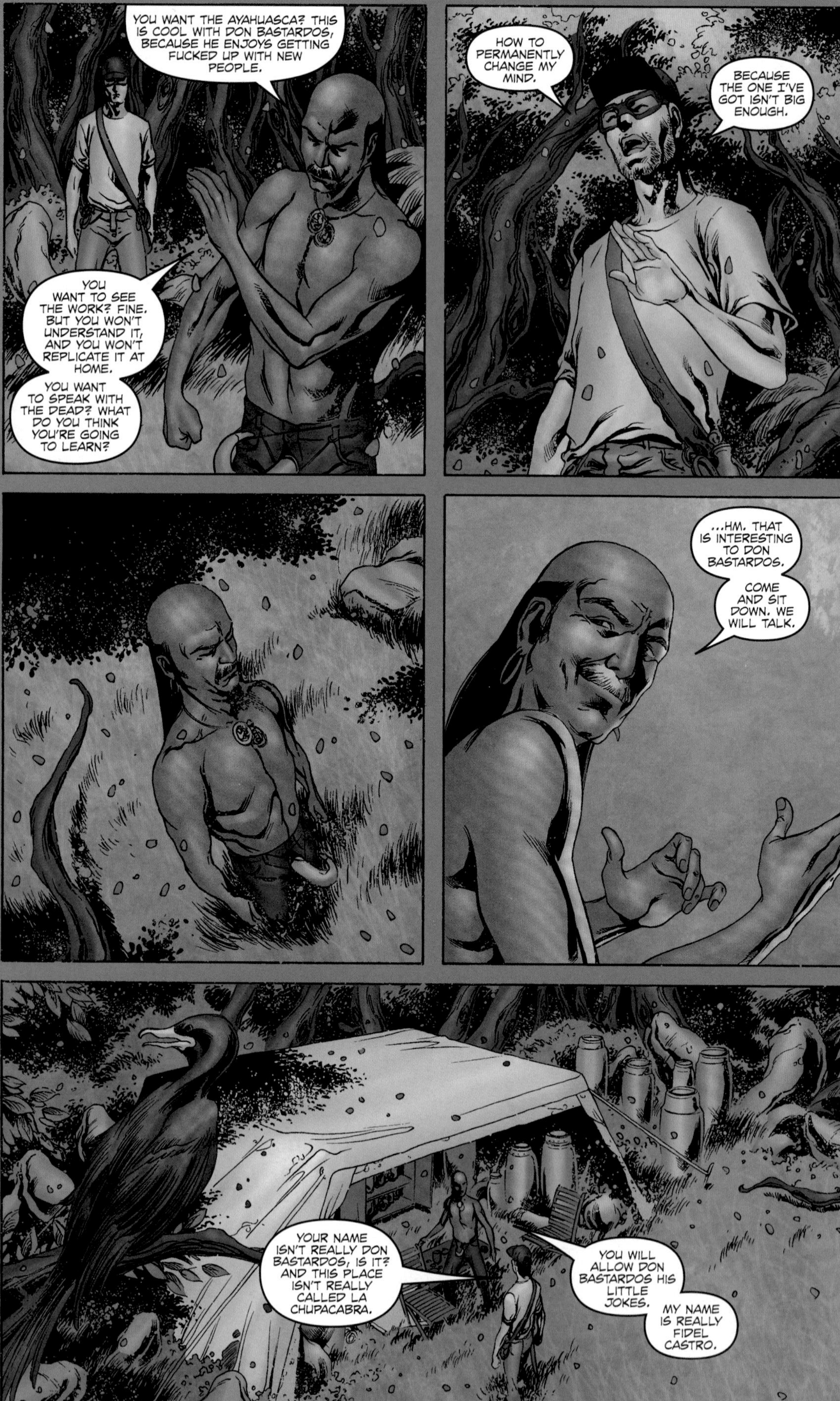
YOU WANT THE AYAHUASCA? THIS IS COOL WITH DON BASTARDOS, BECAUSE HE ENJOYS GETTING FUCKED UP WITH NEW PEOPLE.
YOU WANT TO SEE THE WORK? FINE. BUT YOU WON'T UNDERSTAND IT, AND YOU WON'T REPLICATE IT AT HOME.
YOU WANT TO SPEAK WITH THE DEAD? WHAT DO YOU THINK YOU'RE GOING TO LEARN?
HOW TO PERMANENTLY CHANGE MY MIND.
BECAUSE THE ONE I'VE GOT ISN'T BIG ENOUGH.
...HM. THAT IS INTERESTING TO DON BASTARDOS.
COME AND SIT DOWN. WE WILL TALK.
YOUR NAME ISN'T REALLY DON BASTARDOS, IS IT? AND THIS PLACE ISN'T REALLY CALLED LA CHUPACABRA.
YOU WILL ALLOW DON BASTARDOS HIS LITTLE JOKES.
MY NAME IS REALLY FIDEL CASTRO.

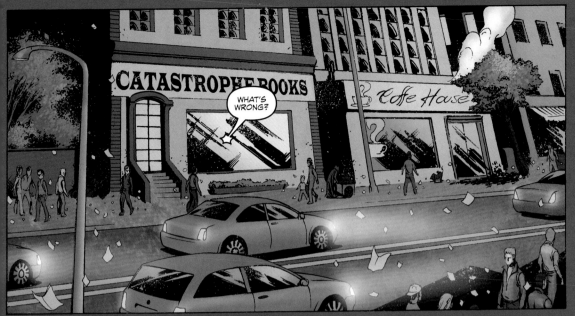

WHAT'S WRONG?

IT'S JOHN. THAT'S JOHN ON THE RADIO. JOHN'S BACK.

I THOUGHT... HELL, I THOUGHT HE WAS DEAD BY NOW.

WHY?

HE HAD A BREAKDOWN. I MEAN, HE REALLY LOST IT. AND THEN, ONE DAY, HE WAS JUST... GONE.

NOT A WORD, NOT A NOTE, NOTHING.

IT TOOK ME SO LONG TO GET OVER THAT.

AND NOW...

SING

SO WHAT IS IT? I MEAN, REALLY?

IS IT THAT YOU'D RESIGNED YOURSELF TO HIS BEING DEAD? IS IT THAT YOUR CREEPY NUTBAG EX-BOYFRIEND'S BACK?

OR IS IT THAT HE DIDN'T COME TO SEE YOU FIRST?

SING

YOU DIDN'T KNOW HIM. YOU WEREN'T AROUND FOR THOSE LAST FEW WEEKS BEFORE HE LEFT.

HE WAS CRAZY. I MEAN, HE REALLY FUCKING LOST IT. HE WAS... SCARY.

AND WHEN I LISTEN TO HIM THERE NOW... HE'S GOT THAT SAME WEIRD EDGE IN HIS VOICE.

SING

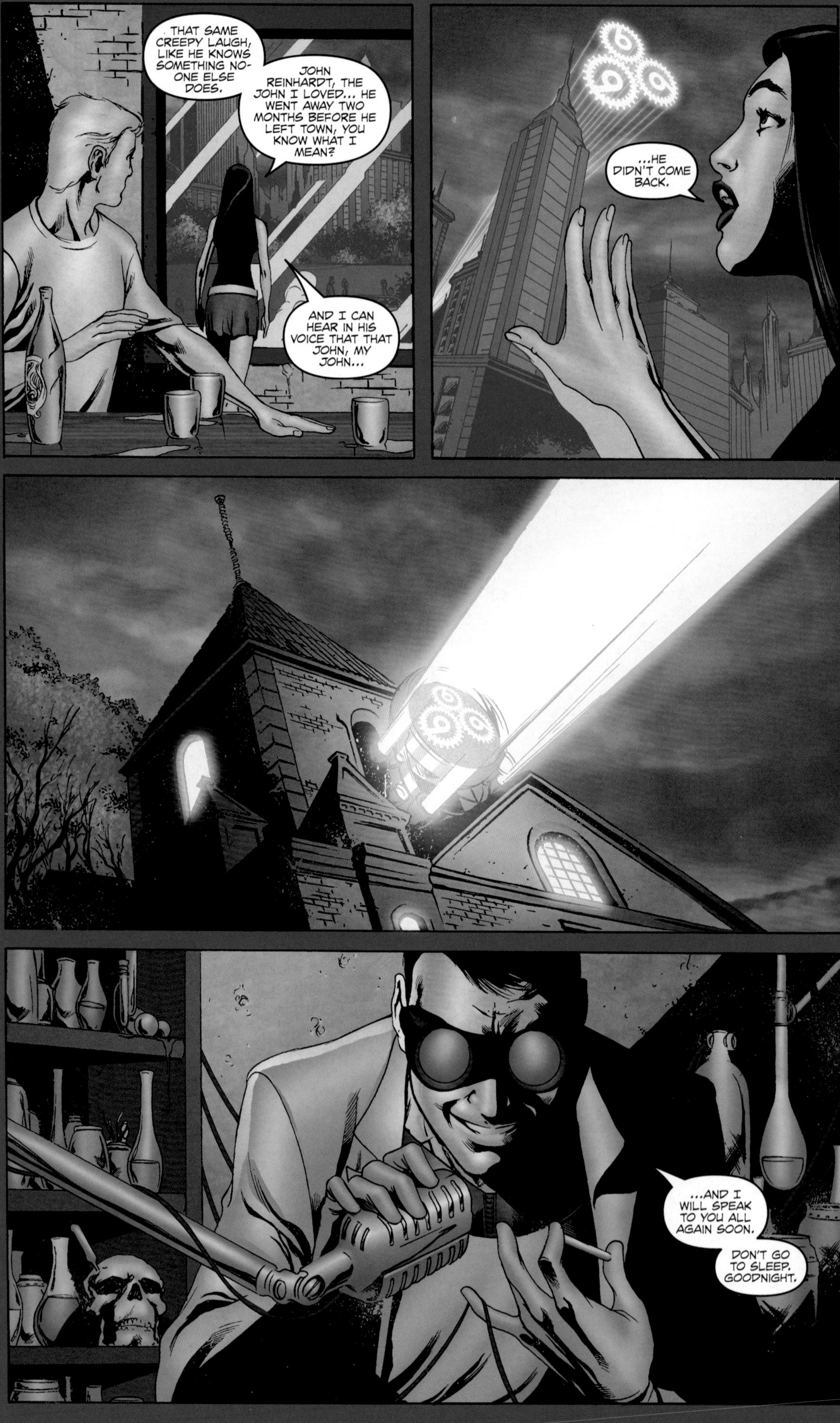
THAT SAME CREEPY LAUGH, LIKE HE KNOWS SOMETHING NO-ONE ELSE DOES.
JOHN REINHARDT, THE JOHN I LOVED... HE WENT AWAY TWO MONTHS BEFORE HE LEFT TOWN, YOU KNOW WHAT I MEAN?
AND I CAN HEAR IN HIS VOICE THAT THAT JOHN, MY JOHN...
...HE DIDN'T COME BACK.
...AND I WILL SPEAK TO YOU ALL AGAIN SOON.
DON'T GO TO SLEEP. GOODNIGHT.

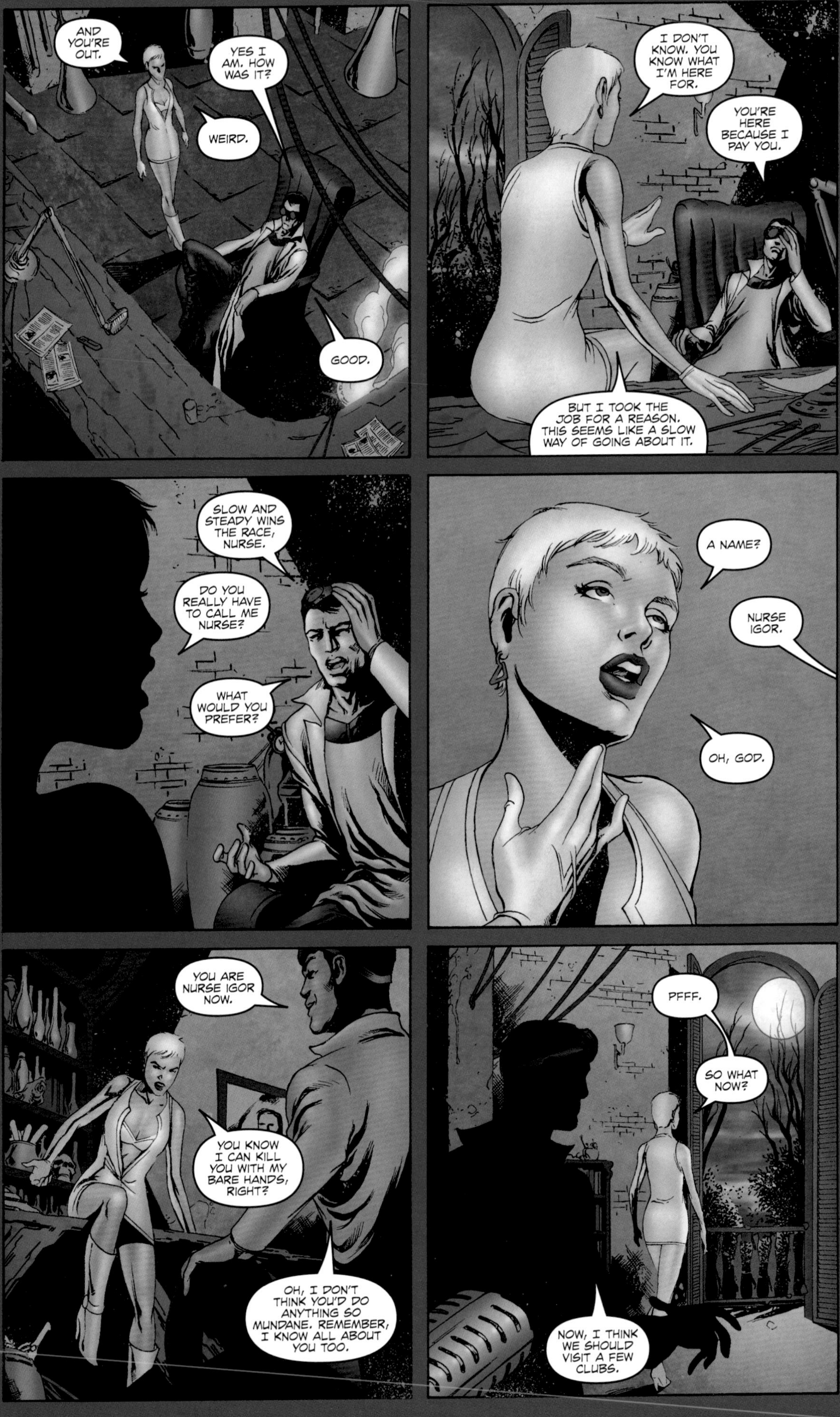
AND YOU'RE OUT.
YES I AM. HOW WAS IT?
WEIRD.
GOOD.
I DON'T KNOW. YOU KNOW WHAT I'M HERE FOR.
YOU'RE HERE BECAUSE I PAY YOU.
BUT I TOOK THE JOB FOR A REASON. THIS SEEMS LIKE A SLOW WAY OF GOING ABOUT IT.
SLOW AND STEADY WINS THE RACE, NURSE.
DO YOU REALLY HAVE TO CALL ME NURSE?
WHAT WOULD YOU PREFER?
A NAME?
NURSE IGOR.
OH, GOD.
YOU ARE NURSE IGOR NOW.
YOU KNOW I CAN KILL YOU WITH MY BARE HANDS, RIGHT?
OH, I DON'T THINK YOU'D DO ANYTHING SO MUNDANE. REMEMBER, I KNOW ALL ABOUT YOU TOO.
PFFF.
SO WHAT NOW?
NOW, I THINK WE SHOULD VISIT A FEW CLUBS.

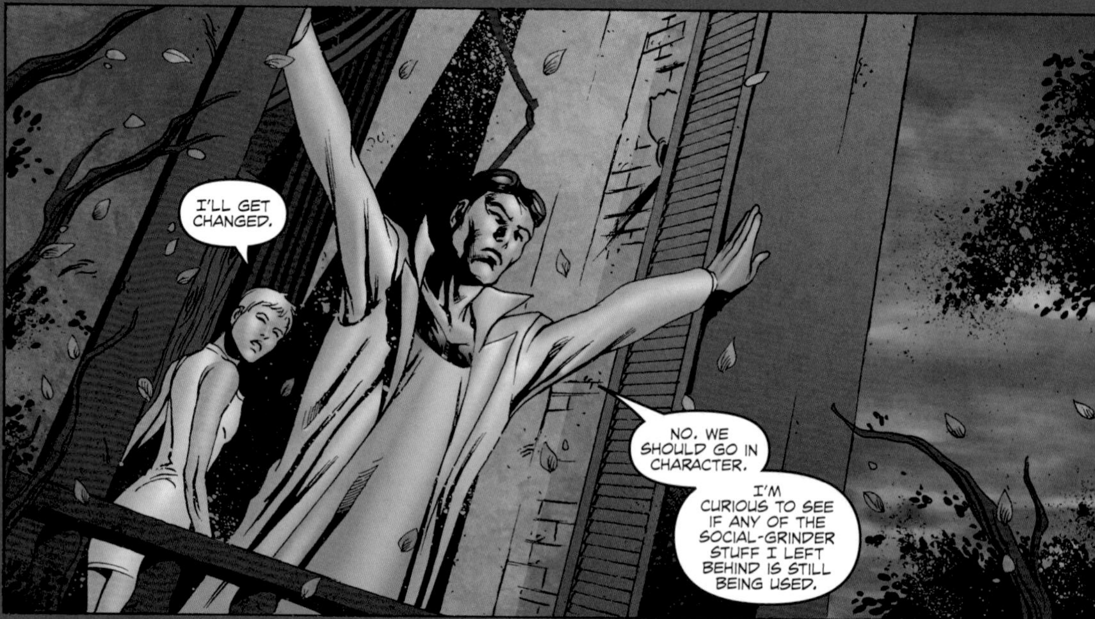
I'LL GET CHANGED.
NO. WE SHOULD GO IN CHARACTER.
I'M CURIOUS TO SEE IF ANY OF THE SOCIAL-GRINDER STUFF I LEFT BEHIND IS STILL BEING USED.

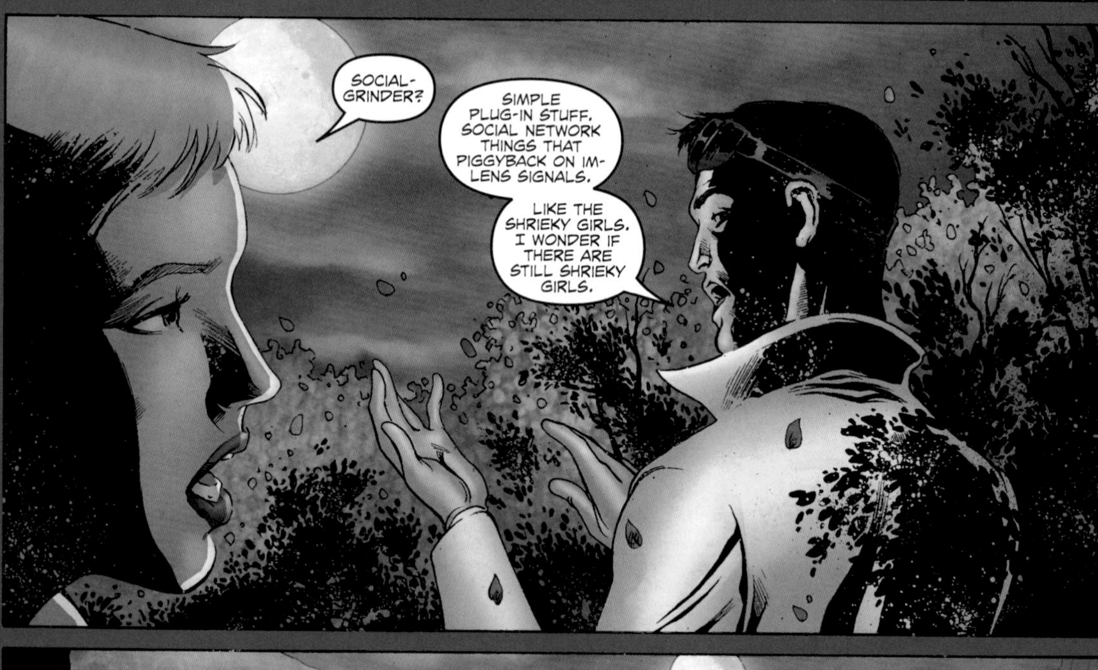
SOCIAL-GRINDER?
SIMPLE PLUG-IN STUFF. SOCIAL NETWORK THINGS THAT PIGGYBACK ON IM-LENS SIGNALS.
LIKE THE SHRIEKY GIRLS. I WONDER IF THERE ARE STILL SHRIEKY GIRLS.

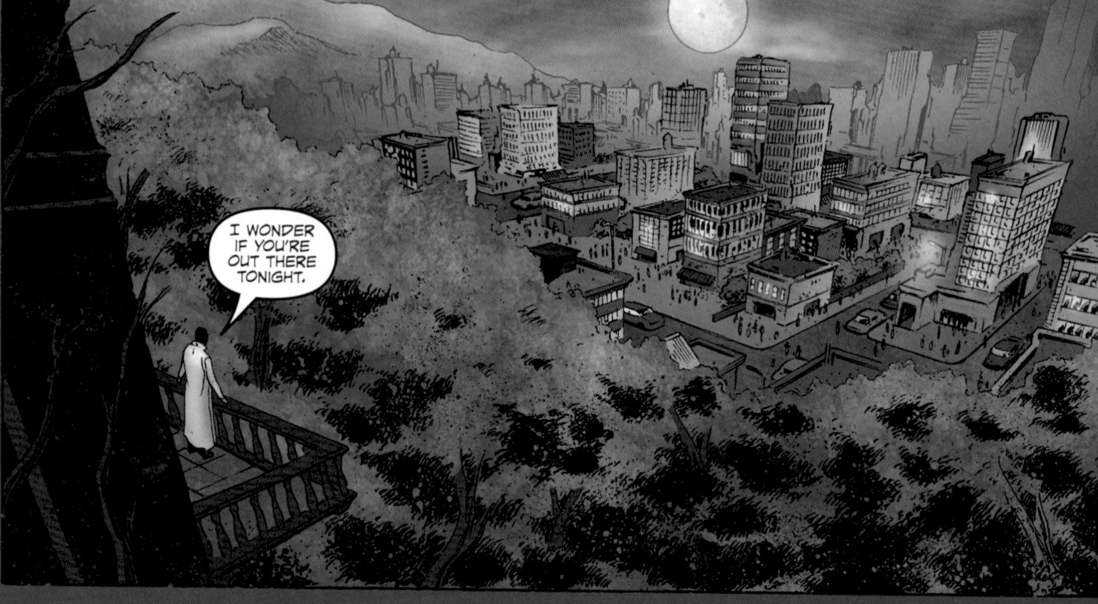
I WONDER IF YOU'RE OUT THERE TONIGHT.

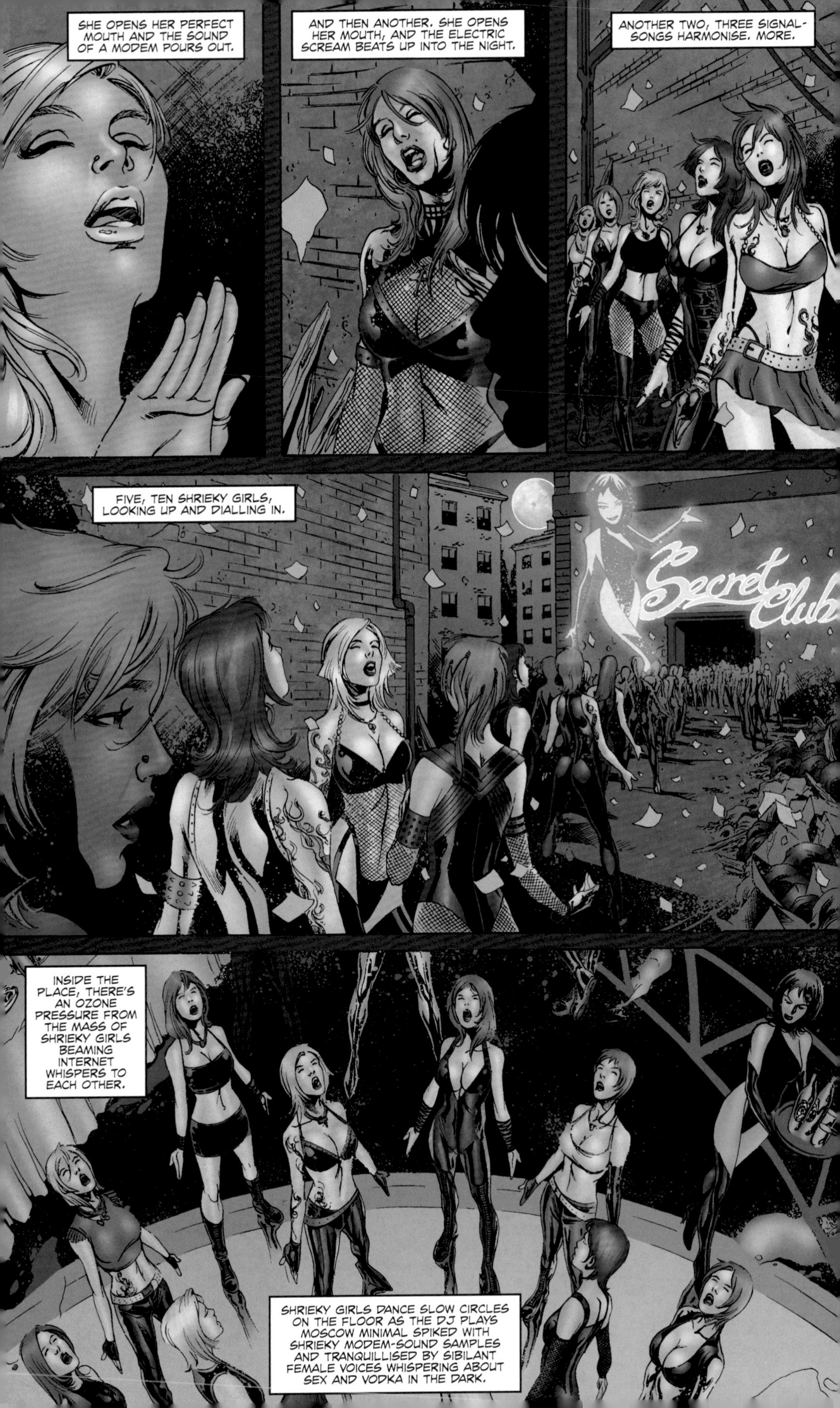
SHE OPENS HER PERFECT MOUTH AND THE SOUND OF A MODEM POURS OUT.
AND THEN ANOTHER. SHE OPENS HER MOUTH, AND THE ELECTRIC SCREAM BEATS UP INTO THE NIGHT.
ANOTHER TWO, THREE SIGNAL-SONGS HARMONISE. MORE.
FIVE, TEN SHRIEKY GIRLS, LOOKING UP AND DIALLING IN.
Secret Club
INSIDE THE PLACE, THERE'S AN OZONE PRESSURE FROM THE MASS OF SHRIEKY GIRLS BEAMING INTERNET WHISPERS TO EACH OTHER.
SHRIEKY GIRLS DANCE SLOW CIRCLES ON THE FLOOR AS THE DJ PLAYS MOSCOW MINIMAL SPIKED WITH SHRIEKY MODEM-SOUND SAMPLES AND TRANQUILLISED BY SIBILANT FEMALE VOICES WHISPERING ABOUT SEX AND VODKA IN THE DARK.

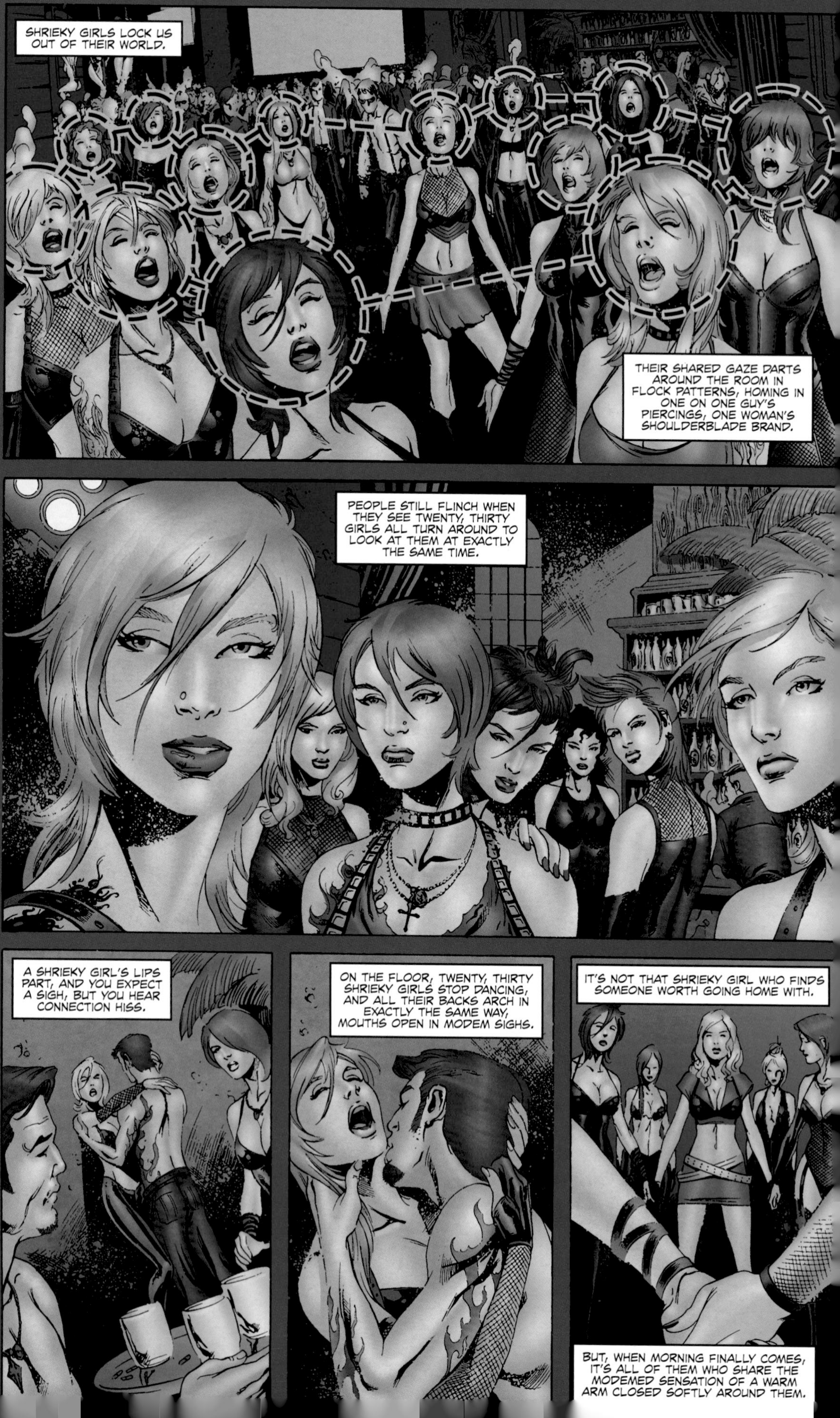

SHRIEKY GIRLS LOCK US OUT OF THEIR WORLD.
THEIR SHARED GAZE DARTS AROUND THE ROOM IN FLOCK PATTERNS, HOMING IN ONE ON ONE GUY'S PIERCINGS, ONE WOMAN'S SHOULDERBLADE BRAND.
PEOPLE STILL FLINCH WHEN THEY SEE TWENTY, THIRTY GIRLS ALL TURN AROUND TO LOOK AT THEM AT EXACTLY THE SAME TIME.
A SHRIEKY GIRL'S LIPS PART, AND YOU EXPECT A SIGH, BUT YOU HEAR CONNECTION HISS.
ON THE FLOOR, TWENTY, THIRTY SHRIEKY GIRLS STOP DANCING, AND ALL THEIR BACKS ARCH IN EXACTLY THE SAME WAY, MOUTHS OPEN IN MODEM SIGHS.
IT'S NOT THAT SHRIEKY GIRL WHO FINDS SOMEONE WORTH GOING HOME WITH.
BUT, WHEN MORNING FINALLY COMES, IT'S ALL OF THEM WHO SHARE THE MODEMED SENSATION OF A WARM ARM CLOSED SOFTLY AROUND THEM.

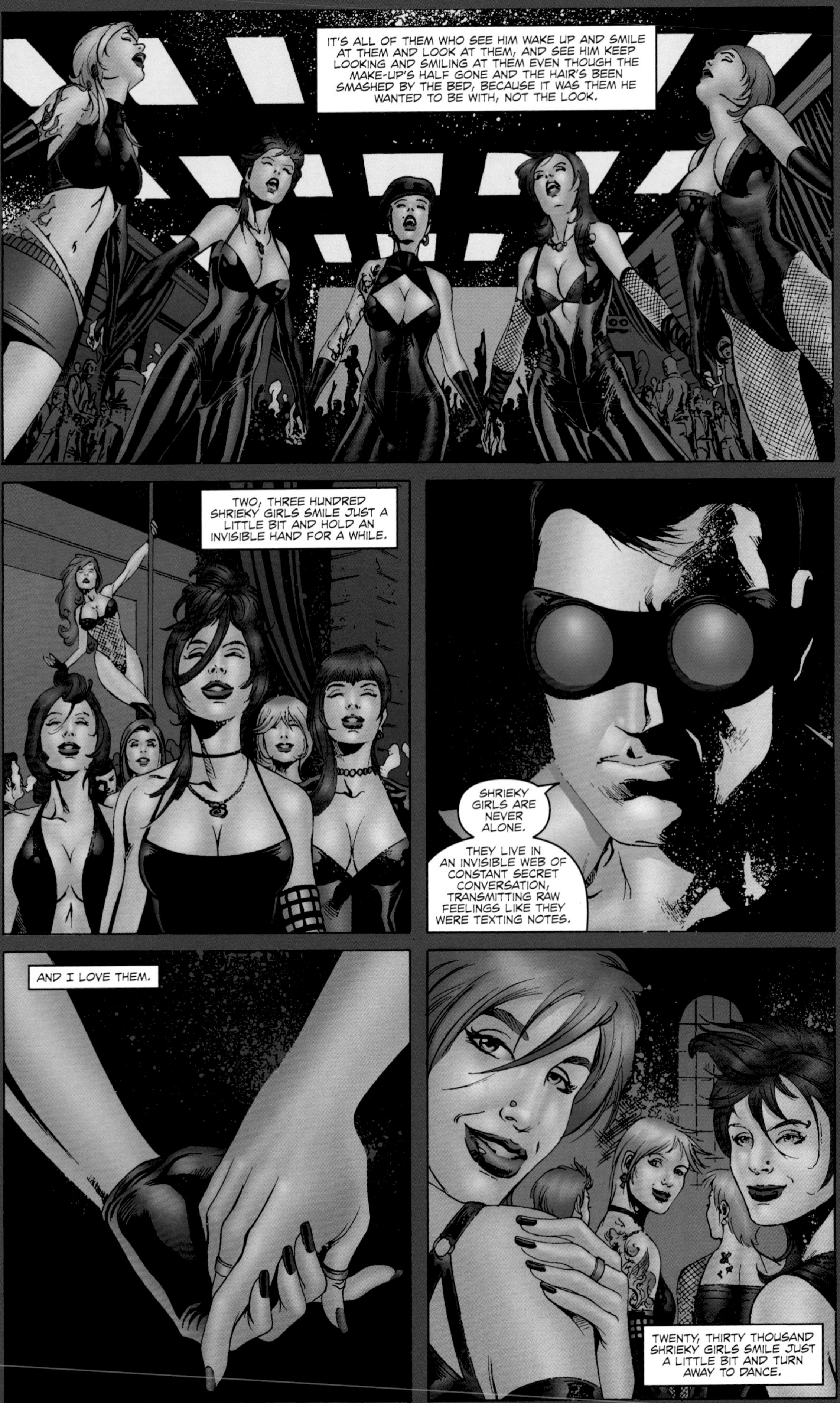
IT'S ALL OF THEM WHO SEE HIM WAKE UP AND SMILE AT THEM AND LOOK AT THEM, AND SEE HIM KEEP LOOKING AND SMILING AT THEM EVEN THOUGH THE MAKE-UP'S HALF GONE AND THE HAIR'S BEEN SMASHED BY THE BED, BECAUSE IT WAS THEM HE WANTED TO BE WITH, NOT THE LOOK.
TWO, THREE HUNDRED SHRIEKY GIRLS SMILE JUST A LITTLE BIT AND HOLD AN INVISIBLE HAND FOR A WHILE.
SHRIEKY GIRLS ARE NEVER ALONE.
THEY LIVE IN AN INVISIBLE WEB OF CONSTANT SECRET CONVERSATION, TRANSMITTING RAW FEELINGS LIKE THEY WERE TEXTING NOTES.
AND I LOVE THEM.
TWENTY, THIRTY THOUSAND SHRIEKY GIRLS SMILE JUST A LITTLE BIT AND TURN AWAY TO DANCE.

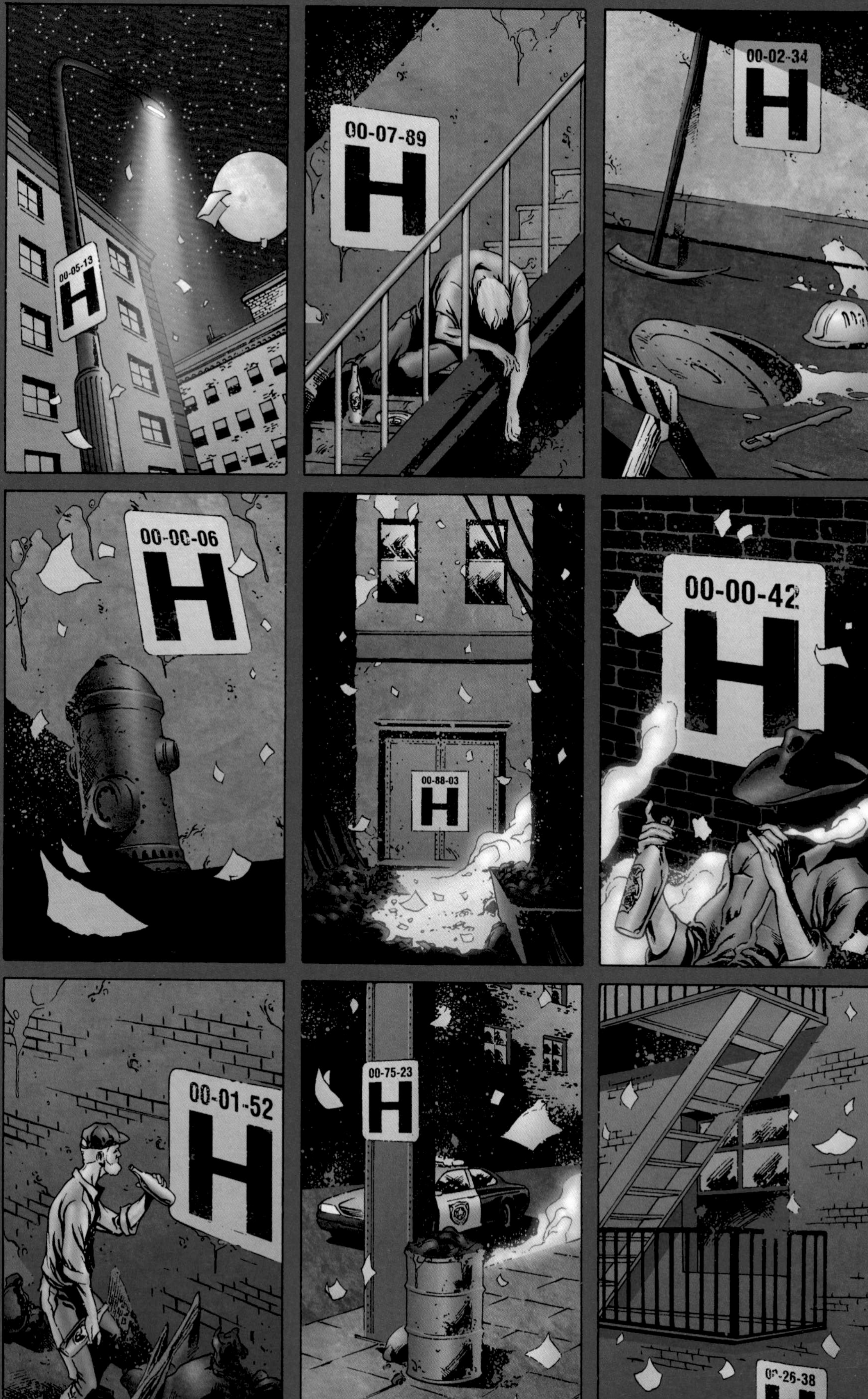

00-05-13
H
00-07-89
H
00-02-34
H
00-00-06
H
00-88-03
H
00-00-42
H
00-01-52
H
00-75-23
H
26-38
H

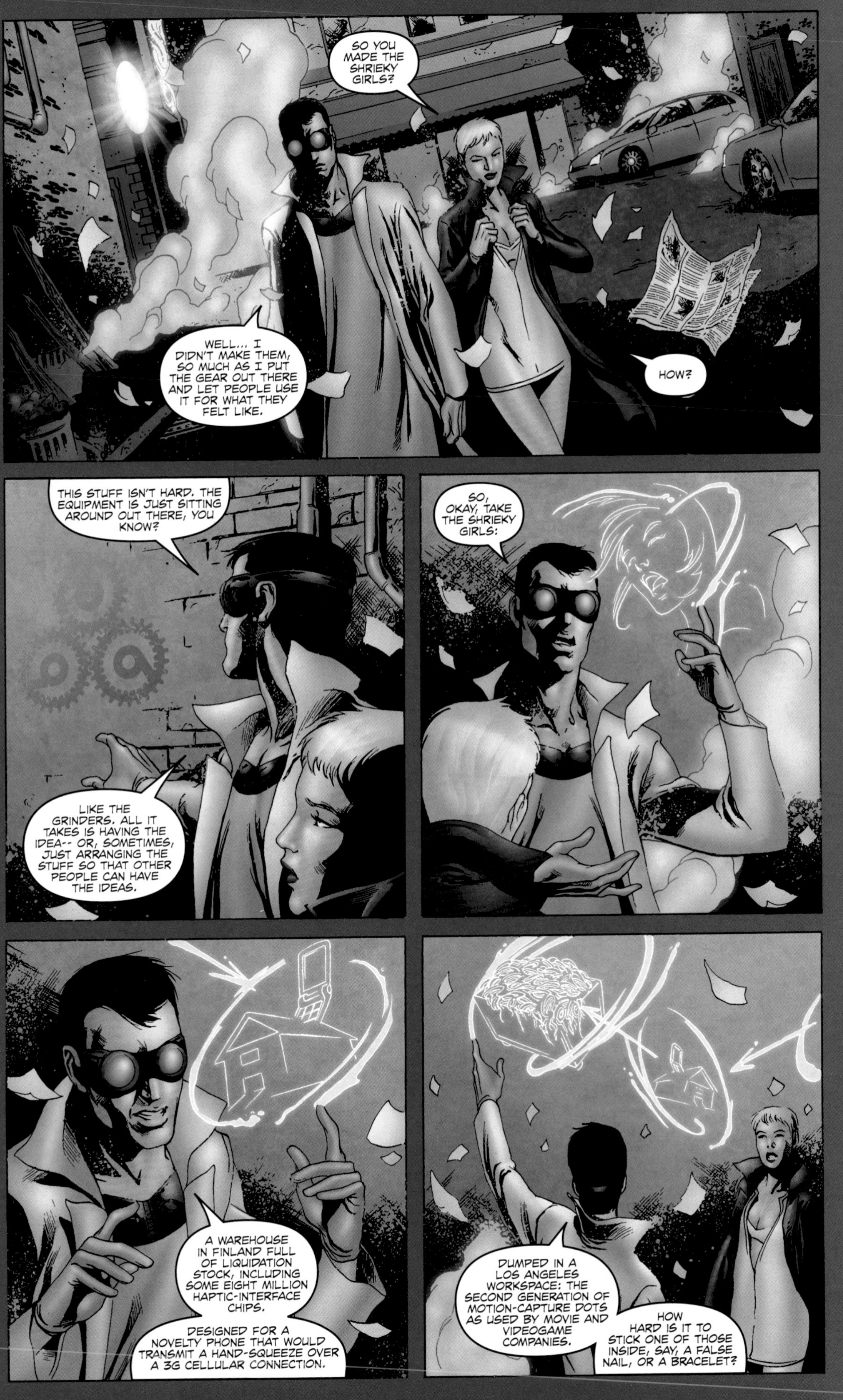

SO YOU MADE THE SHRIEKY GIRLS?
WELL... I DIDN'T MAKE THEM, SO MUCH AS I PUT THE GEAR OUT THERE AND LET PEOPLE USE IT FOR WHAT THEY FELT LIKE.
HOW?
THIS STUFF ISN'T HARD. THE EQUIPMENT IS JUST SITTING AROUND OUT THERE, YOU KNOW?
LIKE THE GRINDERS. ALL IT TAKES IS HAVING THE IDEA-- OR, SOMETIMES, JUST ARRANGING THE STUFF SO THAT OTHER PEOPLE CAN HAVE THE IDEAS.
SO, OKAY, TAKE THE SHRIEKY GIRLS:
A WAREHOUSE IN FINLAND FULL OF LIQUIDATION STOCK, INCLUDING SOME EIGHT MILLION HAPTIC-INTERFACE CHIPS.
DESIGNED FOR A NOVELTY PHONE THAT WOULD TRANSMIT A HAND-SQUEEZE OVER A 3G CELLULAR CONNECTION.
DUMPED IN A LOS ANGELES WORKSPACE: THE SECOND GENERATION OF MOTION-CAPTURE DOTS AS USED BY MOVIE AND VIDEOGAME COMPANIES.
HOW HARD IS IT TO STICK ONE OF THOSE INSIDE, SAY, A FALSE NAIL, OR A BRACELET?

ANSWER: IT'S NOT, REALLY. I CAN TEACH ANYONE WITH OPPOSABLE THUMBS HOW TO DO IT INSIDE AN HOUR.

THE TRICK IS IN HAVING THE IDEA, AND THE MONEY TO TEST IT OUT. AND EVEN THEN, Y'KNOW, THE OBTAINING OF MONEY IS AS MUCH AN ENGINEERING PROBLEM AS ANYTHING.

ANYWAY: THE SHRIEKY GIRL SYSTEM IS LITERALLY JUST HALF A DOZEN ABANDONED OBJECTS AND CHEAP ELECTRONIC RIGGING.

YOU'VE GOT TO REMEMBER, THE WORLD'S FULL OF THIS KIND OF CRAP. I CAN BUY A LANDFILL'S WORTH OF FAULTY OR OUTDATED BLUETOOTH EARPIECES OUT OF INDIA FOR A PENNY EACH.

SURE, THAT MIGHT MEAN I ACTUALLY NEED A COUPLE HUNDRED THOUSAND DOLLARS. BUT IF I *HAVE* THAT...

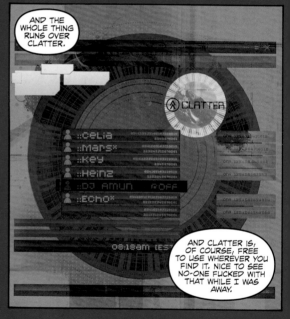

AND THE WHOLE THING RUNS OVER CLATTER.

CLATTER

::celia
::mars×
::key
::Heinz
::DJ AMUN   @OFF
::echo×

08:18am [ES]

AND CLATTER IS, OF COURSE, FREE TO USE WHEREVER YOU FIND IT. NICE TO SEE NO-ONE FUCKED WITH THAT WHILE I WAS AWAY.

CLATTER'S YOURS?

I BUILT CLATTER.

I BUILT A LOT OF STUFF.

WHAT ARE THESE THINGS? I THOUGHT THEY WERE FOR PUBLIC UTILITIES OR SOMETHING, BUT...

AH, THE H-PLATES.

YEAH. PEOPLE THINK THEY'RE FOR THE FIRE DEPARTMENT, OR THE WATER COMPANY, OR EVEN THE POLICE.

09-77-01
H

THEY'RE NOT.

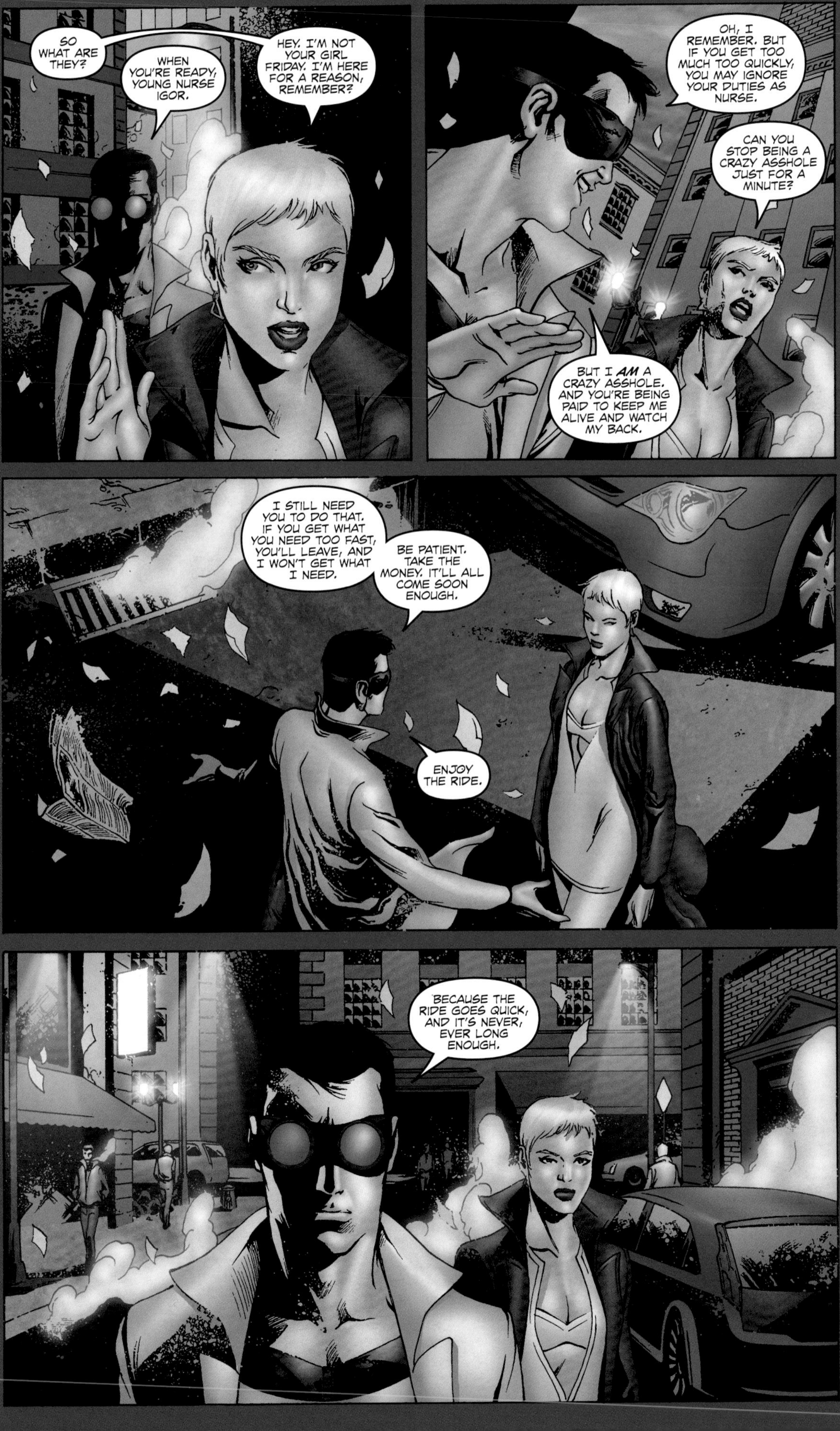
SO WHAT ARE THEY?
WHEN YOU'RE READY, YOUNG NURSE IGOR.
HEY. I'M NOT YOUR GIRL FRIDAY. I'M HERE FOR A REASON, REMEMBER?
OH, I REMEMBER. BUT IF YOU GET TOO MUCH TOO QUICKLY, YOU MAY IGNORE YOUR DUTIES AS NURSE.
CAN YOU STOP BEING A CRAZY ASSHOLE JUST FOR A MINUTE?
BUT I *AM* A CRAZY ASSHOLE. AND YOU'RE BEING PAID TO KEEP ME ALIVE AND WATCH MY BACK.
I STILL NEED YOU TO DO THAT. IF YOU GET WHAT YOU NEED TOO FAST, YOU'LL LEAVE, AND I WON'T GET WHAT I NEED.
BE PATIENT. TAKE THE MONEY. IT'LL ALL COME SOON ENOUGH.
ENJOY THE RIDE.
'BECAUSE THE RIDE GOES QUICK, AND IT'S NEVER, EVER LONG ENOUGH.

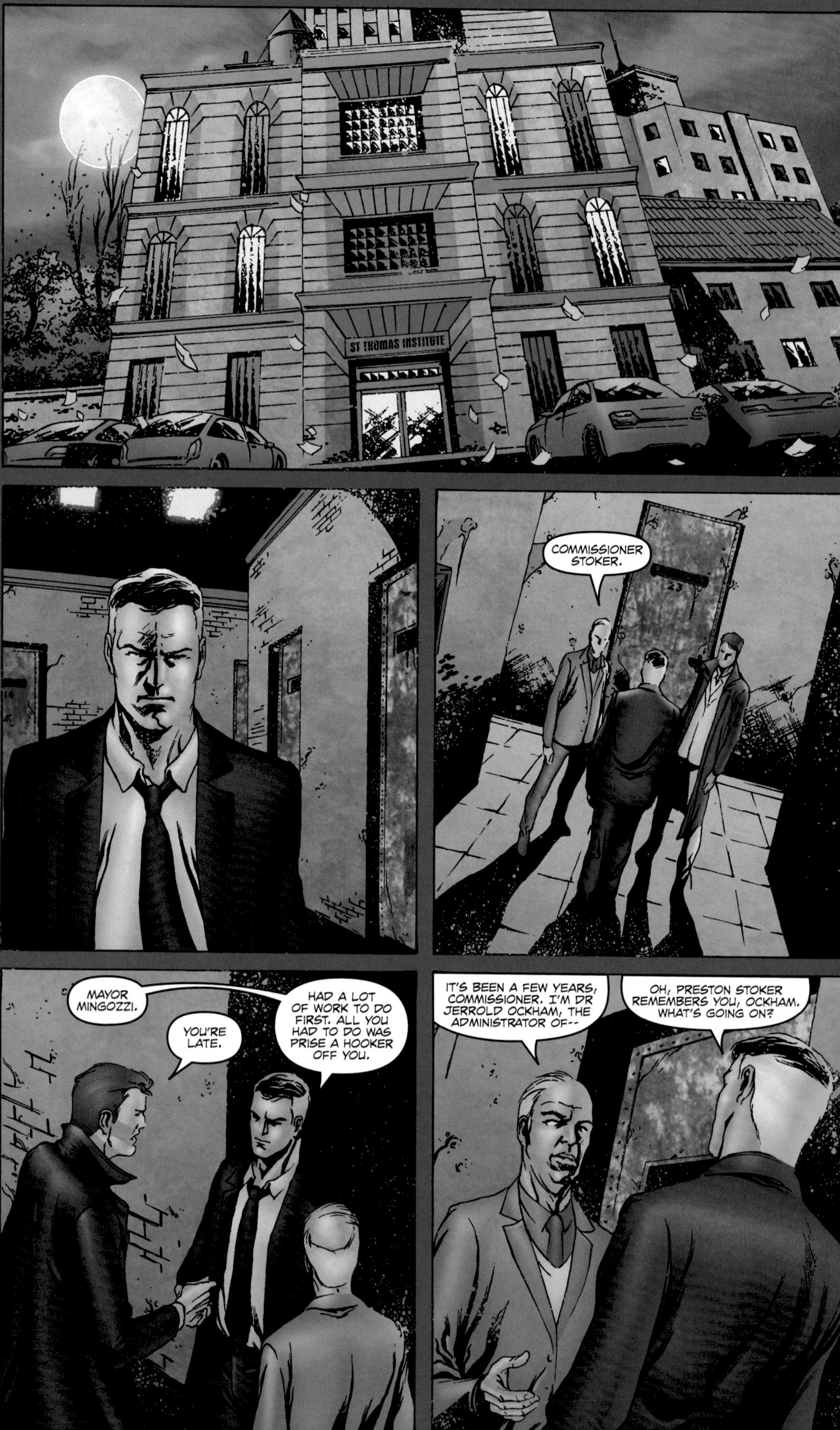

ST THOMAS INSTITUTE
COMMISSIONER STOKER.
MAYOR MINGOZZI.
YOU'RE LATE.
HAD A LOT OF WORK TO DO FIRST. ALL YOU HAD TO DO WAS PRISE A HOOKER OFF YOU.
IT'S BEEN A FEW YEARS, COMMISSIONER. I'M DR JERROLD OCKHAM, THE ADMINISTRATOR OF--
OH, PRESTON STOKER REMEMBERS YOU, OCKHAM. WHAT'S GOING ON?

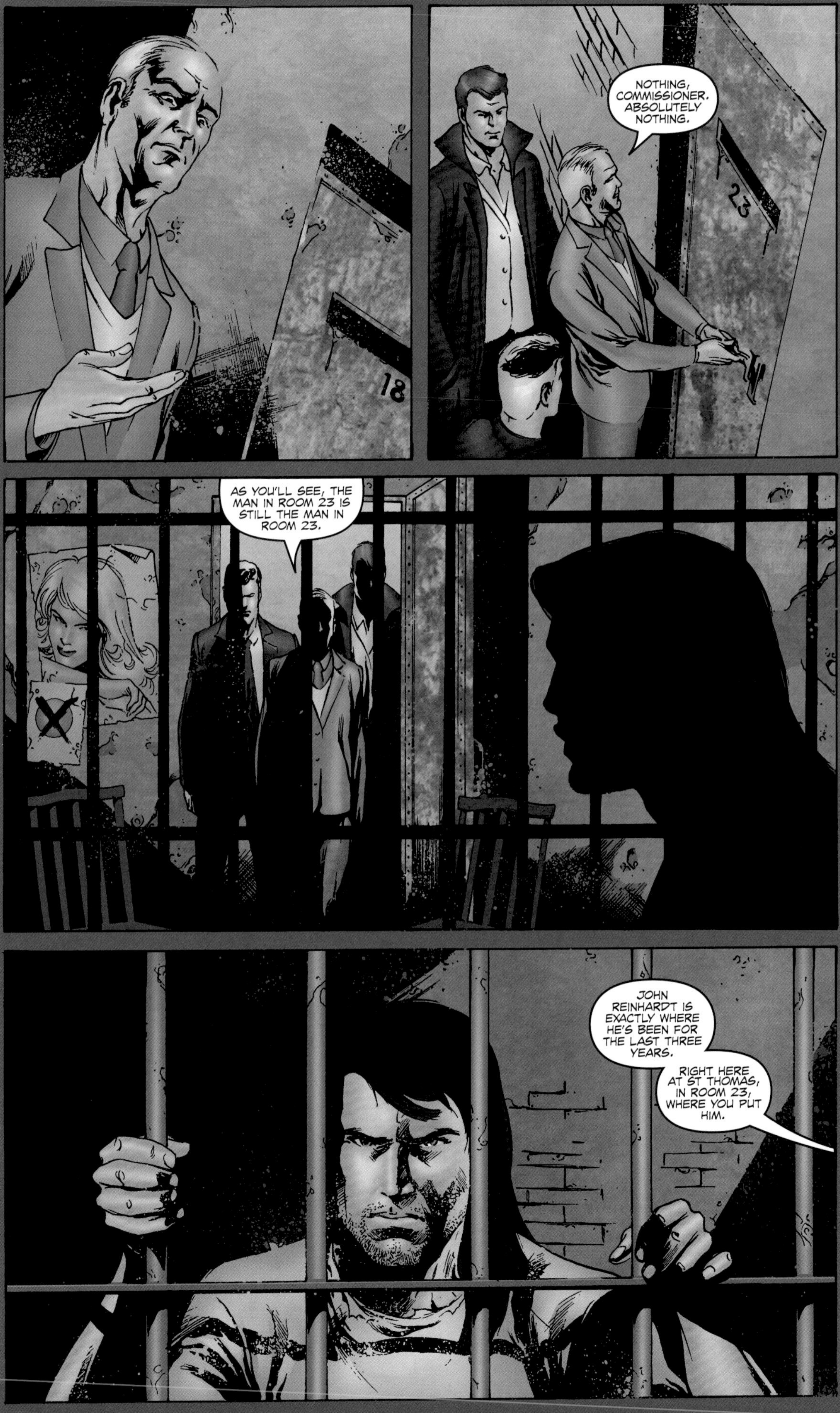
NOTHING, COMMISSIONER. ABSOLUTELY NOTHING.
AS YOU'LL SEE, THE MAN IN ROOM 23 IS STILL THE MAN IN ROOM 23.
JOHN REINHARDT IS EXACTLY WHERE HE'S BEEN FOR THE LAST THREE YEARS.
RIGHT HERE AT ST THOMAS, IN ROOM 23, WHERE YOU PUT HIM.

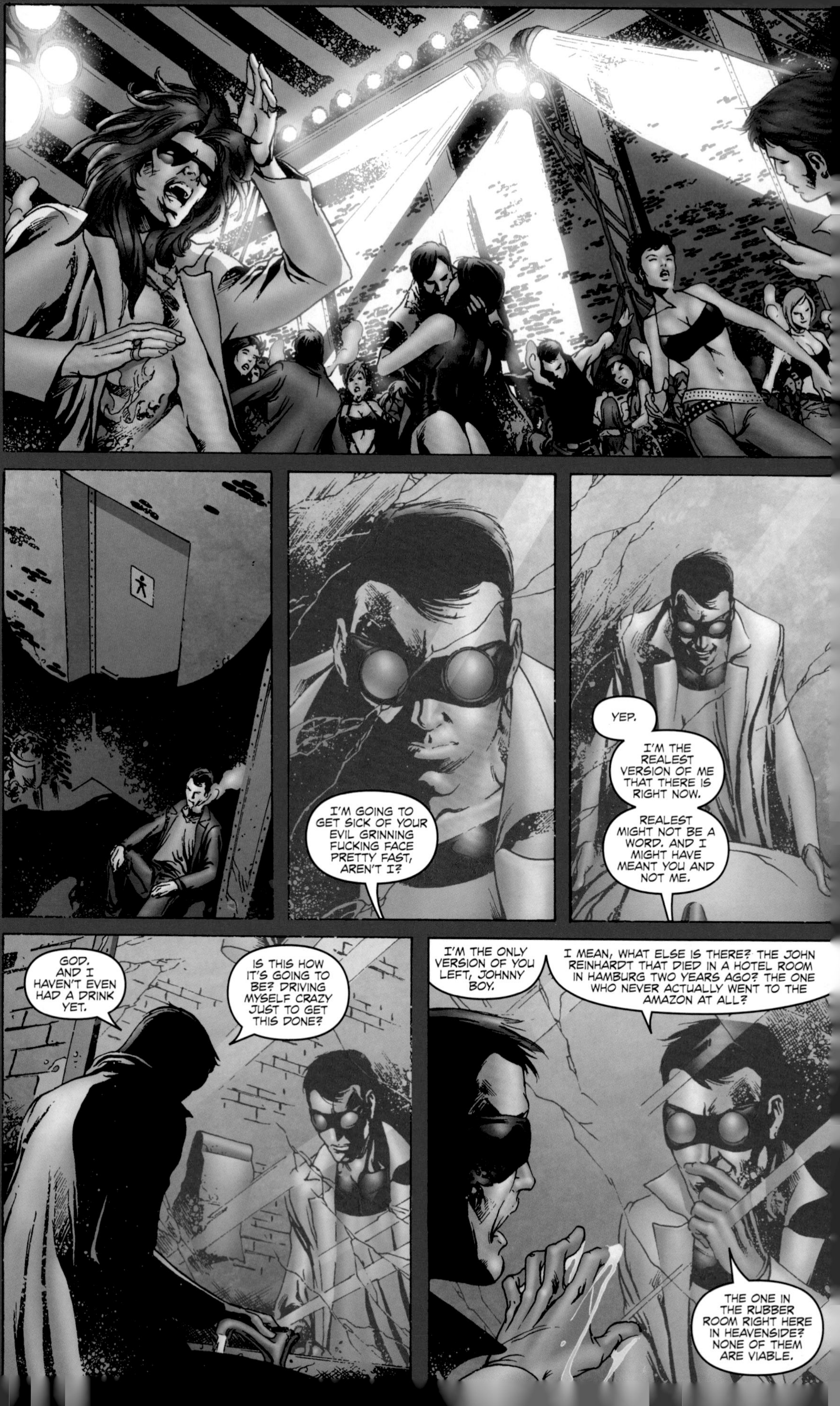
I'M GOING TO GET SICK OF YOUR EVIL GRINNING FUCKING FACE PRETTY FAST, AREN'T I?
YEP.
I'M THE REALEST VERSION OF ME THAT THERE IS RIGHT NOW.
REALEST MIGHT NOT BE A WORD. AND I MIGHT HAVE MEANT YOU AND NOT ME.
GOD. AND I HAVEN'T EVEN HAD A DRINK YET.
IS THIS HOW IT'S GOING TO BE? DRIVING MYSELF CRAZY JUST TO GET THIS DONE?
I'M THE ONLY VERSION OF YOU LEFT, JOHNNY BOY.
I MEAN, WHAT ELSE IS THERE? THE JOHN REINHARDT THAT DIED IN A HOTEL ROOM IN HAMBURG TWO YEARS AGO? THE ONE WHO NEVER ACTUALLY WENT TO THE AMAZON AT ALL?
THE ONE IN THE RUBBER ROOM RIGHT HERE IN HEAVENSIDE? NONE OF THEM ARE VIABLE.

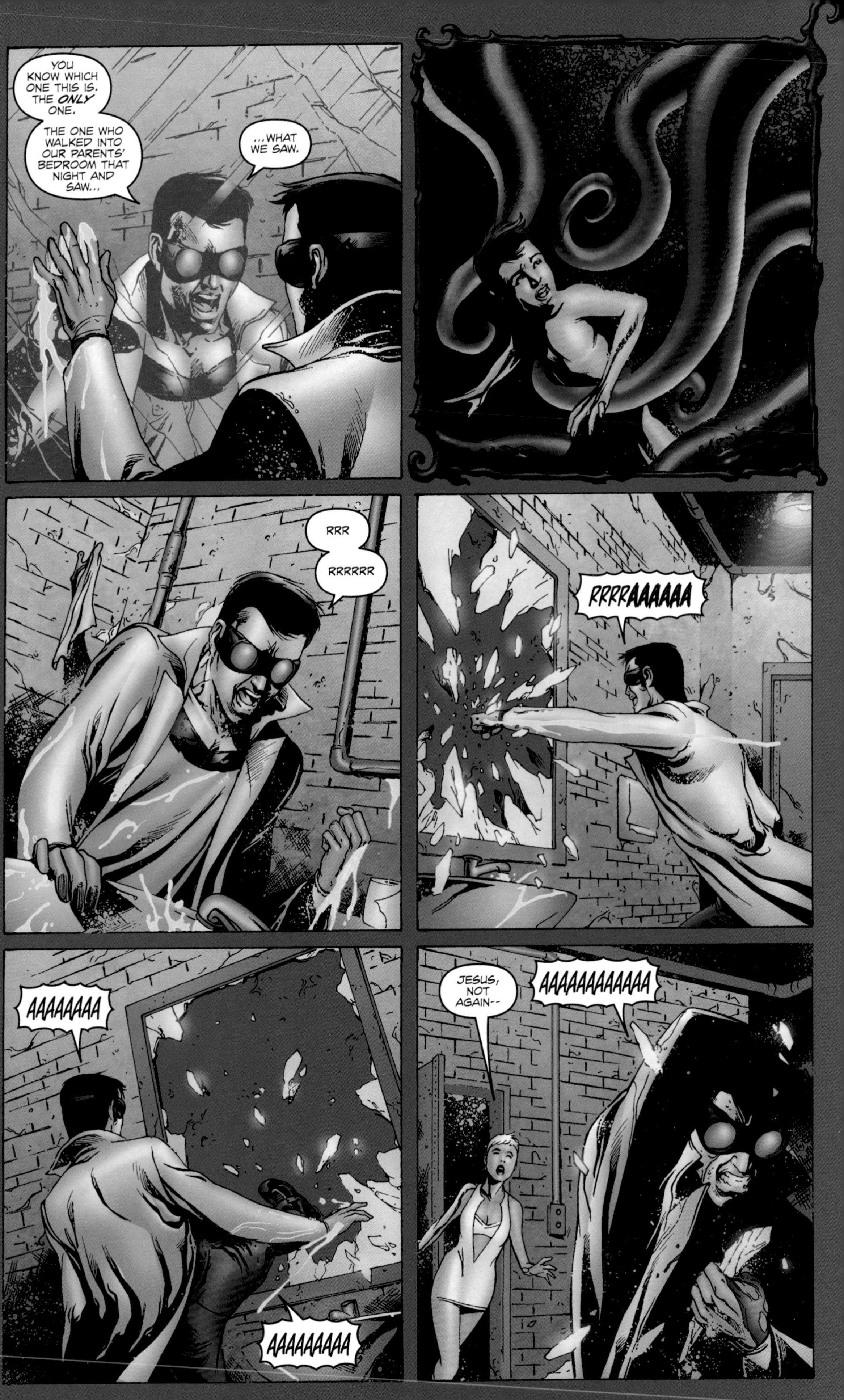
YOU KNOW WHICH ONE THIS IS. THE *ONLY* ONE.
THE ONE WHO WALKED INTO OUR PARENTS' BEDROOM THAT NIGHT AND SAW...
...WHAT WE SAW.
RRR
RRRRRR
RRRRAAAAAA
AAAAAAAA
AAAAAAAAA
JESUS, NOT AGAIN--
AAAAAAAAAAAA

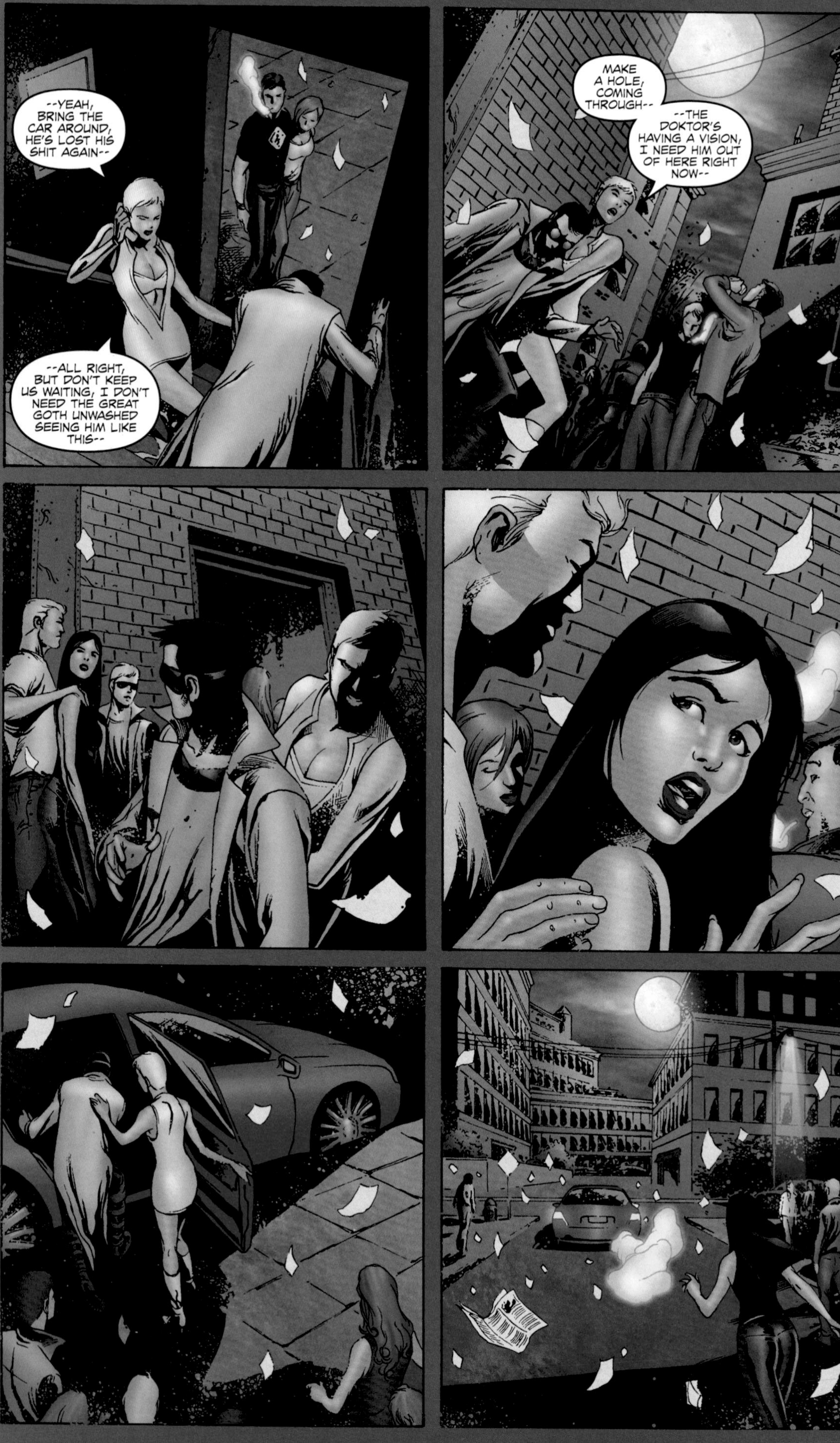
--YEAH, BRING THE CAR AROUND, HE'S LOST HIS SHIT AGAIN--
--ALL RIGHT, BUT DON'T KEEP US WAITING, I DON'T NEED THE GREAT GOTH UNWASHED SEEING HIM LIKE THIS--
MAKE A HOLE, COMING THROUGH--
--THE DOKTOR'S HAVING A VISION, I NEED HIM OUT OF HERE RIGHT NOW--

PART THREE

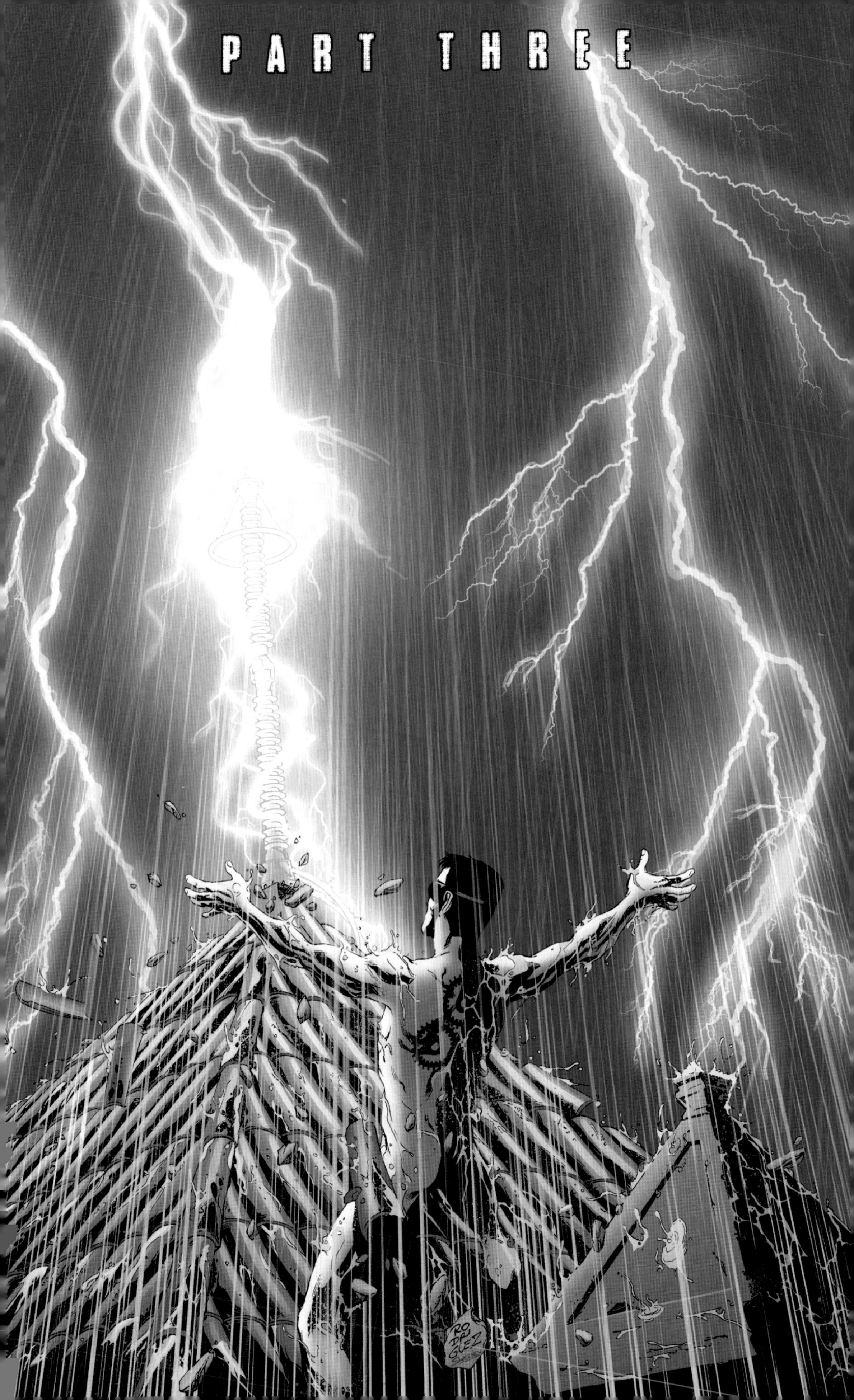

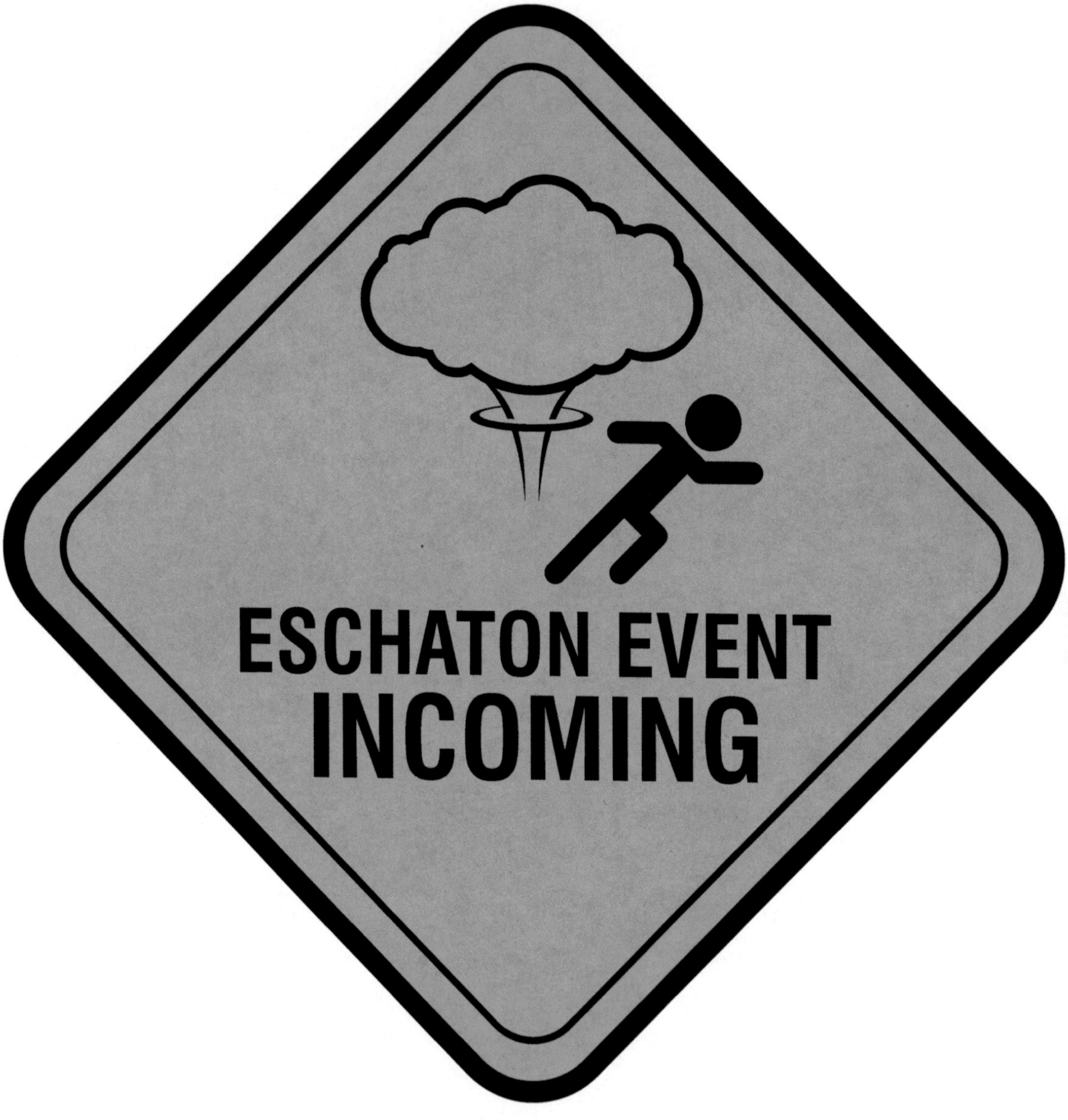
ESCHATON EVENT
INCOMING

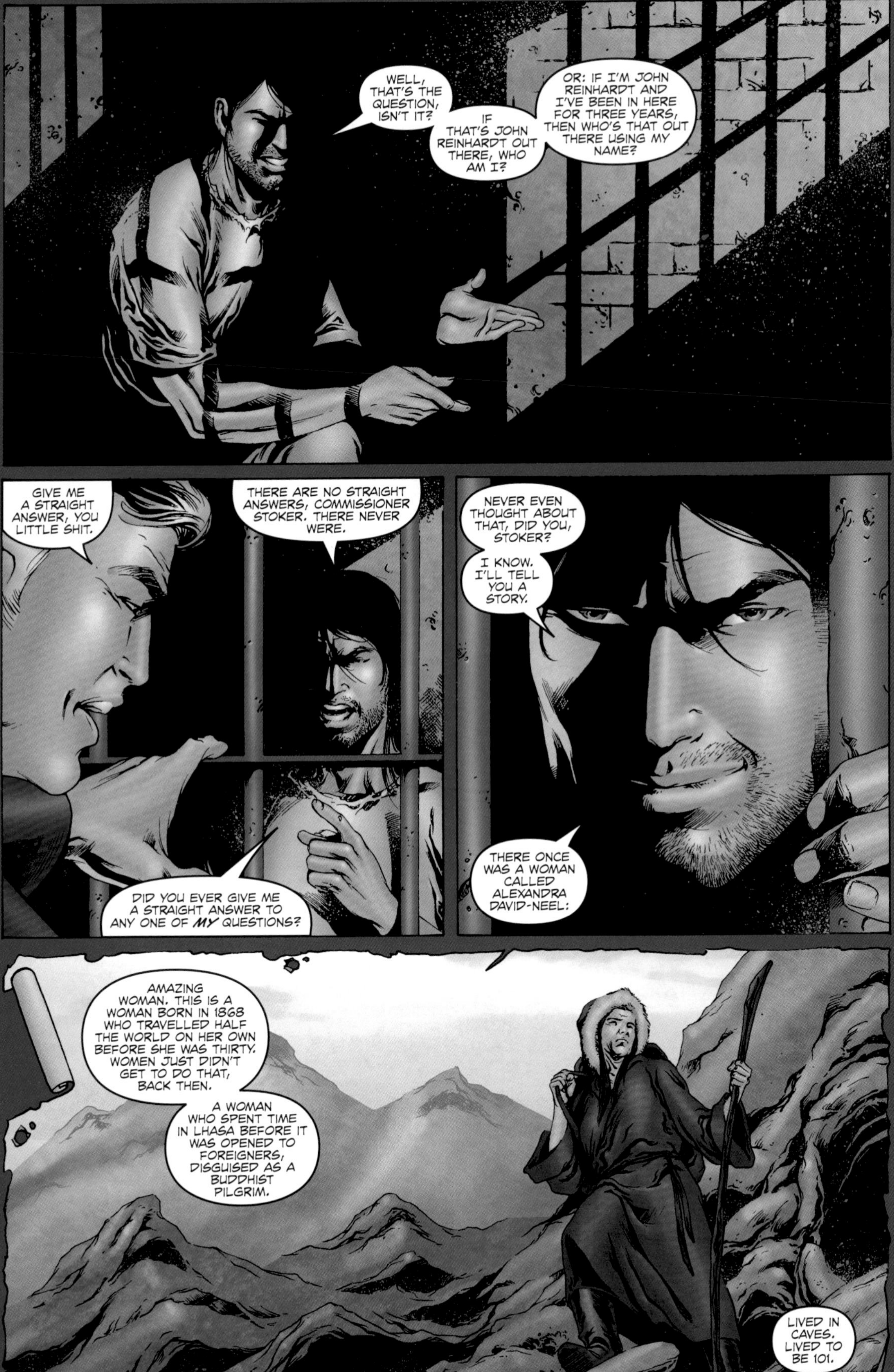

WELL, THAT'S THE QUESTION, ISN'T IT?
IF THAT'S JOHN REINHARDT OUT THERE, WHO AM I?
OR: IF I'M JOHN REINHARDT AND I'VE BEEN IN HERE FOR THREE YEARS, THEN WHO'S THAT OUT THERE USING MY NAME?
GIVE ME A STRAIGHT ANSWER, YOU LITTLE SHIT.
THERE ARE NO STRAIGHT ANSWERS, COMMISSIONER STOKER. THERE NEVER WERE.
DID YOU EVER GIVE ME A STRAIGHT ANSWER TO ANY ONE OF MY QUESTIONS?
NEVER EVEN THOUGHT ABOUT THAT, DID YOU, STOKER?
I KNOW. I'LL TELL YOU A STORY.
THERE ONCE WAS A WOMAN CALLED ALEXANDRA DAVID-NEEL:
AMAZING WOMAN. THIS IS A WOMAN BORN IN 1868 WHO TRAVELLED HALF THE WORLD ON HER OWN BEFORE SHE WAS THIRTY. WOMEN JUST DIDN'T GET TO DO THAT, BACK THEN.
A WOMAN WHO SPENT TIME IN LHASA BEFORE IT WAS OPENED TO FOREIGNERS, DISGUISED AS A BUDDHIST PILGRIM.
LIVED IN CAVES. LIVED TO BE 101.

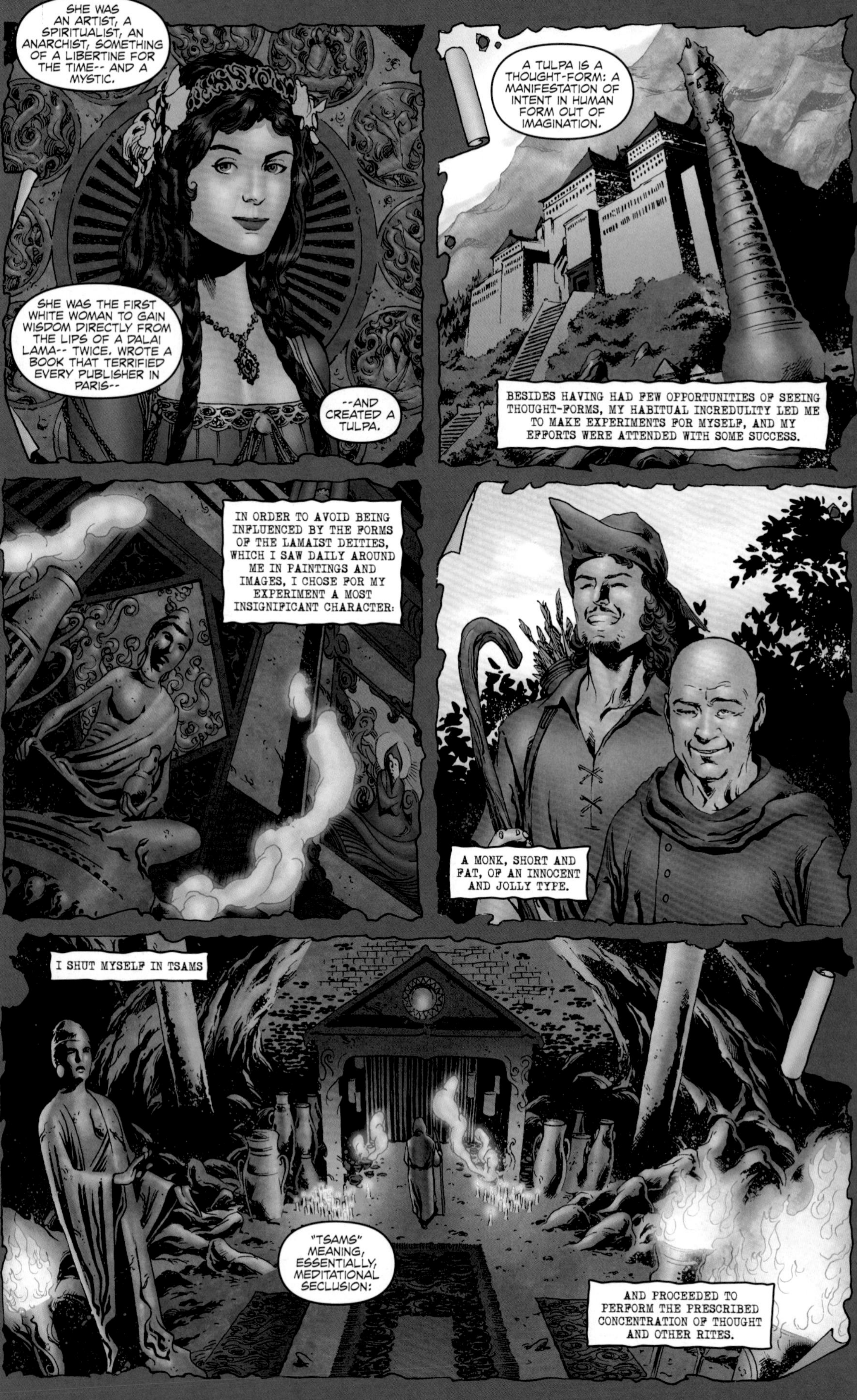
SHE WAS AN ARTIST, A SPIRITUALIST, AN ANARCHIST, SOMETHING OF A LIBERTINE FOR THE TIME-- AND A MYSTIC.
SHE WAS THE FIRST WHITE WOMAN TO GAIN WISDOM DIRECTLY FROM THE LIPS OF A DALAI LAMA-- TWICE. WROTE A BOOK THAT TERRIFIED EVERY PUBLISHER IN PARIS--
--AND CREATED A TULPA.
A TULPA IS A THOUGHT-FORM: A MANIFESTATION OF INTENT IN HUMAN FORM OUT OF IMAGINATION.
BESIDES HAVING HAD FEW OPPORTUNITIES OF SEEING THOUGHT-FORMS, MY HABITUAL INCREDULITY LED ME TO MAKE EXPERIMENTS FOR MYSELF, AND MY EFFORTS WERE ATTENDED WITH SOME SUCCESS.
IN ORDER TO AVOID BEING INFLUENCED BY THE FORMS OF THE LAMAIST DEITIES, WHICH I SAW DAILY AROUND ME IN PAINTINGS AND IMAGES, I CHOSE FOR MY EXPERIMENT A MOST INSIGNIFICANT CHARACTER:
A MONK, SHORT AND FAT, OF AN INNOCENT AND JOLLY TYPE.
I SHUT MYSELF IN TSAMS
"TSAMS" MEANING, ESSENTIALLY, MEDITATIONAL SECLUSION:
AND PROCEEDED TO PERFORM THE PRESCRIBED CONCENTRATION OF THOUGHT AND OTHER RITES.

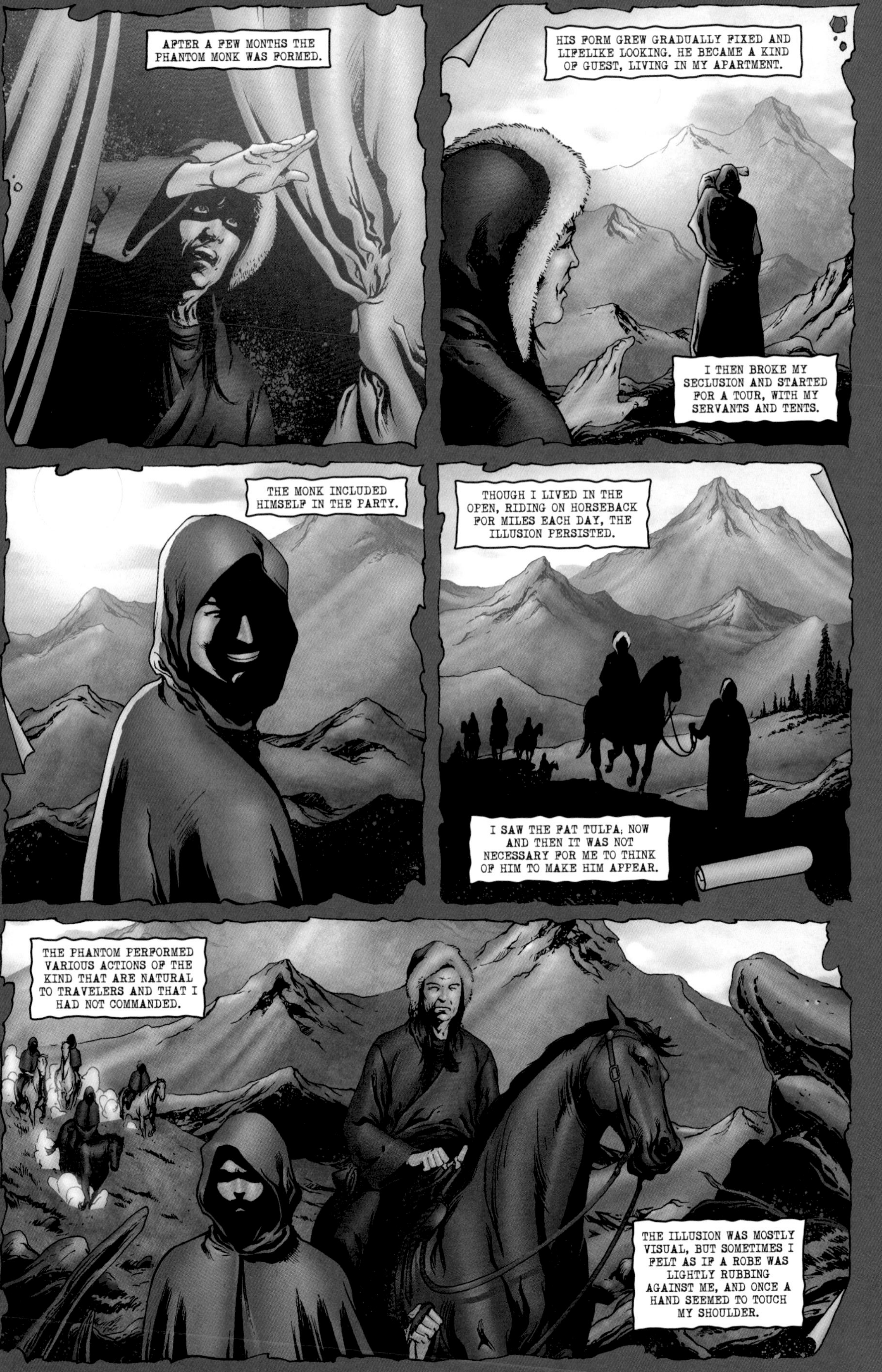
AFTER A FEW MONTHS THE PHANTOM MONK WAS FORMED.
HIS FORM GREW GRADUALLY FIXED AND LIFELIKE LOOKING. HE BECAME A KIND OF GUEST, LIVING IN MY APARTMENT.
I THEN BROKE MY SECLUSION AND STARTED FOR A TOUR, WITH MY SERVANTS AND TENTS.
THE MONK INCLUDED HIMSELF IN THE PARTY.
THOUGH I LIVED IN THE OPEN, RIDING ON HORSEBACK FOR MILES EACH DAY, THE ILLUSION PERSISTED.
I SAW THE FAT TULPA; NOW AND THEN IT WAS NOT NECESSARY FOR ME TO THINK OF HIM TO MAKE HIM APPEAR.
THE PHANTOM PERFORMED VARIOUS ACTIONS OF THE KIND THAT ARE NATURAL TO TRAVELERS AND THAT I HAD NOT COMMANDED.
THE ILLUSION WAS MOSTLY VISUAL, BUT SOMETIMES I FELT AS IF A ROBE WAS LIGHTLY RUBBING AGAINST ME, AND ONCE A HAND SEEMED TO TOUCH MY SHOULDER.

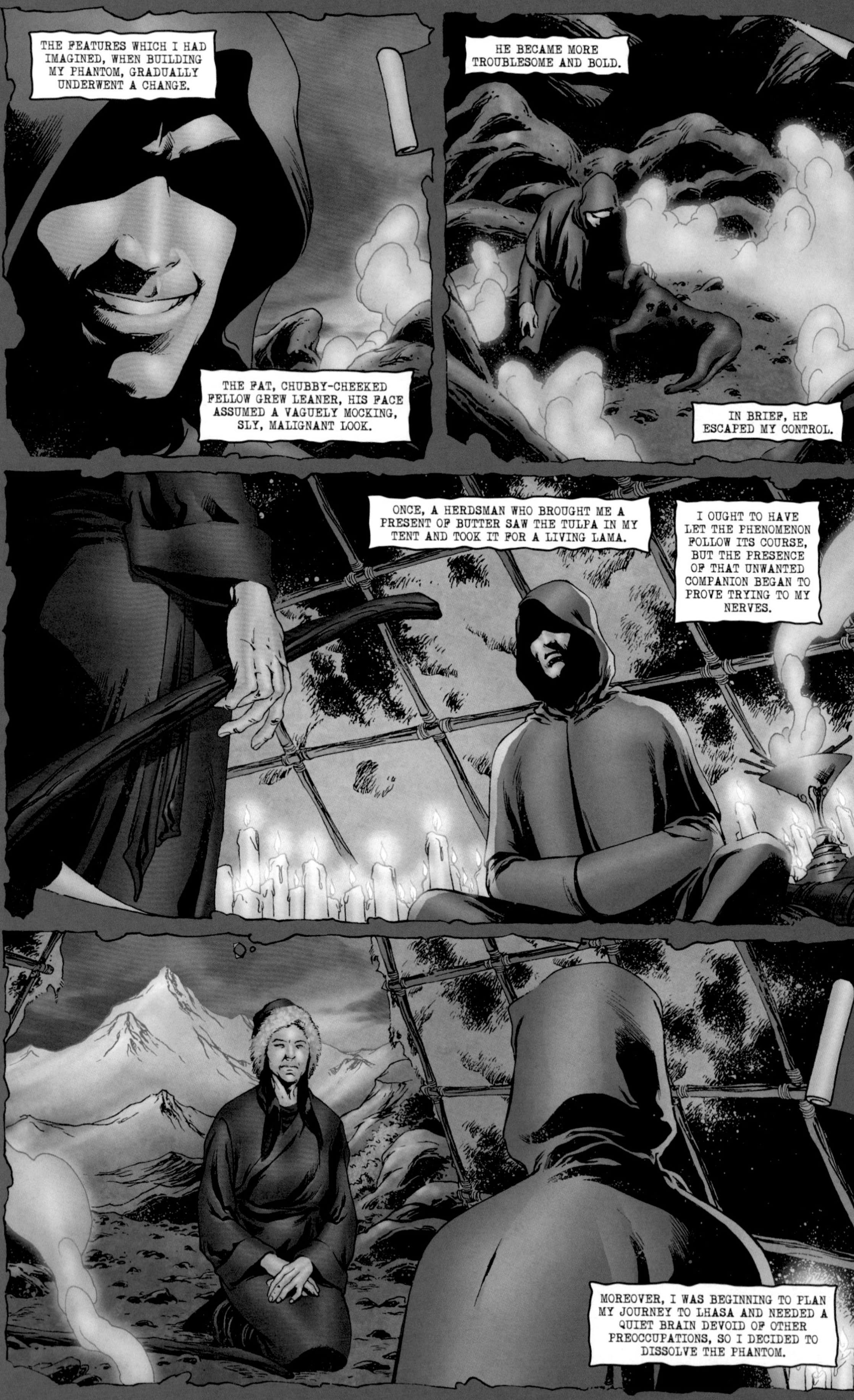
THE FEATURES WHICH I HAD IMAGINED, WHEN BUILDING MY PHANTOM, GRADUALLY UNDERWENT A CHANGE.
THE FAT, CHUBBY-CHEEKED FELLOW GREW LEANER, HIS FACE ASSUMED A VAGUELY MOCKING, SLY, MALIGNANT LOOK.
HE BECAME MORE TROUBLESOME AND BOLD.
IN BRIEF, HE ESCAPED MY CONTROL.
ONCE, A HERDSMAN WHO BROUGHT ME A PRESENT OF BUTTER SAW THE TULPA IN MY TENT AND TOOK IT FOR A LIVING LAMA.
I OUGHT TO HAVE LET THE PHENOMENON FOLLOW ITS COURSE, BUT THE PRESENCE OF THAT UNWANTED COMPANION BEGAN TO PROVE TRYING TO MY NERVES.
MOREOVER, I WAS BEGINNING TO PLAN MY JOURNEY TO LHASA AND NEEDED A QUIET BRAIN DEVOID OF OTHER PREOCCUPATIONS, SO I DECIDED TO DISSOLVE THE PHANTOM.

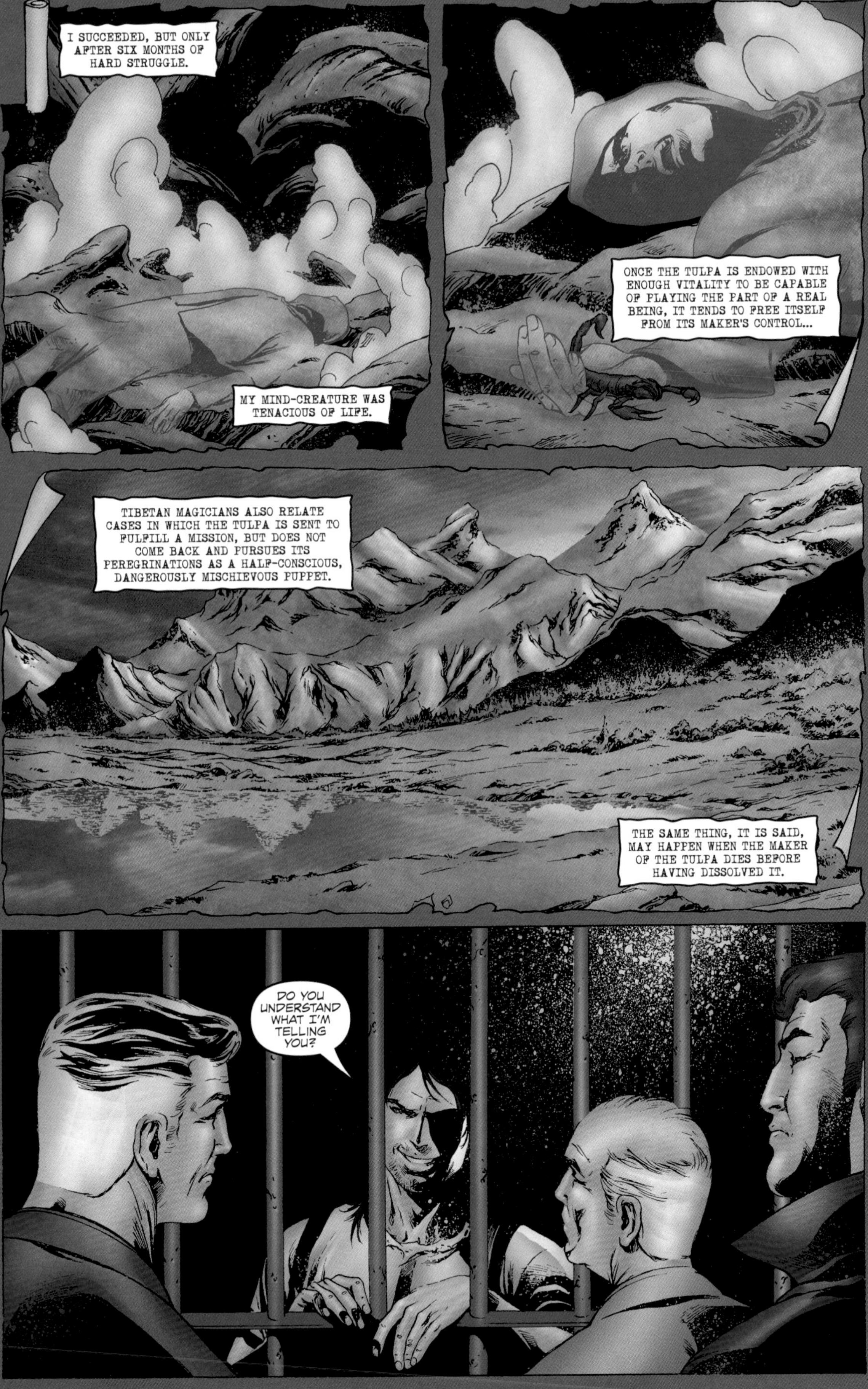

I SUCCEEDED, BUT ONLY AFTER SIX MONTHS OF HARD STRUGGLE.
MY MIND-CREATURE WAS TENACIOUS OF LIFE.
ONCE THE TULPA IS ENDOWED WITH ENOUGH VITALITY TO BE CAPABLE OF PLAYING THE PART OF A REAL BEING, IT TENDS TO FREE ITSELF FROM ITS MAKER'S CONTROL...
TIBETAN MAGICIANS ALSO RELATE CASES IN WHICH THE TULPA IS SENT TO FULFILL A MISSION, BUT DOES NOT COME BACK AND PURSUES ITS PEREGRINATIONS AS A HALF-CONSCIOUS, DANGEROUSLY MISCHIEVOUS PUPPET.
THE SAME THING, IT IS SAID, MAY HAPPEN WHEN THE MAKER OF THE TULPA DIES BEFORE HAVING DISSOLVED IT.
DO YOU UNDERSTAND WHAT I'M TELLING YOU?

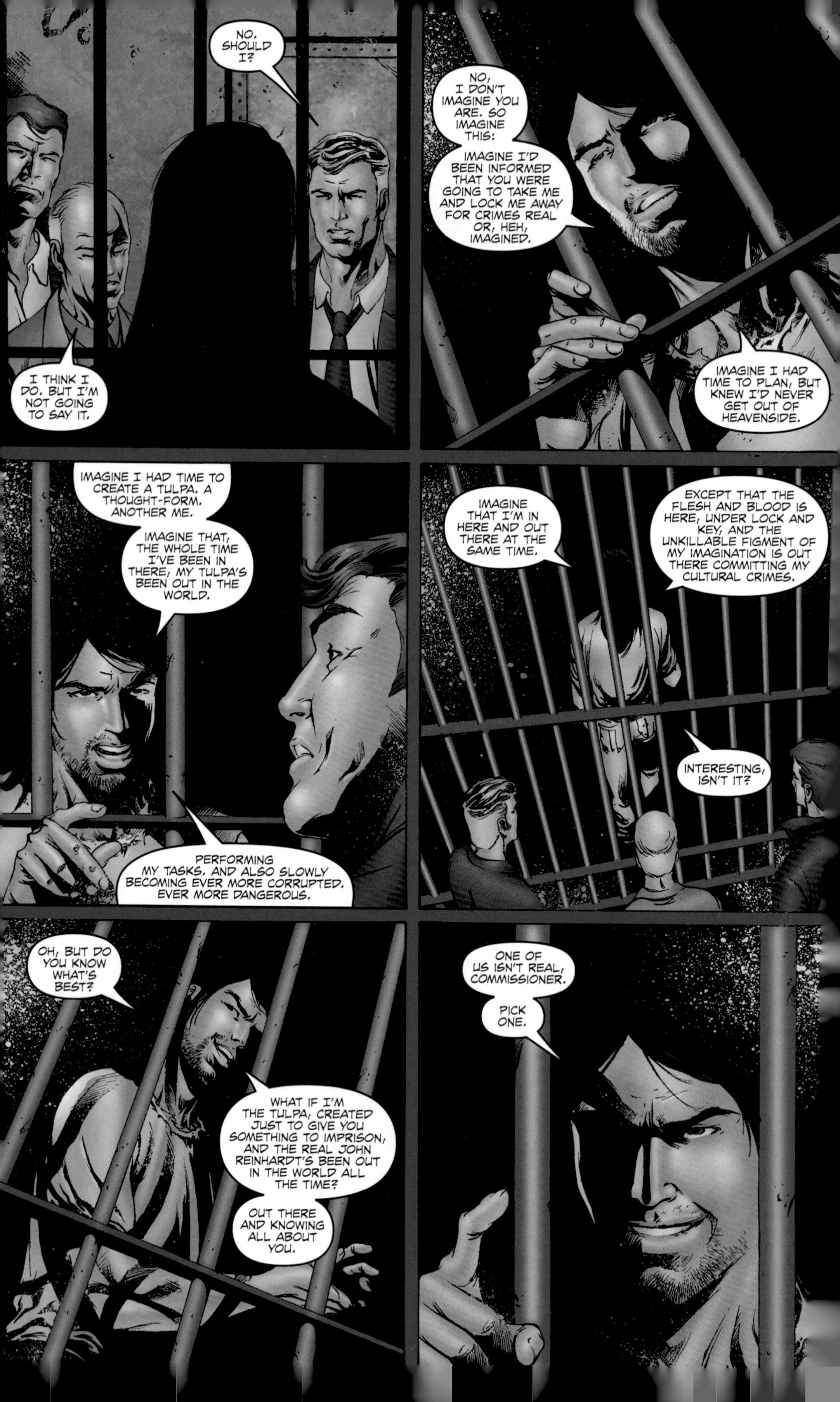
NO. SHOULD I?
I THINK I DO. BUT I'M NOT GOING TO SAY IT.
NO, I DON'T IMAGINE YOU ARE. SO IMAGINE THIS:
IMAGINE I'D BEEN INFORMED THAT YOU WERE GOING TO TAKE ME AND LOCK ME AWAY FOR CRIMES REAL OR, HEH, IMAGINED.
IMAGINE I HAD TIME TO PLAN, BUT KNEW I'D NEVER GET OUT OF HEAVENSIDE.
IMAGINE I HAD TIME TO CREATE A TULPA. A THOUGHT-FORM. ANOTHER ME.
IMAGINE THAT, THE WHOLE TIME I'VE BEEN IN THERE, MY TULPA'S BEEN OUT IN THE WORLD.
PERFORMING MY TASKS. AND ALSO SLOWLY BECOMING EVER MORE CORRUPTED. EVER MORE DANGEROUS.
IMAGINE THAT I'M IN HERE AND OUT THERE AT THE SAME TIME.
EXCEPT THAT THE FLESH AND BLOOD IS HERE, UNDER LOCK AND KEY, AND THE UNKILLABLE FIGMENT OF MY IMAGINATION IS OUT THERE COMMITTING MY CULTURAL CRIMES.
INTERESTING, ISN'T IT?
OH, BUT DO YOU KNOW WHAT'S BEST?
WHAT IF I'M THE TULPA, CREATED JUST TO GIVE YOU SOMETHING TO IMPRISON, AND THE REAL JOHN REINHARDT'S BEEN OUT IN THE WORLD ALL THE TIME?
OUT THERE AND KNOWING ALL ABOUT YOU.
ONE OF US ISN'T REAL, COMMISSIONER.
PICK ONE.

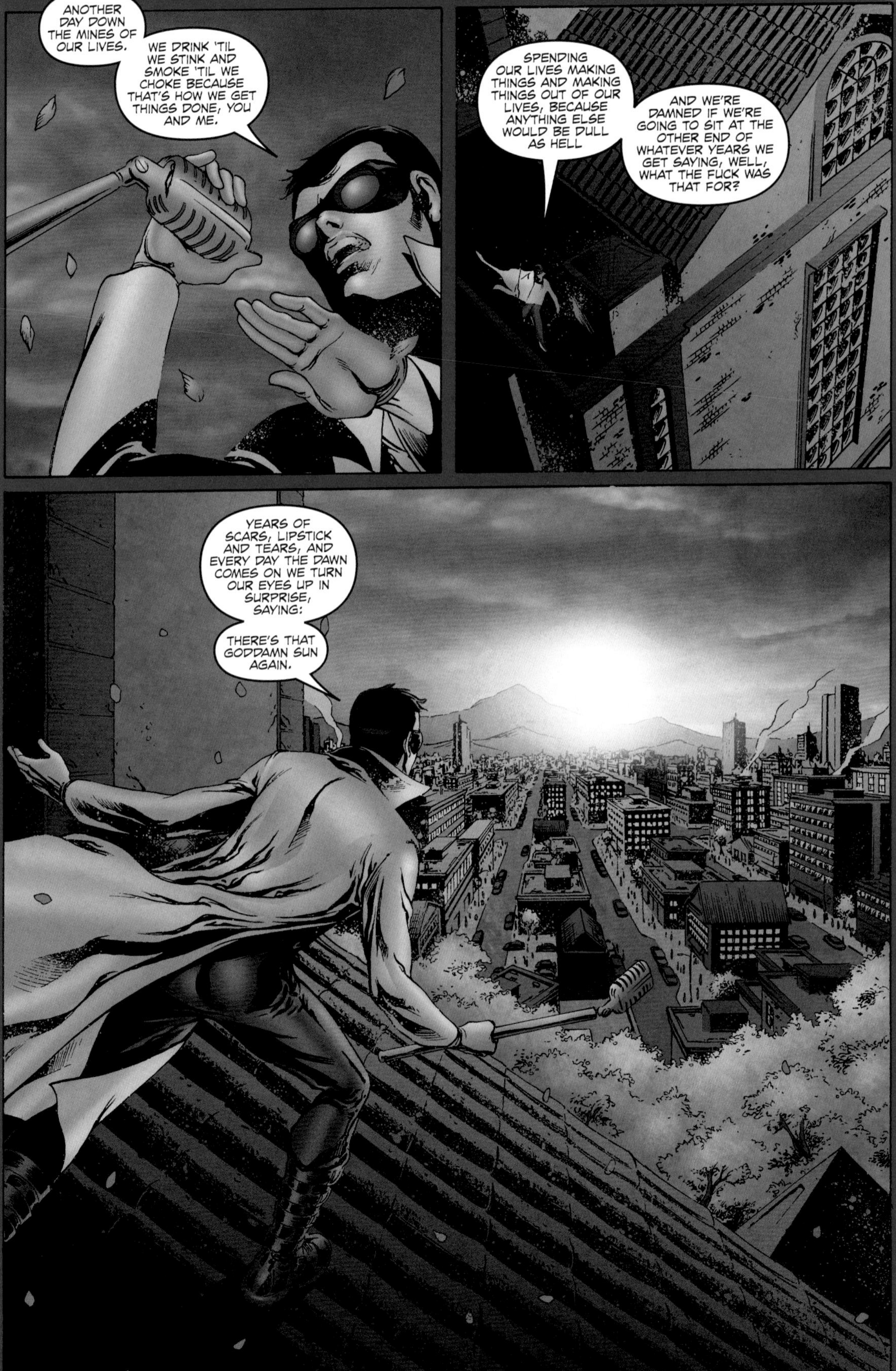
ANOTHER DAY DOWN THE MINES OF OUR LIVES.
WE DRINK 'TIL WE STINK AND SMOKE 'TIL WE CHOKE BECAUSE THAT'S HOW WE GET THINGS DONE, YOU AND ME.
SPENDING OUR LIVES MAKING THINGS AND MAKING THINGS OUT OF OUR LIVES, BECAUSE ANYTHING ELSE WOULD BE DULL AS HELL
AND WE'RE DAMNED IF WE'RE GOING TO SIT AT THE OTHER END OF WHATEVER YEARS WE GET SAYING, WELL, WHAT THE FUCK WAS THAT FOR?
YEARS OF SCARS, LIPSTICK AND TEARS, AND EVERY DAY THE DAWN COMES ON WE TURN OUR EYES UP IN SURPRISE, SAYING:
THERE'S THAT GODDAMN SUN AGAIN.

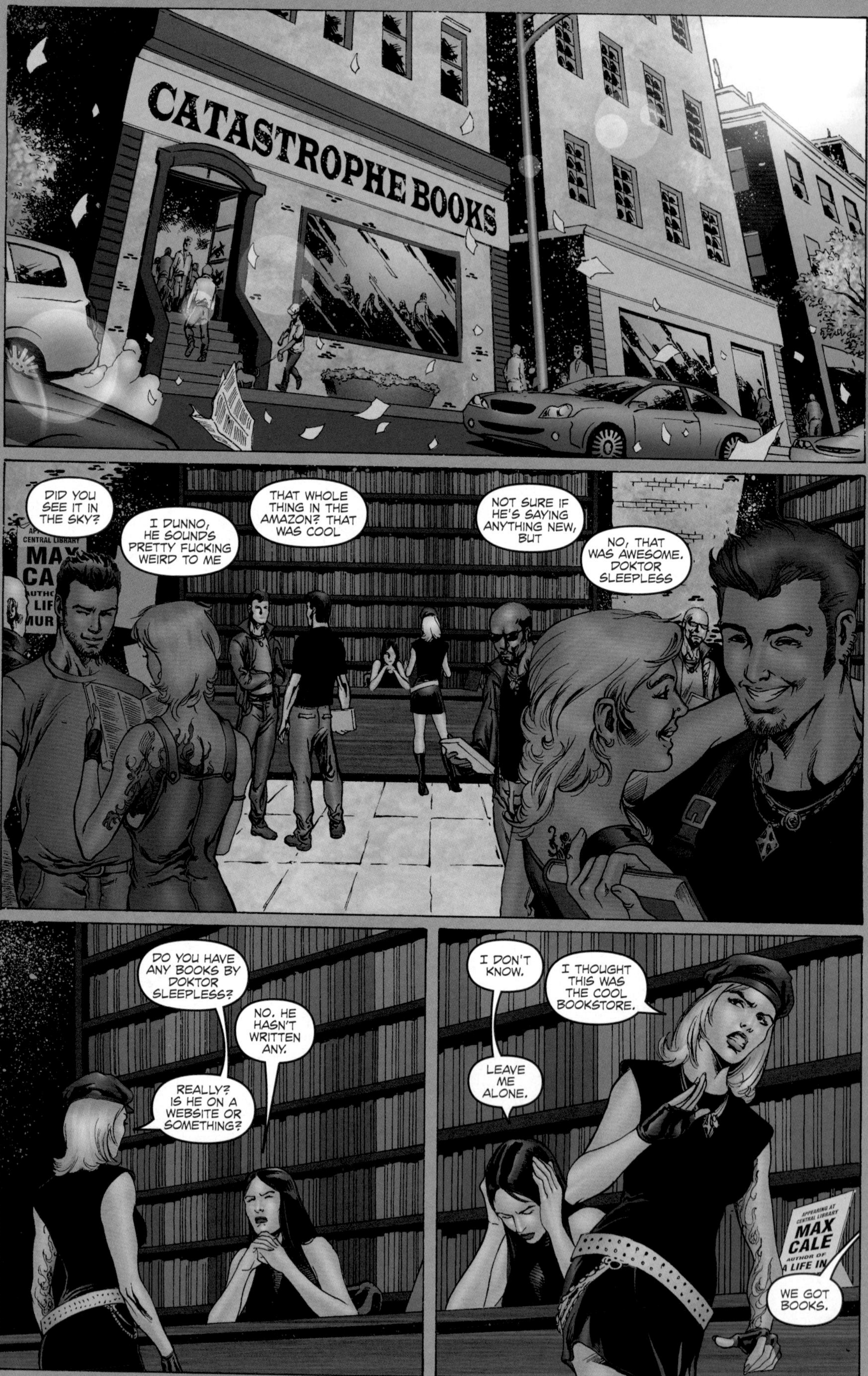
CATASTROPHE BOOKS
DID YOU SEE IT IN THE SKY?
I DUNNO, HE SOUNDS PRETTY FUCKING WEIRD TO ME
THAT WHOLE THING IN THE AMAZON? THAT WAS COOL
NOT SURE IF HE'S SAYING ANYTHING NEW, BUT
NO, THAT WAS AWESOME. DOKTOR SLEEPLESS
DO YOU HAVE ANY BOOKS BY DOKTOR SLEEPLESS?
NO. HE HASN'T WRITTEN ANY.
REALLY? IS HE ON A WEBSITE OR SOMETHING?
I DON'T KNOW.
I THOUGHT THIS WAS THE COOL BOOKSTORE.
LEAVE ME ALONE.
APPEARING AT CENTRAL LIBRARY
MAX CALE
AUTHOR OF
A LIFE IN
WE GOT BOOKS.

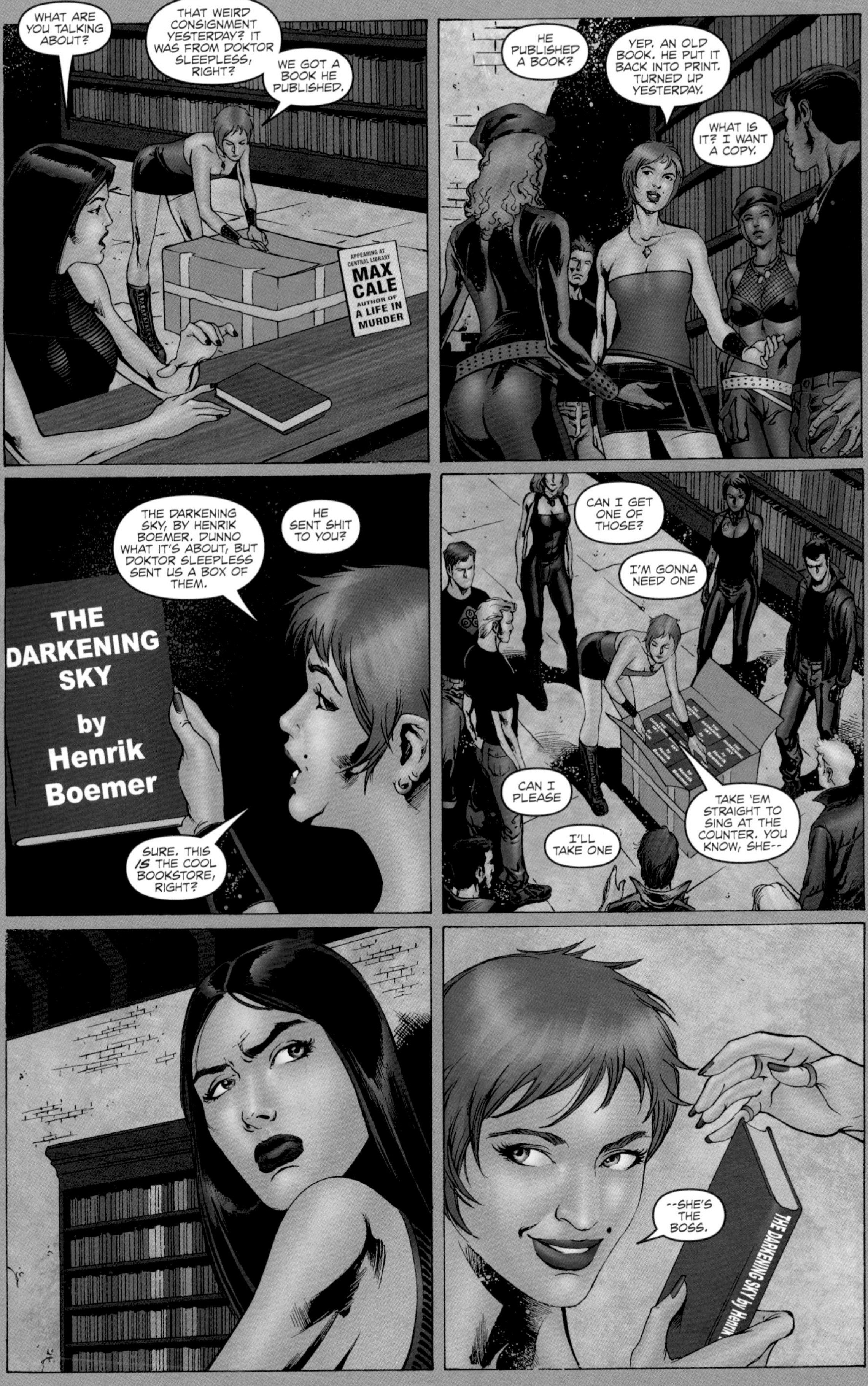
WHAT ARE YOU TALKING ABOUT?
THAT WEIRD CONSIGNMENT YESTERDAY? IT WAS FROM DOKTOR SLEEPLESS, RIGHT?
WE GOT A BOOK HE PUBLISHED.
APPEARING AT CENTRAL LIBRARY MAX CALE AUTHOR OF A LIFE IN MURDER
HE PUBLISHED A BOOK?
YEP. AN OLD BOOK. HE PUT IT BACK INTO PRINT. TURNED UP YESTERDAY.
WHAT IS IT? I WANT A COPY.
THE DARKENING SKY, BY HENRIK BOEMER. DUNNO WHAT IT'S ABOUT, BUT DOKTOR SLEEPLESS SENT US A BOX OF THEM.
HE SENT SHIT TO YOU?
THE DARKENING SKY by Henrik Boemer
SURE. THIS *IS* THE COOL BOOKSTORE, RIGHT?
CAN I GET ONE OF THOSE?
I'M GONNA NEED ONE
CAN I PLEASE
I'LL TAKE ONE
TAKE 'EM STRAIGHT TO SING AT THE COUNTER. YOU KNOW, SHE--
--SHE'S THE BOSS.
THE DARKENING SKY by Henrik

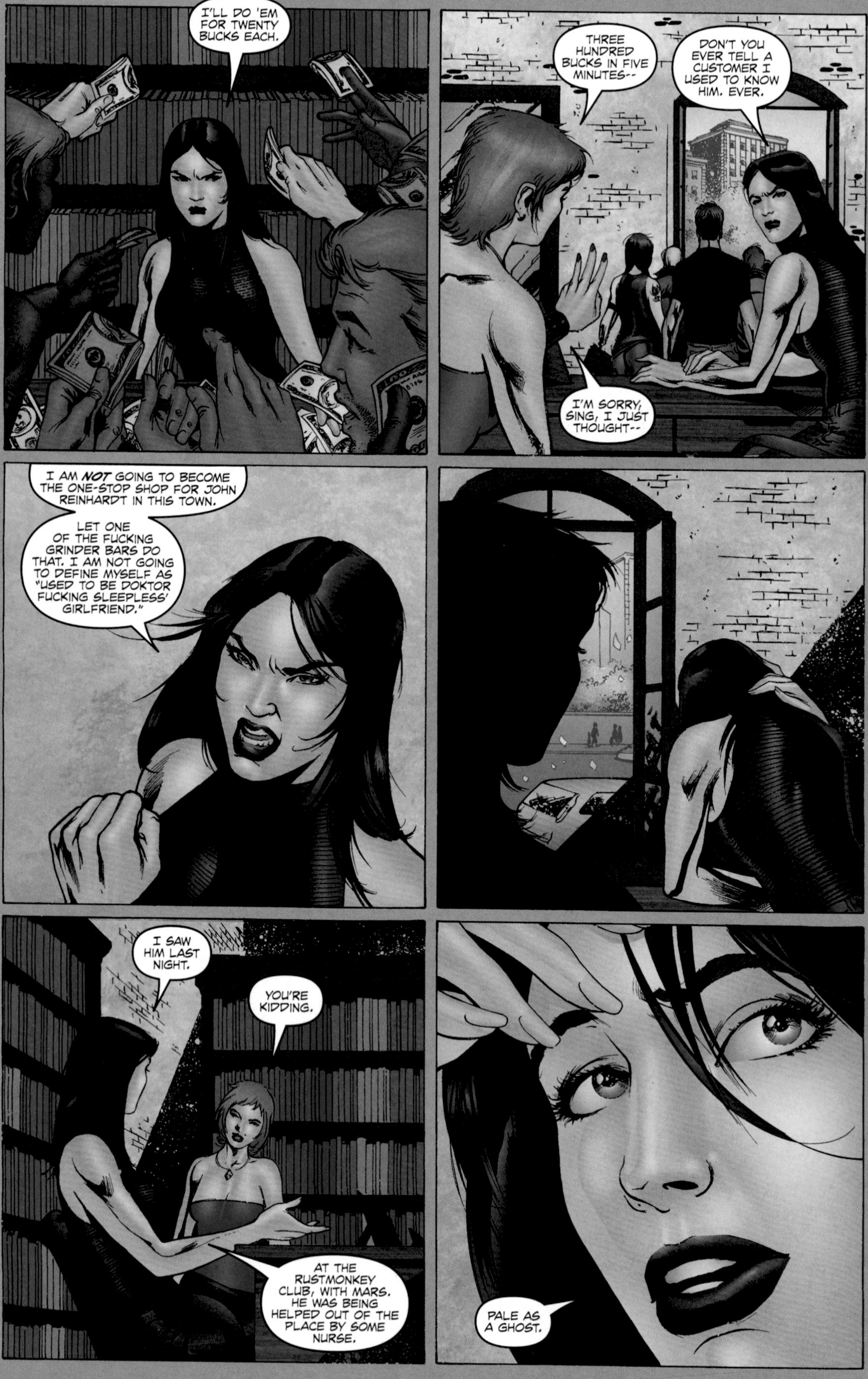
I'LL DO 'EM FOR TWENTY BUCKS EACH.
THREE HUNDRED BUCKS IN FIVE MINUTES--
DON'T YOU EVER TELL A CUSTOMER I USED TO KNOW HIM. EVER.
I'M SORRY, SING, I JUST THOUGHT--
I AM *NOT* GOING TO BECOME THE ONE-STOP SHOP FOR JOHN REINHARDT IN THIS TOWN.
LET ONE OF THE FUCKING GRINDER BARS DO THAT. I AM NOT GOING TO DEFINE MYSELF AS "USED TO BE DOKTOR FUCKING SLEEPLESS' GIRLFRIEND."
I SAW HIM LAST NIGHT.
YOU'RE KIDDING.
AT THE RUSTMONKEY CLUB, WITH MARS. HE WAS BEING HELPED OUT OF THE PLACE BY SOME NURSE.
PALE AS A GHOST.

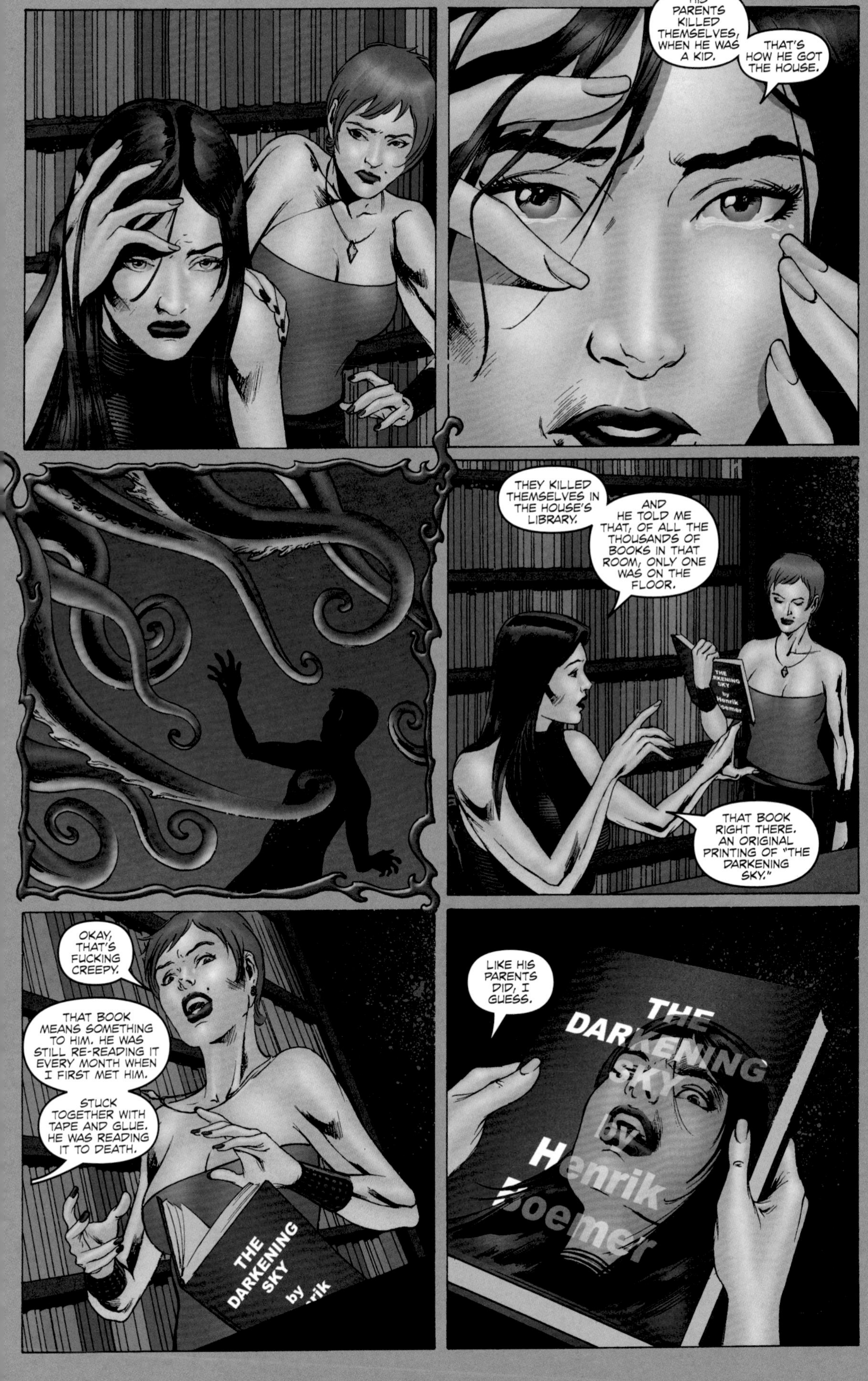
HIS PARENTS KILLED THEMSELVES, WHEN HE WAS A KID.
THAT'S HOW HE GOT THE HOUSE.
THEY KILLED THEMSELVES IN THE HOUSE'S LIBRARY.
AND HE TOLD ME THAT, OF ALL THE THOUSANDS OF BOOKS IN THAT ROOM, ONLY ONE WAS ON THE FLOOR.
THE DARKENING SKY by Henrik Boemer
THAT BOOK RIGHT THERE. AN ORIGINAL PRINTING OF "THE DARKENING SKY."
OKAY, THAT'S FUCKING CREEPY.
THAT BOOK MEANS SOMETHING TO HIM. HE WAS STILL RE-READING IT EVERY MONTH WHEN I FIRST MET HIM.
STUCK TOGETHER WITH TAPE AND GLUE. HE WAS READING IT TO DEATH.
THE DARKENING SKY by
LIKE HIS PARENTS DID, I GUESS.
THE DARKENING SKY by Henrik

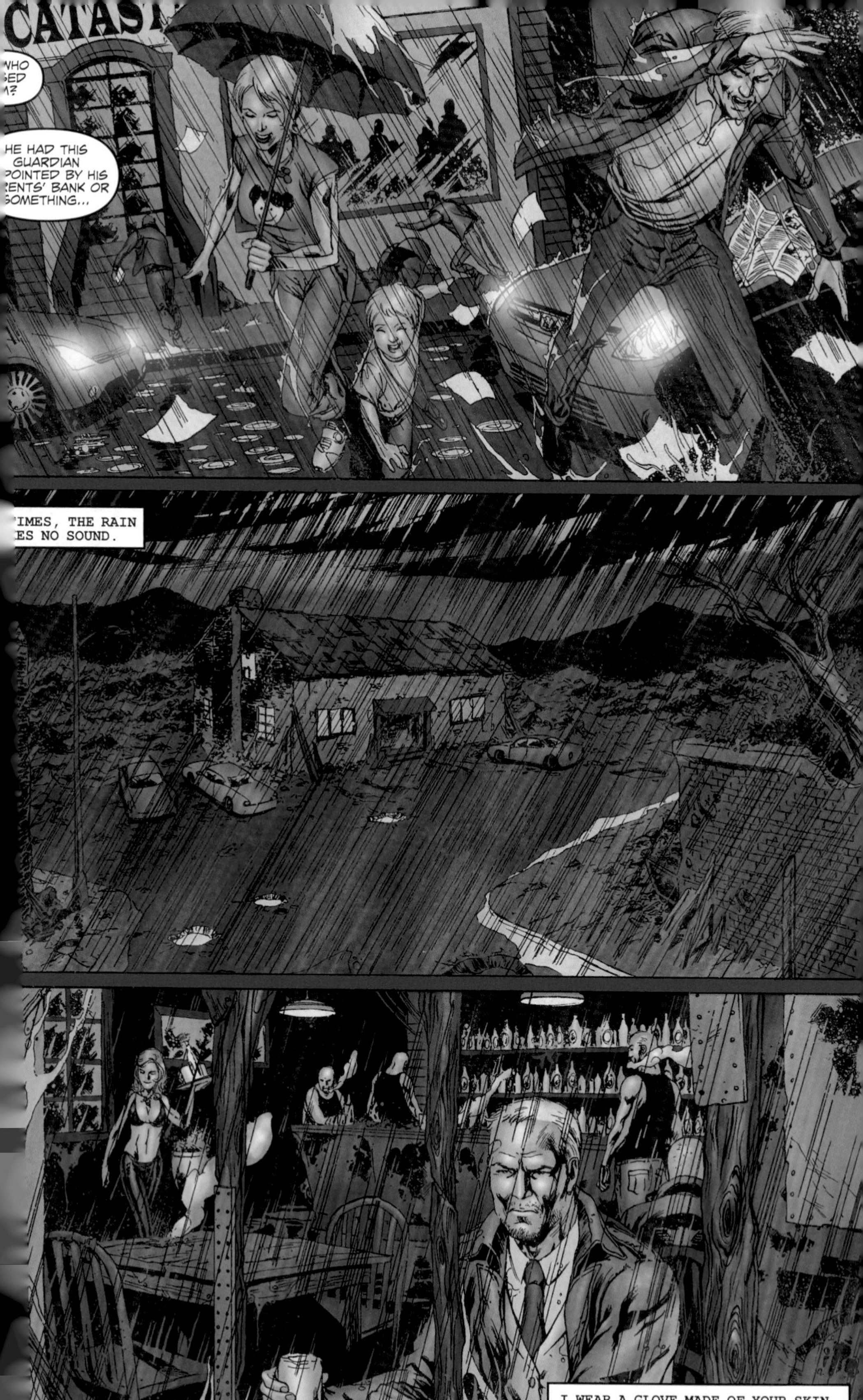
CATAST
WHO
SED
M?
HE HAD THIS
GUARDIAN
POINTED BY HIS
RENTS' BANK OR
SOMETHING...
TIMES, THE RAIN
ES NO SOUND.
I WEAR A GLOVE MADE OF YOUR SKIN. IT'S THE COLOUR OF RAIN, SOFT AND GREY. IT MAKES NO SOUND, NOW, AS I FLEX MY FINGERS INSIDE IT.

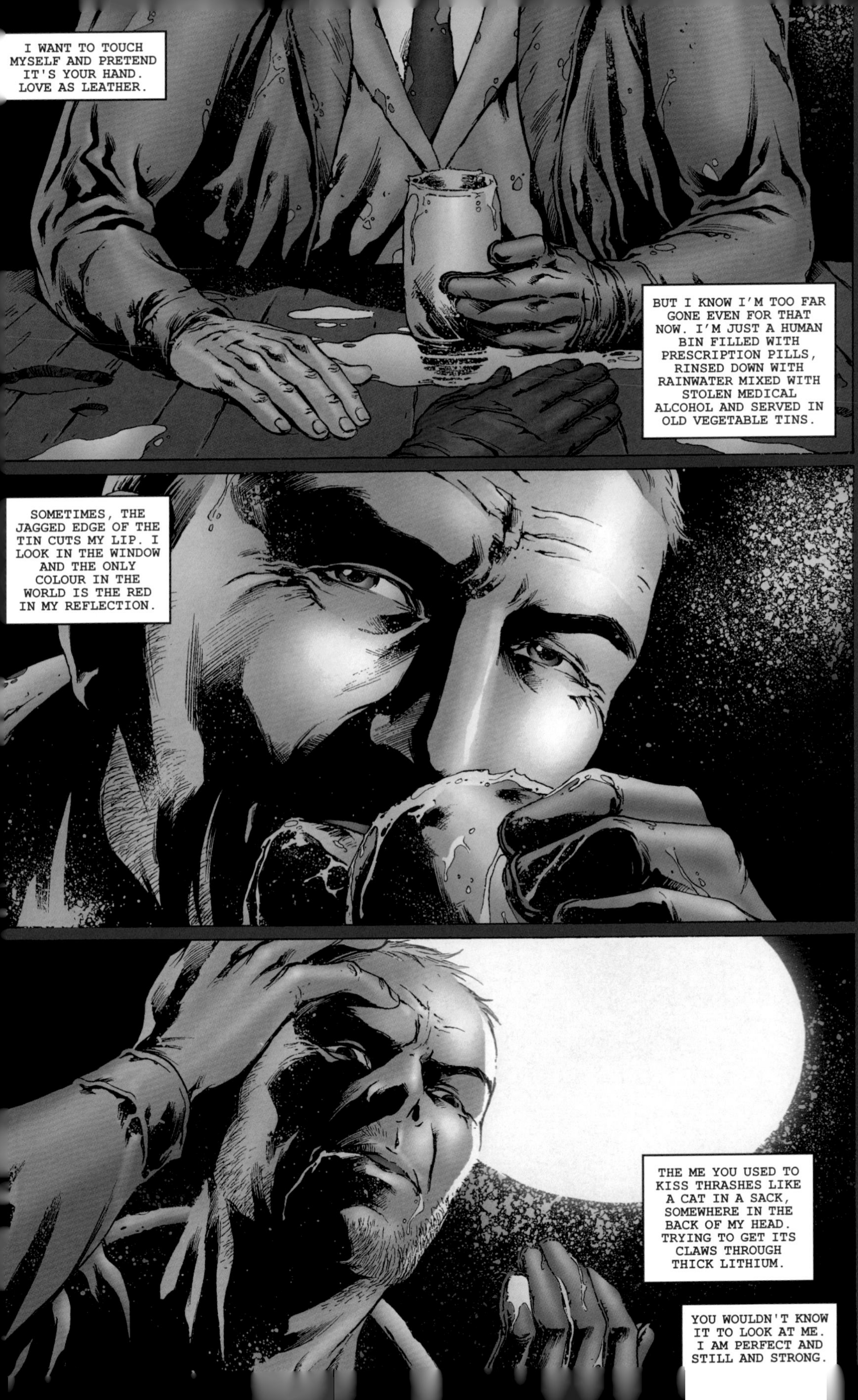
I WANT TO TOUCH MYSELF AND PRETEND IT'S YOUR HAND. LOVE AS LEATHER.
BUT I KNOW I'M TOO FAR GONE EVEN FOR THAT NOW. I'M JUST A HUMAN BIN FILLED WITH PRESCRIPTION PILLS, RINSED DOWN WITH RAINWATER MIXED WITH STOLEN MEDICAL ALCOHOL AND SERVED IN OLD VEGETABLE TINS.
SOMETIMES, THE JAGGED EDGE OF THE TIN CUTS MY LIP. I LOOK IN THE WINDOW AND THE ONLY COLOUR IN THE WORLD IS THE RED IN MY REFLECTION.
THE ME YOU USED TO KISS THRASHES LIKE A CAT IN A SACK, SOMEWHERE IN THE BACK OF MY HEAD. TRYING TO GET ITS CLAWS THROUGH THICK LITHIUM.
YOU WOULDN'T KNOW IT TO LOOK AT ME. I AM PERFECT AND STILL AND STRONG.

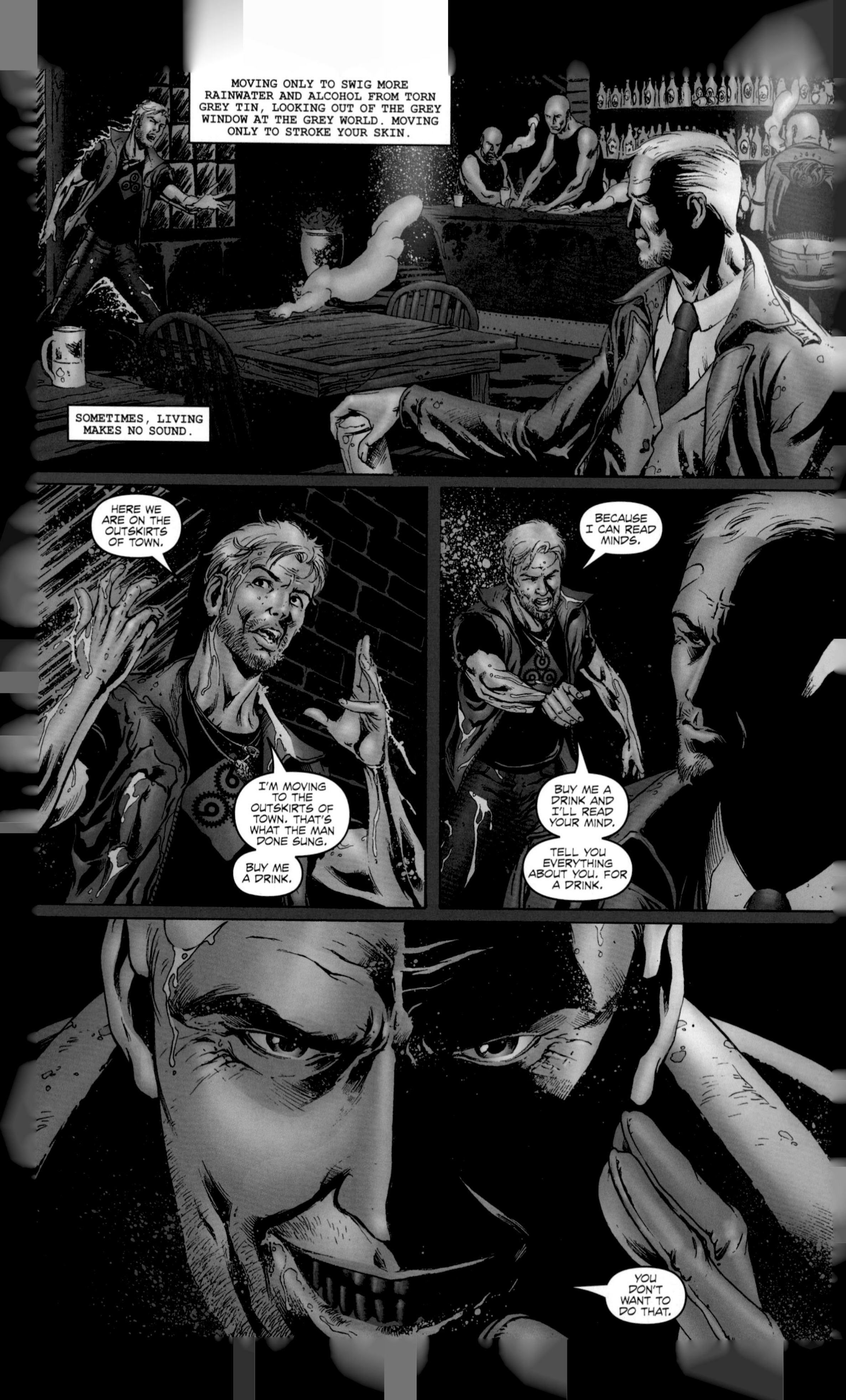
MOVING ONLY TO SWIG MORE RAINWATER AND ALCOHOL FROM TORN GREY TIN, LOOKING OUT OF THE GREY WINDOW AT THE GREY WORLD. MOVING ONLY TO STROKE YOUR SKIN.
SOMETIMES, LIVING MAKES NO SOUND.
HERE WE ARE ON THE OUTSKIRTS OF TOWN.
I'M MOVING TO THE OUTSKIRTS OF TOWN. THAT'S WHAT THE MAN DONE SUNG.
BUY ME A DRINK.
BECAUSE I CAN READ MINDS.
BUY ME A DRINK AND I'LL READ YOUR MIND.
TELL YOU EVERYTHING ABOUT YOU. FOR A DRINK.
YOU DON'T WANT TO DO THAT.

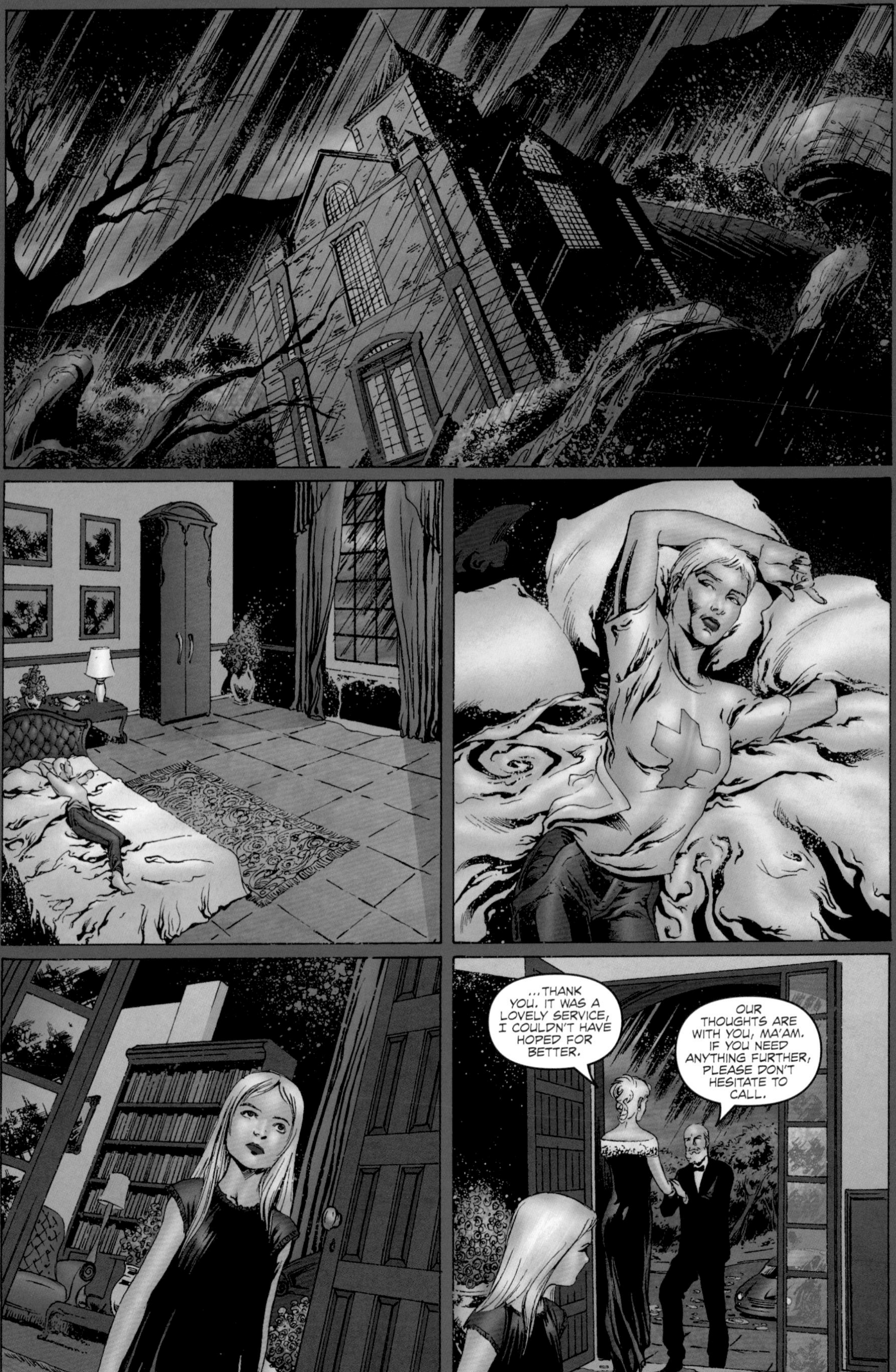
...THANK YOU. IT WAS A LOVELY SERVICE, I COULDN'T HAVE HOPED FOR BETTER.
OUR THOUGHTS ARE WITH YOU, MA'AM. IF YOU NEED ANYTHING FURTHER, PLEASE DON'T HESITATE TO CALL.

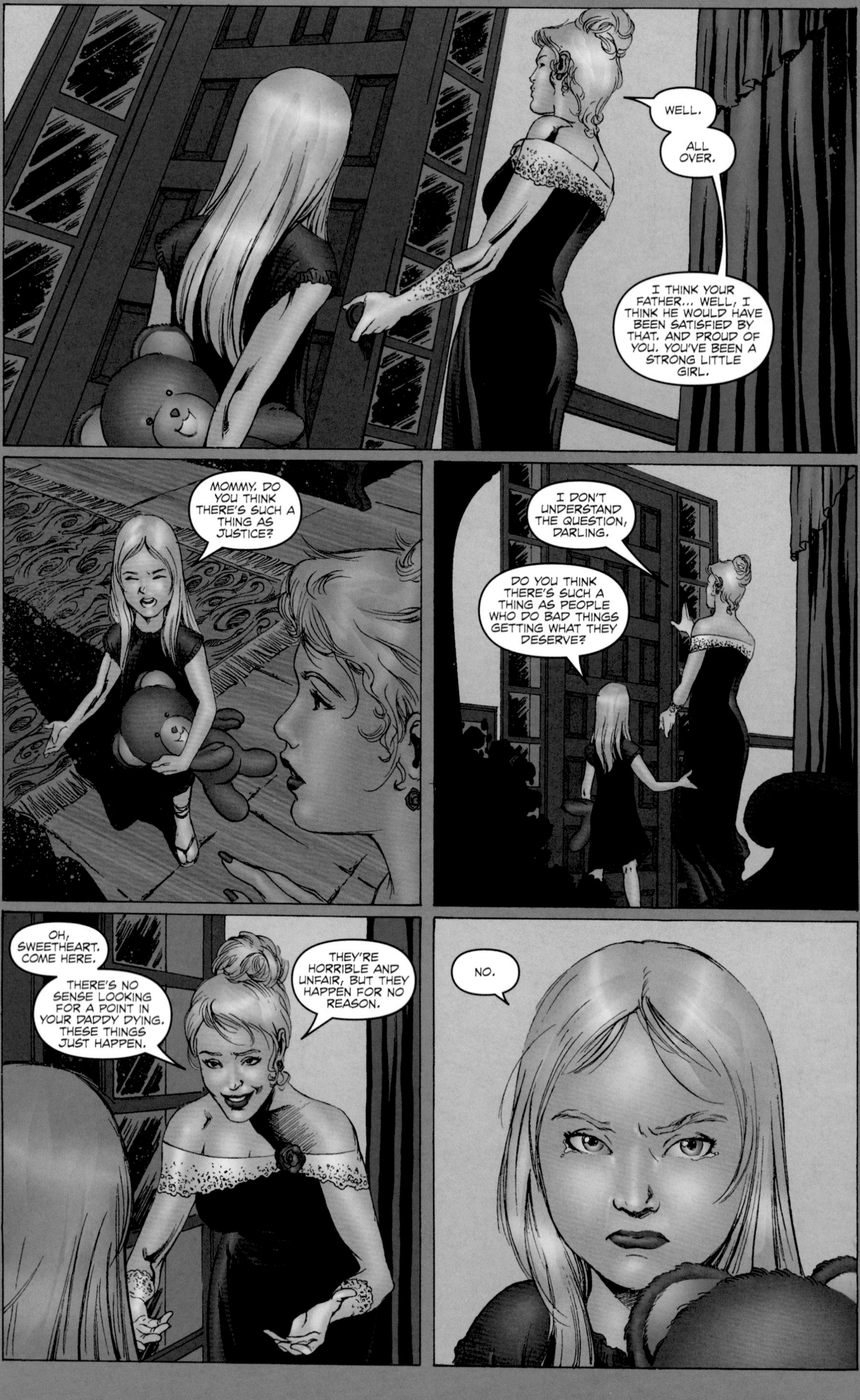
WELL.
ALL OVER.
I THINK YOUR FATHER... WELL, I THINK HE WOULD HAVE BEEN SATISFIED BY THAT. AND PROUD OF YOU. YOU'VE BEEN A STRONG LITTLE GIRL.
MOMMY, DO YOU THINK THERE'S SUCH A THING AS JUSTICE?
I DON'T UNDERSTAND THE QUESTION, DARLING.
DO YOU THINK THERE'S SUCH A THING AS PEOPLE WHO DO BAD THINGS GETTING WHAT THEY DESERVE?
OH, SWEETHEART. COME HERE.
THERE'S NO SENSE LOOKING FOR A POINT IN YOUR DADDY DYING. THESE THINGS JUST HAPPEN.
THEY'RE HORRIBLE AND UNFAIR, BUT THEY HAPPEN FOR NO REASON.
NO.

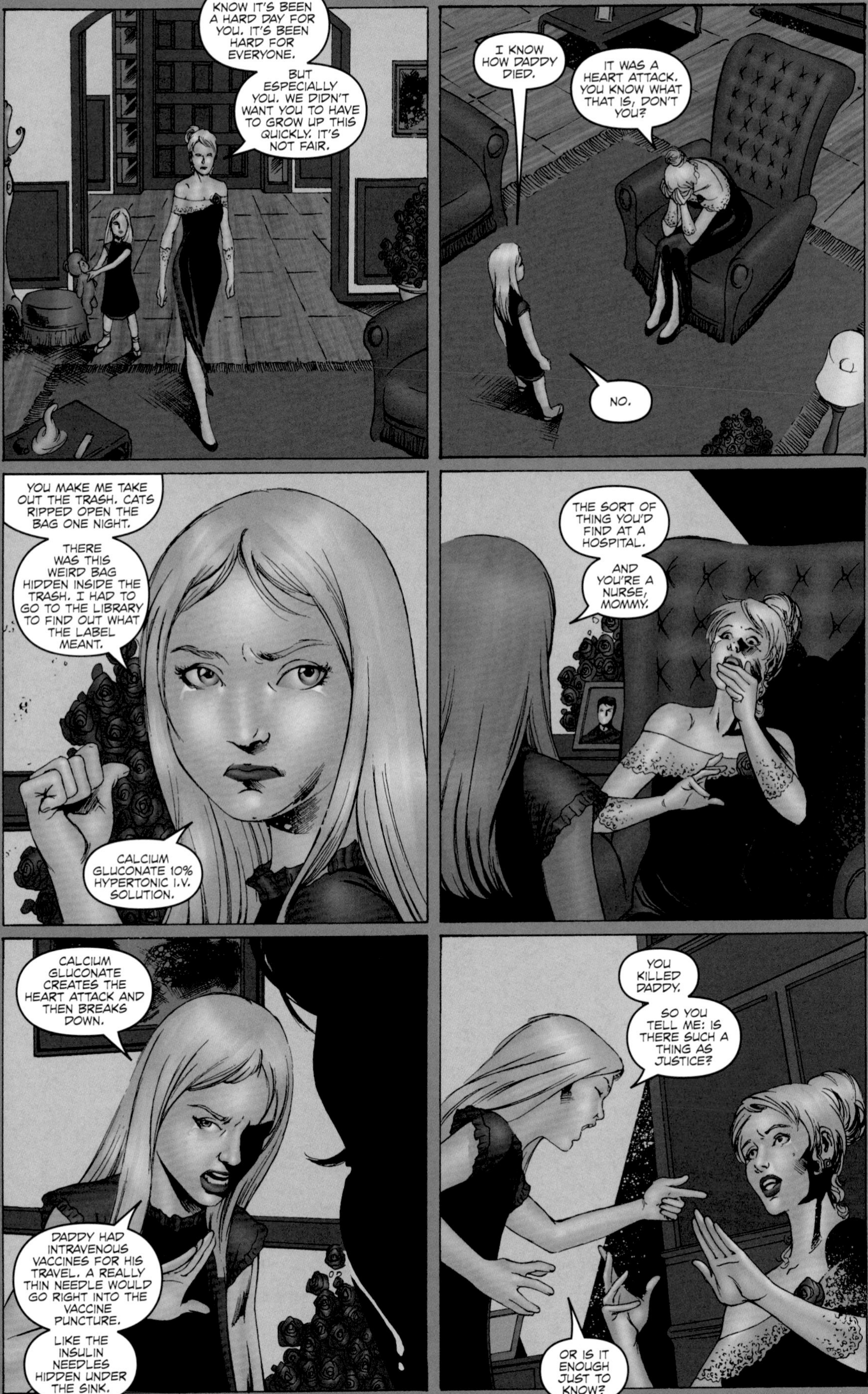
PLEASE... I KNOW IT'S BEEN A HARD DAY FOR YOU. IT'S BEEN HARD FOR EVERYONE.
BUT ESPECIALLY YOU. WE DIDN'T WANT YOU TO HAVE TO GROW UP THIS QUICKLY. IT'S NOT FAIR.
I KNOW HOW DADDY DIED.
IT WAS A HEART ATTACK. YOU KNOW WHAT THAT IS, DON'T YOU?
NO.
YOU MAKE ME TAKE OUT THE TRASH. CATS RIPPED OPEN THE BAG ONE NIGHT.
THERE WAS THIS WEIRD BAG HIDDEN INSIDE THE TRASH. I HAD TO GO TO THE LIBRARY TO FIND OUT WHAT THE LABEL MEANT.
CALCIUM GLUCONATE 10% HYPERTONIC I.V. SOLUTION.
THE SORT OF THING YOU'D FIND AT A HOSPITAL.
AND YOU'RE A NURSE, MOMMY.
CALCIUM GLUCONATE CREATES THE HEART ATTACK AND THEN BREAKS DOWN.
DADDY HAD INTRAVENOUS VACCINES FOR HIS TRAVEL. A REALLY THIN NEEDLE WOULD GO RIGHT INTO THE VACCINE PUNCTURE.
LIKE THE INSULIN NEEDLES HIDDEN UNDER THE SINK.
YOU KILLED DADDY.
SO YOU TELL ME: IS THERE SUCH A THING AS JUSTICE?
OR IS IT ENOUGH JUST TO KNOW?

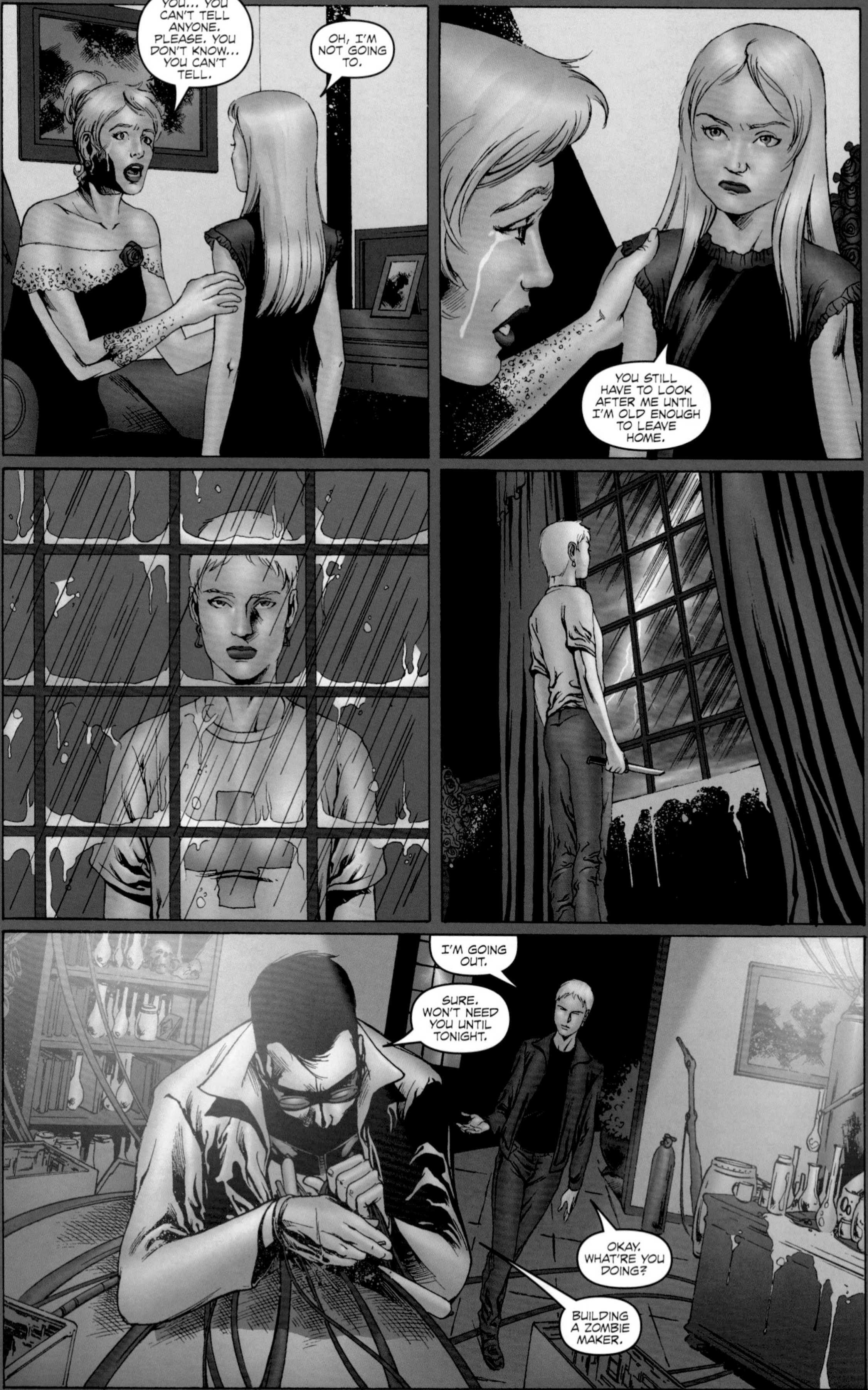
YOU... YOU CAN'T TELL ANYONE. PLEASE. YOU DON'T KNOW... YOU CAN'T TELL.
OH, I'M NOT GOING TO.
YOU STILL HAVE TO LOOK AFTER ME UNTIL I'M OLD ENOUGH TO LEAVE HOME.
I'M GOING OUT.
SURE. WON'T NEED YOU UNTIL TONIGHT.
OKAY. WHAT'RE YOU DOING?
BUILDING A ZOMBIE MAKER.

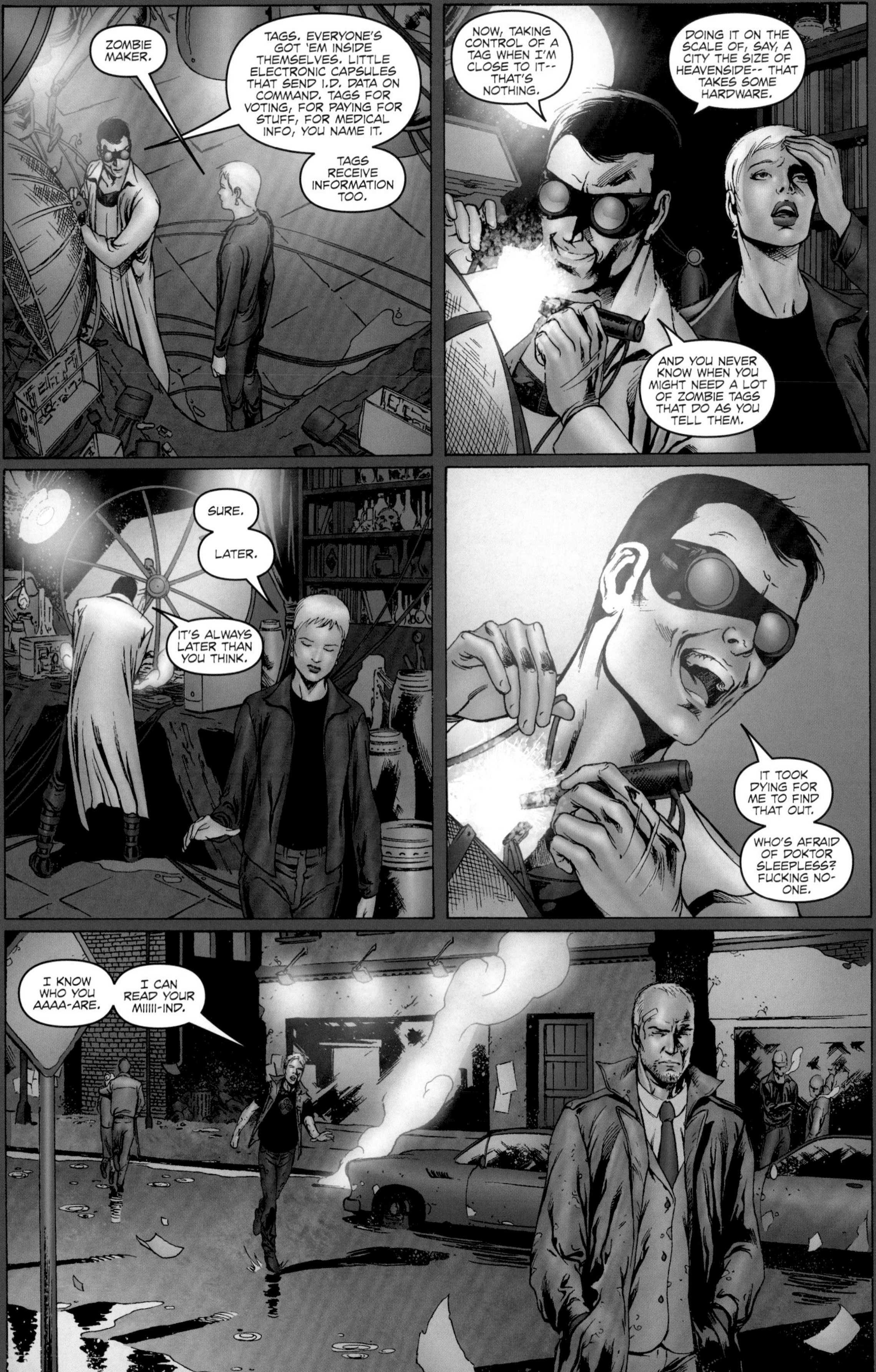
ZOMBIE MAKER.
TAGS. EVERYONE'S GOT 'EM INSIDE THEMSELVES. LITTLE ELECTRONIC CAPSULES THAT SEND I.D. DATA ON COMMAND. TAGS FOR VOTING, FOR PAYING FOR STUFF, FOR MEDICAL INFO, YOU NAME IT.
TAGS RECEIVE INFORMATION TOO.
NOW, TAKING CONTROL OF A TAG WHEN I'M CLOSE TO IT-- THAT'S NOTHING.
DOING IT ON THE SCALE OF, SAY, A CITY THE SIZE OF HEAVENSIDE-- THAT TAKES SOME HARDWARE.
AND YOU NEVER KNOW WHEN YOU MIGHT NEED A LOT OF ZOMBIE TAGS THAT DO AS YOU TELL THEM.
SURE.
LATER.
IT'S ALWAYS LATER THAN YOU THINK.
IT TOOK DYING FOR ME TO FIND THAT OUT.
WHO'S AFRAID OF DOKTOR SLEEPLESS? FUCKING NO-ONE.
I KNOW WHO YOU AAAA-ARE.
I CAN READ YOUR MIIIII-IND.

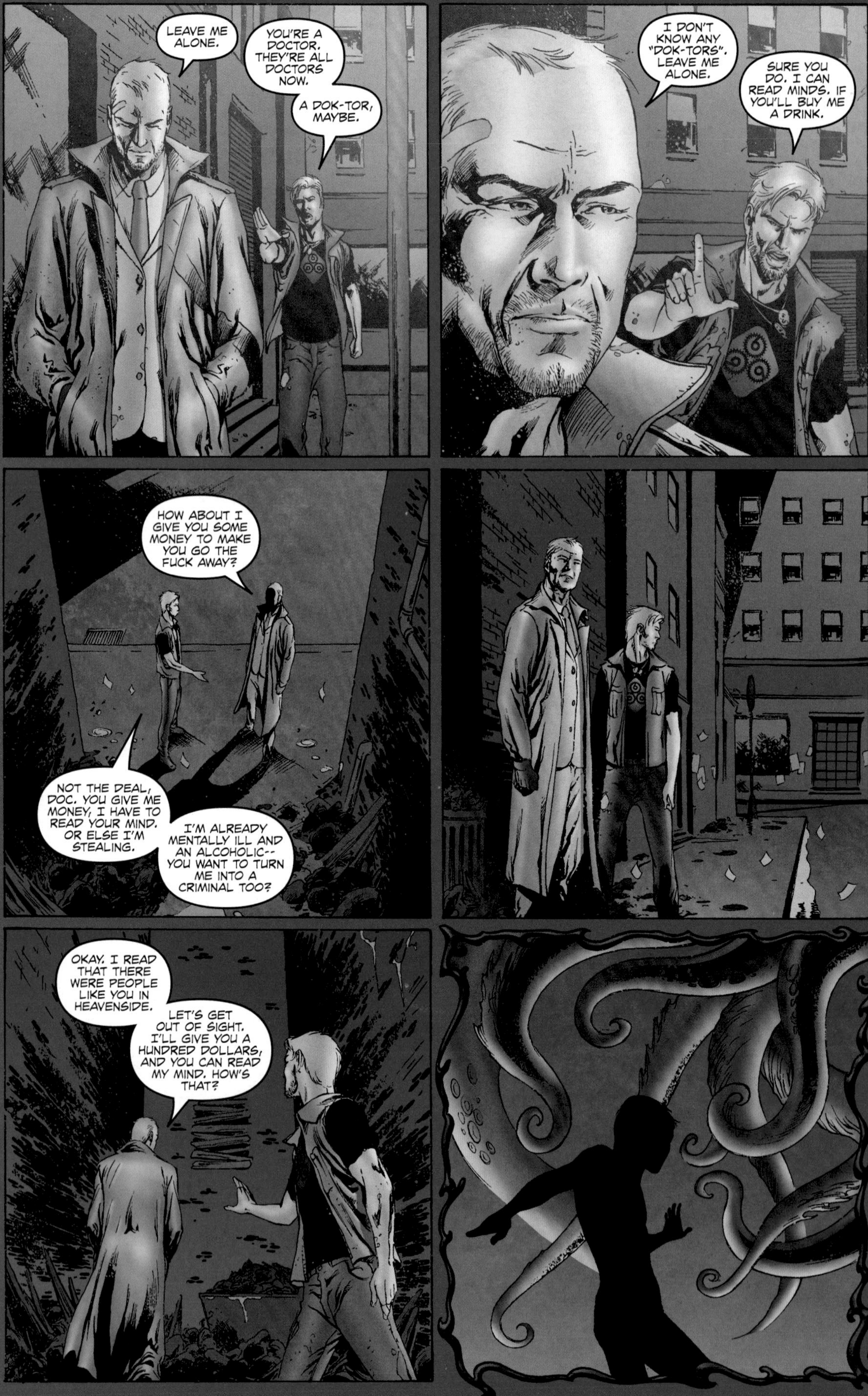

LEAVE ME ALONE.
YOU'RE A DOCTOR. THEY'RE ALL DOCTORS NOW.
A DOK-TOR, MAYBE.
I DON'T KNOW ANY "DOK-TORS". LEAVE ME ALONE.
SURE YOU DO. I CAN READ MINDS. IF YOU'LL BUY ME A DRINK.
HOW ABOUT I GIVE YOU SOME MONEY TO MAKE YOU GO THE FUCK AWAY?
NOT THE DEAL, DOC. YOU GIVE ME MONEY, I HAVE TO READ YOUR MIND. OR ELSE I'M STEALING.
I'M ALREADY MENTALLY ILL AND AN ALCOHOLIC-- YOU WANT TO TURN ME INTO A CRIMINAL TOO?
OKAY. I READ THAT THERE WERE PEOPLE LIKE YOU IN HEAVENSIDE.
LET'S GET OUT OF SIGHT. I'LL GIVE YOU A HUNDRED DOLLARS, AND YOU CAN READ MY MIND. HOW'S THAT?

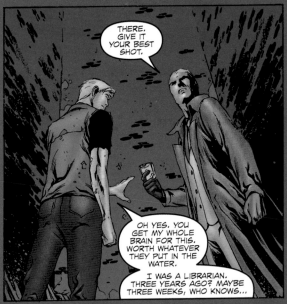

THERE. GIVE IT YOUR BEST SHOT.

OH YES. YOU GET MY WHOLE BRAIN FOR THIS. WORTH WHATEVER THEY PUT IN THE WATER.

I WAS A LIBRARIAN. THREE YEARS AGO? MAYBE THREE WEEKS, WHO KNOWS...

NAAAAA.

NGG.

YES. YOU SEE THAT? I PUT THAT RIGHT THERE FOR YOU.

MR AND MRS REINHARDT, JUST THE WAY I FOUND THEM THAT MORNING, ALL THOSE YEARS AGO.

DOCTOR. DOCTOR.

DR ALBERT CANNON. YOU BECAME HIS LEGAL GUARDIAN AFTER THEY DIED. APPOINTED BY THE BANK YOU WORKED FOR.

YOU RAISED JOHN REINHARDT.

"RAISED" IS A LITTLE STRONG. BUT I TRIED TO GUIDE HIM, TRIED AND FAILED. AND NOW LOOK.

NOW LOOK AT THE MESS I HAVE TO CLEAR UP.

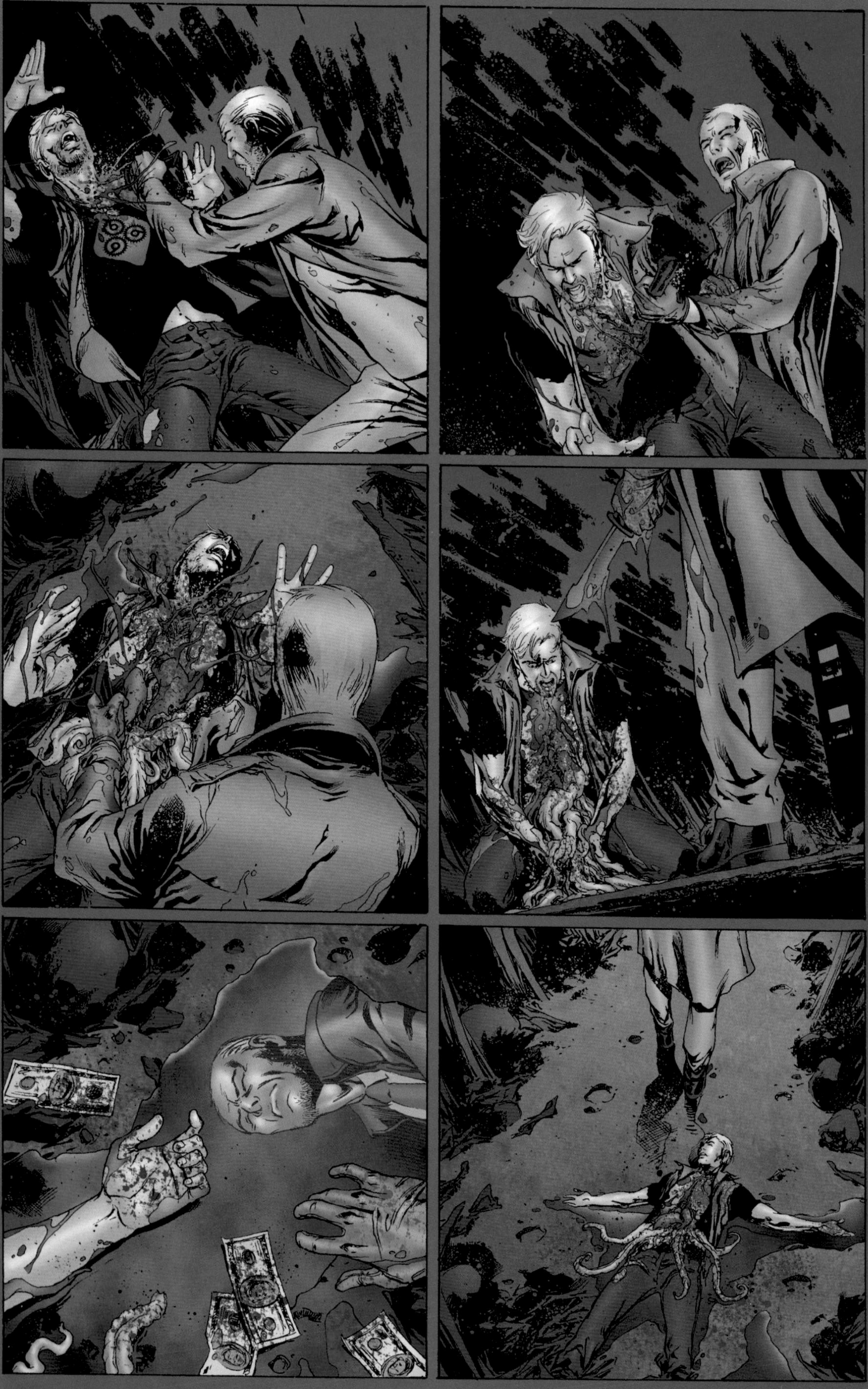

PART FOUR

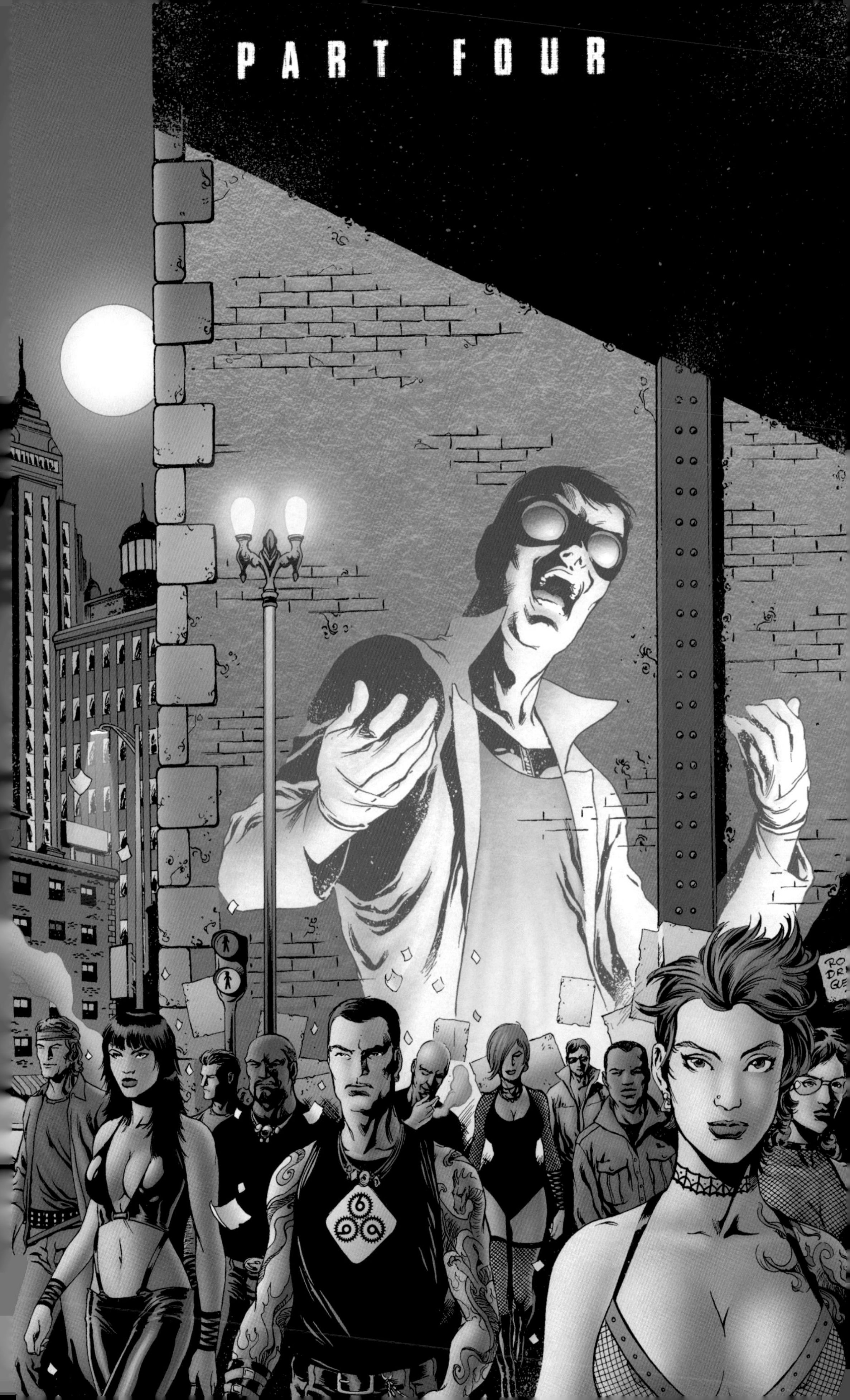

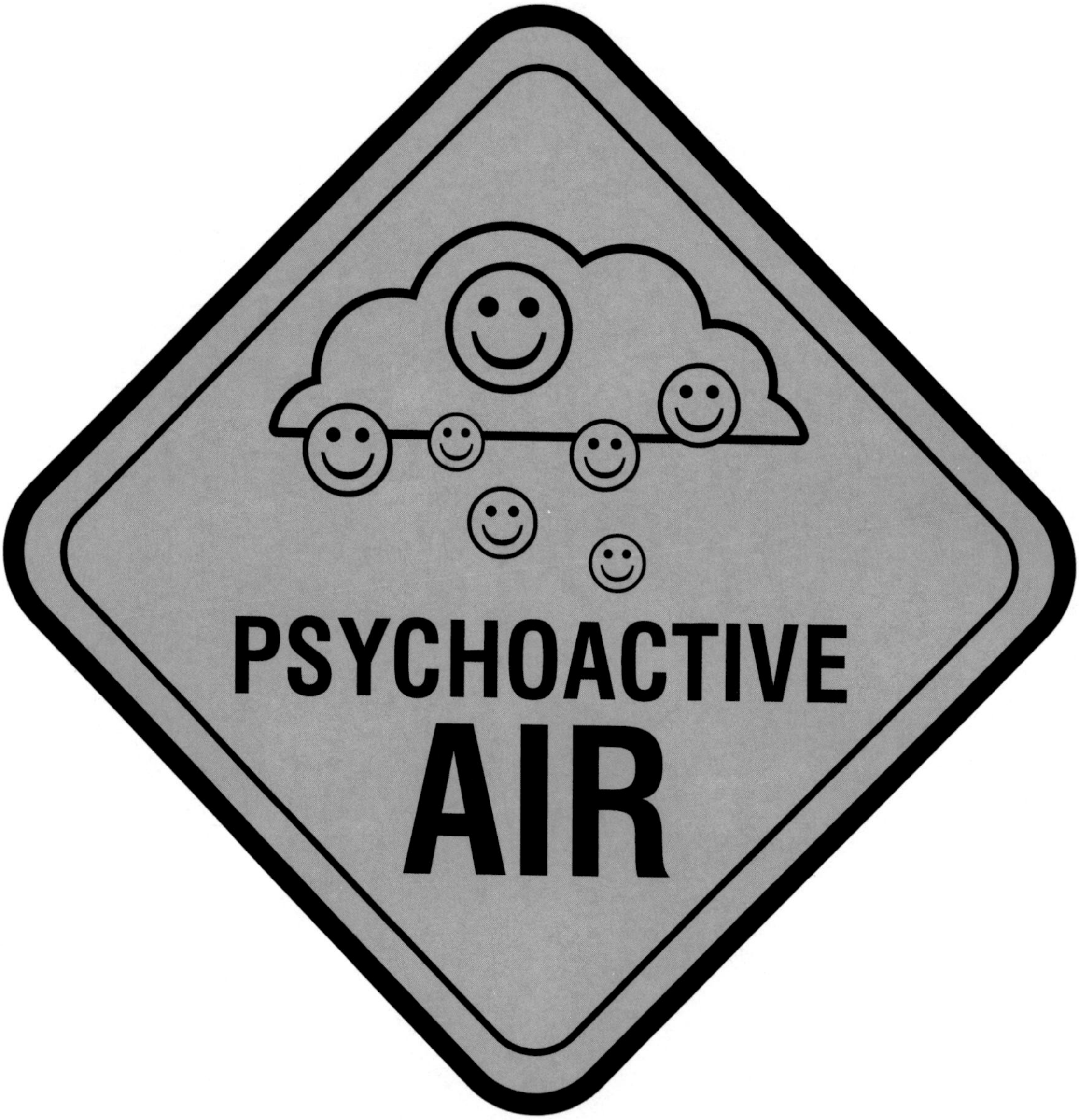
PSYCHOACTIVE
AIR

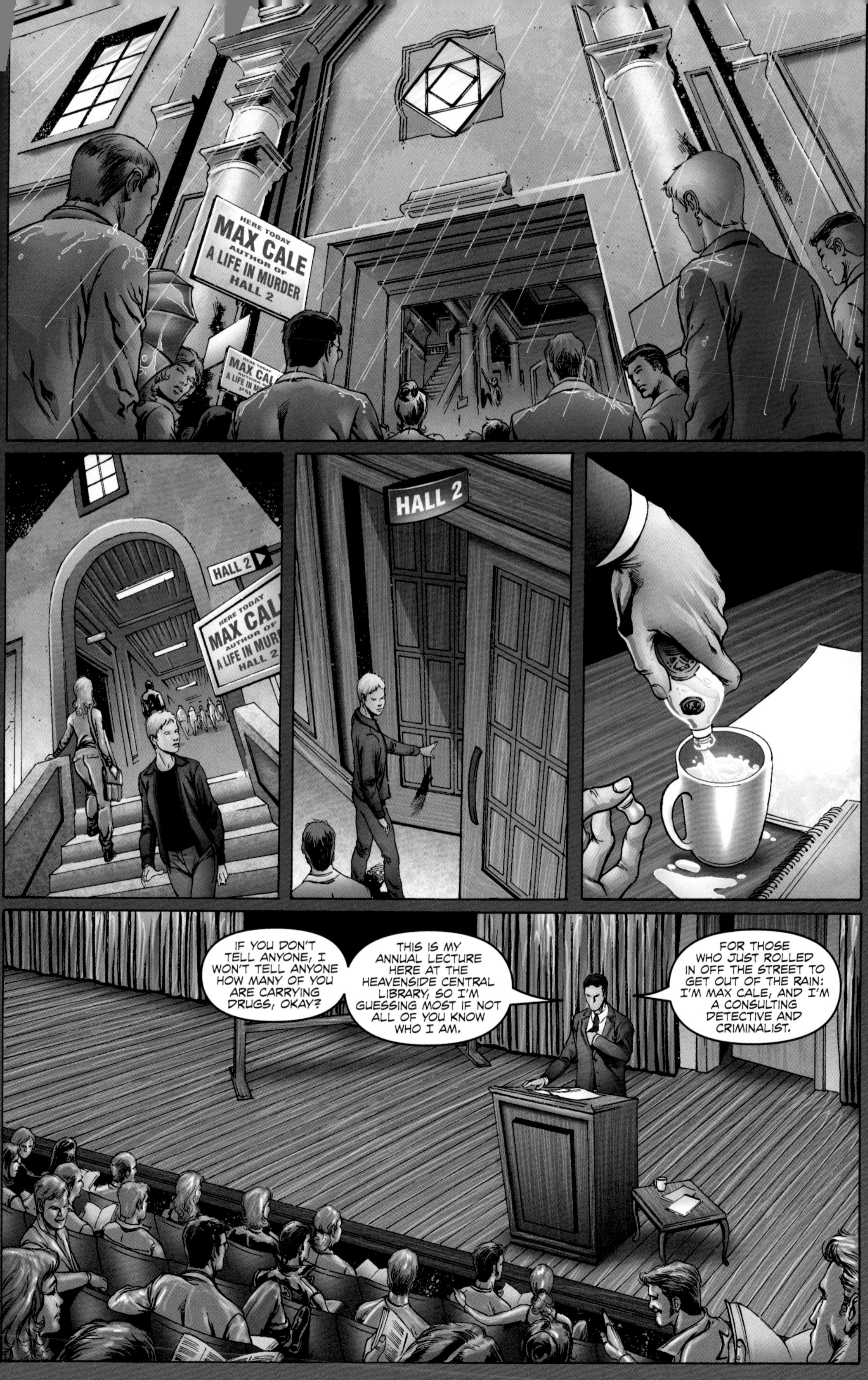
HERE TODAY
MAX CALE
AUTHOR OF
A LIFE IN MURDER
HALL 2
HALL 2
HALL 2
IF YOU DON'T TELL ANYONE, I WON'T TELL ANYONE HOW MANY OF YOU ARE CARRYING DRUGS, OKAY?
THIS IS MY ANNUAL LECTURE HERE AT THE HEAVENSIDE CENTRAL LIBRARY, SO I'M GUESSING MOST IF NOT ALL OF YOU KNOW WHO I AM.
FOR THOSE WHO JUST ROLLED IN OFF THE STREET TO GET OUT OF THE RAIN: I'M MAX CALE, AND I'M A CONSULTING DETECTIVE AND CRIMINALIST.

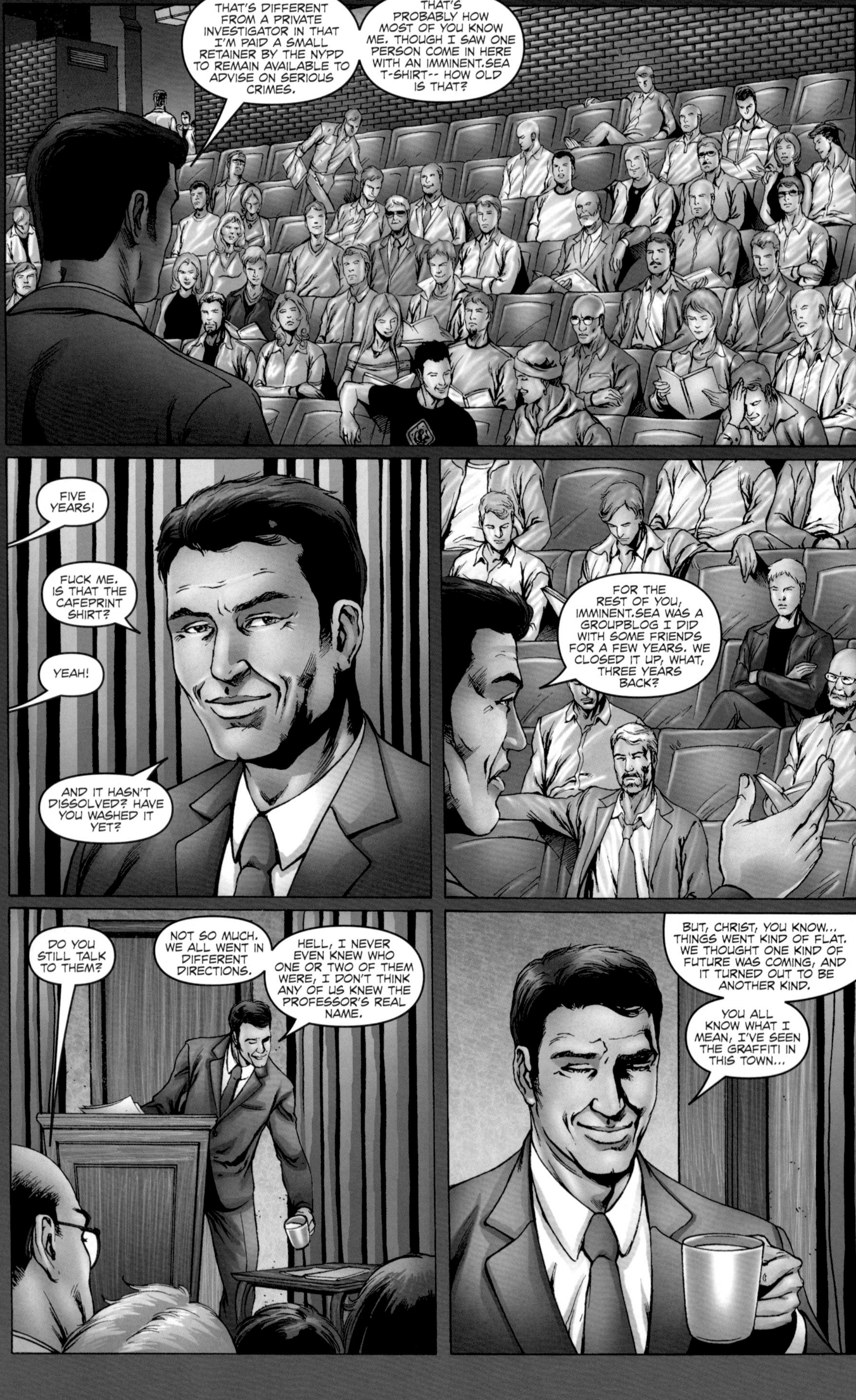
THAT'S DIFFERENT FROM A PRIVATE INVESTIGATOR IN THAT I'M PAID A SMALL RETAINER BY THE NYPD TO REMAIN AVAILABLE TO ADVISE ON SERIOUS CRIMES.
THAT'S PROBABLY HOW MOST OF YOU KNOW ME. THOUGH I SAW ONE PERSON COME IN HERE WITH AN IMMINENT.SEA T-SHIRT-- HOW OLD IS THAT?
FIVE YEARS!
FUCK ME. IS THAT THE CAFEPRINT SHIRT?
YEAH!
AND IT HASN'T DISSOLVED? HAVE YOU WASHED IT YET?
FOR THE REST OF YOU, IMMINENT.SEA WAS A GROUPBLOG I DID WITH SOME FRIENDS FOR A FEW YEARS. WE CLOSED IT UP, WHAT, THREE YEARS BACK?
DO YOU STILL TALK TO THEM?
NOT SO MUCH. WE ALL WENT IN DIFFERENT DIRECTIONS.
HELL, I NEVER EVEN KNEW WHO ONE OR TWO OF THEM WERE, I DON'T THINK ANY OF US KNEW THE PROFESSOR'S REAL NAME.
BUT, CHRIST, YOU KNOW... THINGS WENT KIND OF FLAT. WE THOUGHT ONE KIND OF FUTURE WAS COMING, AND IT TURNED OUT TO BE ANOTHER KIND.
YOU ALL KNOW WHAT I MEAN, I'VE SEEN THE GRAFFITI IN THIS TOWN...

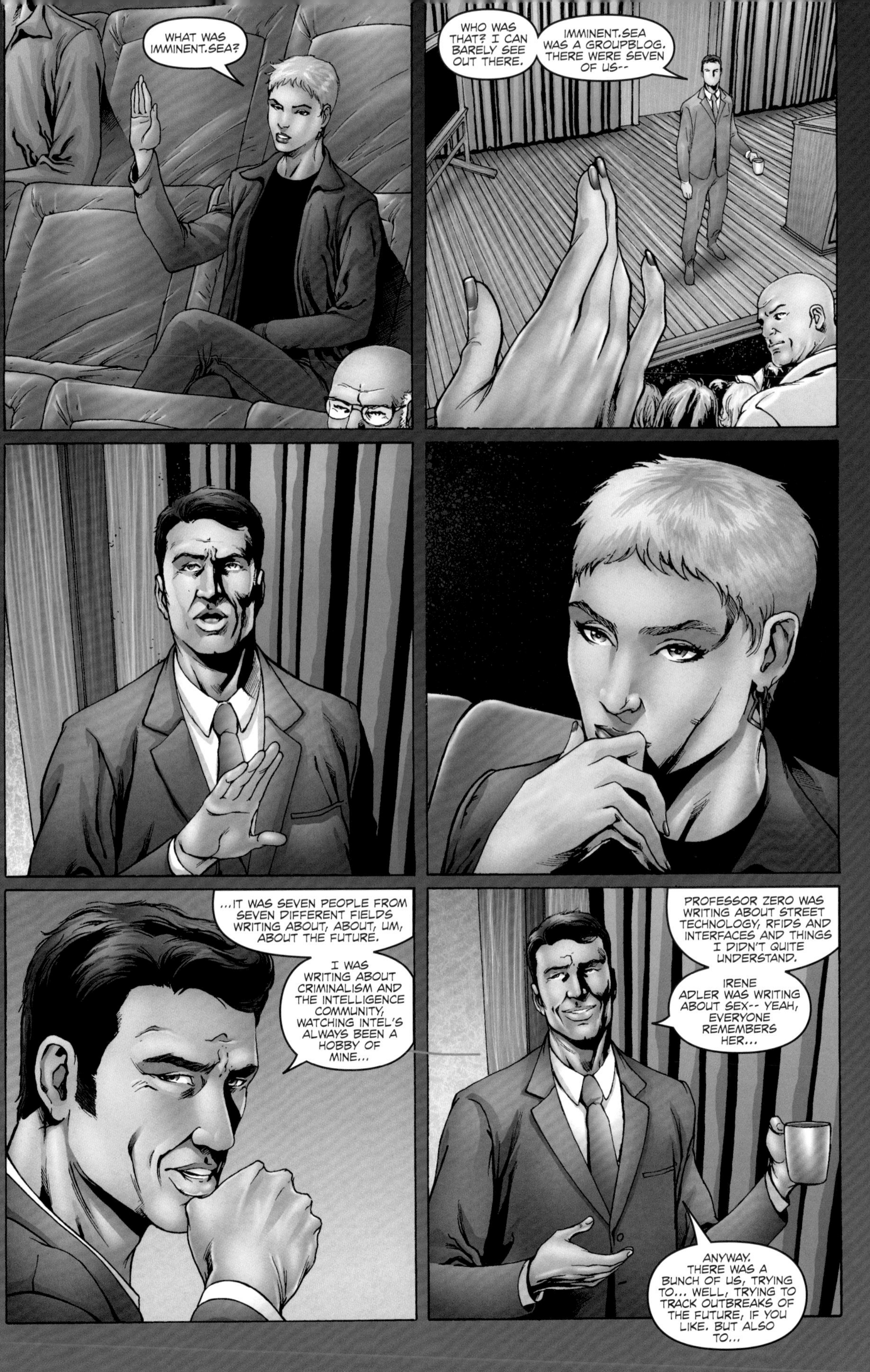
WHAT WAS IMMINENT.SEA?
WHO WAS THAT? I CAN BARELY SEE OUT THERE.
IMMINENT.SEA WAS A GROUPBLOG. THERE WERE SEVEN OF US--
...IT WAS SEVEN PEOPLE FROM SEVEN DIFFERENT FIELDS WRITING ABOUT, ABOUT, UM, ABOUT THE FUTURE.
I WAS WRITING ABOUT CRIMINALISM AND THE INTELLIGENCE COMMUNITY, WATCHING INTEL'S ALWAYS BEEN A HOBBY OF MINE...
PROFESSOR ZERO WAS WRITING ABOUT STREET TECHNOLOGY, RFIDS AND INTERFACES AND THINGS I DIDN'T QUITE UNDERSTAND.
IRENE ADLER WAS WRITING ABOUT SEX-- YEAH, EVERYONE REMEMBERS HER...
ANYWAY. THERE WAS A BUNCH OF US, TRYING TO... WELL, TRYING TO TRACK OUTBREAKS OF THE FUTURE, IF YOU LIKE. BUT ALSO TO...

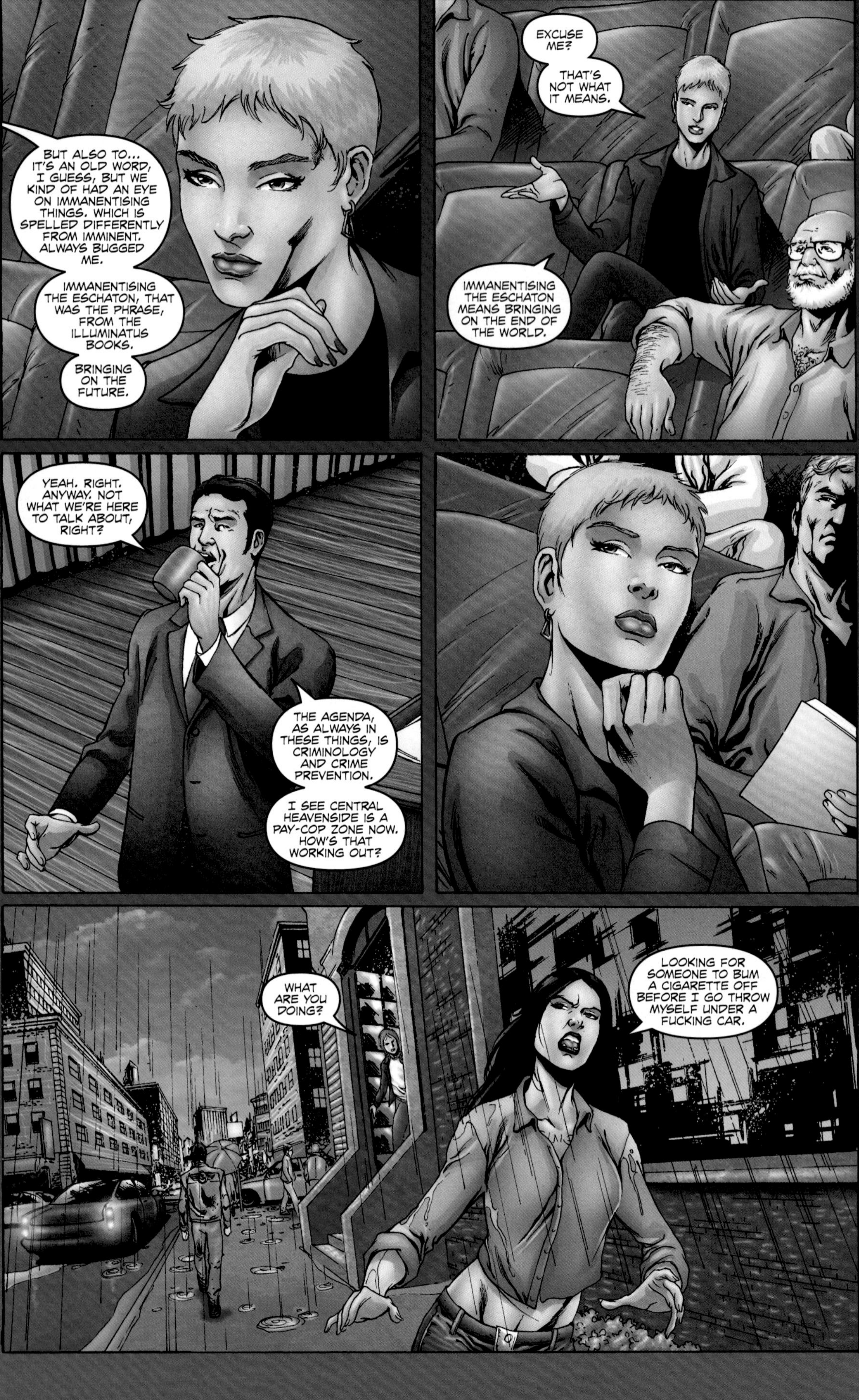
BUT ALSO TO... IT'S AN OLD WORD, I GUESS, BUT WE KIND OF HAD AN EYE ON IMMANENTISING THINGS. WHICH IS SPELLED DIFFERENTLY FROM IMMINENT. ALWAYS BUGGED ME.
IMMANENTISING THE ESCHATON, THAT WAS THE PHRASE, FROM THE ILLUMINATUS BOOKS.
BRINGING ON THE FUTURE.
EXCUSE ME?
THAT'S NOT WHAT IT MEANS.
IMMANENTISING THE ESCHATON MEANS BRINGING ON THE END OF THE WORLD.
YEAH. RIGHT. ANYWAY. NOT WHAT WE'RE HERE TO TALK ABOUT, RIGHT?
THE AGENDA, AS ALWAYS IN THESE THINGS, IS CRIMINOLOGY AND CRIME PREVENTION.
I SEE CENTRAL HEAVENSIDE IS A PAY-COP ZONE NOW. HOW'S THAT WORKING OUT?
WHAT ARE YOU DOING?
LOOKING FOR SOMEONE TO BUM A CIGARETTE OFF BEFORE I GO THROW MYSELF UNDER A FUCKING CAR.

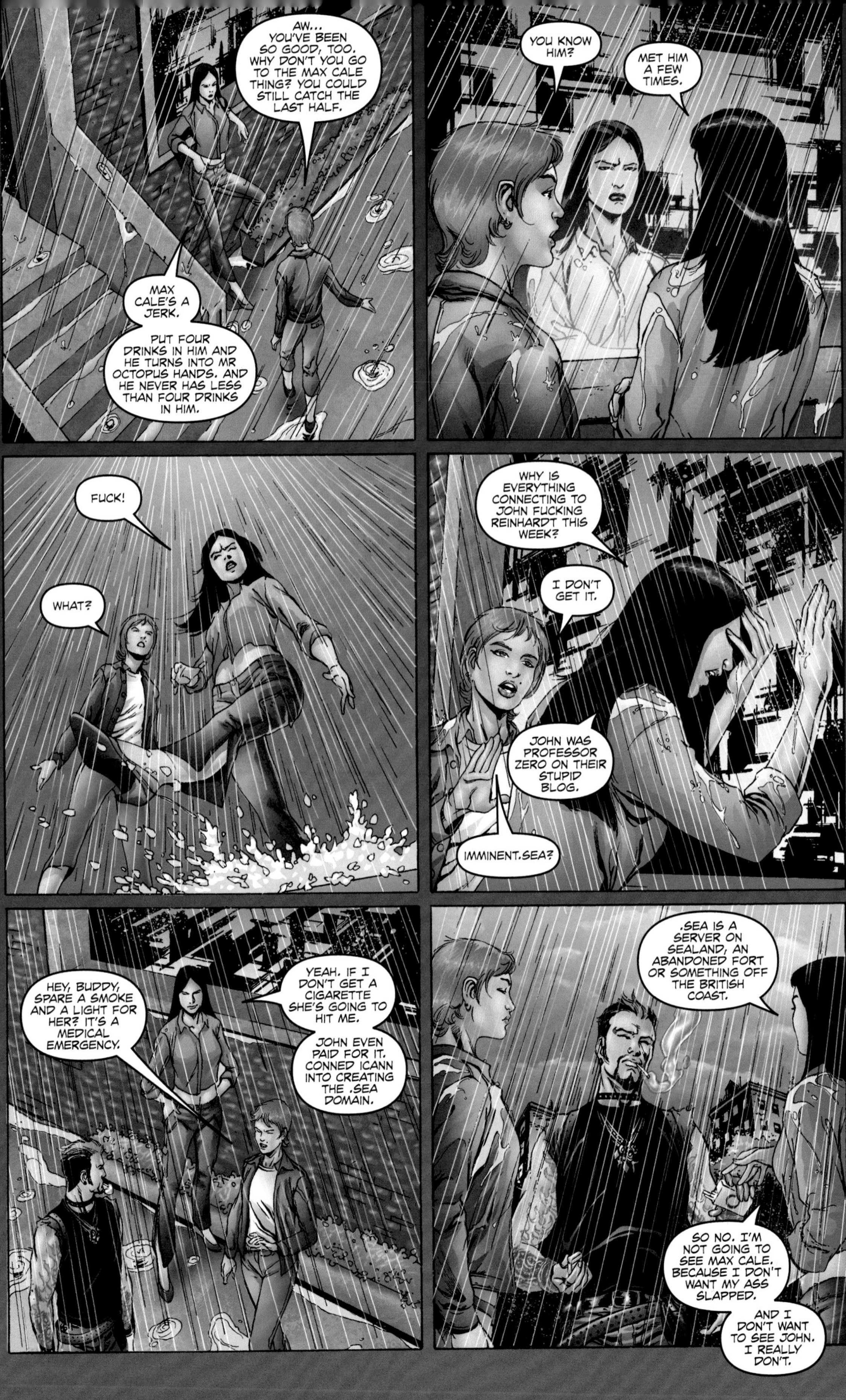
AW... YOU'VE BEEN SO GOOD, TOO. WHY DON'T YOU GO TO THE MAX CALE THING? YOU COULD STILL CATCH THE LAST HALF.
MAX CALE'S A JERK.
PUT FOUR DRINKS IN HIM AND HE TURNS INTO MR OCTOPUS HANDS. AND HE NEVER HAS LESS THAN FOUR DRINKS IN HIM.
YOU KNOW HIM?
MET HIM A FEW TIMES.
FUCK!
WHAT?
WHY IS EVERYTHING CONNECTING TO JOHN FUCKING REINHARDT THIS WEEK?
I DON'T GET IT.
JOHN WAS PROFESSOR ZERO ON THEIR STUPID BLOG.
IMMINENT.SEA?
HEY, BUDDY, SPARE A SMOKE AND A LIGHT FOR HER? IT'S A MEDICAL EMERGENCY.
YEAH. IF I DON'T GET A CIGARETTE SHE'S GOING TO HIT ME.
JOHN EVEN PAID FOR IT. CONNED ICANN INTO CREATING THE .SEA DOMAIN.
.SEA IS A SERVER ON SEALAND, AN ABANDONED FORT OR SOMETHING OFF THE BRITISH COAST.
SO NO. I'M NOT GOING TO SEE MAX CALE. BECAUSE I DON'T WANT MY ASS SLAPPED.
AND I DON'T WANT TO SEE JOHN. I REALLY DON'T.

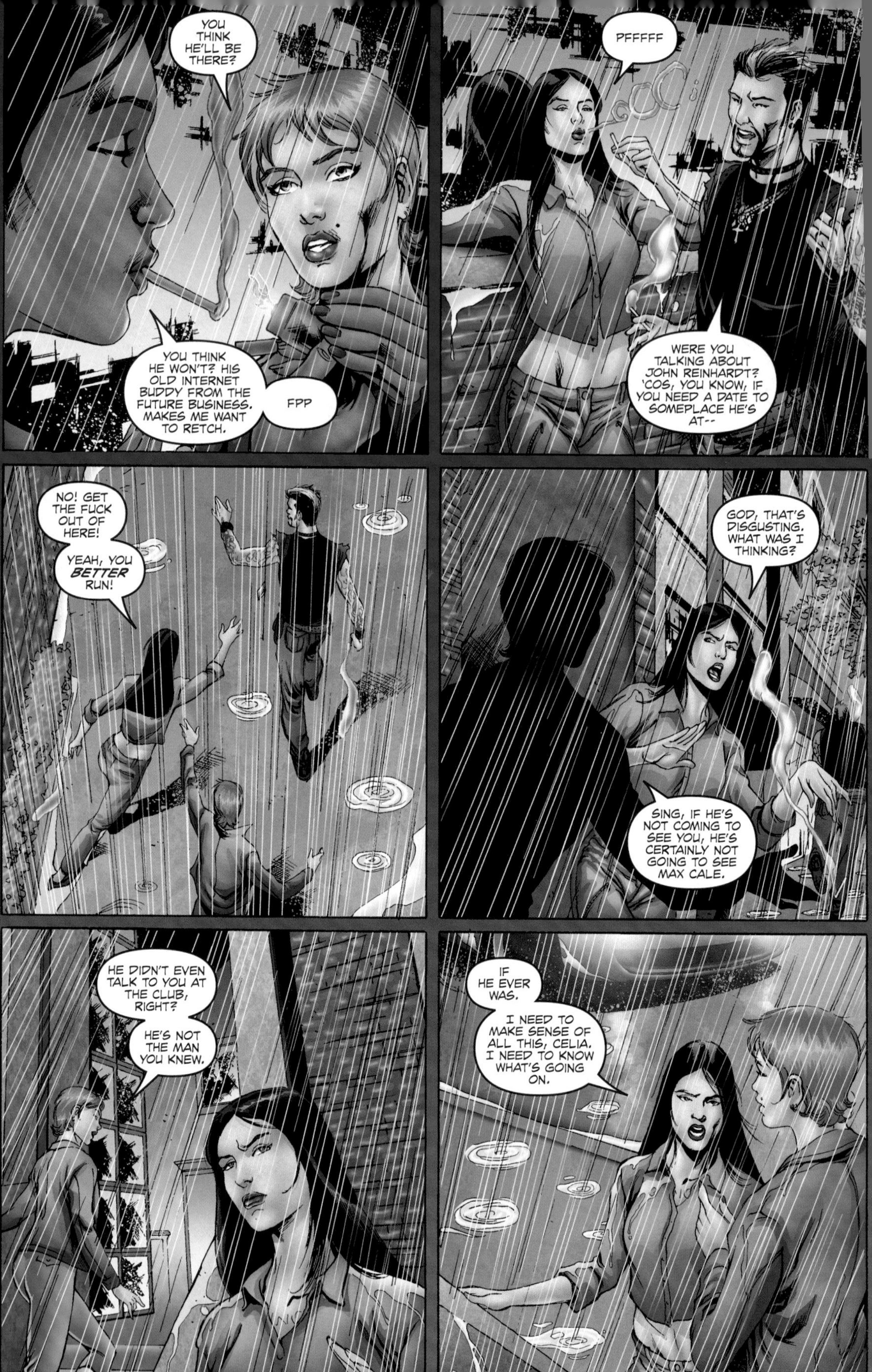

YOU THINK HE'LL BE THERE?
YOU THINK HE WON'T? HIS OLD INTERNET BUDDY FROM THE FUTURE BUSINESS. MAKES ME WANT TO RETCH.
FPP
PFFFFF
WERE YOU TALKING ABOUT JOHN REINHARDT? 'COS, YOU KNOW, IF YOU NEED A DATE TO SOMEPLACE HE'S AT--
NO! GET THE FUCK OUT OF HERE!
YEAH, YOU BETTER RUN!
GOD, THAT'S DISGUSTING. WHAT WAS I THINKING?
SING, IF HE'S NOT COMING TO SEE YOU, HE'S CERTAINLY NOT GOING TO SEE MAX CALE.
HE DIDN'T EVEN TALK TO YOU AT THE CLUB, RIGHT?
HE'S NOT THE MAN YOU KNEW.
IF HE EVER WAS.
I NEED TO MAKE SENSE OF ALL THIS, CELIA. I NEED TO KNOW WHAT'S GOING ON.

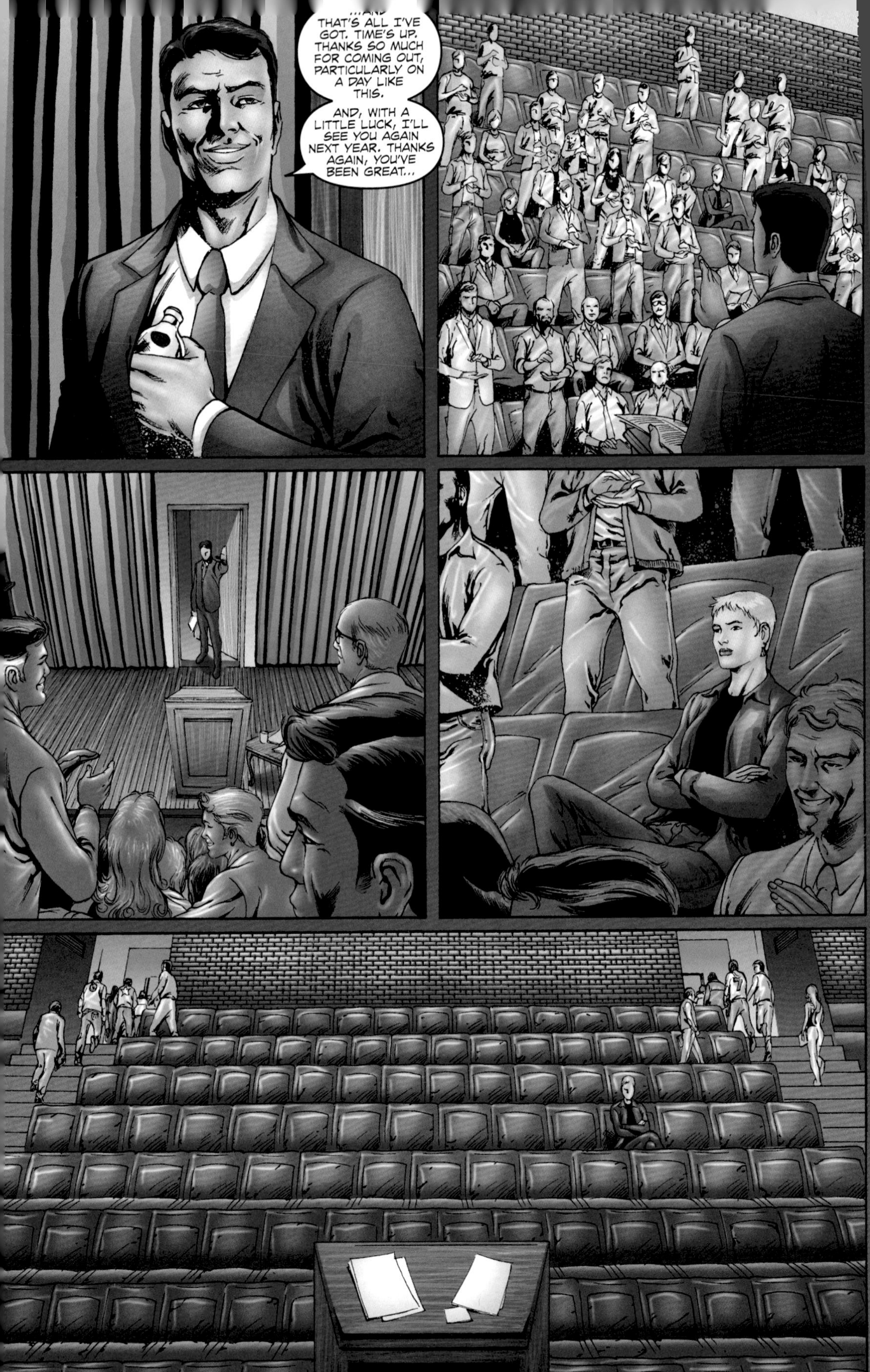
THAT'S ALL I'VE GOT. TIME'S UP. THANKS SO MUCH FOR COMING OUT, PARTICULARLY ON A DAY LIKE THIS.
AND, WITH A LITTLE LUCK, I'LL SEE YOU AGAIN NEXT YEAR. THANKS AGAIN, YOU'VE BEEN GREAT...

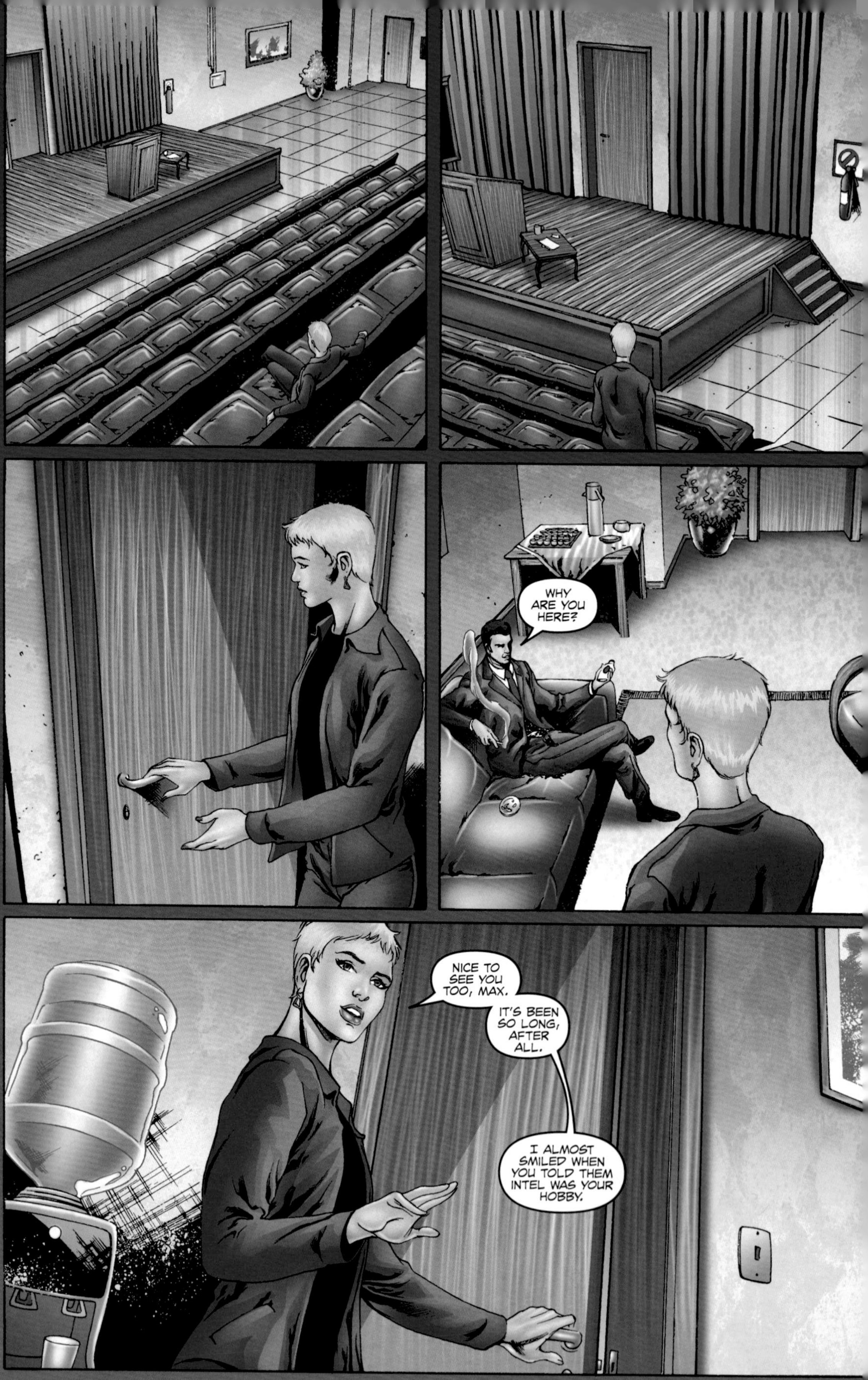
WHY ARE YOU HERE?
NICE TO SEE YOU TOO, MAX.
IT'S BEEN SO LONG, AFTER ALL.
I ALMOST SMILED WHEN YOU TOLD THEM INTEL WAS YOUR HOBBY.

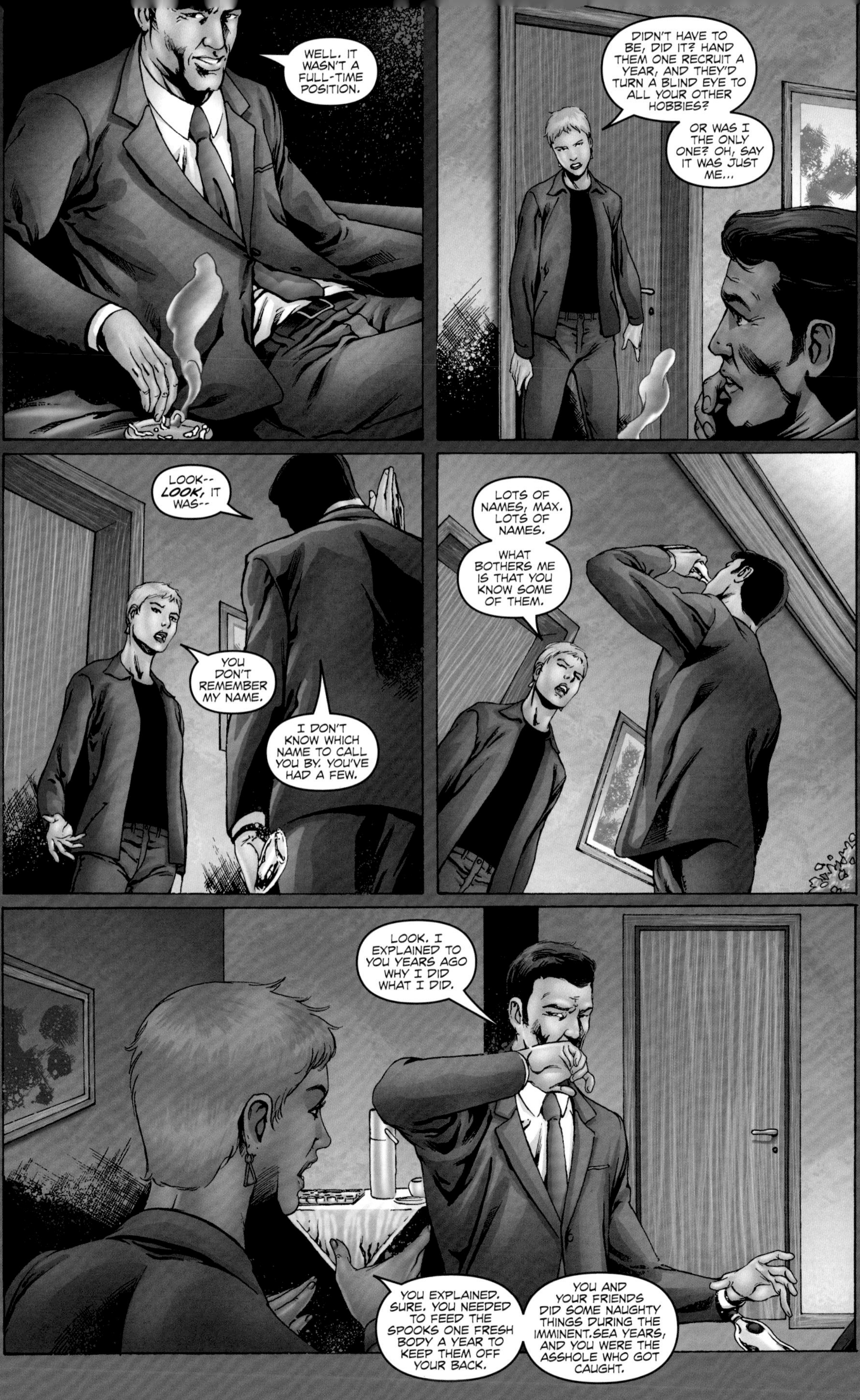
WELL. IT WASN'T A FULL-TIME POSITION.
DIDN'T HAVE TO BE, DID IT? HAND THEM ONE RECRUIT A YEAR, AND THEY'D TURN A BLIND EYE TO ALL YOUR OTHER HOBBIES?
OR WAS I THE ONLY ONE? OH, SAY IT WAS JUST ME...
LOOK-- LOOK, IT WAS--
YOU DON'T REMEMBER MY NAME.
I DON'T KNOW WHICH NAME TO CALL YOU BY. YOU'VE HAD A FEW.
LOTS OF NAMES, MAX. LOTS OF NAMES.
WHAT BOTHERS ME IS THAT YOU KNOW SOME OF THEM.
LOOK. I EXPLAINED TO YOU YEARS AGO WHY I DID WHAT I DID.
YOU EXPLAINED. SURE. YOU NEEDED TO FEED THE SPOOKS ONE FRESH BODY A YEAR TO KEEP THEM OFF YOUR BACK.
YOU AND YOUR FRIENDS DID SOME NAUGHTY THINGS DURING THE IMMINENT.SEA YEARS, AND YOU WERE THE ASSHOLE WHO GOT CAUGHT.

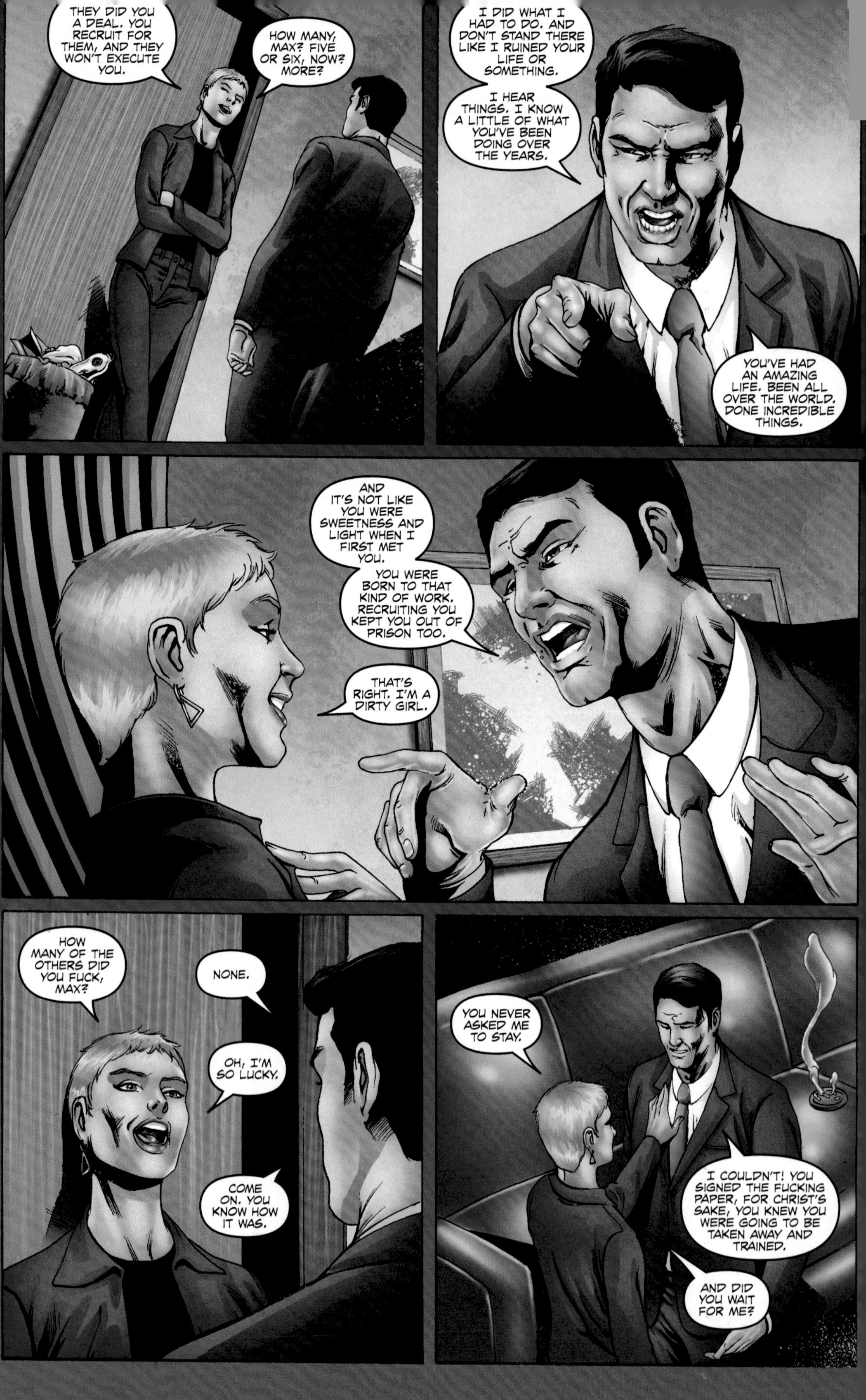
THEY DID YOU A DEAL. YOU RECRUIT FOR THEM, AND THEY WON'T EXECUTE YOU.
HOW MANY, MAX? FIVE OR SIX, NOW? MORE?
I DID WHAT I HAD TO DO. AND DON'T STAND THERE LIKE I RUINED YOUR LIFE OR SOMETHING.
I HEAR THINGS. I KNOW A LITTLE OF WHAT YOU'VE BEEN DOING OVER THE YEARS.
YOU'VE HAD AN AMAZING LIFE. BEEN ALL OVER THE WORLD. DONE INCREDIBLE THINGS.
AND IT'S NOT LIKE YOU WERE SWEETNESS AND LIGHT WHEN I FIRST MET YOU.
YOU WERE BORN TO THAT KIND OF WORK. RECRUITING YOU KEPT YOU OUT OF PRISON TOO.
THAT'S RIGHT. I'M A DIRTY GIRL.
HOW MANY OF THE OTHERS DID YOU FUCK, MAX?
NONE.
OH, I'M SO LUCKY.
COME ON. YOU KNOW HOW IT WAS.
YOU NEVER ASKED ME TO STAY.
I COULDN'T! YOU SIGNED THE FUCKING PAPER, FOR CHRIST'S SAKE, YOU KNEW YOU WERE GOING TO BE TAKEN AWAY AND TRAINED.
AND DID YOU WAIT FOR ME?

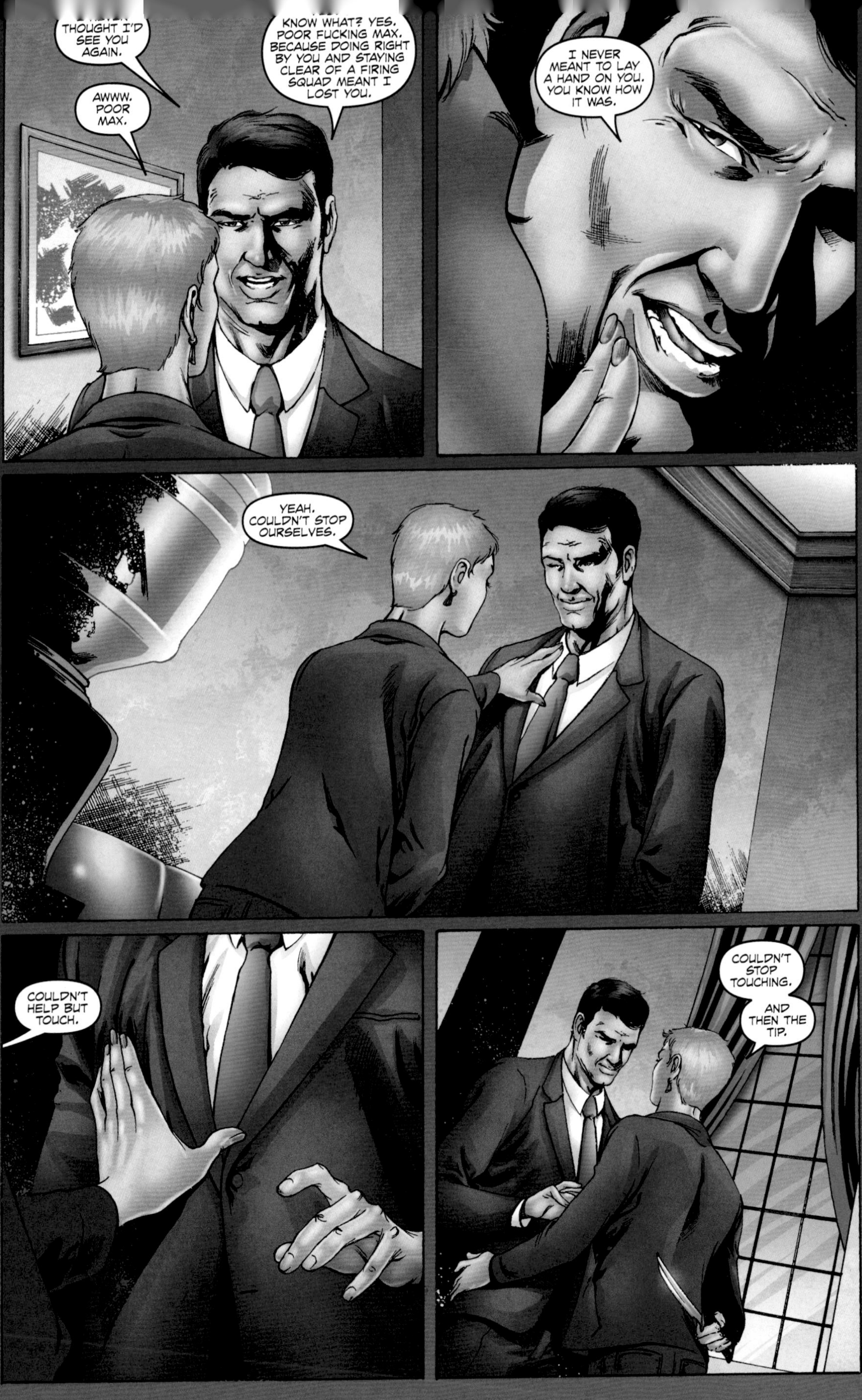
THOUGHT I'D SEE YOU AGAIN.
AWWW. POOR MAX.
KNOW WHAT? YES. POOR FUCKING MAX. BECAUSE DOING RIGHT BY YOU AND STAYING CLEAR OF A FIRING SQUAD MEANT I LOST YOU.
I NEVER MEANT TO LAY A HAND ON YOU. YOU KNOW HOW IT WAS.
YEAH. COULDN'T STOP OURSELVES.
COULDN'T HELP BUT TOUCH.
COULDN'T STOP TOUCHING.
AND THEN THE TIP.

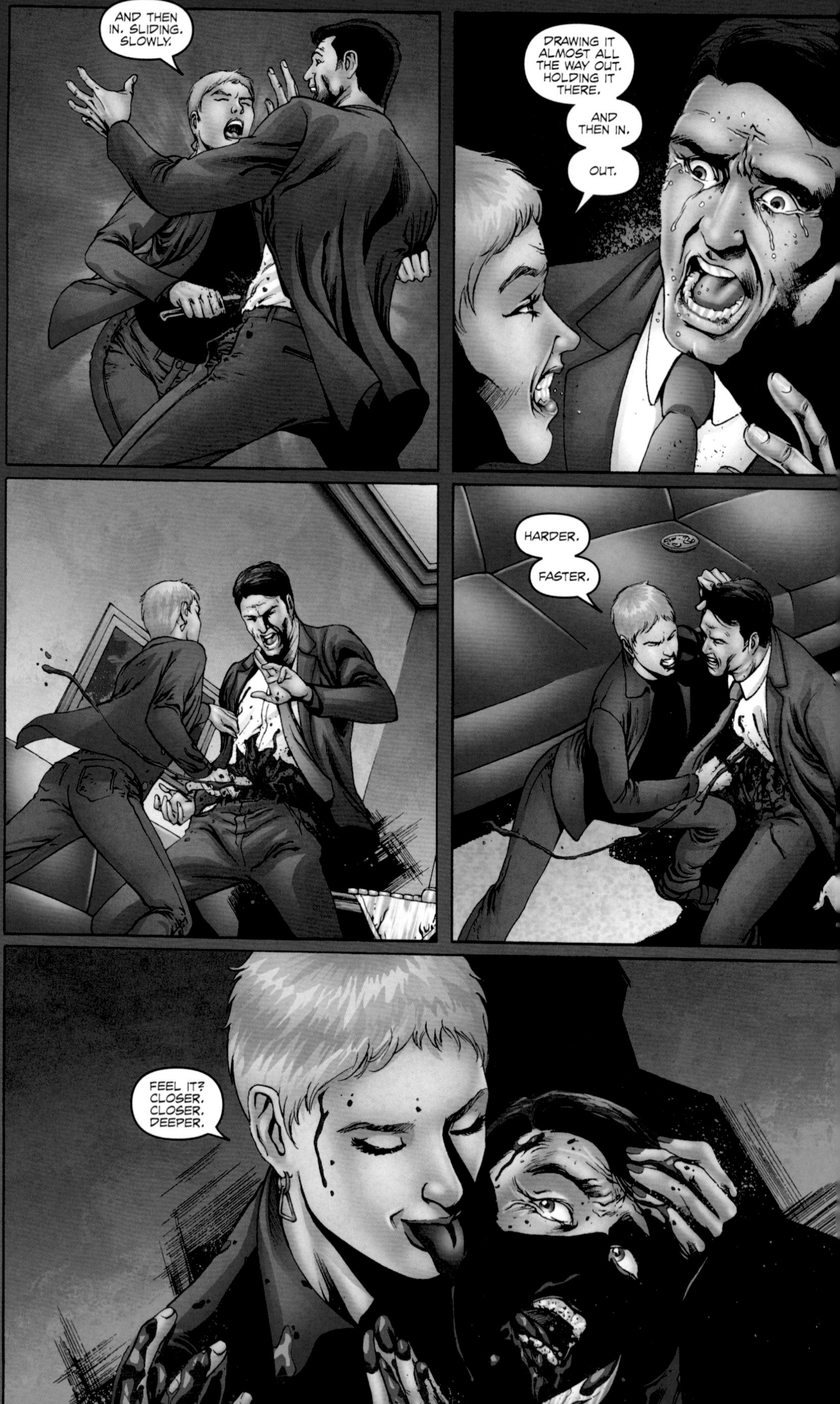
AND THEN IN. SLIDING. SLOWLY.
DRAWING IT ALMOST ALL THE WAY OUT. HOLDING IT THERE.
AND THEN IN.
OUT.
HARDER.
FASTER.
FEEL IT? CLOSER. CLOSER. DEEPER.

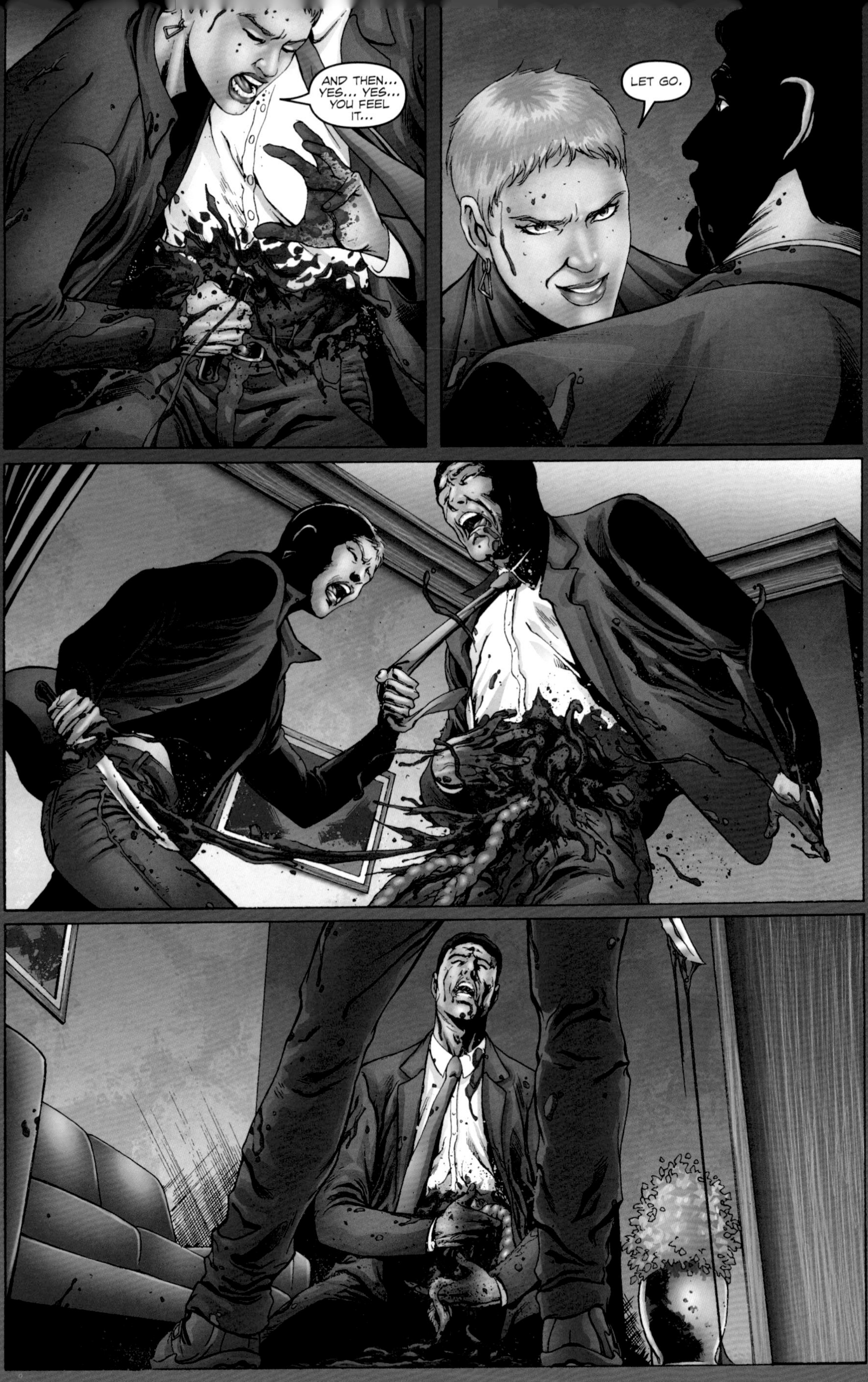
AND THEN... YES... YES... YOU FEEL IT...
LET GO.

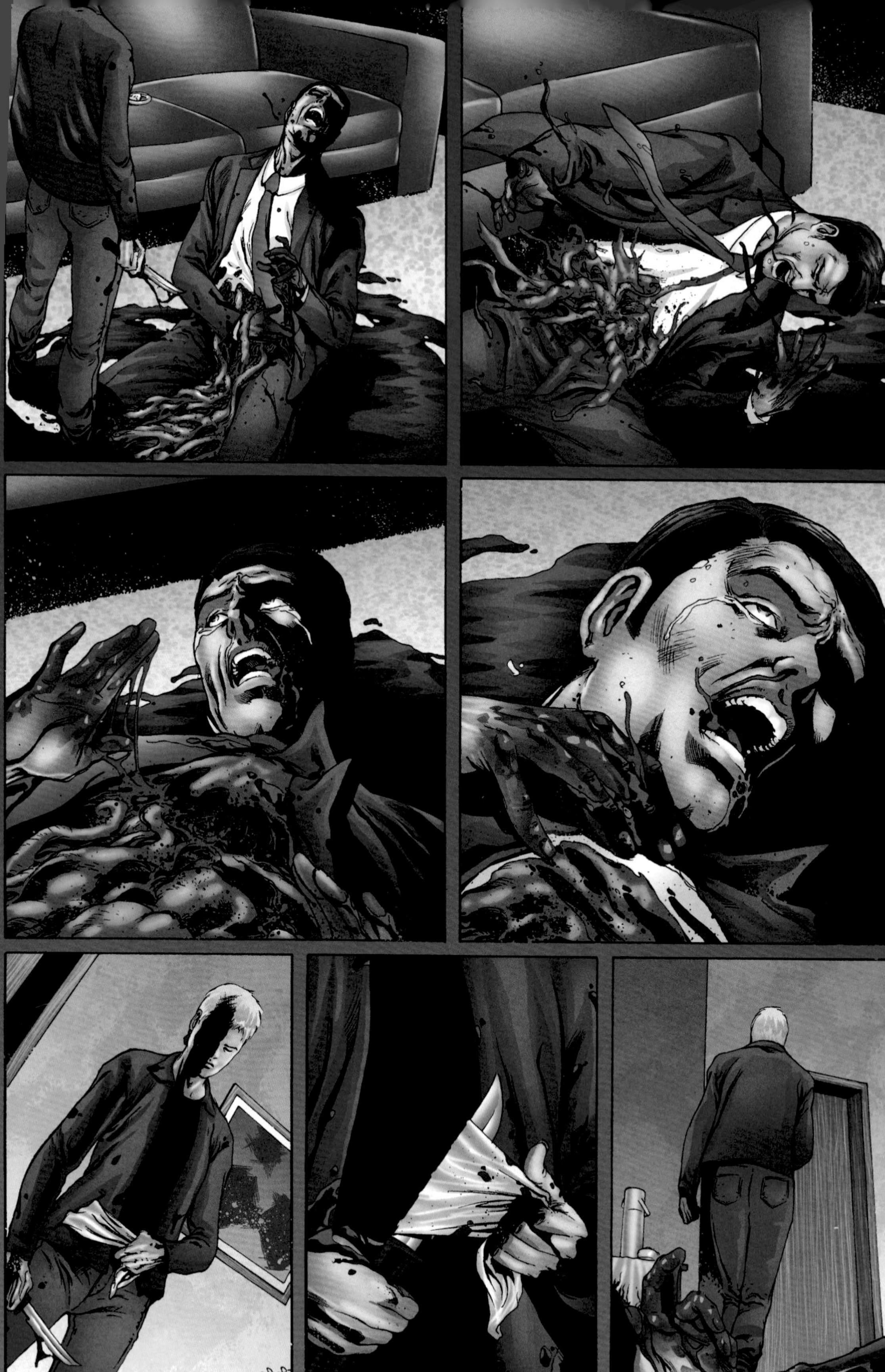

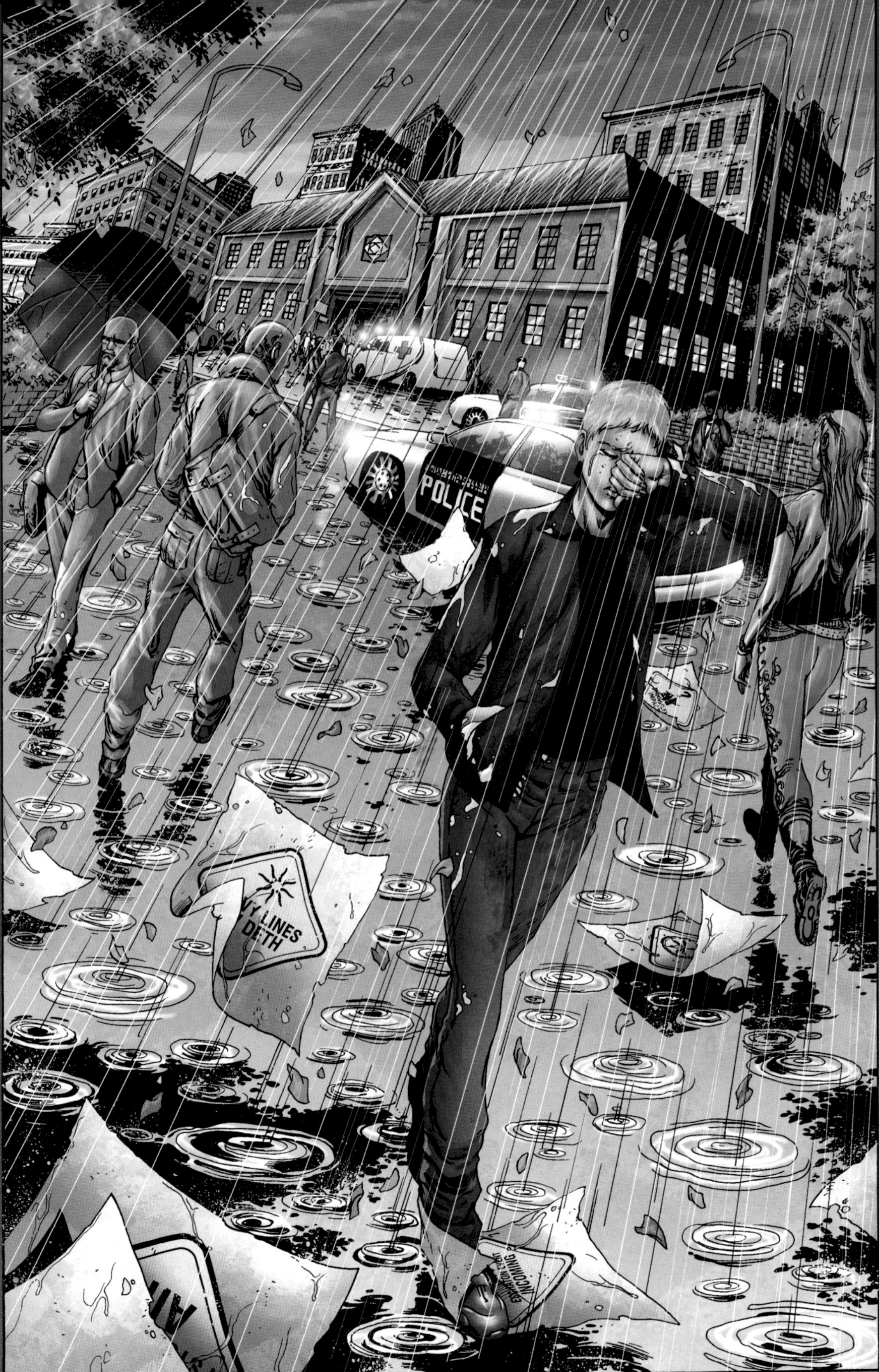
POLICE

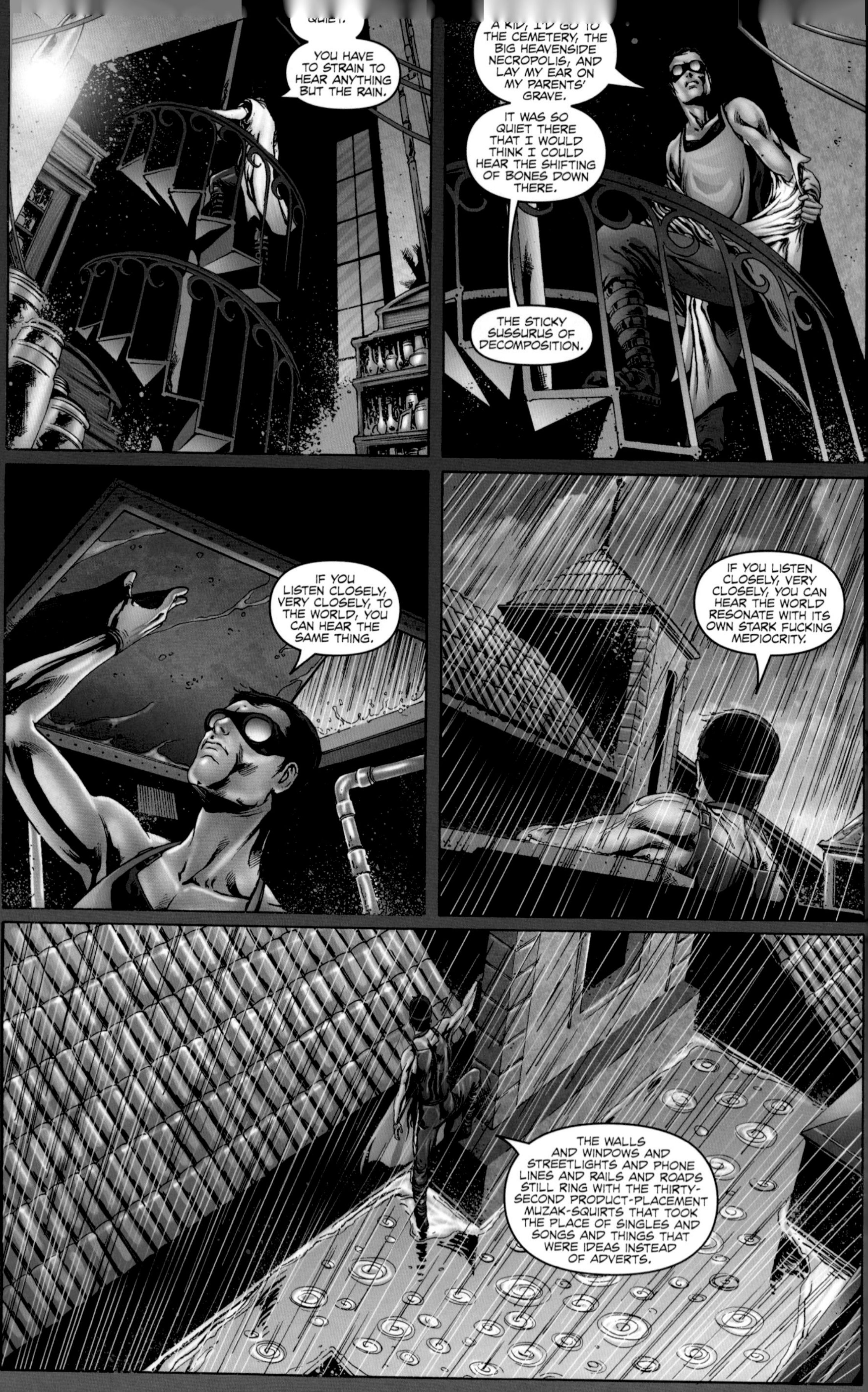
QUIET.
YOU HAVE TO STRAIN TO HEAR ANYTHING BUT THE RAIN.
A KID, I'D GO TO THE CEMETERY, THE BIG HEAVENSIDE NECROPOLIS, AND LAY MY EAR ON MY PARENTS' GRAVE.
IT WAS SO QUIET THERE THAT I WOULD THINK I COULD HEAR THE SHIFTING OF BONES DOWN THERE.
THE STICKY SUSSURUS OF DECOMPOSITION.
IF YOU LISTEN CLOSELY, VERY CLOSELY, TO THE WORLD, YOU CAN HEAR THE SAME THING.
IF YOU LISTEN CLOSELY, VERY CLOSELY, YOU CAN HEAR THE WORLD RESONATE WITH ITS OWN STARK FUCKING MEDIOCRITY.
THE WALLS AND WINDOWS AND STREETLIGHTS AND PHONE LINES AND RAILS AND ROADS STILL RING WITH THE THIRTY-SECOND PRODUCT-PLACEMENT MUZAK-SQUIRTS THAT TOOK THE PLACE OF SINGLES AND SONGS AND THINGS THAT WERE IDEAS INSTEAD OF ADVERTS.

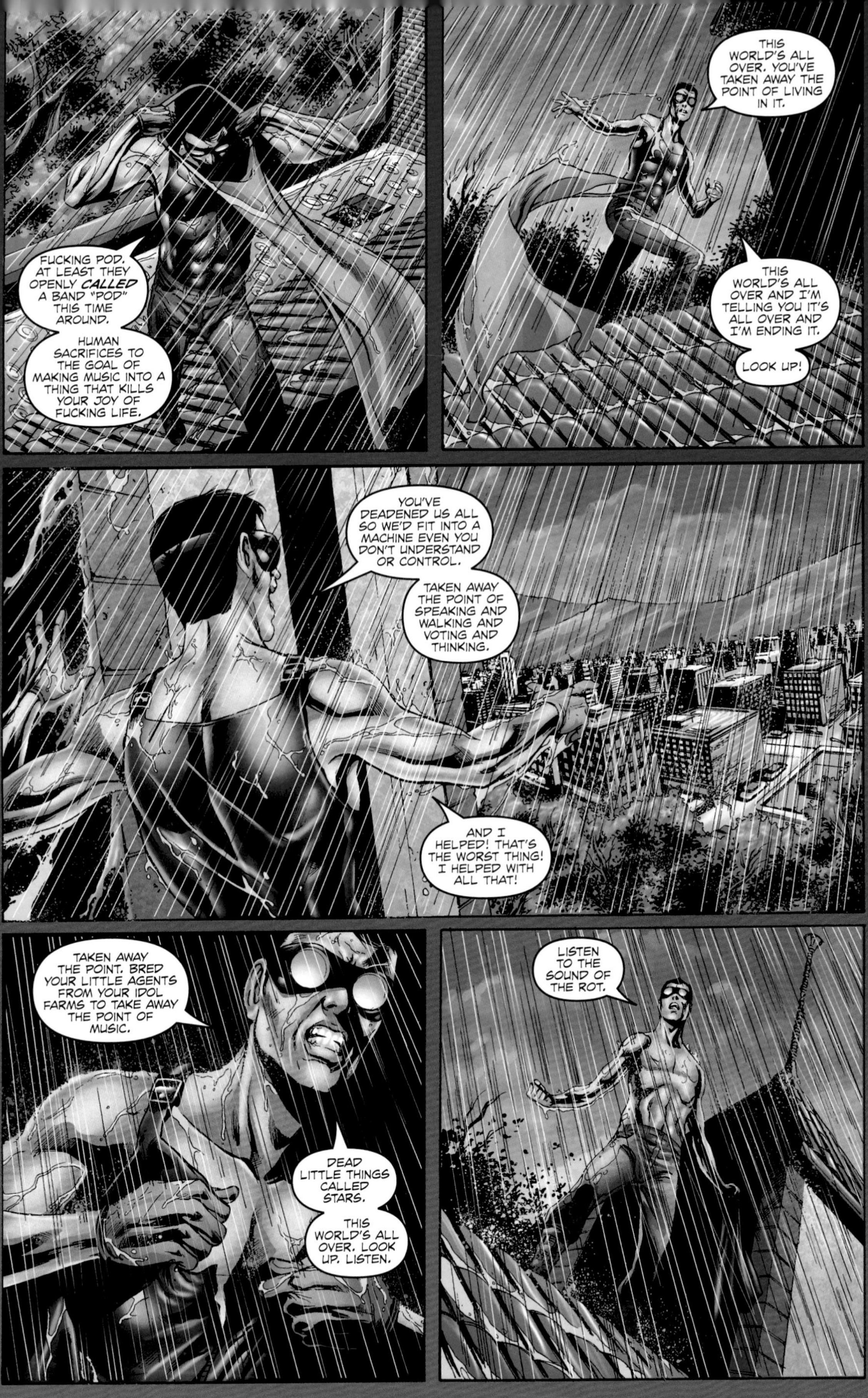
FUCKING POD. AT LEAST THEY OPENLY *CALLED* A BAND "POD" THIS TIME AROUND.
HUMAN SACRIFICES TO THE GOAL OF MAKING MUSIC INTO A THING THAT KILLS YOUR JOY OF FUCKING LIFE.
THIS WORLD'S ALL OVER. YOU'VE TAKEN AWAY THE POINT OF LIVING IN IT.
THIS WORLD'S ALL OVER AND I'M TELLING YOU IT'S ALL OVER AND I'M ENDING IT.
LOOK UP!
YOU'VE DEADENED US ALL SO WE'D FIT INTO A MACHINE EVEN YOU DON'T UNDERSTAND OR CONTROL.
TAKEN AWAY THE POINT OF SPEAKING AND WALKING AND VOTING AND THINKING.
AND I HELPED! THAT'S THE WORST THING! I HELPED WITH ALL THAT!
TAKEN AWAY THE POINT. BRED YOUR LITTLE AGENTS FROM YOUR IDOL FARMS TO TAKE AWAY THE POINT OF MUSIC.
DEAD LITTLE THINGS CALLED STARS.
THIS WORLD'S ALL OVER. LOOK UP. LISTEN.
LISTEN TO THE SOUND OF THE ROT.

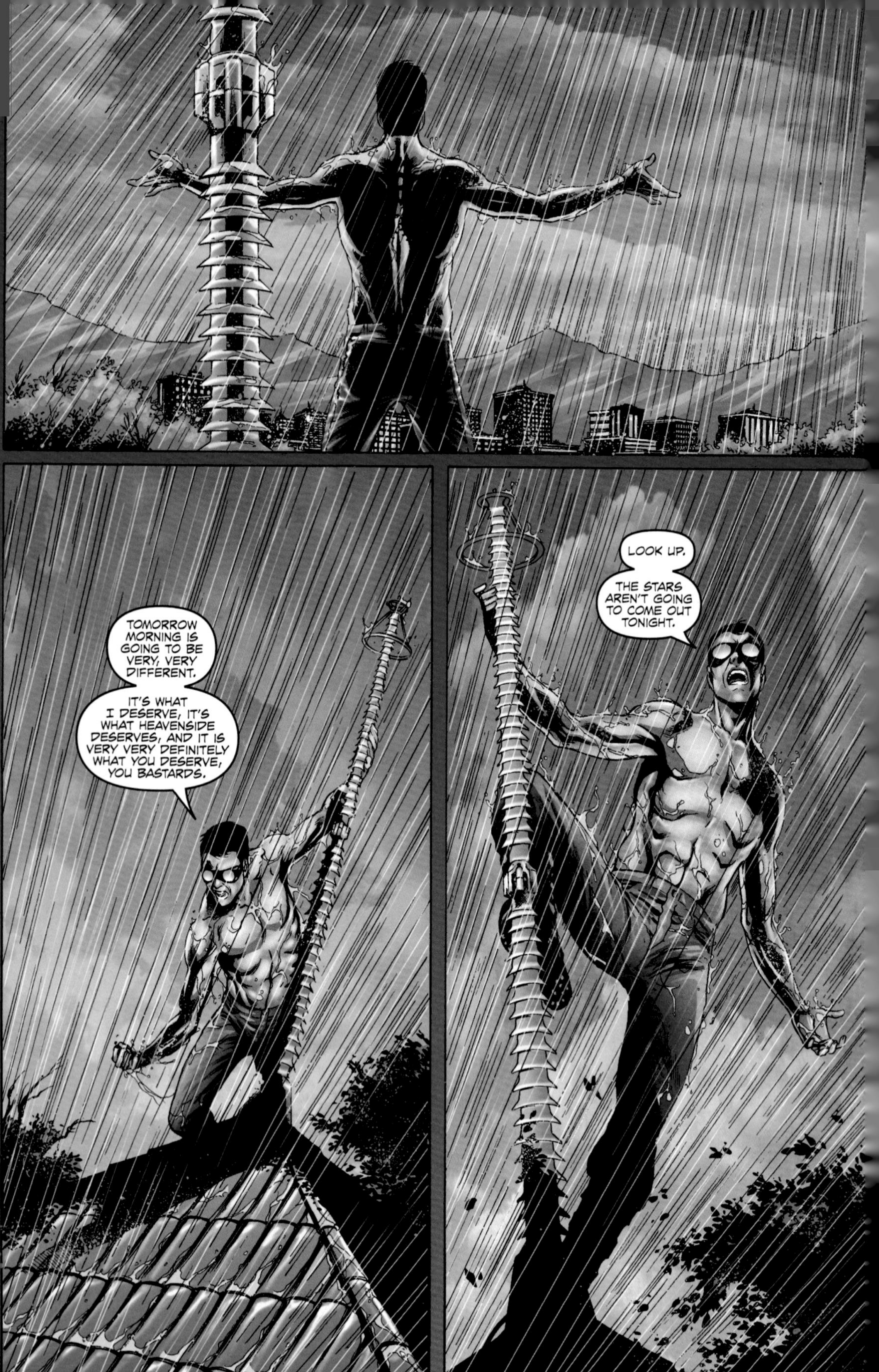
TOMORROW MORNING IS GOING TO BE VERY, VERY DIFFERENT.
IT'S WHAT I DESERVE, IT'S WHAT HEAVENSIDE DESERVES, AND IT IS VERY VERY DEFINITELY WHAT YOU DESERVE, YOU BASTARDS.
LOOK UP.
THE STARS AREN'T GOING TO COME OUT TONIGHT.

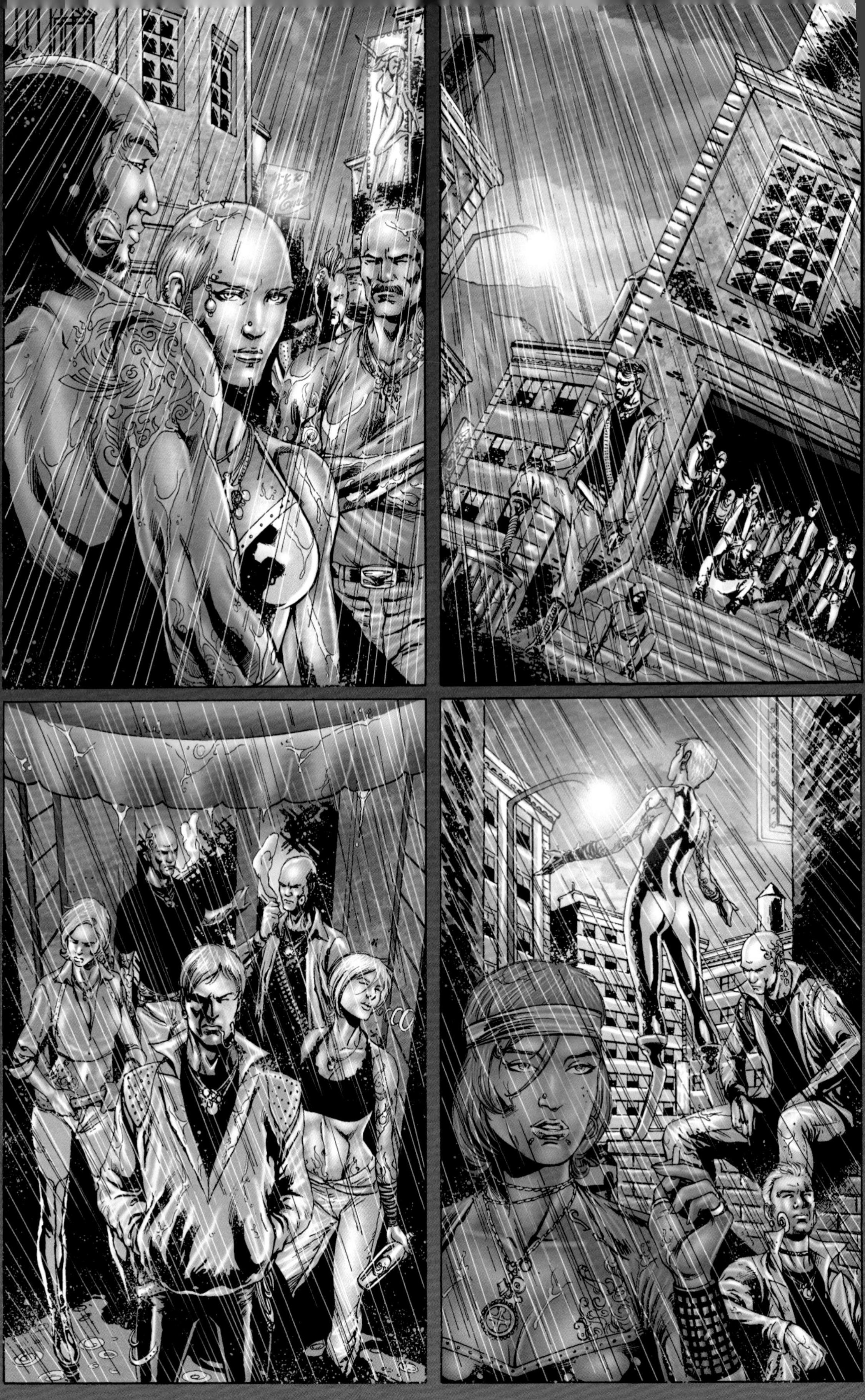

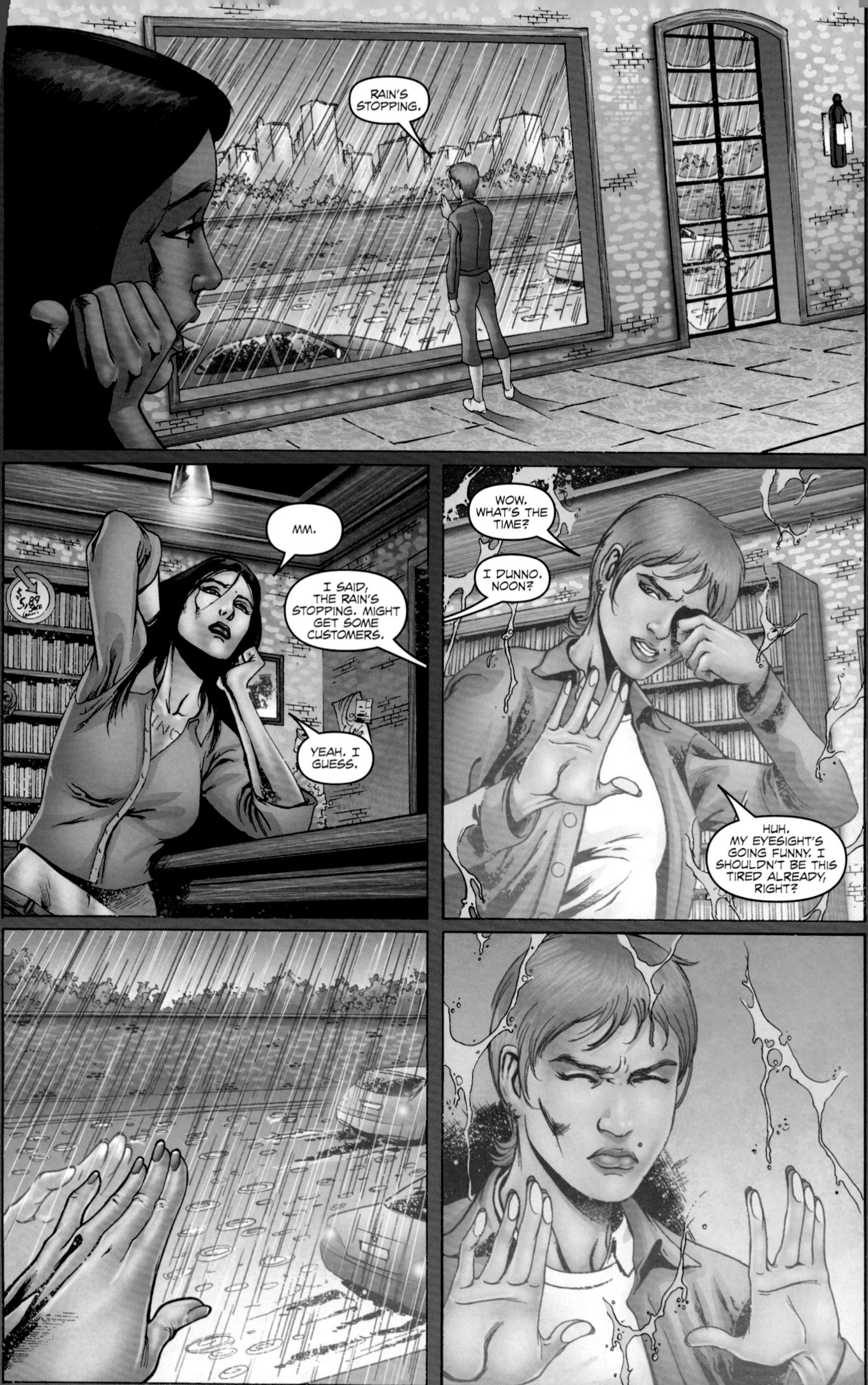
RAIN'S STOPPING.
MM.
I SAID, THE RAIN'S STOPPING. MIGHT GET SOME CUSTOMERS.
YEAH. I GUESS.
WOW. WHAT'S THE TIME?
I DUNNO. NOON?
HUH. MY EYESIGHT'S GOING FUNNY. I SHOULDN'T BE THIS TIRED ALREADY, RIGHT?

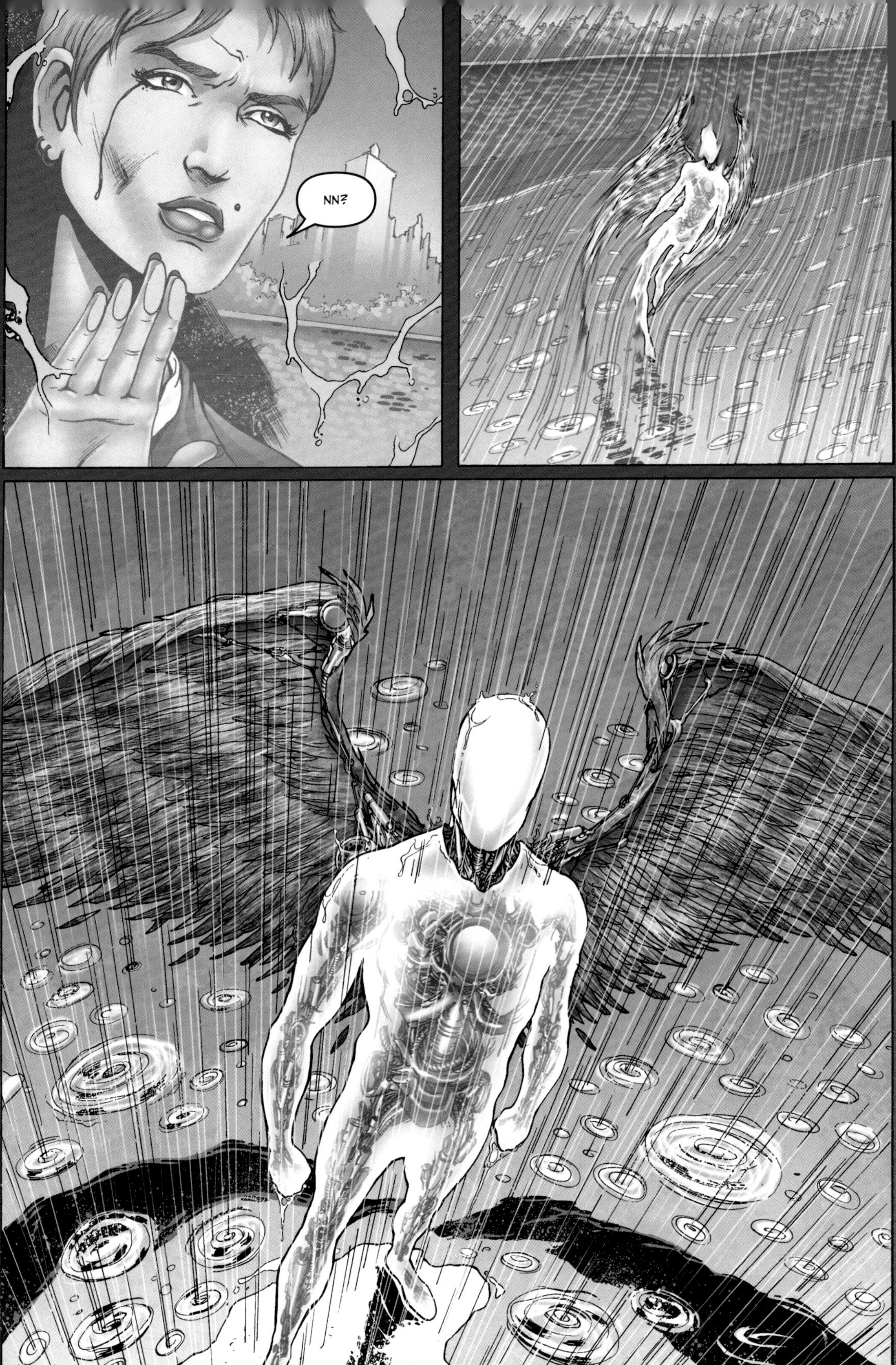
NN?

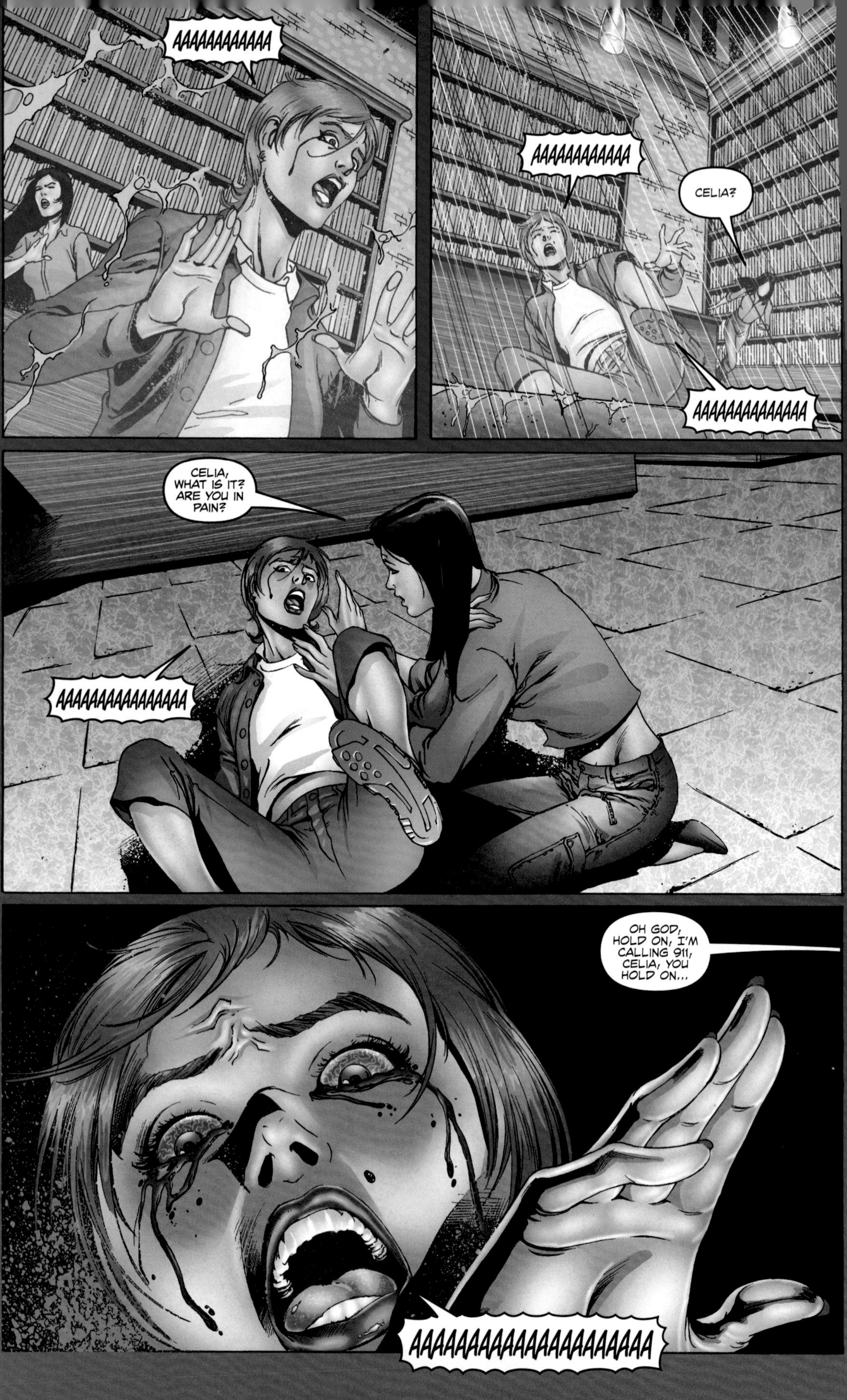

AAAAAAAAAAAA
AAAAAAAAAAAA
CELIA?
AAAAAAAAAAAAAA
CELIA, WHAT IS IT? ARE YOU IN PAIN?
AAAAAAAAAAAAAAAA
OH GOD, HOLD ON, I'M CALLING 911, CELIA, YOU HOLD ON...
AAAAAAAAAAAAAAAAAAAAAA

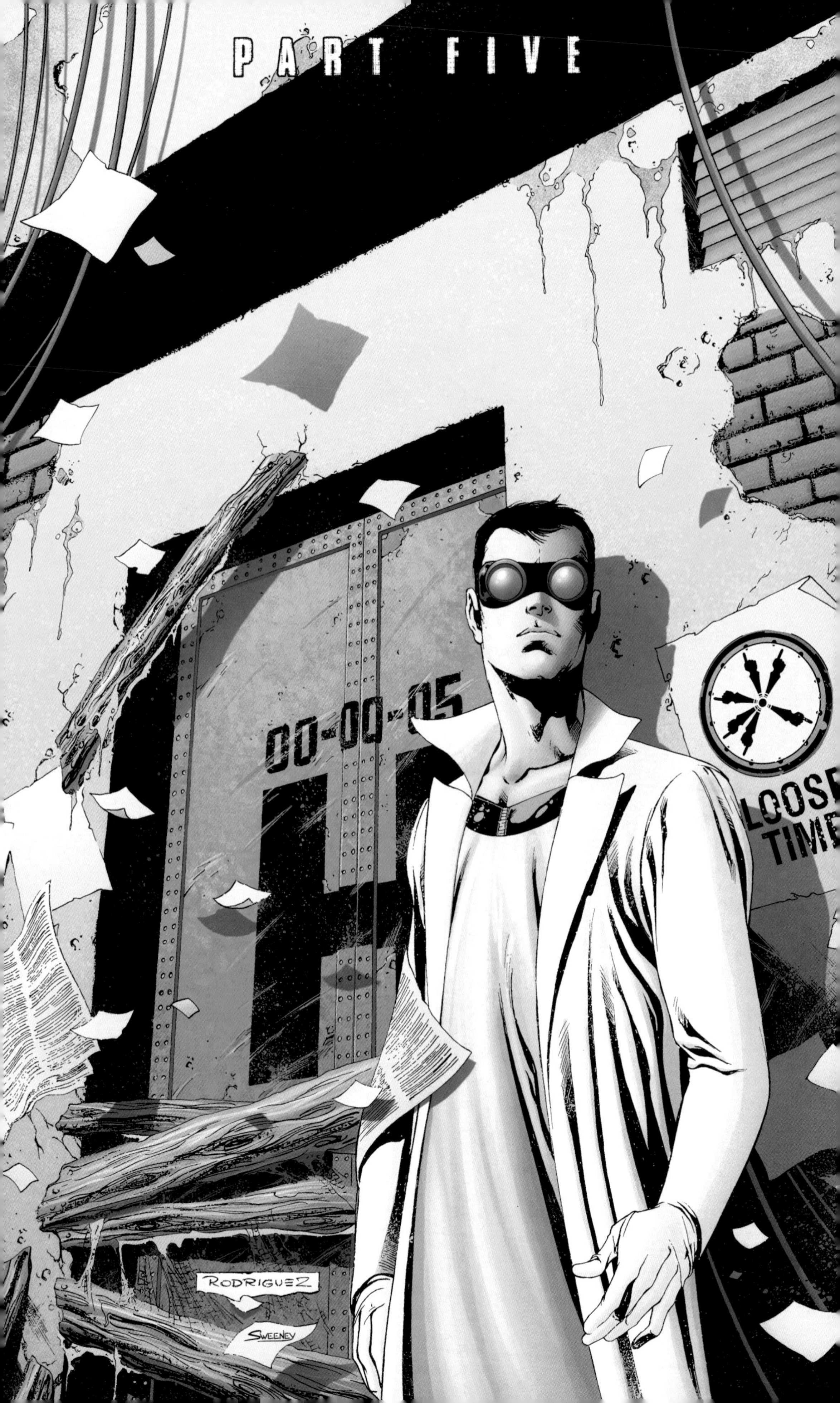
PART FIVE
00-00-05
LOOSE
TIME
RODRIGUEZ
SWEENEY

LOOSE
TIME

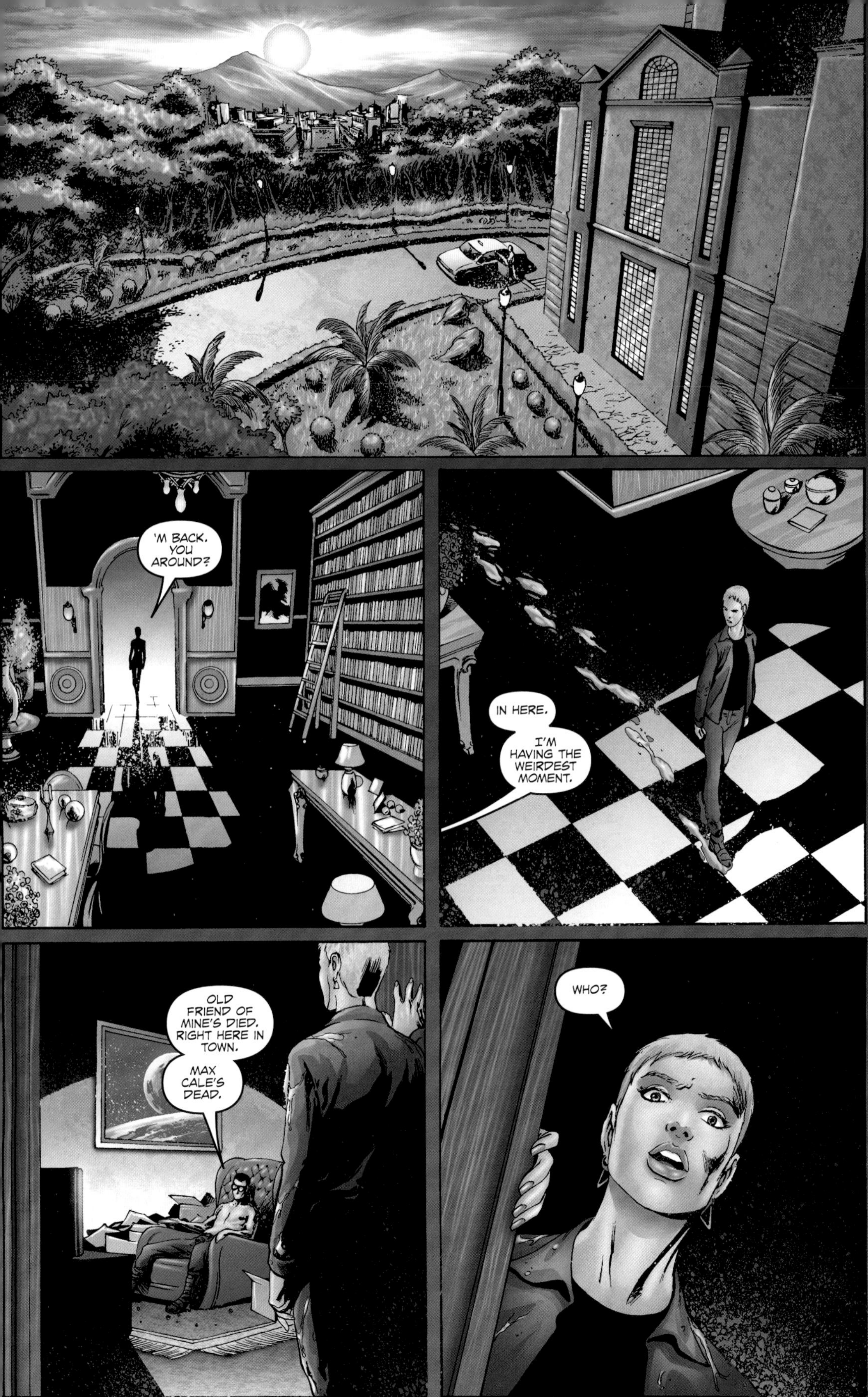
'M BACK. YOU AROUND?
IN HERE.
I'M HAVING THE WEIRDEST MOMENT.
OLD FRIEND OF MINE'S DIED. RIGHT HERE IN TOWN.
MAX CALE'S DEAD.
WHO?

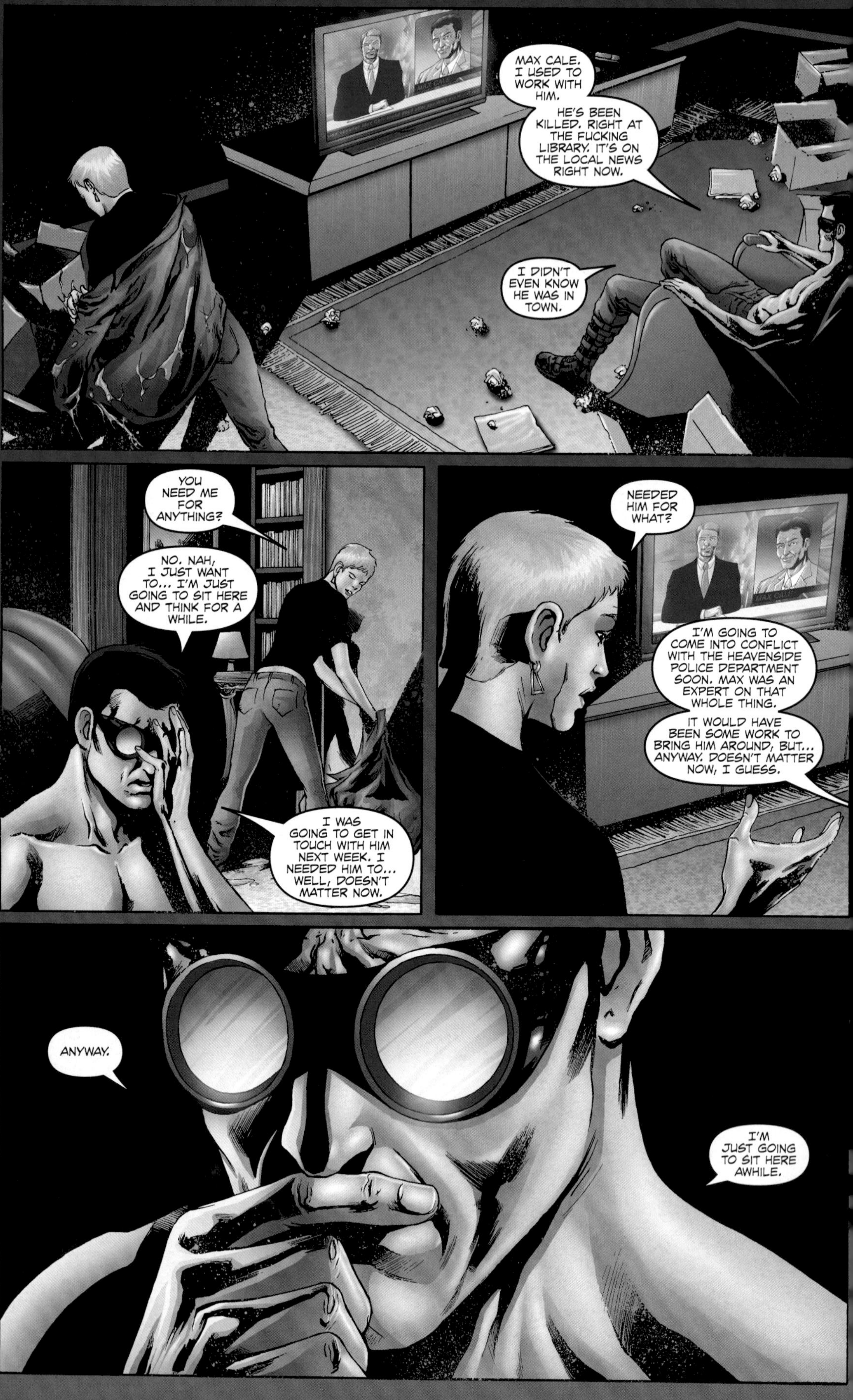
MAX CALE. I USED TO WORK WITH HIM.
HE'S BEEN KILLED. RIGHT AT THE FUCKING LIBRARY. IT'S ON THE LOCAL NEWS RIGHT NOW.
I DIDN'T EVEN KNOW HE WAS IN TOWN.
YOU NEED ME FOR ANYTHING?
NO. NAH, I JUST WANT TO... I'M JUST GOING TO SIT HERE AND THINK FOR A WHILE.
I WAS GOING TO GET IN TOUCH WITH HIM NEXT WEEK. I NEEDED HIM TO... WELL, DOESN'T MATTER NOW.
NEEDED HIM FOR WHAT?
I'M GOING TO COME INTO CONFLICT WITH THE HEAVENSIDE POLICE DEPARTMENT SOON. MAX WAS AN EXPERT ON THAT WHOLE THING.
IT WOULD HAVE BEEN SOME WORK TO BRING HIM AROUND, BUT... ANYWAY. DOESN'T MATTER NOW, I GUESS.
ANYWAY.
I'M JUST GOING TO SIT HERE AWHILE.

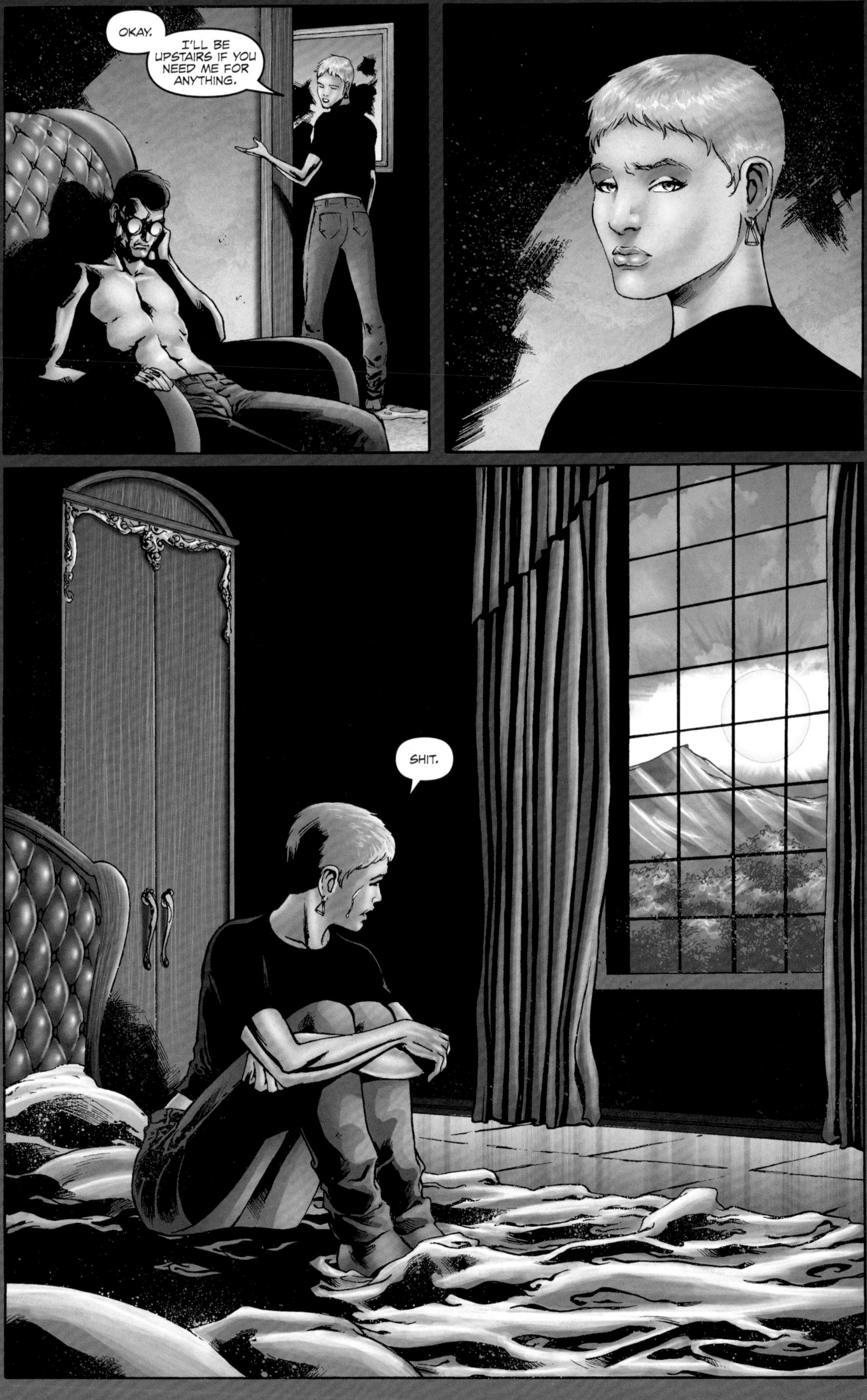
OKAY.
I'LL BE UPSTAIRS IF YOU NEED ME FOR ANYTHING.
SHIT.

HEAVENSIDE GENERAL HOSPITAL

DOCTOR?

HM?

I BROUGHT CELIA IN, CELIA RUSH, SHE'S IN THERE...

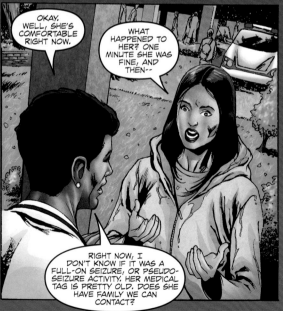

OKAY. WELL, SHE'S COMFORTABLE RIGHT NOW.

WHAT HAPPENED TO HER? ONE MINUTE SHE WAS FINE, AND THEN--

RIGHT NOW, I DON'T KNOW IF IT WAS A FULL-ON SEIZURE, OR PSEUDO-SEIZURE ACTIVITY. HER MEDICAL TAG IS PRETTY OLD. DOES SHE HAVE FAMILY WE CAN CONTACT?

OH, GOD. IS IT THAT BAD?

THE INSURANCE ON HER TAG IS CAPPED. I WANT TO GET HER INTO AN MRI, BUT THAT COST WILL LIMIT THE MEDS I CAN GIVE HER.

WHAT'S WRONG WITH HER?

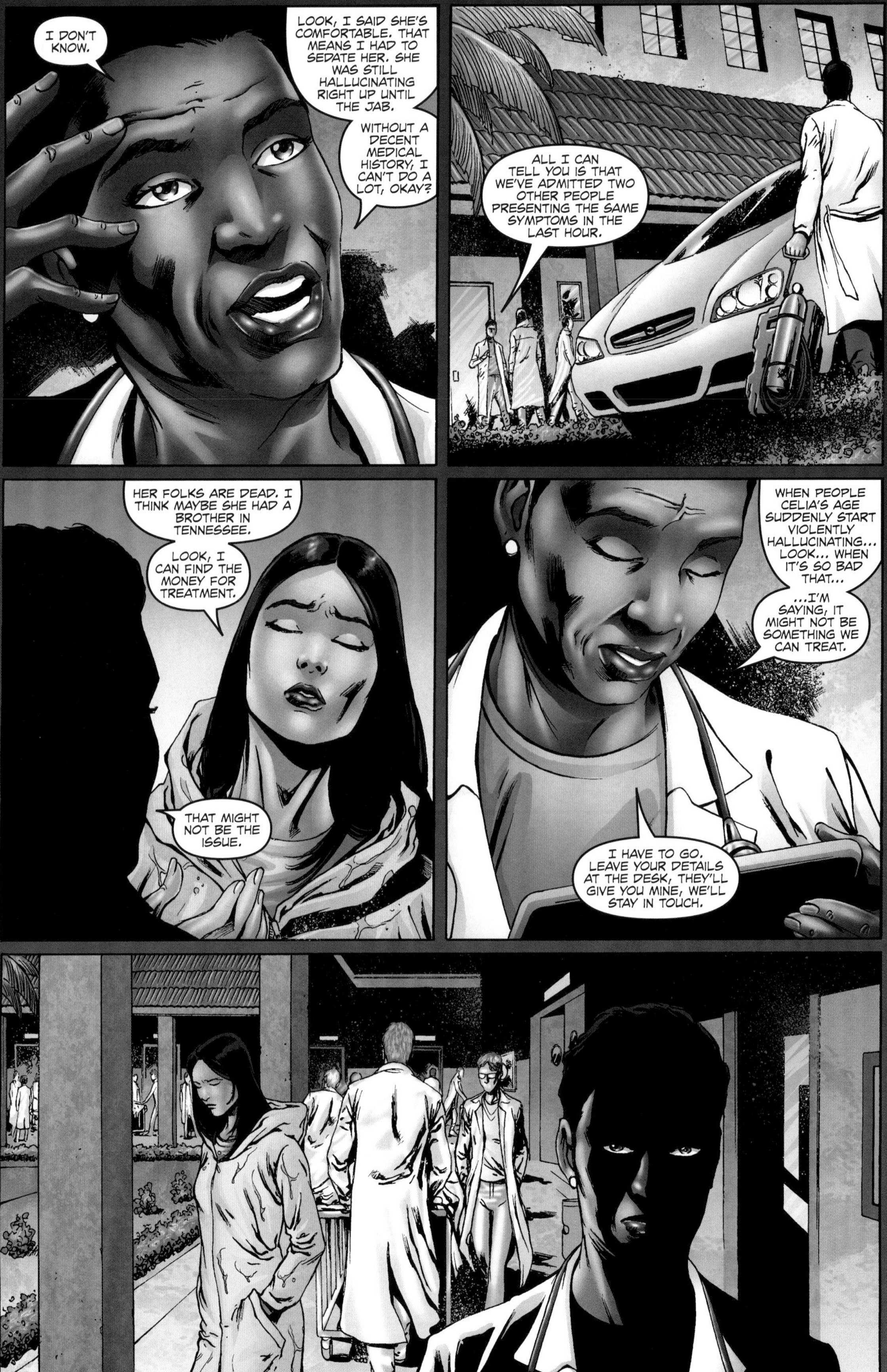
I DON'T KNOW.
LOOK, I SAID SHE'S COMFORTABLE. THAT MEANS I HAD TO SEDATE HER. SHE WAS STILL HALLUCINATING RIGHT UP UNTIL THE JAB.
WITHOUT A DECENT MEDICAL HISTORY, I CAN'T DO A LOT, OKAY?
ALL I CAN TELL YOU IS THAT WE'VE ADMITTED TWO OTHER PEOPLE PRESENTING THE SAME SYMPTOMS IN THE LAST HOUR.
HER FOLKS ARE DEAD. I THINK MAYBE SHE HAD A BROTHER IN TENNESSEE.
LOOK, I CAN FIND THE MONEY FOR TREATMENT.
THAT MIGHT NOT BE THE ISSUE.
WHEN PEOPLE CELIA'S AGE SUDDENLY START VIOLENTLY HALLUCINATING... LOOK... WHEN IT'S SO BAD THAT...
...I'M SAYING, IT MIGHT NOT BE SOMETHING WE CAN TREAT.
I HAVE TO GO. LEAVE YOUR DETAILS AT THE DESK, THEY'LL GIVE YOU MINE, WE'LL STAY IN TOUCH.

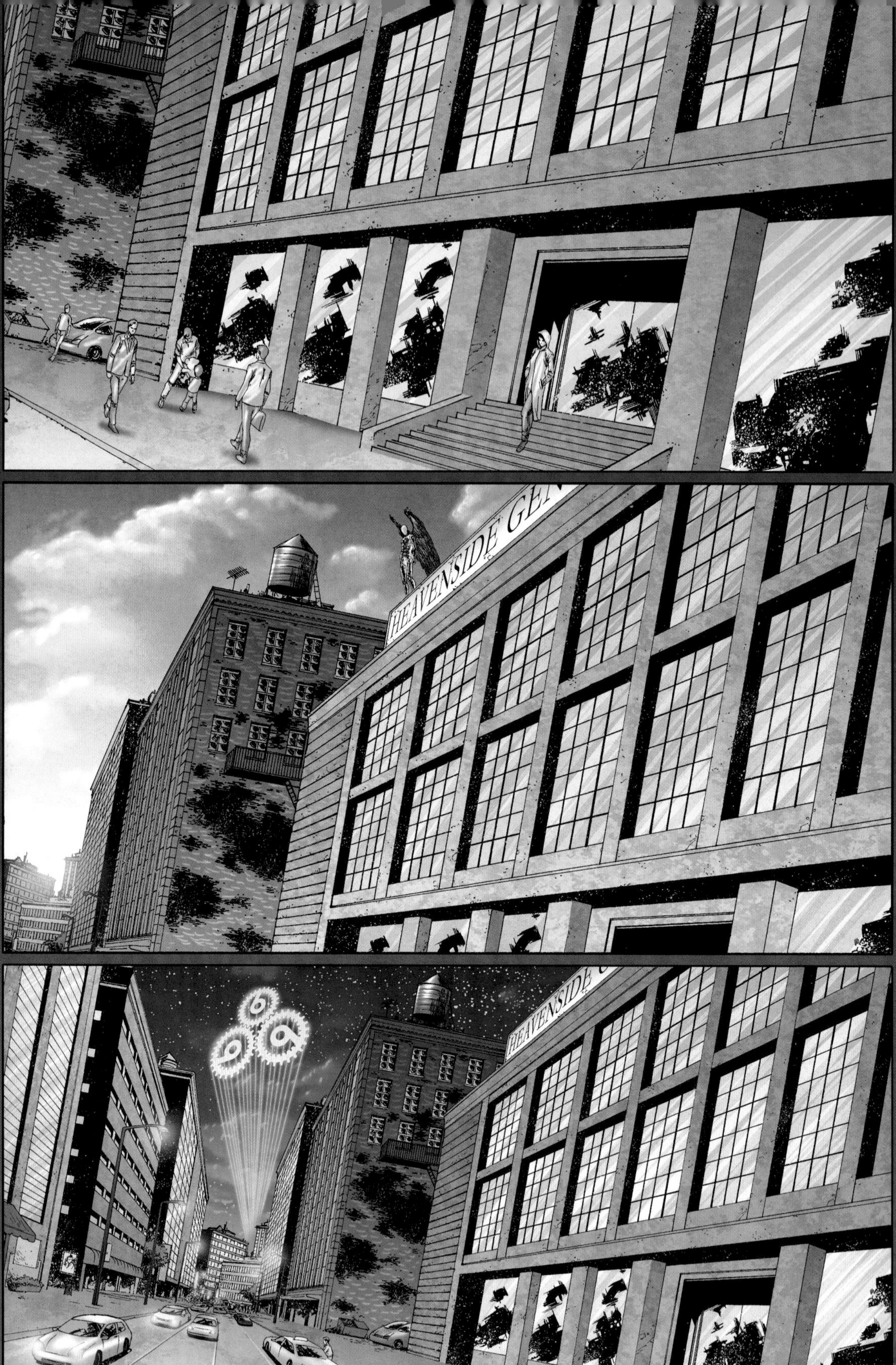
HEAVENSIDE GEN
HEAVENSIDE

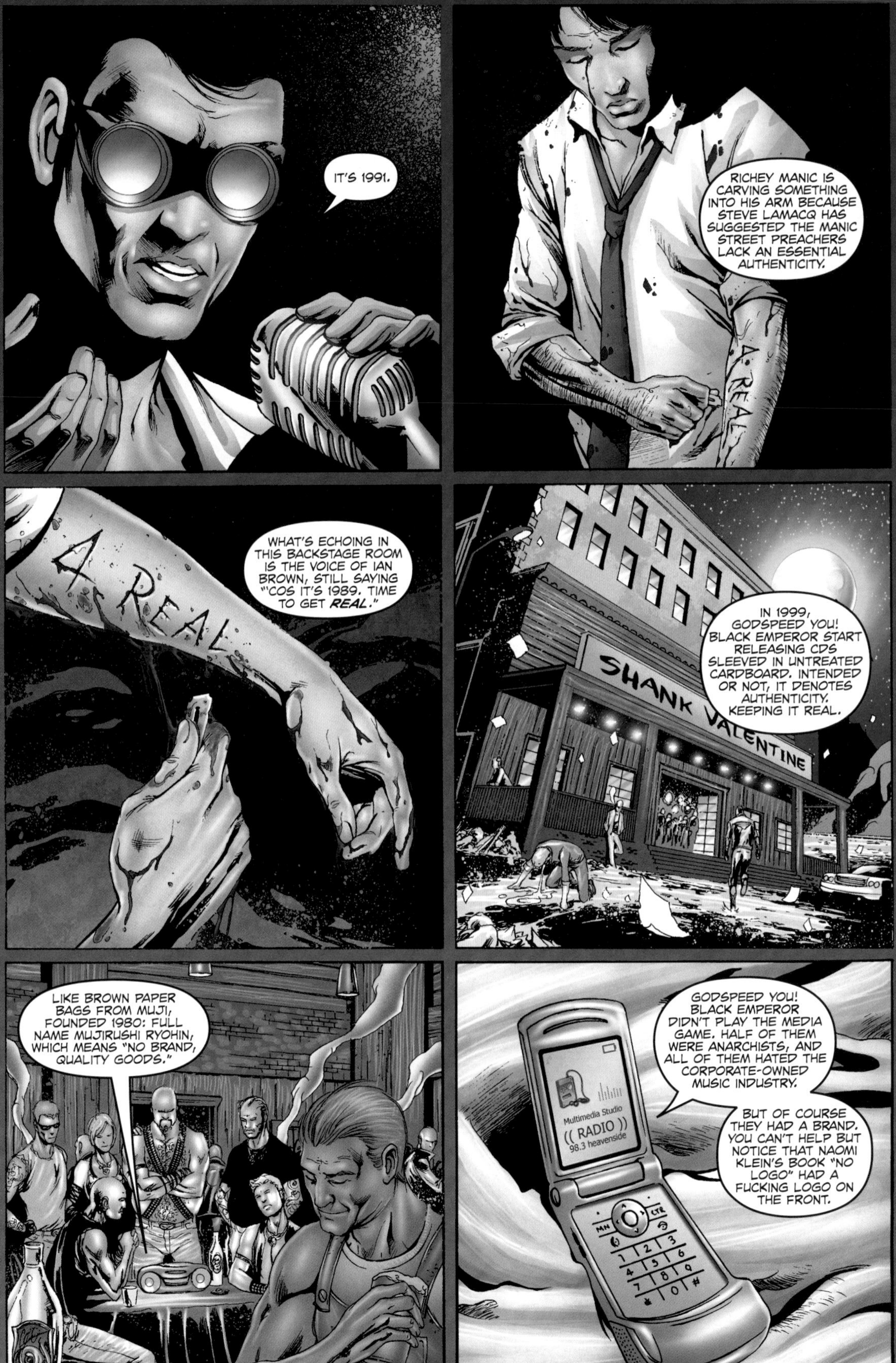
IT'S 1991.
RICHEY MANIC IS CARVING SOMETHING INTO HIS ARM BECAUSE STEVE LAMACQ HAS SUGGESTED THE MANIC STREET PREACHERS LACK AN ESSENTIAL AUTHENTICITY.
4 REAL
WHAT'S ECHOING IN THIS BACKSTAGE ROOM IS THE VOICE OF IAN BROWN, STILL SAYING "COS IT'S 1989. TIME TO GET ***REAL***."
4 REAL
SHANK VALENTINE
IN 1999, GODSPEED YOU! BLACK EMPEROR START RELEASING CDS SLEEVED IN UNTREATED CARDBOARD. INTENDED OR NOT, IT DENOTES AUTHENTICITY. KEEPING IT REAL.
LIKE BROWN PAPER BAGS FROM MUJI, FOUNDED 1980: FULL NAME MUJIRUSHI RYOHIN, WHICH MEANS "NO BRAND, QUALITY GOODS."
GODSPEED YOU! BLACK EMPEROR DIDN'T PLAY THE MEDIA GAME. HALF OF THEM WERE ANARCHISTS, AND ALL OF THEM HATED THE CORPORATE-OWNED MUSIC INDUSTRY.
BUT OF COURSE THEY HAD A BRAND. YOU CAN'T HELP BUT NOTICE THAT NAOMI KLEIN'S BOOK "NO LOGO" HAD A FUCKING LOGO ON THE FRONT.
Multimedia Studio
((RADIO))
98.3 heavenside

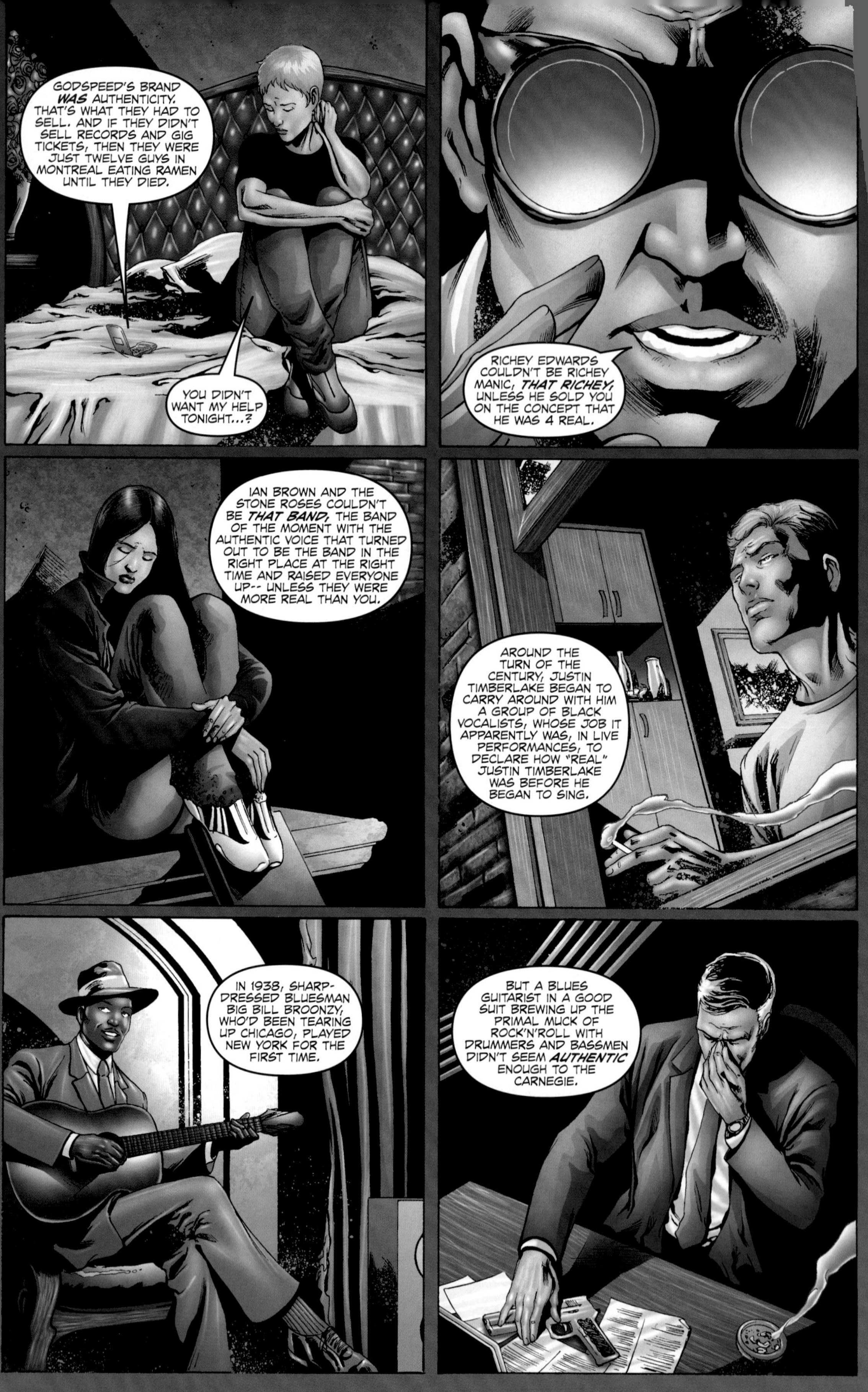
GODSPEED'S BRAND *WAS* AUTHENTICITY. THAT'S WHAT THEY HAD TO SELL. AND IF THEY DIDN'T SELL RECORDS AND GIG TICKETS, THEN THEY WERE JUST TWELVE GUYS IN MONTREAL EATING RAMEN UNTIL THEY DIED.
YOU DIDN'T WANT MY HELP TONIGHT...?
RICHEY EDWARDS COULDN'T BE RICHEY MANIC, *THAT RICHEY,* UNLESS HE SOLD YOU ON THE CONCEPT THAT HE WAS 4 REAL.
IAN BROWN AND THE STONE ROSES COULDN'T BE *THAT BAND,* THE BAND OF THE MOMENT WITH THE AUTHENTIC VOICE THAT TURNED OUT TO BE THE BAND IN THE RIGHT PLACE AT THE RIGHT TIME AND RAISED EVERYONE UP-- UNLESS THEY WERE MORE REAL THAN YOU.
AROUND THE TURN OF THE CENTURY, JUSTIN TIMBERLAKE BEGAN TO CARRY AROUND WITH HIM A GROUP OF BLACK VOCALISTS, WHOSE JOB IT APPARENTLY WAS, IN LIVE PERFORMANCES, TO DECLARE HOW "REAL" JUSTIN TIMBERLAKE WAS BEFORE HE BEGAN TO SING.
IN 1938, SHARP-DRESSED BLUESMAN BIG BILL BROONZY, WHO'D BEEN TEARING UP CHICAGO, PLAYED NEW YORK FOR THE FIRST TIME.
BUT A BLUES GUITARIST IN A GOOD SUIT BREWING UP THE PRIMAL MUCK OF ROCK'N'ROLL WITH DRUMMERS AND BASSMEN DIDN'T SEEM *AUTHENTIC* ENOUGH TO THE CARNEGIE.

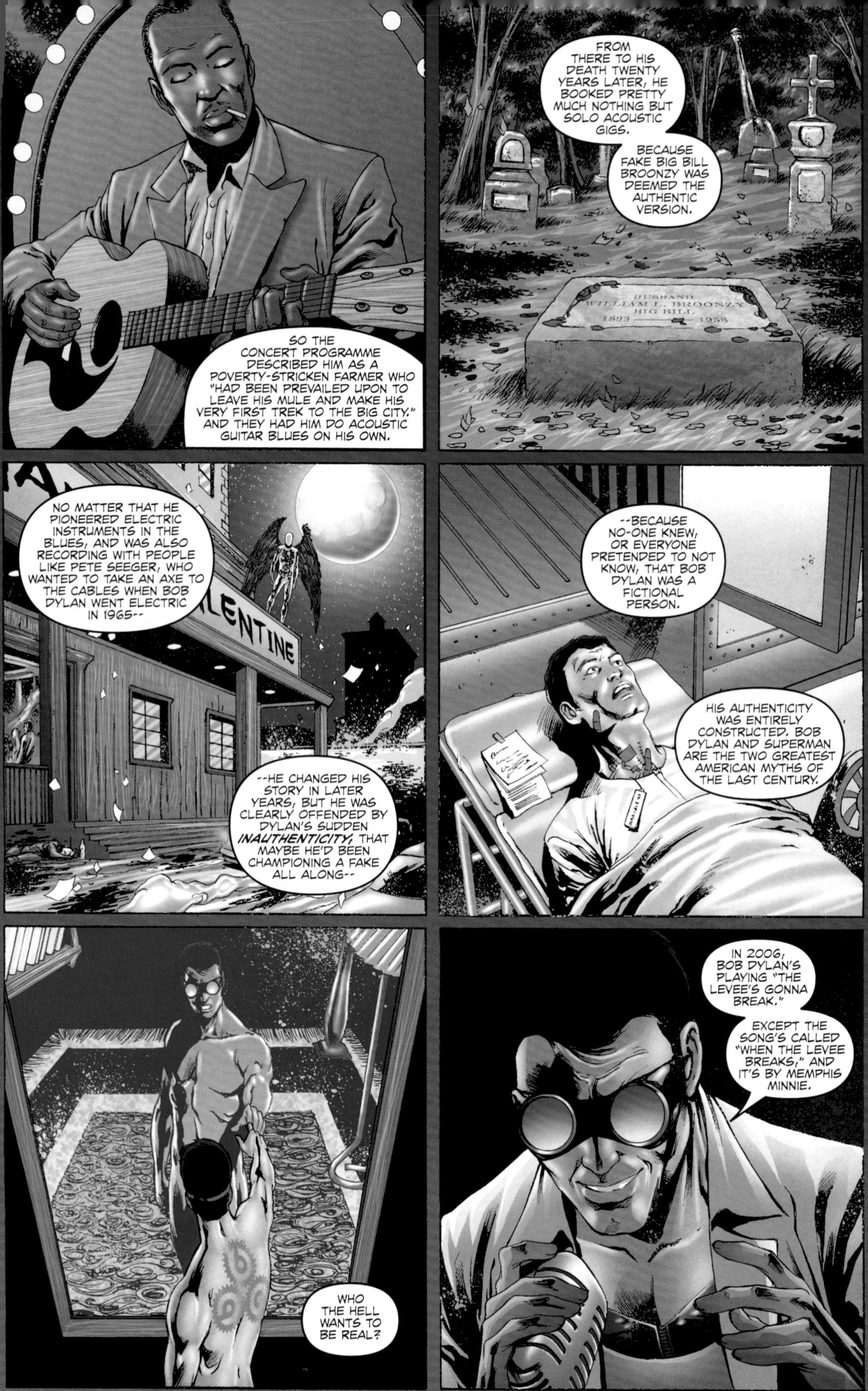

SO THE CONCERT PROGRAMME DESCRIBED HIM AS A POVERTY-STRICKEN FARMER WHO "HAD BEEN PREVAILED UPON TO LEAVE HIS MULE AND MAKE HIS VERY FIRST TREK TO THE BIG CITY." AND THEY HAD HIM DO ACOUSTIC GUITAR BLUES ON HIS OWN.
FROM THERE TO HIS DEATH TWENTY YEARS LATER, HE BOOKED PRETTY MUCH NOTHING BUT SOLO ACOUSTIC GIGS.
BECAUSE FAKE BIG BILL BROONZY WAS DEEMED THE AUTHENTIC VERSION.
HUSBAND
WILLIAM L. BROONZY
BIG BILL
1893 — 1958
NO MATTER THAT HE PIONEERED ELECTRIC INSTRUMENTS IN THE BLUES, AND WAS ALSO RECORDING WITH PEOPLE LIKE PETE SEEGER, WHO WANTED TO TAKE AN AXE TO THE CABLES WHEN BOB DYLAN WENT ELECTRIC IN 1965--
LENTINE
--HE CHANGED HIS STORY IN LATER YEARS, BUT HE WAS CLEARLY OFFENDED BY DYLAN'S SUDDEN *INAUTHENTICITY,* THAT MAYBE HE'D BEEN CHAMPIONING A FAKE ALL ALONG--
--BECAUSE NO-ONE KNEW, OR EVERYONE PRETENDED TO NOT KNOW, THAT BOB DYLAN WAS A FICTIONAL PERSON.
HIS AUTHENTICITY WAS ENTIRELY CONSTRUCTED. BOB DYLAN AND SUPERMAN ARE THE TWO GREATEST AMERICAN MYTHS OF THE LAST CENTURY.
WHO THE HELL WANTS TO BE REAL?
IN 2006, BOB DYLAN'S PLAYING "THE LEVEE'S GONNA BREAK."
EXCEPT THE SONG'S CALLED "WHEN THE LEVEE BREAKS," AND IT'S BY MEMPHIS MINNIE.

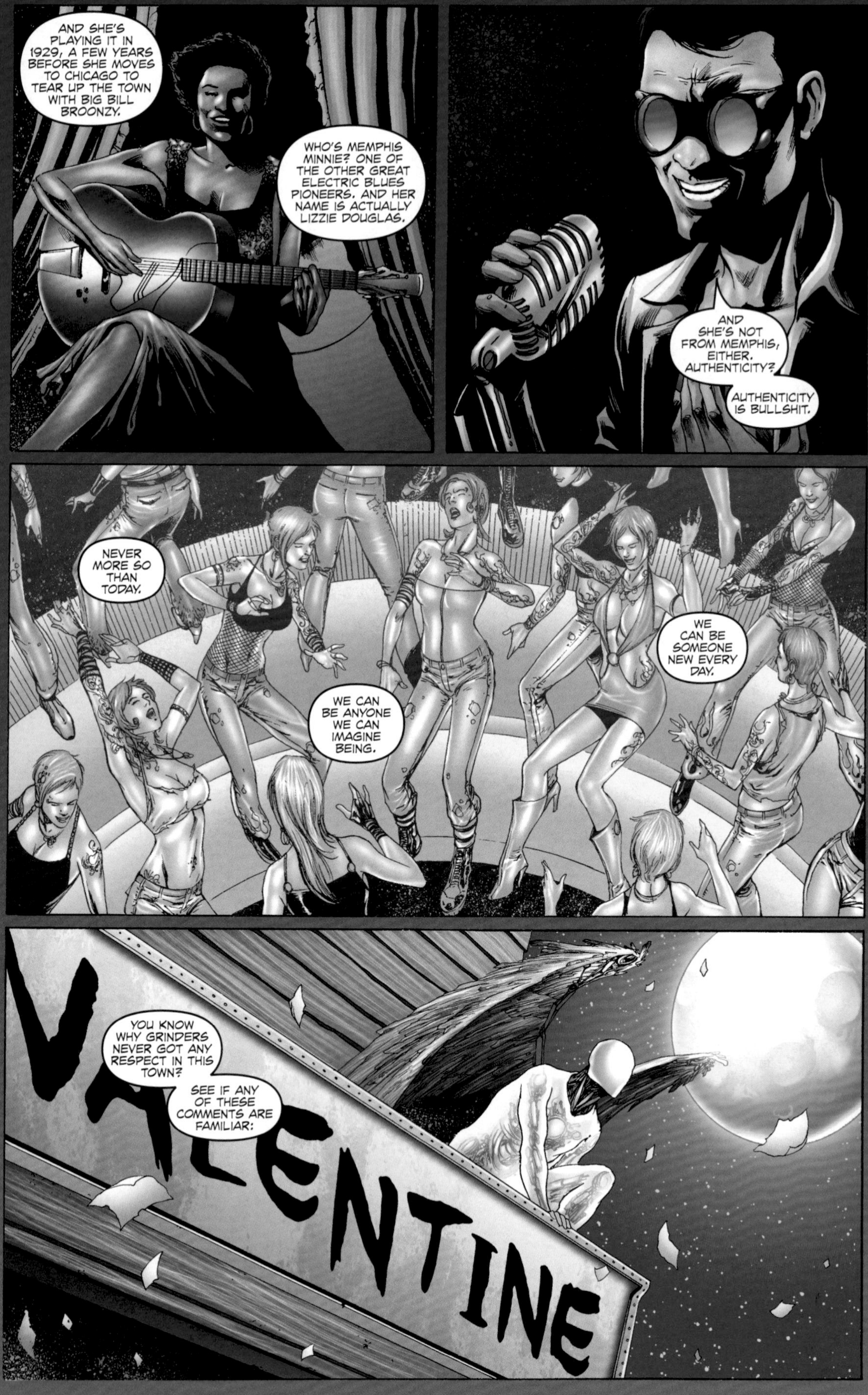
AND SHE'S PLAYING IT IN 1929, A FEW YEARS BEFORE SHE MOVES TO CHICAGO TO TEAR UP THE TOWN WITH BIG BILL BROONZY.
WHO'S MEMPHIS MINNIE? ONE OF THE OTHER GREAT ELECTRIC BLUES PIONEERS. AND HER NAME IS ACTUALLY LIZZIE DOUGLAS.
AND SHE'S NOT FROM MEMPHIS, EITHER. AUTHENTICITY?
AUTHENTICITY IS BULLSHIT.
NEVER MORE SO THAN TODAY.
WE CAN BE ANYONE WE CAN IMAGINE BEING.
WE CAN BE SOMEONE NEW EVERY DAY.
YOU KNOW WHY GRINDERS NEVER GOT ANY RESPECT IN THIS TOWN?
SEE IF ANY OF THESE COMMENTS ARE FAMILIAR:
VALENTINE

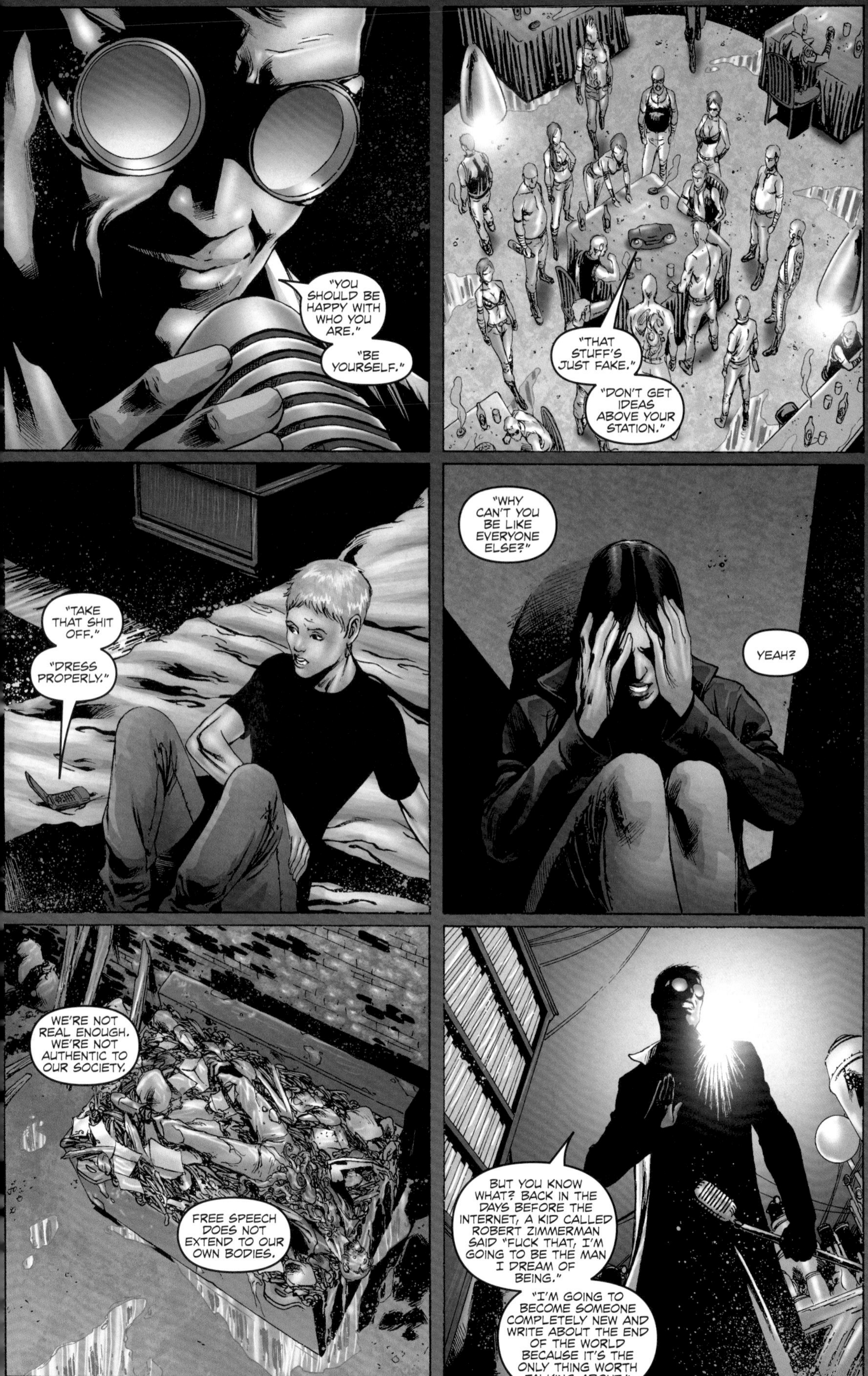
"YOU SHOULD BE HAPPY WITH WHO YOU ARE."
"BE YOURSELF."
"THAT STUFF'S JUST FAKE."
"DON'T GET IDEAS ABOVE YOUR STATION."
"TAKE THAT SHIT OFF."
"DRESS PROPERLY."
"WHY CAN'T YOU BE LIKE EVERYONE ELSE?"
YEAH?
WE'RE NOT REAL ENOUGH. WE'RE NOT AUTHENTIC TO OUR SOCIETY.
FREE SPEECH DOES NOT EXTEND TO OUR OWN BODIES.
BUT YOU KNOW WHAT? BACK IN THE DAYS BEFORE THE INTERNET, A KID CALLED ROBERT ZIMMERMAN SAID "FUCK THAT, I'M GOING TO BE THE MAN I DREAM OF BEING."
"I'M GOING TO BECOME SOMEONE COMPLETELY NEW AND WRITE ABOUT THE END OF THE WORLD BECAUSE IT'S THE ONLY THING WORTH TALKING ABOUT."

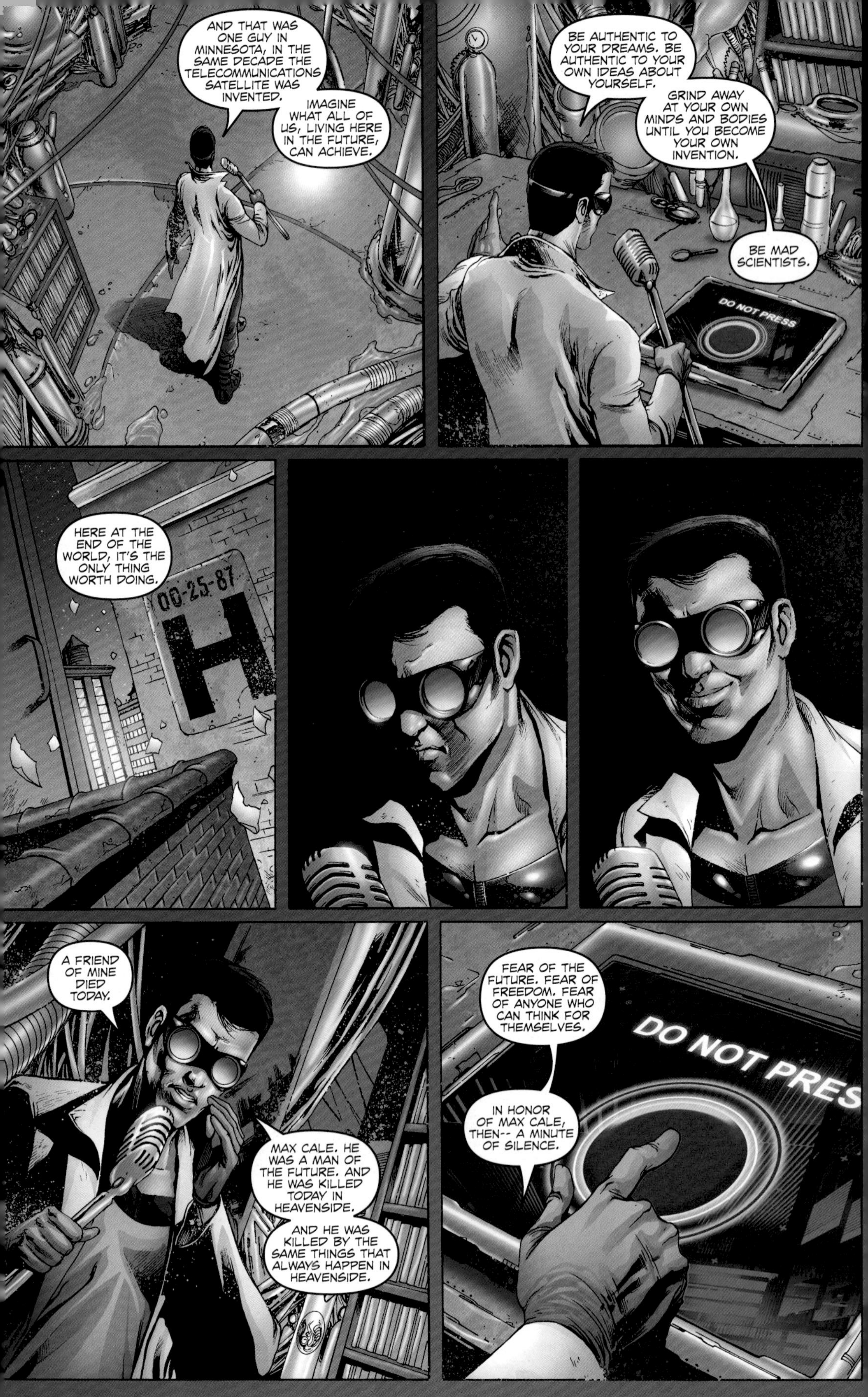
AND THAT WAS ONE GUY IN MINNESOTA, IN THE SAME DECADE THE TELECOMMUNICATIONS SATELLITE WAS INVENTED.
IMAGINE WHAT ALL OF US, LIVING HERE IN THE FUTURE, CAN ACHIEVE.
BE AUTHENTIC TO YOUR DREAMS. BE AUTHENTIC TO YOUR OWN IDEAS ABOUT YOURSELF.
GRIND AWAY AT YOUR OWN MINDS AND BODIES UNTIL YOU BECOME YOUR OWN INVENTION.
BE MAD SCIENTISTS.
DO NOT PRESS
HERE AT THE END OF THE WORLD, IT'S THE ONLY THING WORTH DOING.
00-25-87
H
A FRIEND OF MINE DIED TODAY.
MAX CALE. HE WAS A MAN OF THE FUTURE. AND HE WAS KILLED TODAY IN HEAVENSIDE.
AND HE WAS KILLED BY THE SAME THINGS THAT ALWAYS HAPPEN IN HEAVENSIDE.
FEAR OF THE FUTURE. FEAR OF FREEDOM. FEAR OF ANYONE WHO CAN THINK FOR THEMSELVES.
DO NOT PRES
IN HONOR OF MAX CALE, THEN-- A MINUTE OF SILENCE.

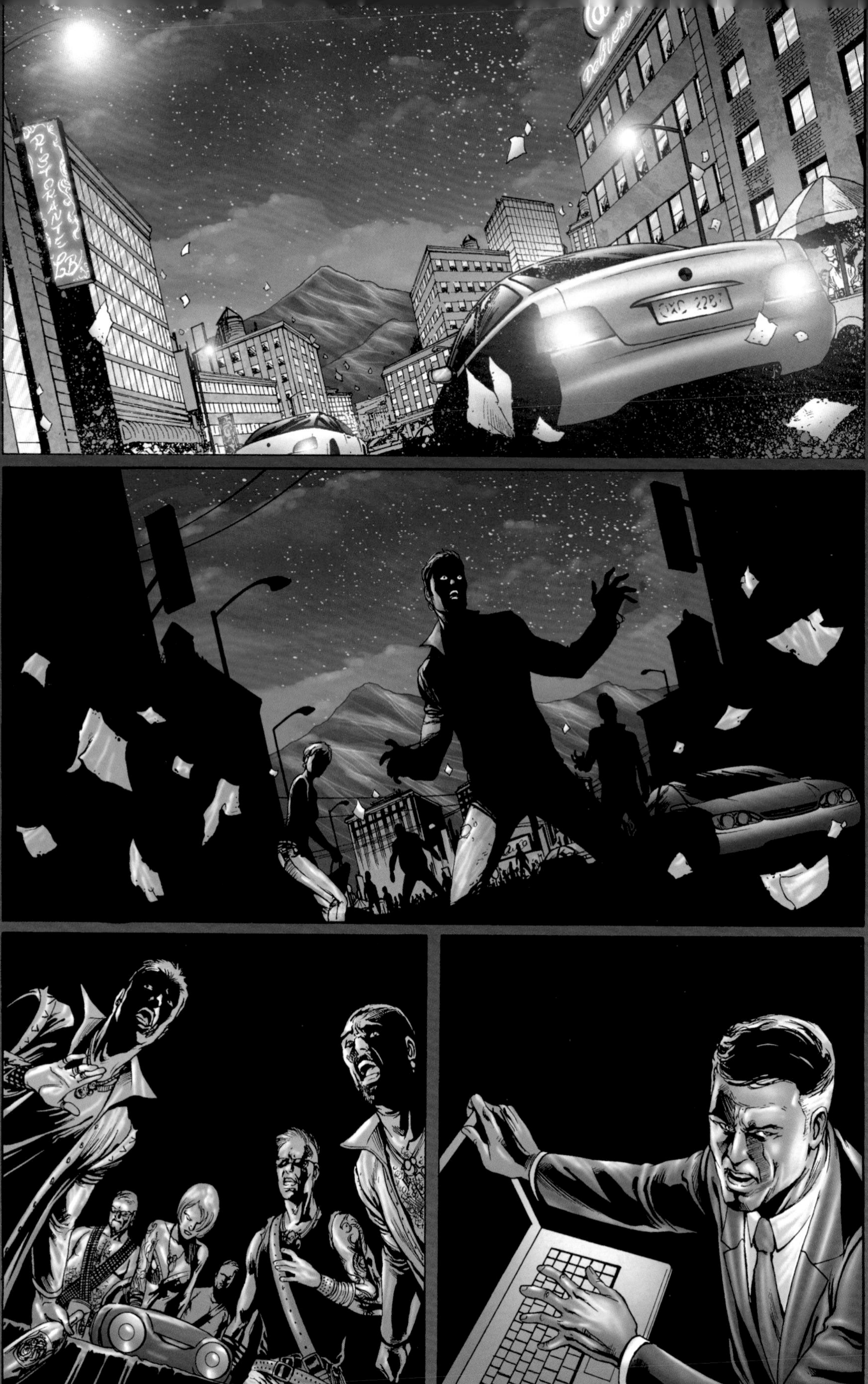
RISTORANTE
LB

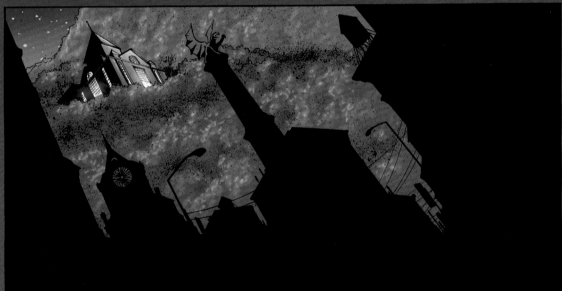

WHAT DID YOU DO?

ME? NOT A THING.

HEAVENSIDE'S GONE DARK, RIGHT ON FUCKING CUE, REINHARDT. WHAT DID YOU--

DOKTOR, PLEASE.

NOW, WE'RE GOING TO HAVE VISITORS SHORTLY, SO PLEASE GET CHANGED AND GET INTO CHARACTER.

OH, AND THROW THAT TABLET IN THE INCINERATOR ON YOUR WAY OUT, WOULD YOU?

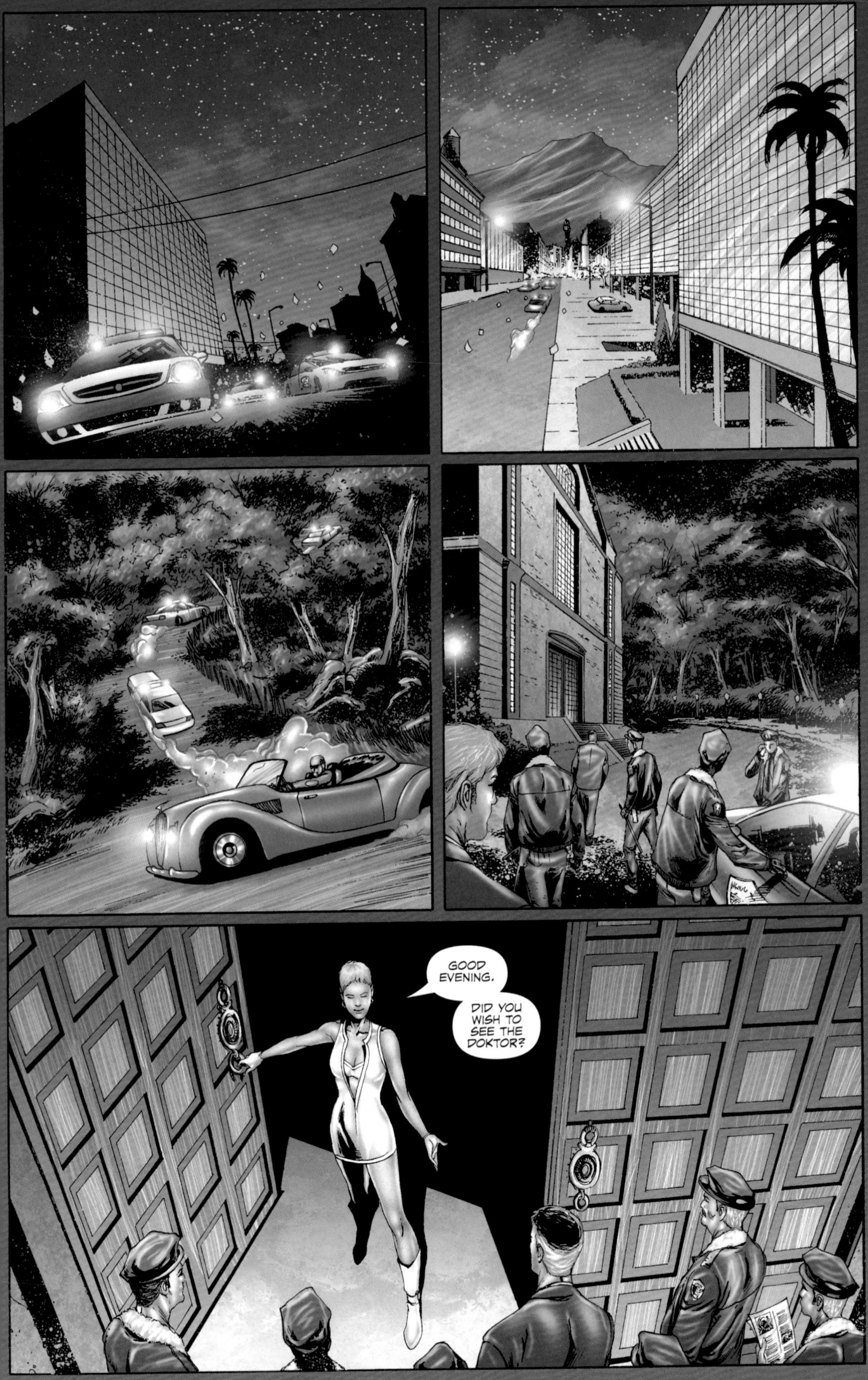
GOOD EVENING.
DID YOU WISH TO SEE THE DOKTOR?

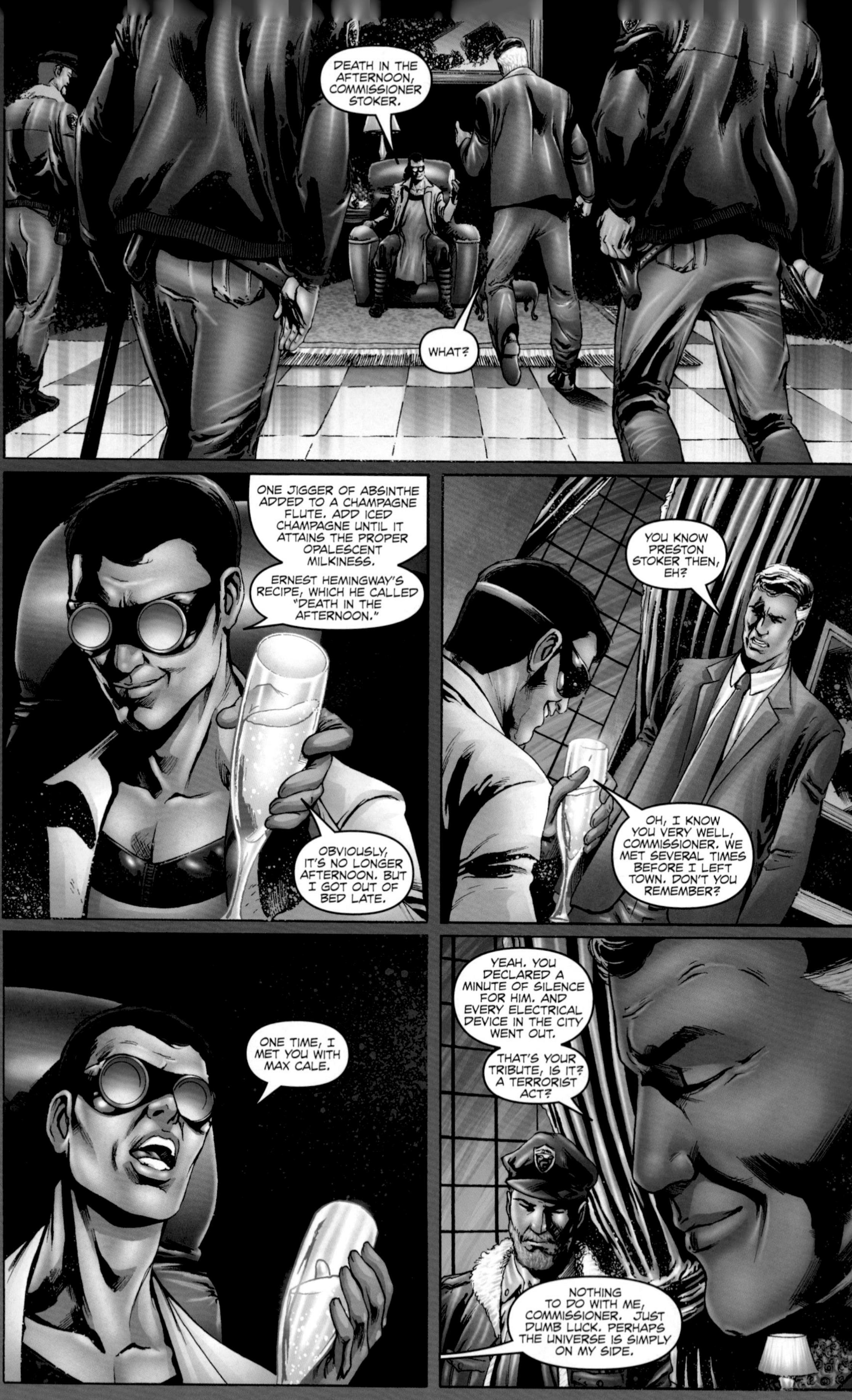
DEATH IN THE AFTERNOON, COMMISSIONER STOKER.
WHAT?
ONE JIGGER OF ABSINTHE ADDED TO A CHAMPAGNE FLUTE. ADD ICED CHAMPAGNE UNTIL IT ATTAINS THE PROPER OPALESCENT MILKINESS.
ERNEST HEMINGWAY'S RECIPE, WHICH HE CALLED "DEATH IN THE AFTERNOON."
OBVIOUSLY, IT'S NO LONGER AFTERNOON. BUT I GOT OUT OF BED LATE.
YOU KNOW PRESTON STOKER THEN, EH?
OH, I KNOW YOU VERY WELL, COMMISSIONER. WE MET SEVERAL TIMES BEFORE I LEFT TOWN. DON'T YOU REMEMBER?
ONE TIME, I MET YOU WITH MAX CALE.
YEAH. YOU DECLARED A MINUTE OF SILENCE FOR HIM. AND EVERY ELECTRICAL DEVICE IN THE CITY WENT OUT.
THAT'S YOUR TRIBUTE, IS IT? A TERRORIST ACT?
NOTHING TO DO WITH ME, COMMISSIONER. JUST DUMB LUCK. PERHAPS THE UNIVERSE IS SIMPLY ON MY SIDE.

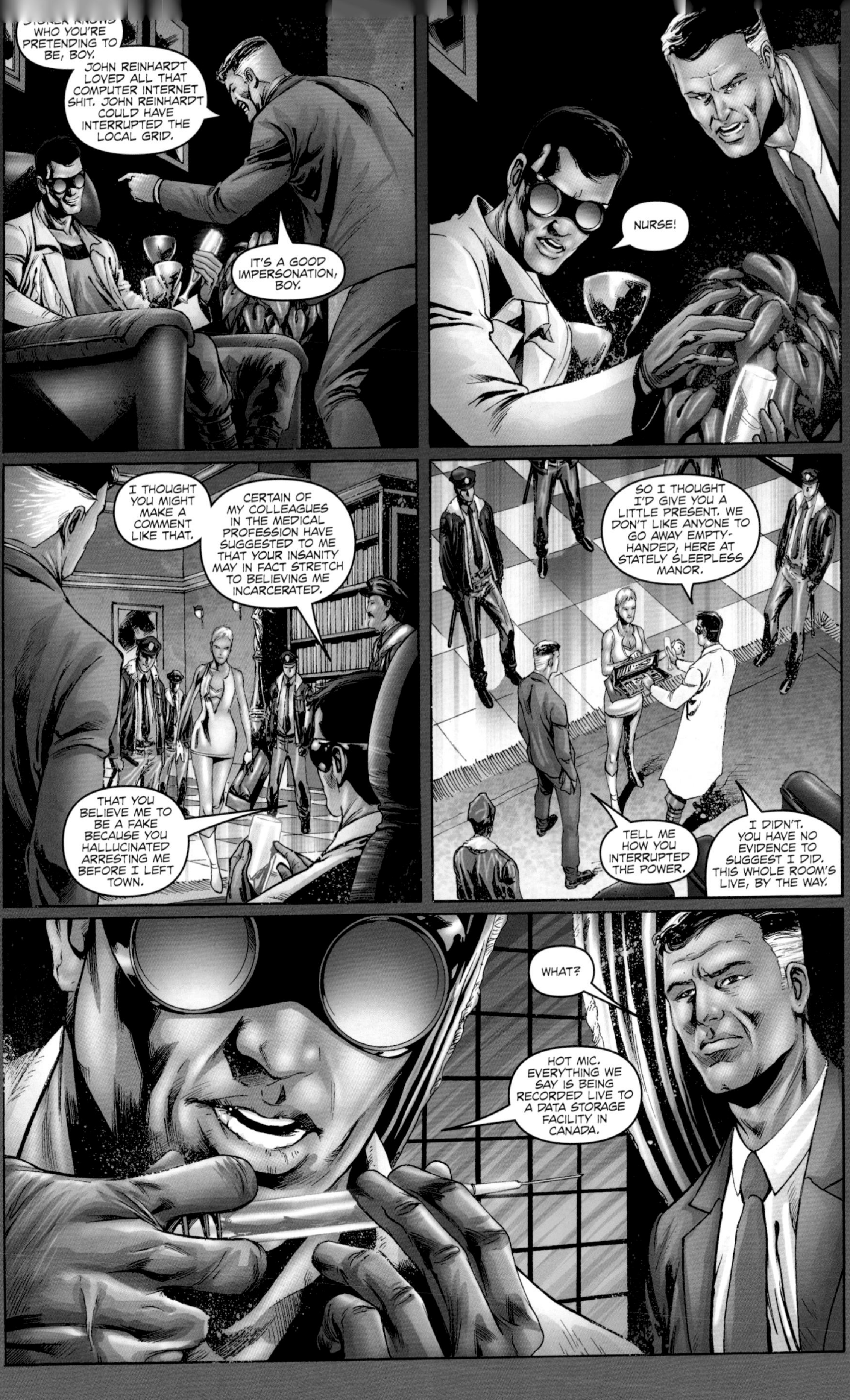

WHO YOU'RE PRETENDING TO BE, BOY.
JOHN REINHARDT LOVED ALL THAT COMPUTER INTERNET SHIT. JOHN REINHARDT COULD HAVE INTERRUPTED THE LOCAL GRID.
IT'S A GOOD IMPERSONATION, BOY.
NURSE!
I THOUGHT YOU MIGHT MAKE A COMMENT LIKE THAT.
CERTAIN OF MY COLLEAGUES IN THE MEDICAL PROFESSION HAVE SUGGESTED TO ME THAT YOUR INSANITY MAY IN FACT STRETCH TO BELIEVING ME INCARCERATED.
THAT YOU BELIEVE ME TO BE A FAKE BECAUSE YOU HALLUCINATED ARRESTING ME BEFORE I LEFT TOWN.
SO I THOUGHT I'D GIVE YOU A LITTLE PRESENT. WE DON'T LIKE ANYONE TO GO AWAY EMPTY-HANDED, HERE AT STATELY SLEEPLESS MANOR.
TELL ME HOW YOU INTERRUPTED THE POWER.
I DIDN'T. YOU HAVE NO EVIDENCE TO SUGGEST I DID. THIS WHOLE ROOM'S LIVE, BY THE WAY.
WHAT?
HOT MIC. EVERYTHING WE SAY IS BEING RECORDED LIVE TO A DATA STORAGE FACILITY IN CANADA.

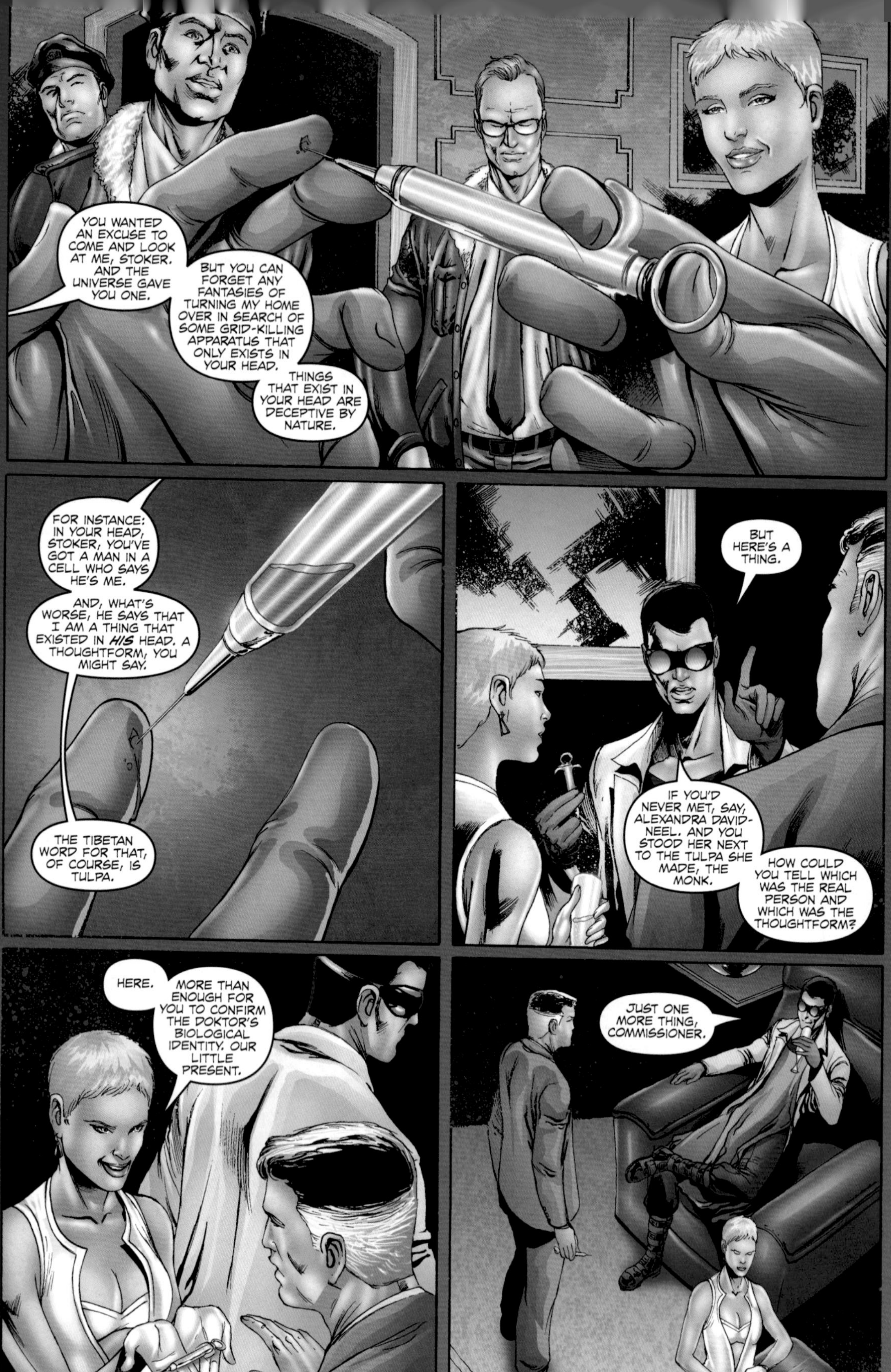
YOU WANTED AN EXCUSE TO COME AND LOOK AT ME, STOKER. AND THE UNIVERSE GAVE YOU ONE.
BUT YOU CAN FORGET ANY FANTASIES OF TURNING MY HOME OVER IN SEARCH OF SOME GRID-KILLING APPARATUS THAT ONLY EXISTS IN YOUR HEAD.
THINGS THAT EXIST IN YOUR HEAD ARE DECEPTIVE BY NATURE.
FOR INSTANCE: IN YOUR HEAD, STOKER, YOU'VE GOT A MAN IN A CELL WHO SAYS HE'S ME.
AND, WHAT'S WORSE, HE SAYS THAT I AM A THING THAT EXISTED IN *HIS* HEAD. A THOUGHTFORM, YOU MIGHT SAY.
THE TIBETAN WORD FOR THAT, OF COURSE, IS TULPA.
BUT HERE'S A THING.
IF YOU'D NEVER MET, SAY, ALEXANDRA DAVID-NEEL. AND YOU STOOD HER NEXT TO THE TULPA SHE MADE, THE MONK.
HOW COULD YOU TELL WHICH WAS THE REAL PERSON AND WHICH WAS THE THOUGHTFORM?
HERE.
MORE THAN ENOUGH FOR YOU TO CONFIRM THE DOKTOR'S BIOLOGICAL IDENTITY. OUR LITTLE PRESENT.
JUST ONE MORE THING, COMMISSIONER.

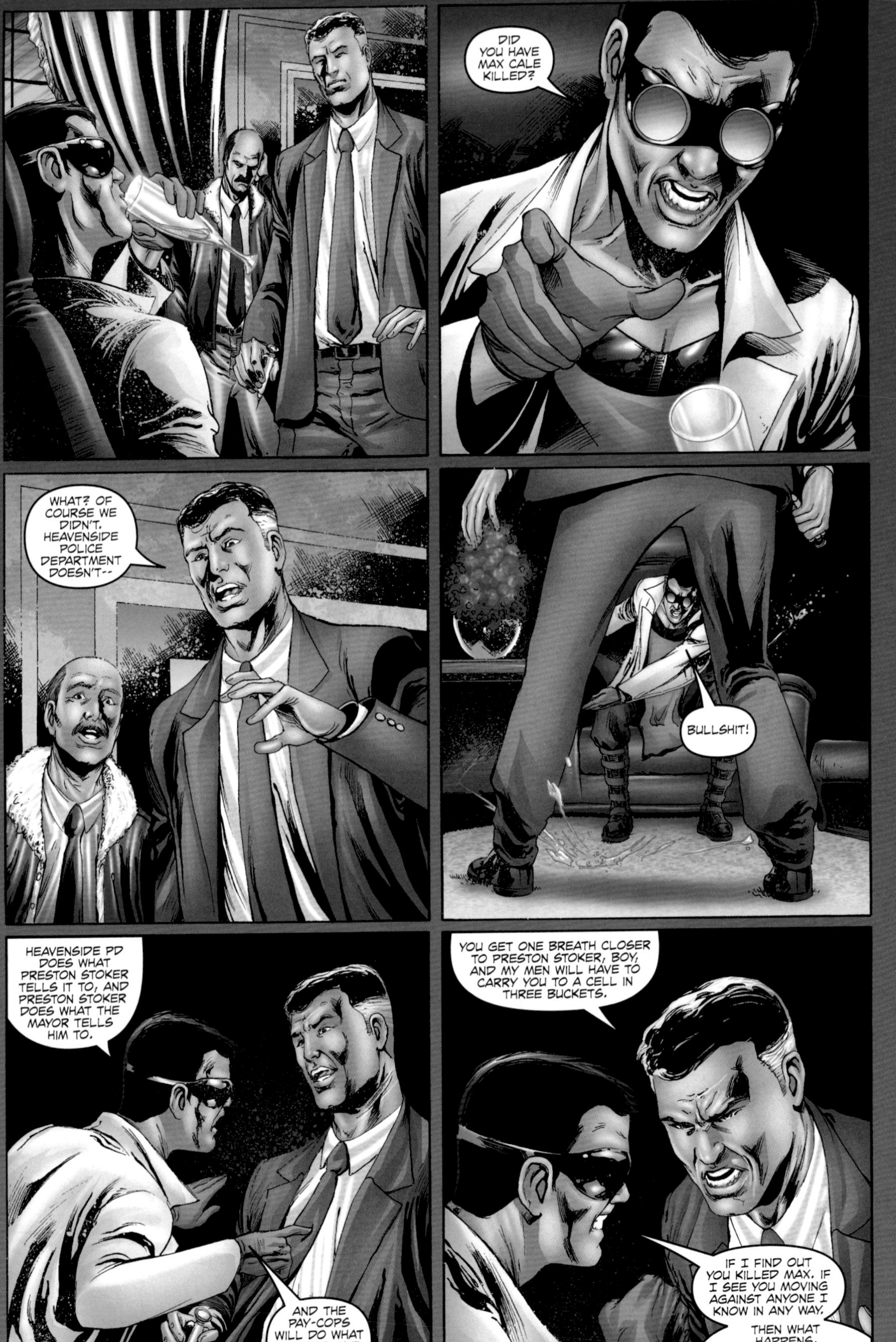
DID YOU HAVE MAX CALE KILLED?
WHAT? OF COURSE WE DIDN'T. HEAVENSIDE POLICE DEPARTMENT DOESN'T--
BULLSHIT!
HEAVENSIDE PD DOES WHAT PRESTON STOKER TELLS IT TO, AND PRESTON STOKER DOES WHAT THE MAYOR TELLS HIM TO.
AND THE PAY-COPS WILL DO WHAT THEY'RE PAID TO DO, WON'T THEY?
YOU GET ONE BREATH CLOSER TO PRESTON STOKER, BOY, AND MY MEN WILL HAVE TO CARRY YOU TO A CELL IN THREE BUCKETS.
IF I FIND OUT YOU KILLED MAX. IF I SEE YOU MOVING AGAINST ANYONE I KNOW IN ANY WAY.
THEN WHAT HAPPENS, COMMISSIONER, WILL NOT BE IN YOUR SLEEP. DO YOU UNDERSTAND ME?

YOU'RE THREATENING A POLICE OFFICER.

NO, I'M NOT, AND I KEEP MANY VERY EXPENSIVE LAWYERS WHO WILL PROVE IT.

I'M WARNING YOU.

THAT. IS A THREAT.

YOU MISUNDERSTAND ME CONSTANTLY, COMMISSIONER.

YOU SEE, MAX CALE WAS PART OF A GROUP OF ROGUE EXPERTS. THE IMMINENT.SEA TEAM. AND THOSE PEOPLE WERE INTO ALL KINDS OF NASTY THINGS.

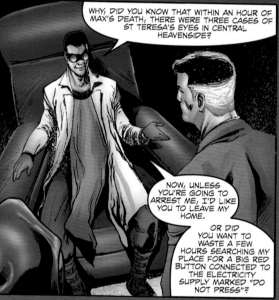

WHY, DID YOU KNOW THAT WITHIN AN HOUR OF MAX'S DEATH, THERE WERE THREE CASES OF ST TERESA'S EYES IN CENTRAL HEAVENSIDE?

NOW, UNLESS YOU'RE GOING TO ARREST ME, I'D LIKE YOU TO LEAVE MY HOME.

OR DID YOU WANT TO WASTE A FEW HOURS SEARCHING MY PLACE FOR A BIG RED BUTTON CONNECTED TO THE ELECTRICITY SUPPLY MARKED "DO NOT PRESS"?

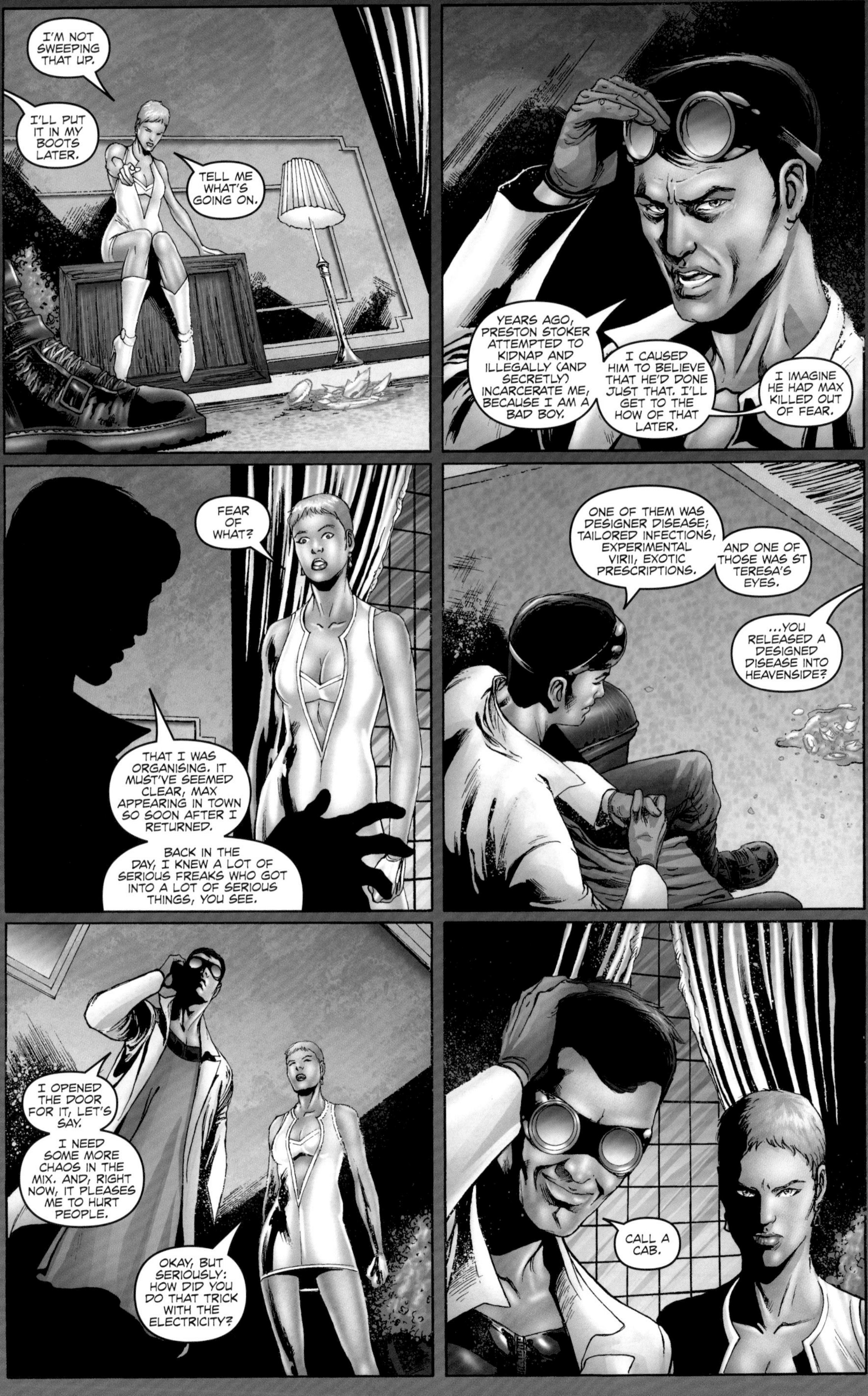
I'M NOT SWEEPING THAT UP.
I'LL PUT IT IN MY BOOTS LATER.
TELL ME WHAT'S GOING ON.
YEARS AGO, PRESTON STOKER ATTEMPTED TO KIDNAP AND ILLEGALLY (AND SECRETLY) INCARCERATE ME, BECAUSE I AM A BAD BOY.
I CAUSED HIM TO BELIEVE THAT HE'D DONE JUST THAT. I'LL GET TO THE HOW OF THAT LATER.
I IMAGINE HE HAD MAX KILLED OUT OF FEAR.
FEAR OF WHAT?
THAT I WAS ORGANISING. IT MUST'VE SEEMED CLEAR, MAX APPEARING IN TOWN SO SOON AFTER I RETURNED.
BACK IN THE DAY, I KNEW A LOT OF SERIOUS FREAKS WHO GOT INTO A LOT OF SERIOUS THINGS, YOU SEE.
ONE OF THEM WAS DESIGNER DISEASE; TAILORED INFECTIONS, EXPERIMENTAL VIRII, EXOTIC PRESCRIPTIONS.
AND ONE OF THOSE WAS ST TERESA'S EYES.
...YOU RELEASED A DESIGNED DISEASE INTO HEAVENSIDE?
I OPENED THE DOOR FOR IT, LET'S SAY.
I NEED SOME MORE CHAOS IN THE MIX. AND, RIGHT NOW, IT PLEASES ME TO HURT PEOPLE.
OKAY, BUT SERIOUSLY: HOW DID YOU DO THAT TRICK WITH THE ELECTRICITY?
CALL A CAB.

DOWN HERE.

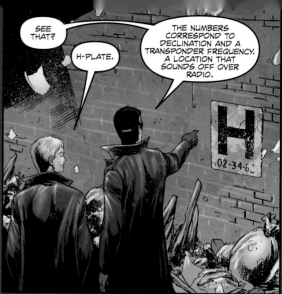

SEE THAT?

H-PLATE.

THE NUMBERS CORRESPOND TO DECLINATION AND A TRANSPONDER FREQUENCY. A LOCATION THAT SOUNDS OFF OVER RADIO.

H

02-34-6

EVERY H-PLATE HAS A DIFFERENT CODE. I HAVE IMPORTANT JUNK IN MY HEAD THAT LETS ME HEAR IT.

AND RIGHT NOW I'M THE ONLY PERSON IN HEAVENSIDE WHO CAN. STOKER'S NOT CLEARED FOR H-PLATES. NEITHER'S THE MAYOR.

THERE WE GO.

NOW, WHAT I DO IS SEND AN ACCESS CODE TO THE DOOR, ALSO EMPLOYING THE ESSENTIAL CRAP I'VE GROUND INTO MY BODY...

GO ON. TAKE A LOOK.

HOLY SHITBALLS.

PART SIX

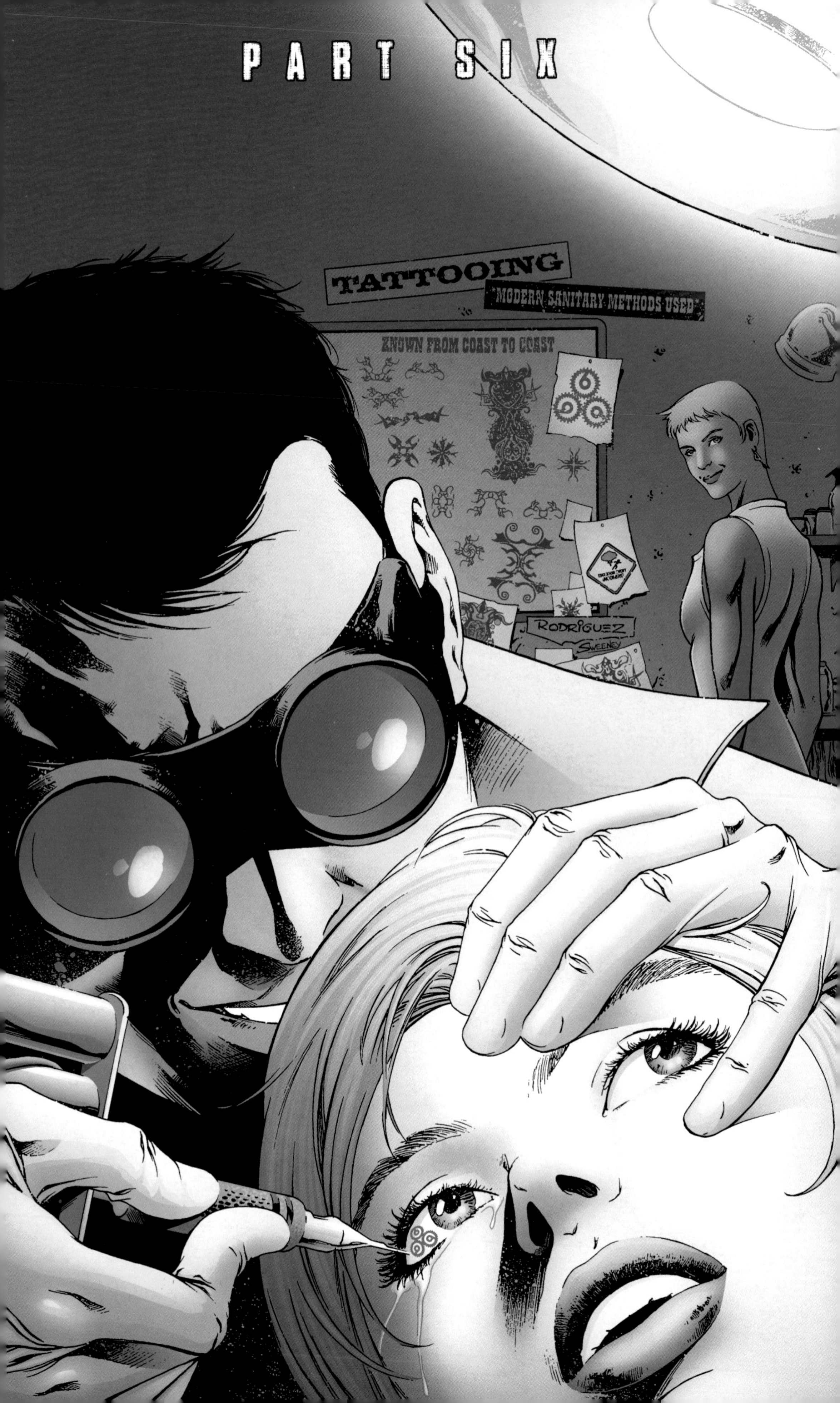
TATTOOING
MODERN SANITARY METHODS USED
KNOWN FROM COAST TO COAST
RODRIGUEZ
SWEENEY

CULTURAL
FLUX

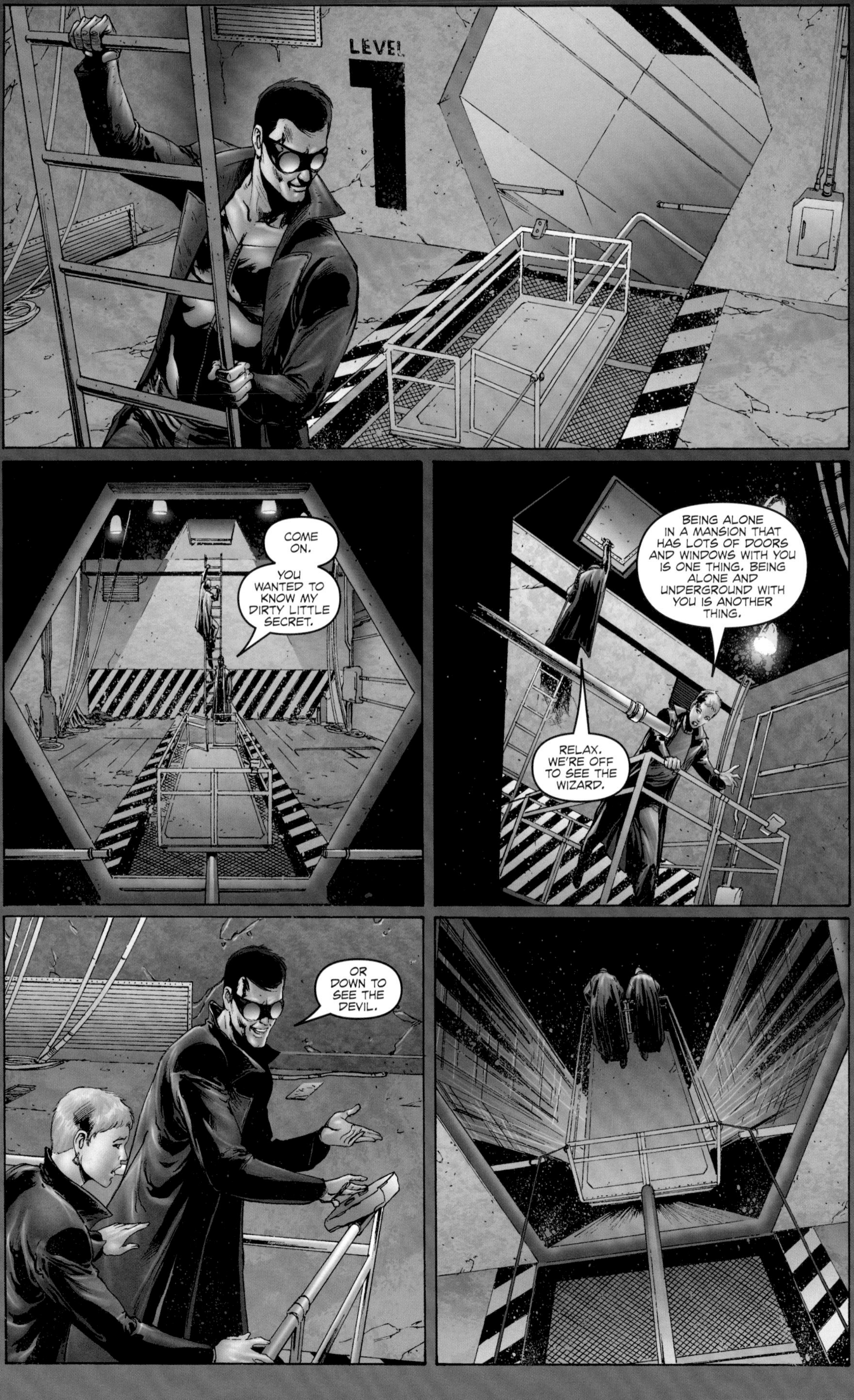
LEVEL 1
COME ON.
YOU WANTED TO KNOW MY DIRTY LITTLE SECRET.
BEING ALONE IN A MANSION THAT HAS LOTS OF DOORS AND WINDOWS WITH YOU IS ONE THING. BEING ALONE AND UNDERGROUND WITH YOU IS ANOTHER THING.
RELAX. WE'RE OFF TO SEE THE WIZARD.
OR DOWN TO SEE THE DEVIL.

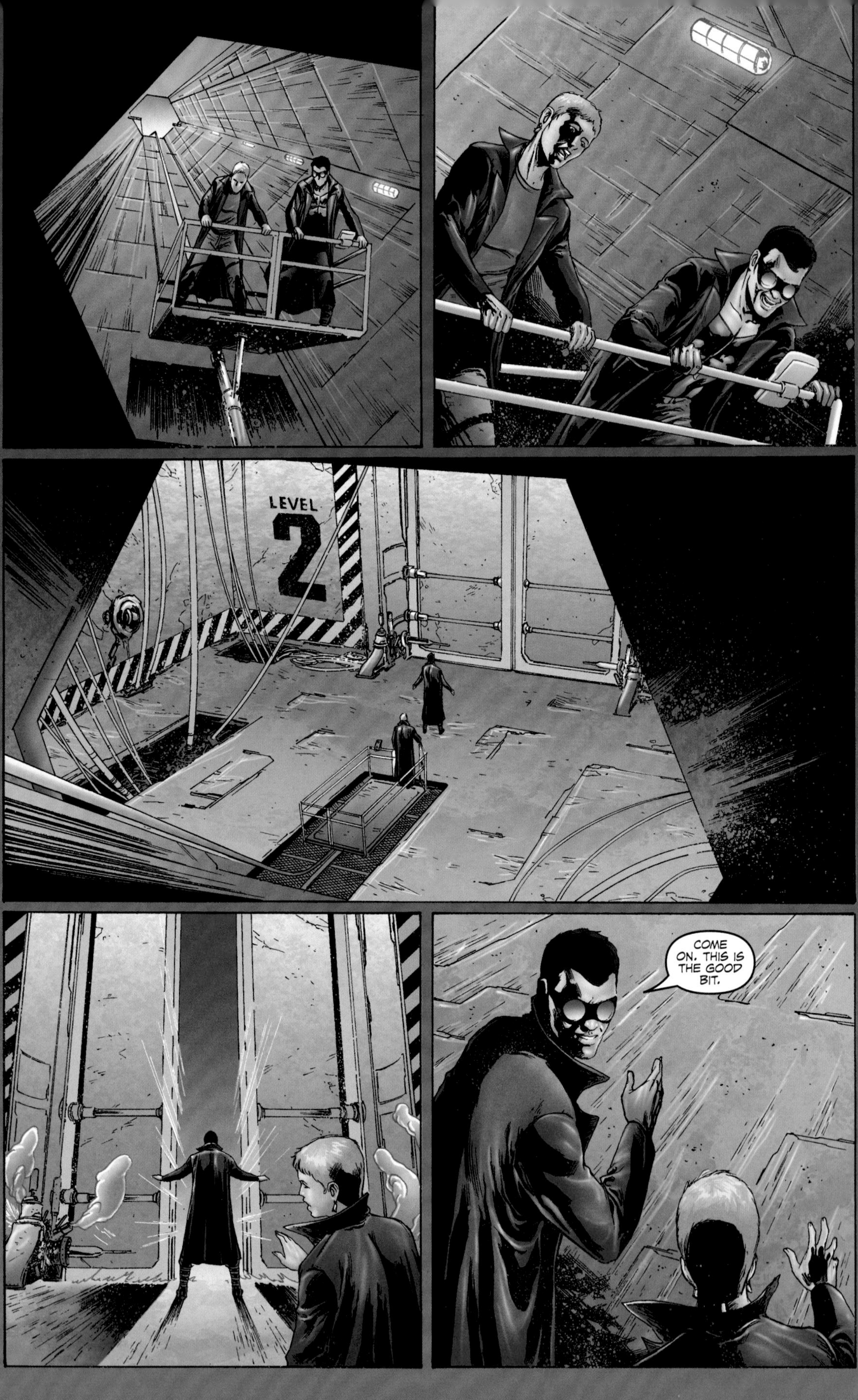
LEVEL 2
COME ON. THIS IS THE GOOD BIT.

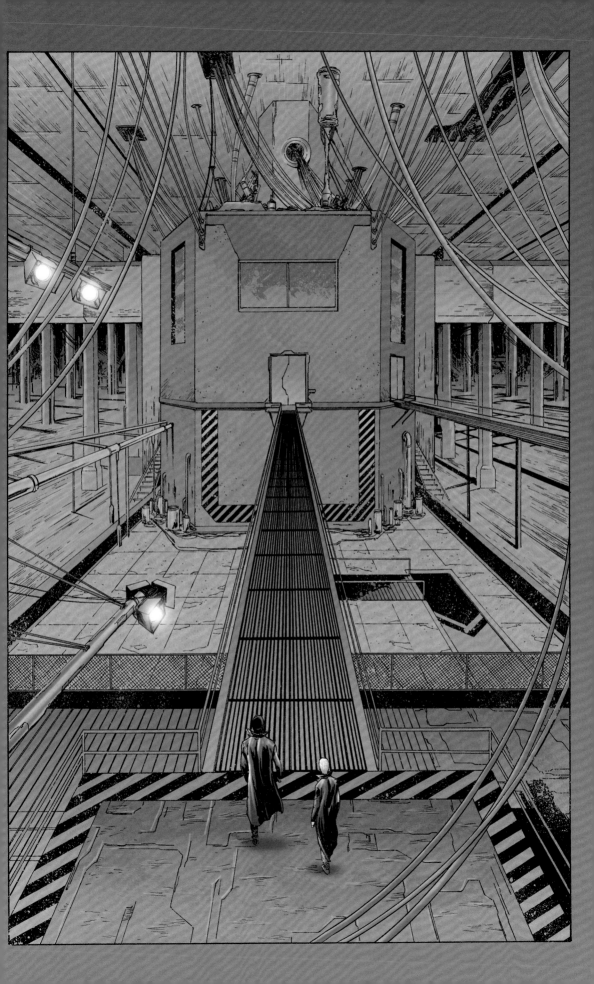

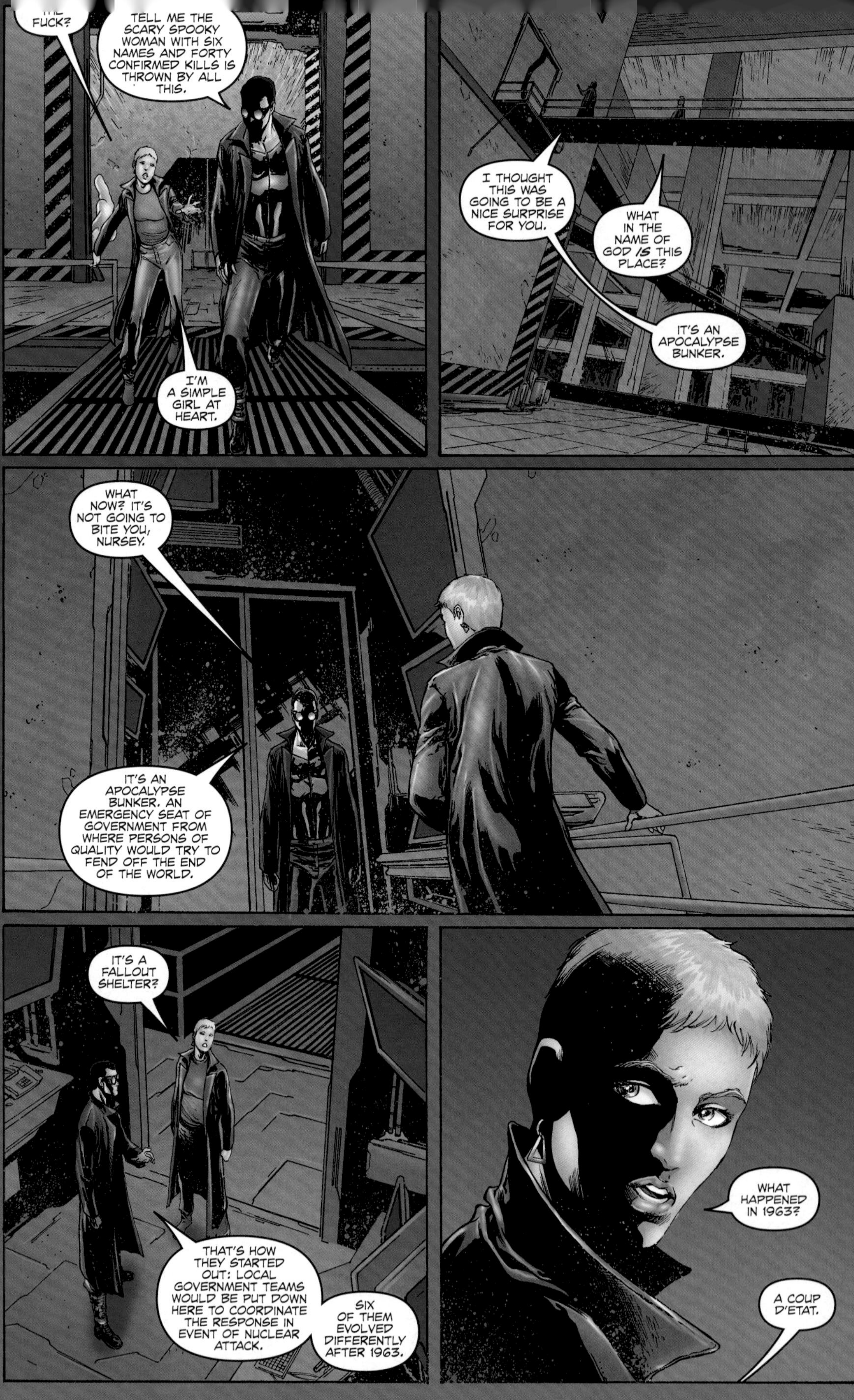

FUCK?
TELL ME THE SCARY SPOOKY WOMAN WITH SIX NAMES AND FORTY CONFIRMED KILLS IS THROWN BY ALL THIS.
I'M A SIMPLE GIRL AT HEART.
I THOUGHT THIS WAS GOING TO BE A NICE SURPRISE FOR YOU.
WHAT IN THE NAME OF GOD IS THIS PLACE?
IT'S AN APOCALYPSE BUNKER.
WHAT NOW? IT'S NOT GOING TO BITE YOU, NURSEY.
IT'S AN APOCALYPSE BUNKER. AN EMERGENCY SEAT OF GOVERNMENT FROM WHERE PERSONS OF QUALITY WOULD TRY TO FEND OFF THE END OF THE WORLD.
IT'S A FALLOUT SHELTER?
THAT'S HOW THEY STARTED OUT: LOCAL GOVERNMENT TEAMS WOULD BE PUT DOWN HERE TO COORDINATE THE RESPONSE IN EVENT OF NUCLEAR ATTACK.
SIX OF THEM EVOLVED DIFFERENTLY AFTER 1963.
WHAT HAPPENED IN 1963?
A COUP D'ETAT.

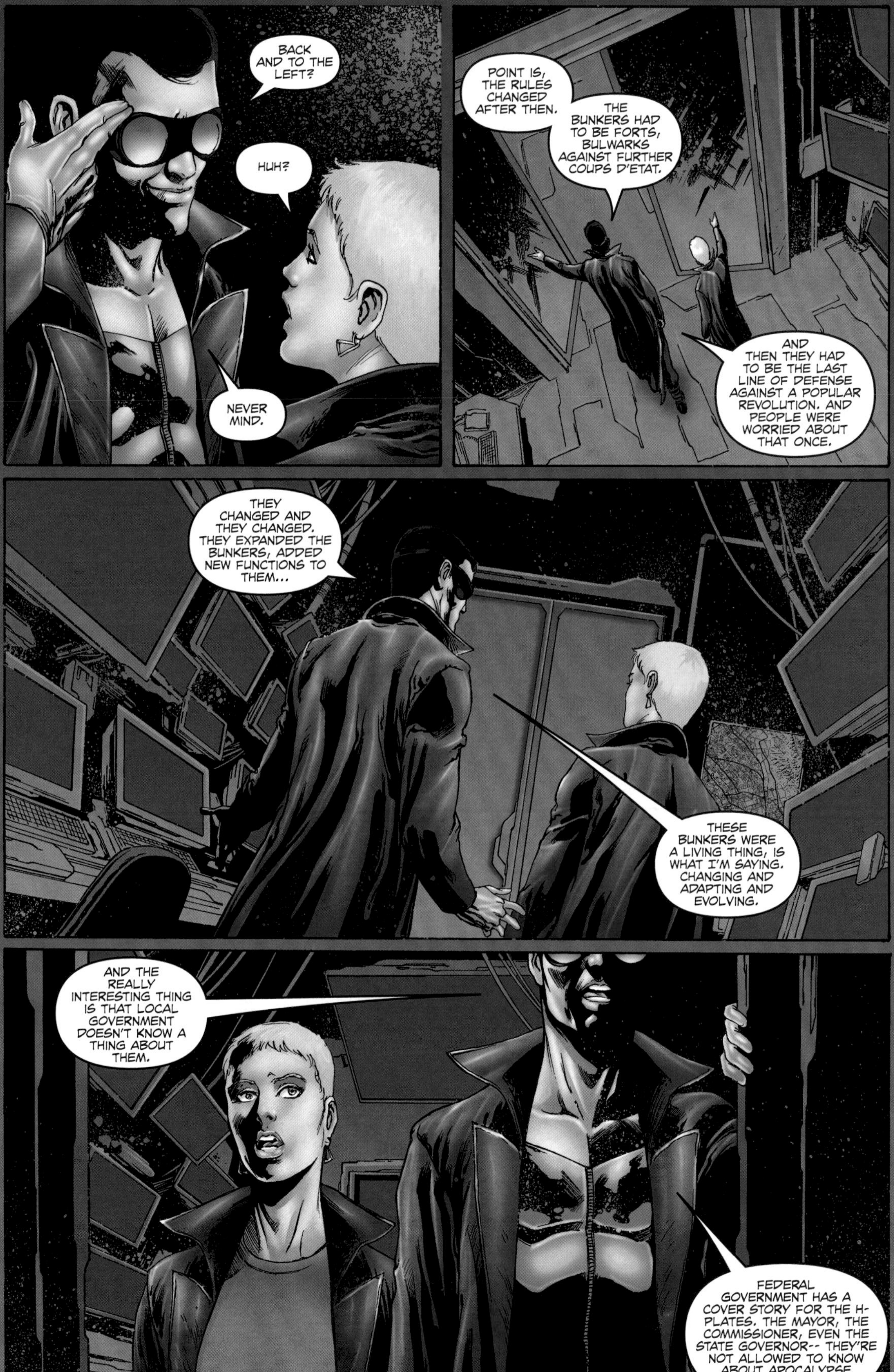
BACK AND TO THE LEFT?
HUH?
NEVER MIND.
POINT IS, THE RULES CHANGED AFTER THEN.
THE BUNKERS HAD TO BE FORTS, BULWARKS AGAINST FURTHER COUPS D'ETAT.
AND THEN THEY HAD TO BE THE LAST LINE OF DEFENSE AGAINST A POPULAR REVOLUTION. AND PEOPLE WERE WORRIED ABOUT THAT ONCE.
THEY CHANGED AND THEY CHANGED. THEY EXPANDED THE BUNKERS, ADDED NEW FUNCTIONS TO THEM...
THESE BUNKERS WERE A LIVING THING, IS WHAT I'M SAYING. CHANGING AND ADAPTING AND EVOLVING.
AND THE REALLY INTERESTING THING IS THAT LOCAL GOVERNMENT DOESN'T KNOW A THING ABOUT THEM.
FEDERAL GOVERNMENT HAS A COVER STORY FOR THE H-PLATES. THE MAYOR, THE COMMISSIONER, EVEN THE STATE GOVERNOR-- THEY'RE NOT ALLOWED TO KNOW ABOUT APOCALYPSE BUNKERS.

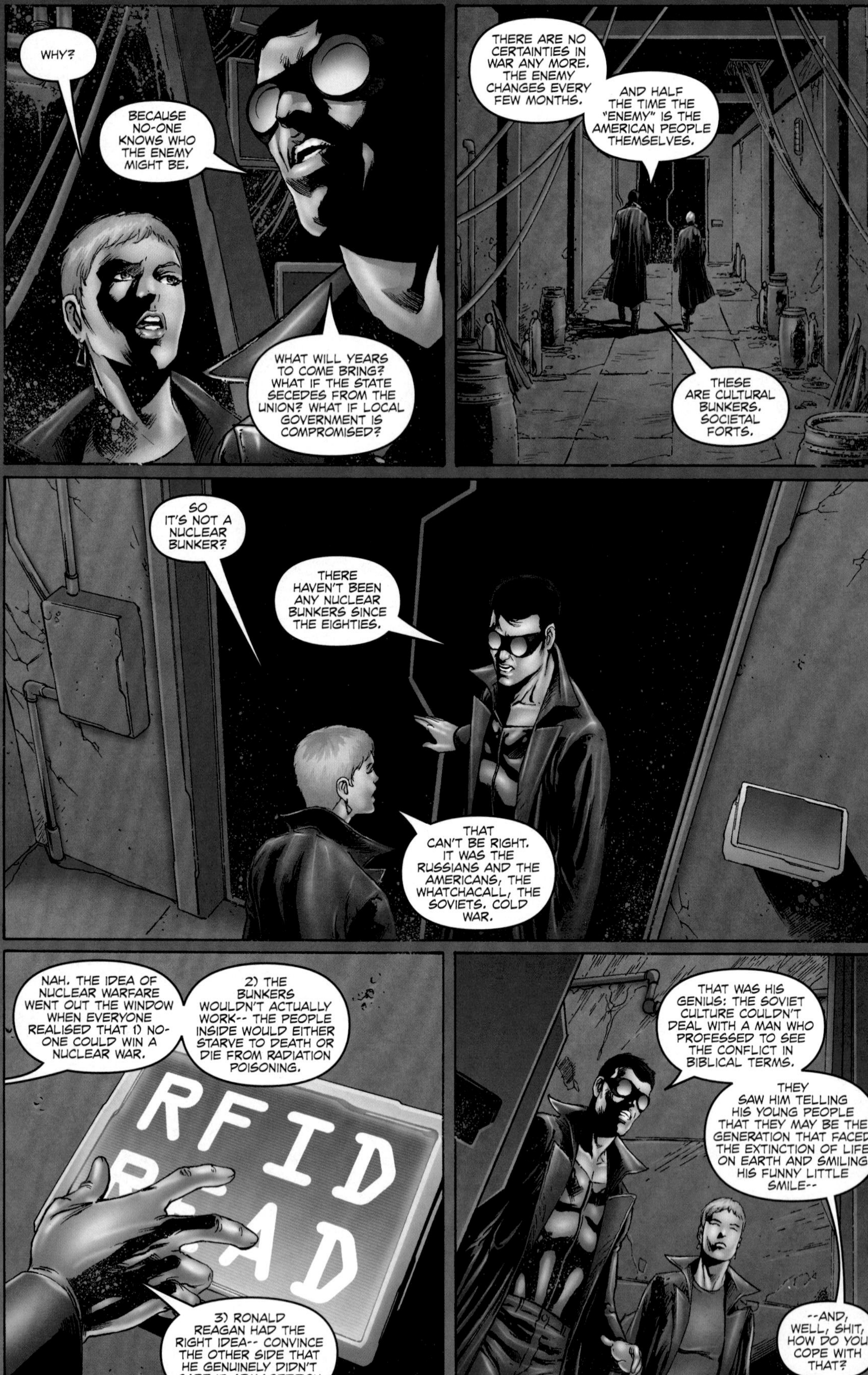
WHY?
BECAUSE NO-ONE KNOWS WHO THE ENEMY MIGHT BE.
WHAT WILL YEARS TO COME BRING? WHAT IF THE STATE SECEDES FROM THE UNION? WHAT IF LOCAL GOVERNMENT IS COMPROMISED?
THERE ARE NO CERTAINTIES IN WAR ANY MORE. THE ENEMY CHANGES EVERY FEW MONTHS.
AND HALF THE TIME THE "ENEMY" IS THE AMERICAN PEOPLE THEMSELVES.
THESE ARE CULTURAL BUNKERS. SOCIETAL FORTS.
SO IT'S NOT A NUCLEAR BUNKER?
THERE HAVEN'T BEEN ANY NUCLEAR BUNKERS SINCE THE EIGHTIES.
THAT CAN'T BE RIGHT. IT WAS THE RUSSIANS AND THE AMERICANS, THE WHATCHACALL, THE SOVIETS. COLD WAR.
NAH. THE IDEA OF NUCLEAR WARFARE WENT OUT THE WINDOW WHEN EVERYONE REALISED THAT 1) NO-ONE COULD WIN A NUCLEAR WAR.
2) THE BUNKERS WOULDN'T ACTUALLY WORK-- THE PEOPLE INSIDE WOULD EITHER STARVE TO DEATH OR DIE FROM RADIATION POISONING.
RFID
3) RONALD REAGAN HAD THE RIGHT IDEA-- CONVINCE THE OTHER SIDE THAT HE GENUINELY DIDN'T CARE IF ARMAGEDDON CAME.
THAT WAS HIS GENIUS: THE SOVIET CULTURE COULDN'T DEAL WITH A MAN WHO PROFESSED TO SEE THE CONFLICT IN BIBLICAL TERMS.
THEY SAW HIM TELLING HIS YOUNG PEOPLE THAT THEY MAY BE THE GENERATION THAT FACED THE EXTINCTION OF LIFE ON EARTH AND SMILING HIS FUNNY LITTLE SMILE--
--AND, WELL, SHIT, HOW DO YOU COPE WITH THAT?

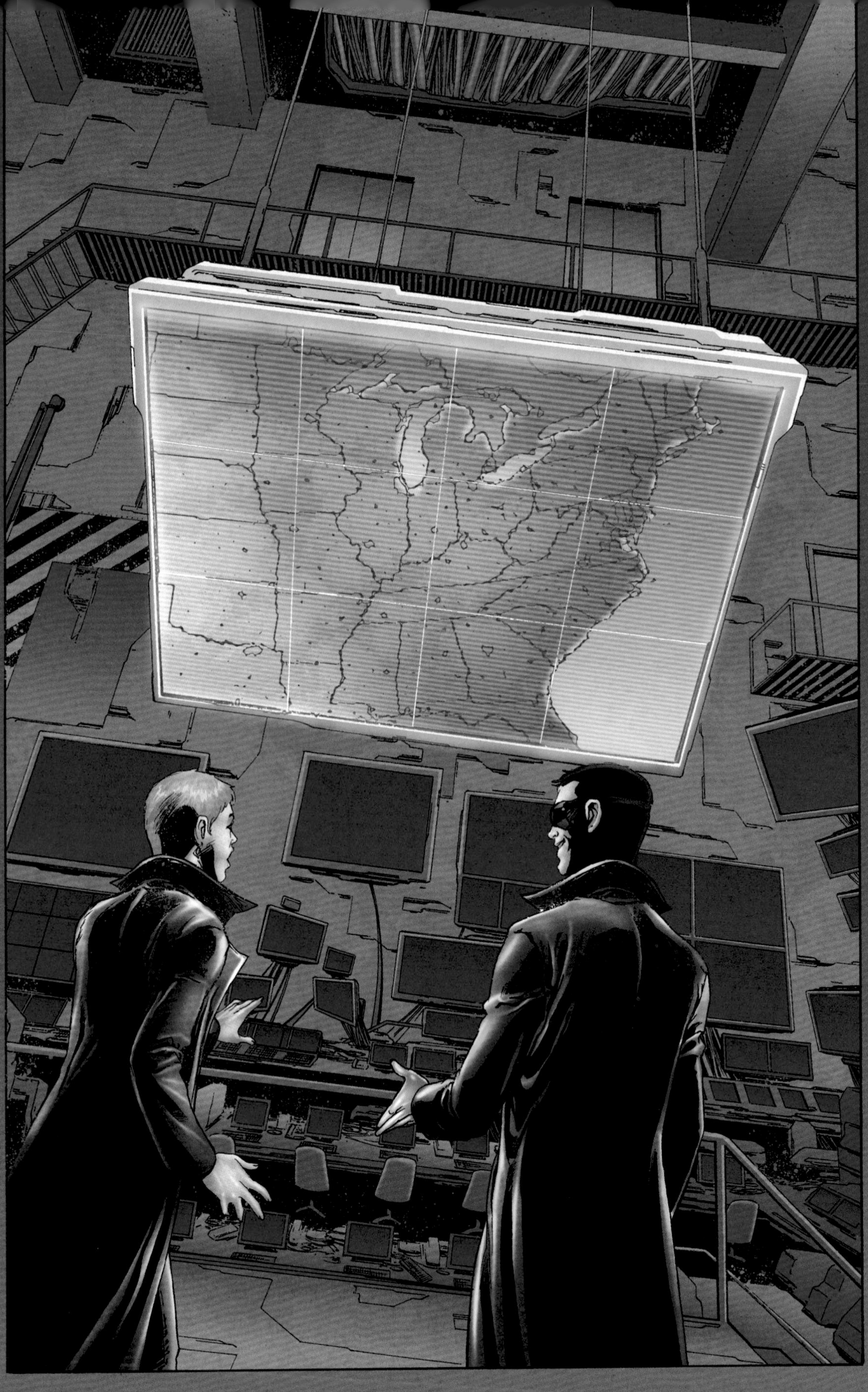

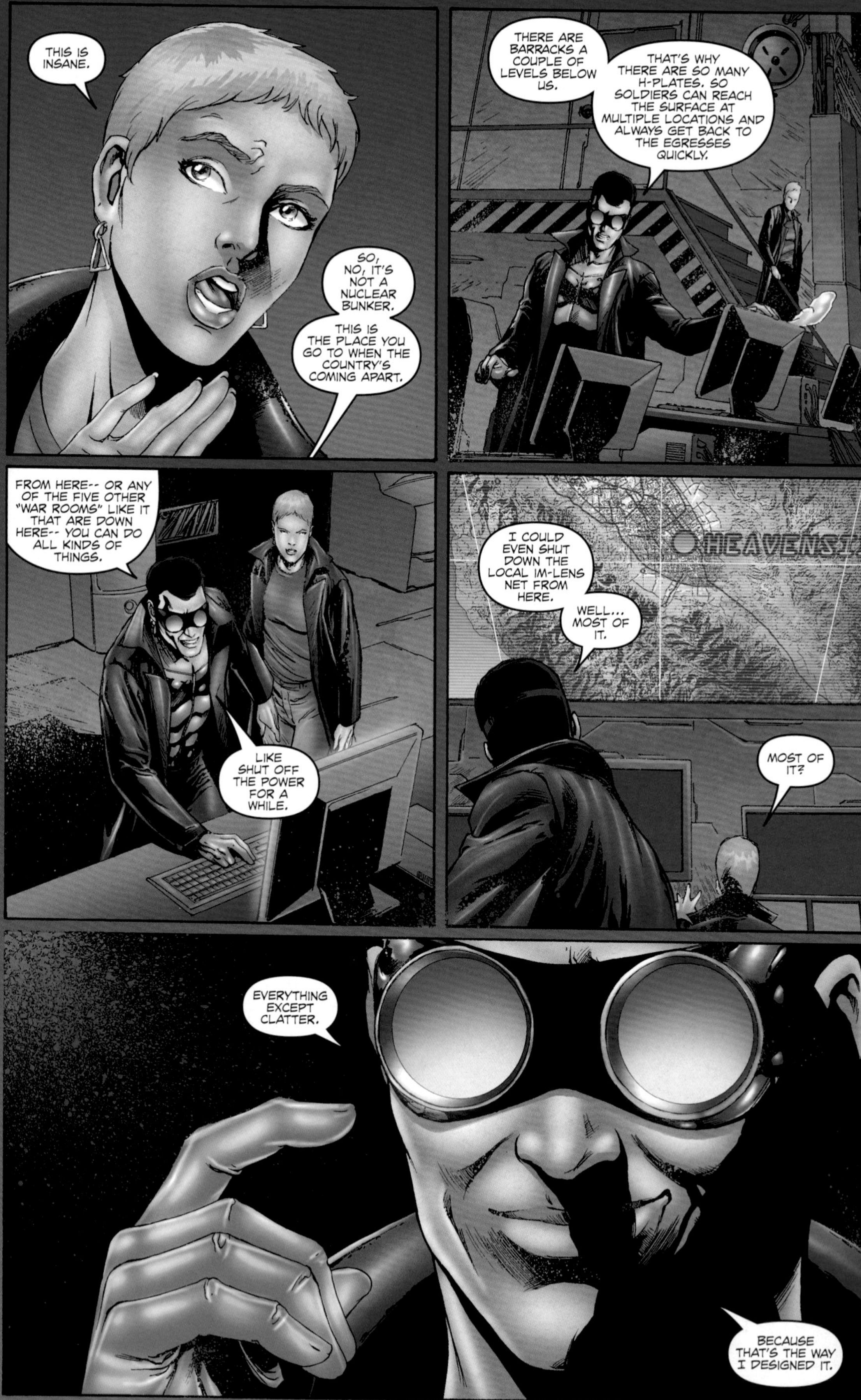
THIS IS INSANE.
SO, NO, IT'S NOT A NUCLEAR BUNKER.
THIS IS THE PLACE YOU GO TO WHEN THE COUNTRY'S COMING APART.
THERE ARE BARRACKS A COUPLE OF LEVELS BELOW US.
THAT'S WHY THERE ARE SO MANY H-PLATES. SO SOLDIERS CAN REACH THE SURFACE AT MULTIPLE LOCATIONS AND ALWAYS GET BACK TO THE EGRESSES QUICKLY.
FROM HERE-- OR ANY OF THE FIVE OTHER "WAR ROOMS" LIKE IT THAT ARE DOWN HERE-- YOU CAN DO ALL KINDS OF THINGS.
LIKE SHUT OFF THE POWER FOR A WHILE.
HEAVENSID
I COULD EVEN SHUT DOWN THE LOCAL IM-LENS NET FROM HERE.
WELL... MOST OF IT.
MOST OF IT?
EVERYTHING EXCEPT CLATTER.
BECAUSE THAT'S THE WAY I DESIGNED IT.

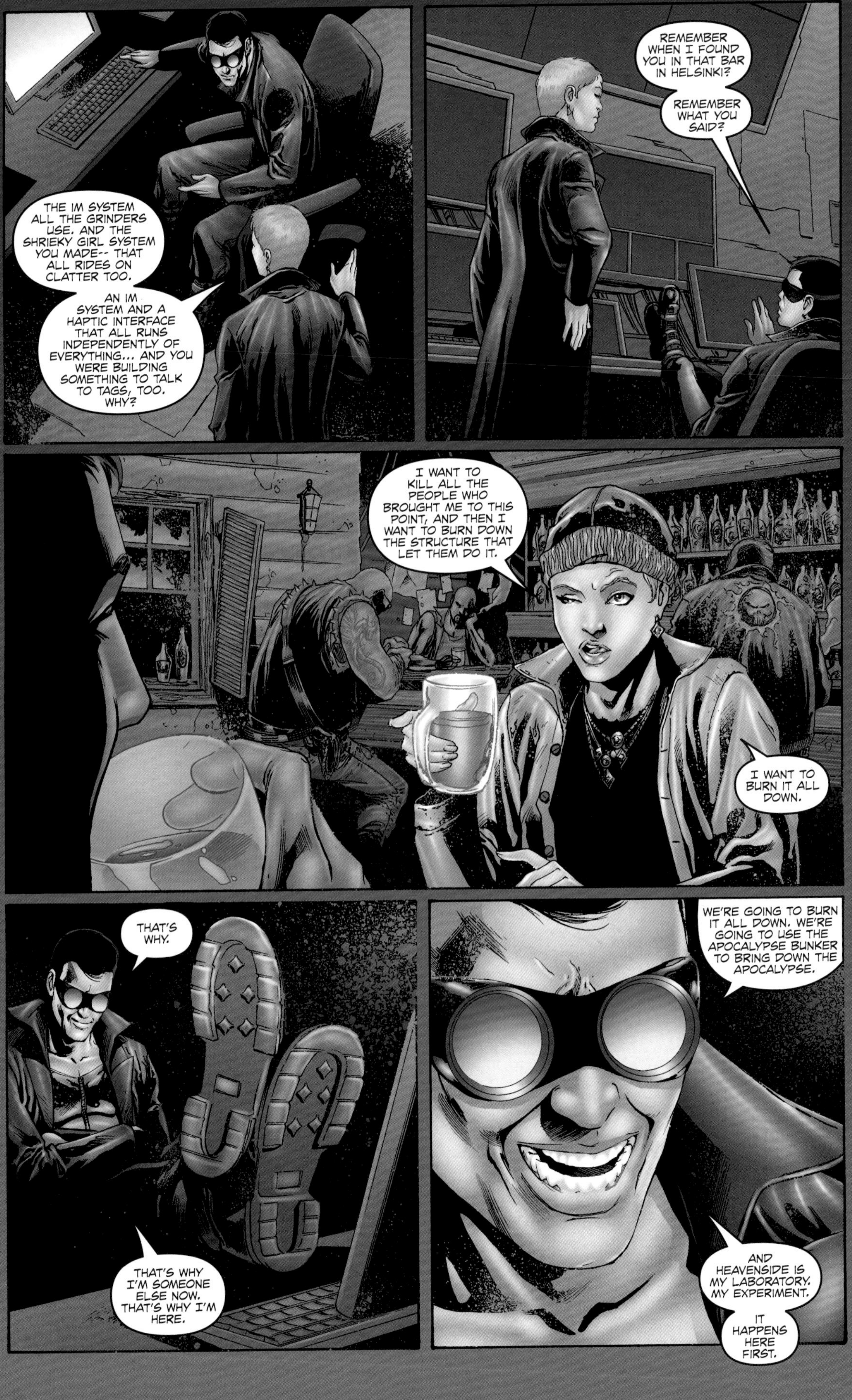
THE IM SYSTEM ALL THE GRINDERS USE. AND THE SHRIEKY GIRL SYSTEM YOU MADE-- THAT ALL RIDES ON CLATTER TOO.
AN IM SYSTEM AND A HAPTIC INTERFACE THAT ALL RUNS INDEPENDENTLY OF EVERYTHING... AND YOU WERE BUILDING SOMETHING TO TALK TO TAGS, TOO. WHY?
REMEMBER WHEN I FOUND YOU IN THAT BAR IN HELSINKI?
REMEMBER WHAT YOU SAID?
I WANT TO KILL ALL THE PEOPLE WHO BROUGHT ME TO THIS POINT, AND THEN I WANT TO BURN DOWN THE STRUCTURE THAT LET THEM DO IT.
I WANT TO BURN IT ALL DOWN.
THAT'S WHY.
THAT'S WHY I'M SOMEONE ELSE NOW. THAT'S WHY I'M HERE.
WE'RE GOING TO BURN IT ALL DOWN. WE'RE GOING TO USE THE APOCALYPSE BUNKER TO BRING DOWN THE APOCALYPSE.
AND HEAVENSIDE IS MY LABORATORY. MY EXPERIMENT.
IT HAPPENS HERE FIRST.

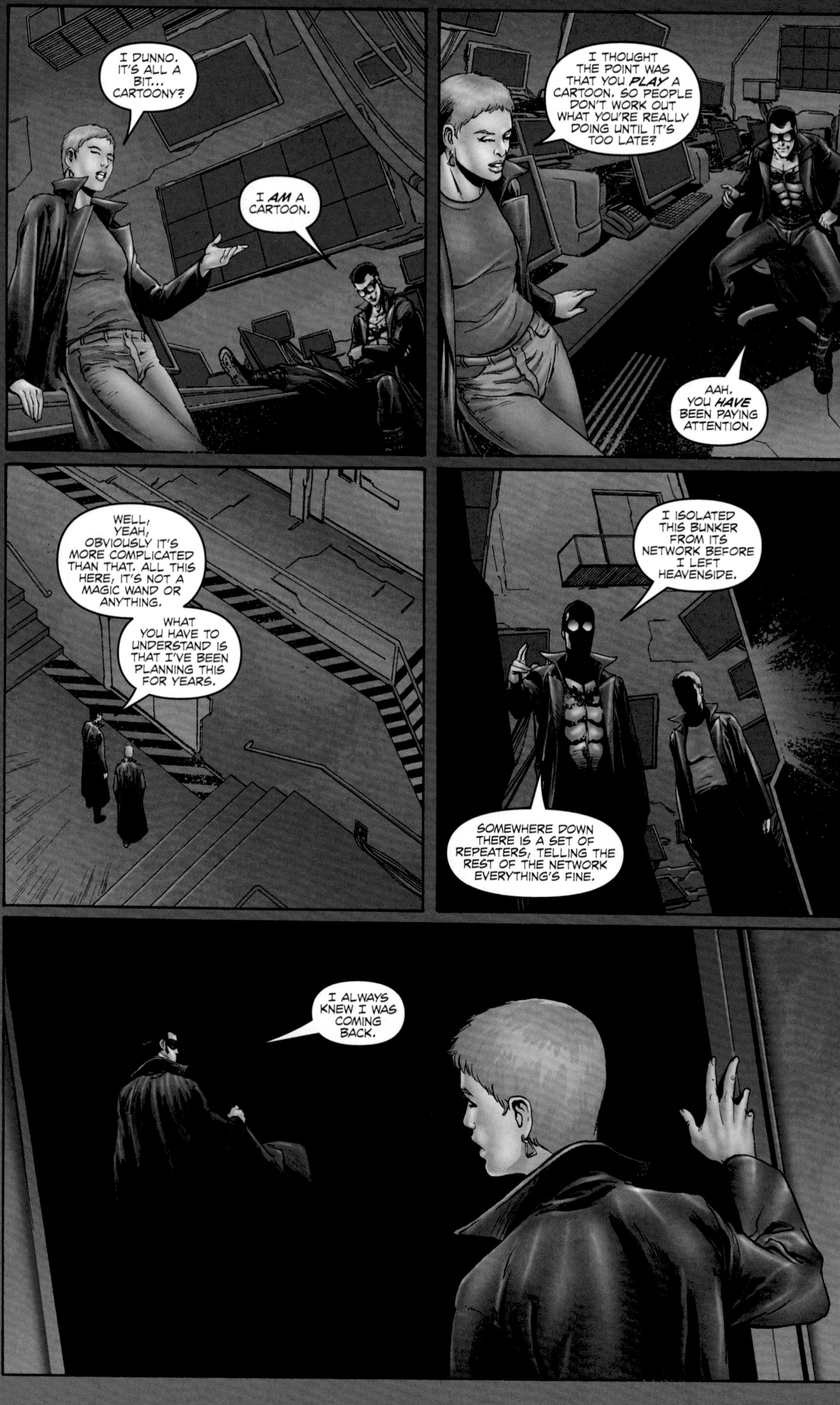

I DUNNO. IT'S ALL A BIT... CARTOONY?
I AM A CARTOON.
I THOUGHT THE POINT WAS THAT YOU PLAY A CARTOON. SO PEOPLE DON'T WORK OUT WHAT YOU'RE REALLY DOING UNTIL IT'S TOO LATE?
AAH. YOU HAVE BEEN PAYING ATTENTION.
WELL, YEAH, OBVIOUSLY IT'S MORE COMPLICATED THAN THAT. ALL THIS HERE, IT'S NOT A MAGIC WAND OR ANYTHING.
WHAT YOU HAVE TO UNDERSTAND IS THAT I'VE BEEN PLANNING THIS FOR YEARS.
I ISOLATED THIS BUNKER FROM ITS NETWORK BEFORE I LEFT HEAVENSIDE.
SOMEWHERE DOWN THERE IS A SET OF REPEATERS, TELLING THE REST OF THE NETWORK EVERYTHING'S FINE.
I ALWAYS KNEW I WAS COMING BACK.

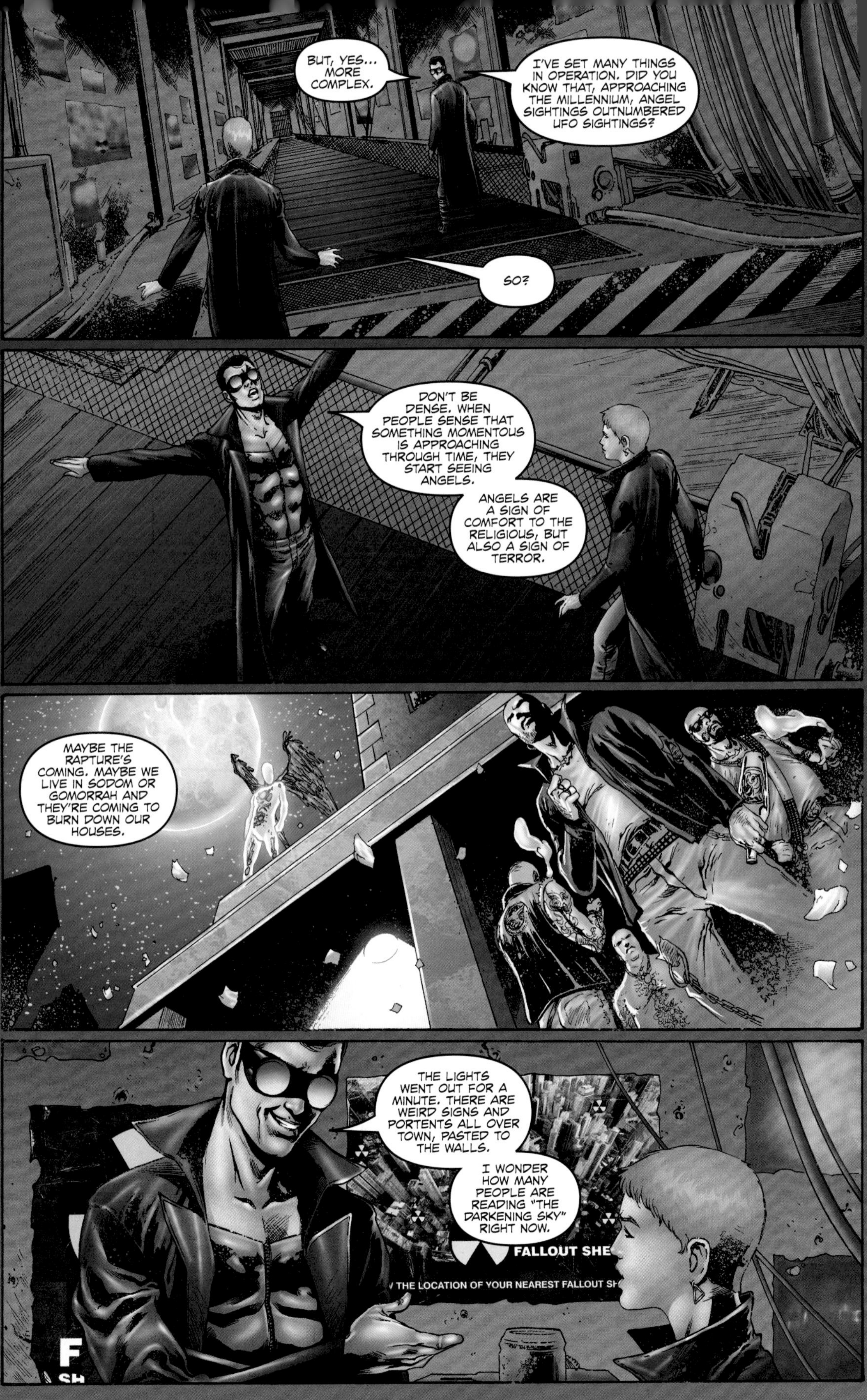
BUT, YES... MORE COMPLEX.
I'VE SET MANY THINGS IN OPERATION. DID YOU KNOW THAT, APPROACHING THE MILLENNIUM, ANGEL SIGHTINGS OUTNUMBERED UFO SIGHTINGS?
SO?
DON'T BE DENSE. WHEN PEOPLE SENSE THAT SOMETHING MOMENTOUS IS APPROACHING THROUGH TIME, THEY START SEEING ANGELS.
ANGELS ARE A SIGN OF COMFORT TO THE RELIGIOUS, BUT ALSO A SIGN OF TERROR.
MAYBE THE RAPTURE'S COMING. MAYBE WE LIVE IN SODOM OR GOMORRAH AND THEY'RE COMING TO BURN DOWN OUR HOUSES.
THE LIGHTS WENT OUT FOR A MINUTE. THERE ARE WEIRD SIGNS AND PORTENTS ALL OVER TOWN, PASTED TO THE WALLS.
I WONDER HOW MANY PEOPLE ARE READING "THE DARKENING SKY" RIGHT NOW.
FALLOUT SHE
THE LOCATION OF YOUR NEAREST FALLOUT SH

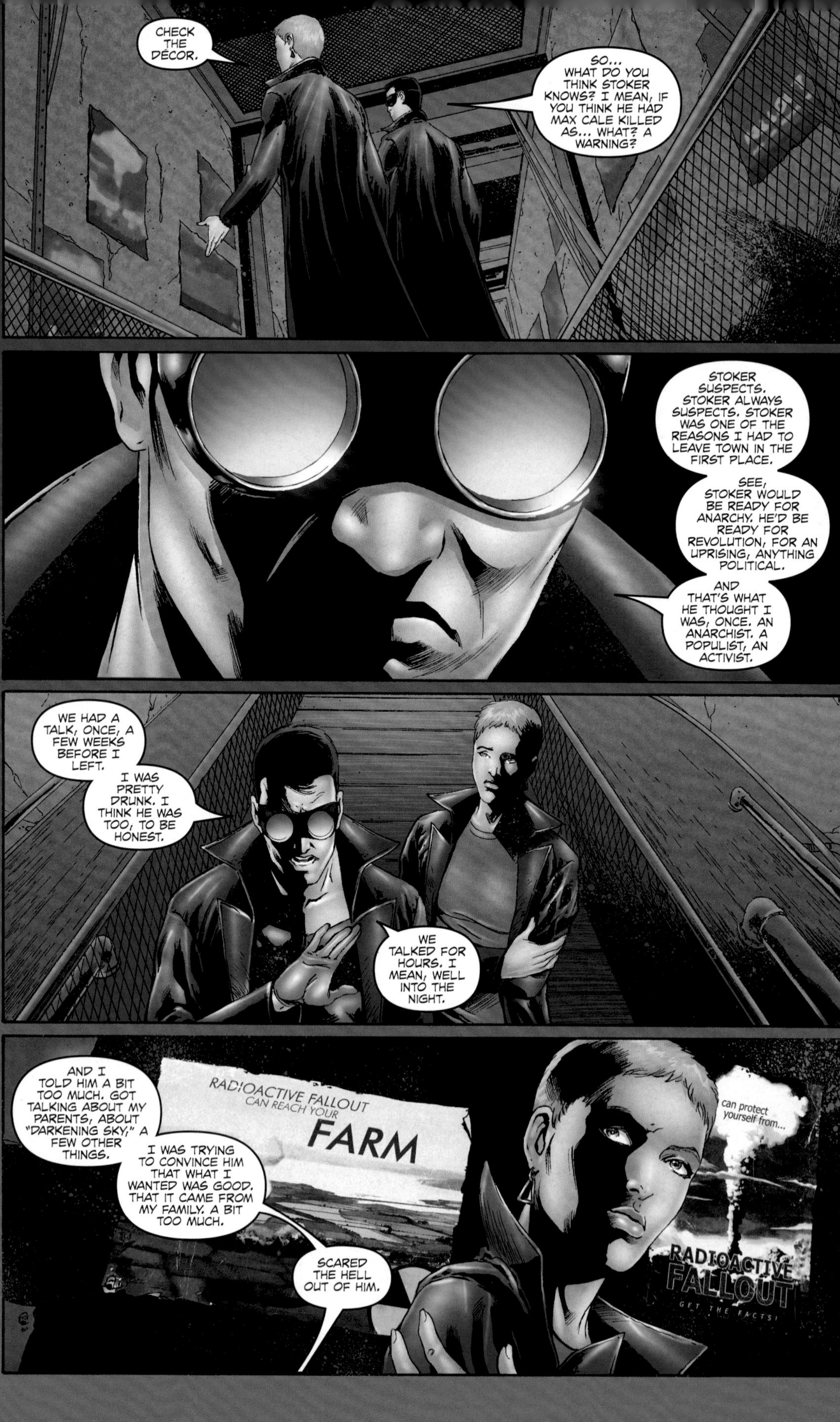
CHECK THE DÉCOR.
SO... WHAT DO YOU THINK STOKER KNOWS? I MEAN, IF YOU THINK HE HAD MAX CALE KILLED AS... WHAT? A WARNING?
STOKER SUSPECTS. STOKER ALWAYS SUSPECTS. STOKER WAS ONE OF THE REASONS I HAD TO LEAVE TOWN IN THE FIRST PLACE.
SEE, STOKER WOULD BE READY FOR ANARCHY. HE'D BE READY FOR REVOLUTION, FOR AN UPRISING, ANYTHING POLITICAL.
AND THAT'S WHAT HE THOUGHT I WAS, ONCE. AN ANARCHIST. A POPULIST, AN ACTIVIST.
WE HAD A TALK, ONCE, A FEW WEEKS BEFORE I LEFT.
I WAS PRETTY DRUNK. I THINK HE WAS TOO, TO BE HONEST.
WE TALKED FOR HOURS. I MEAN, WELL INTO THE NIGHT.
RADIOACTIVE FALLOUT CAN REACH YOUR FARM
can protect yourself from...
RADIOACTIVE FALLOUT
GET THE FACTS!
AND I TOLD HIM A BIT TOO MUCH. GOT TALKING ABOUT MY PARENTS, ABOUT "DARKENING SKY," A FEW OTHER THINGS.
I WAS TRYING TO CONVINCE HIM THAT WHAT I WANTED WAS GOOD. THAT IT CAME FROM MY FAMILY. A BIT TOO MUCH.
SCARED THE HELL OUT OF HIM.

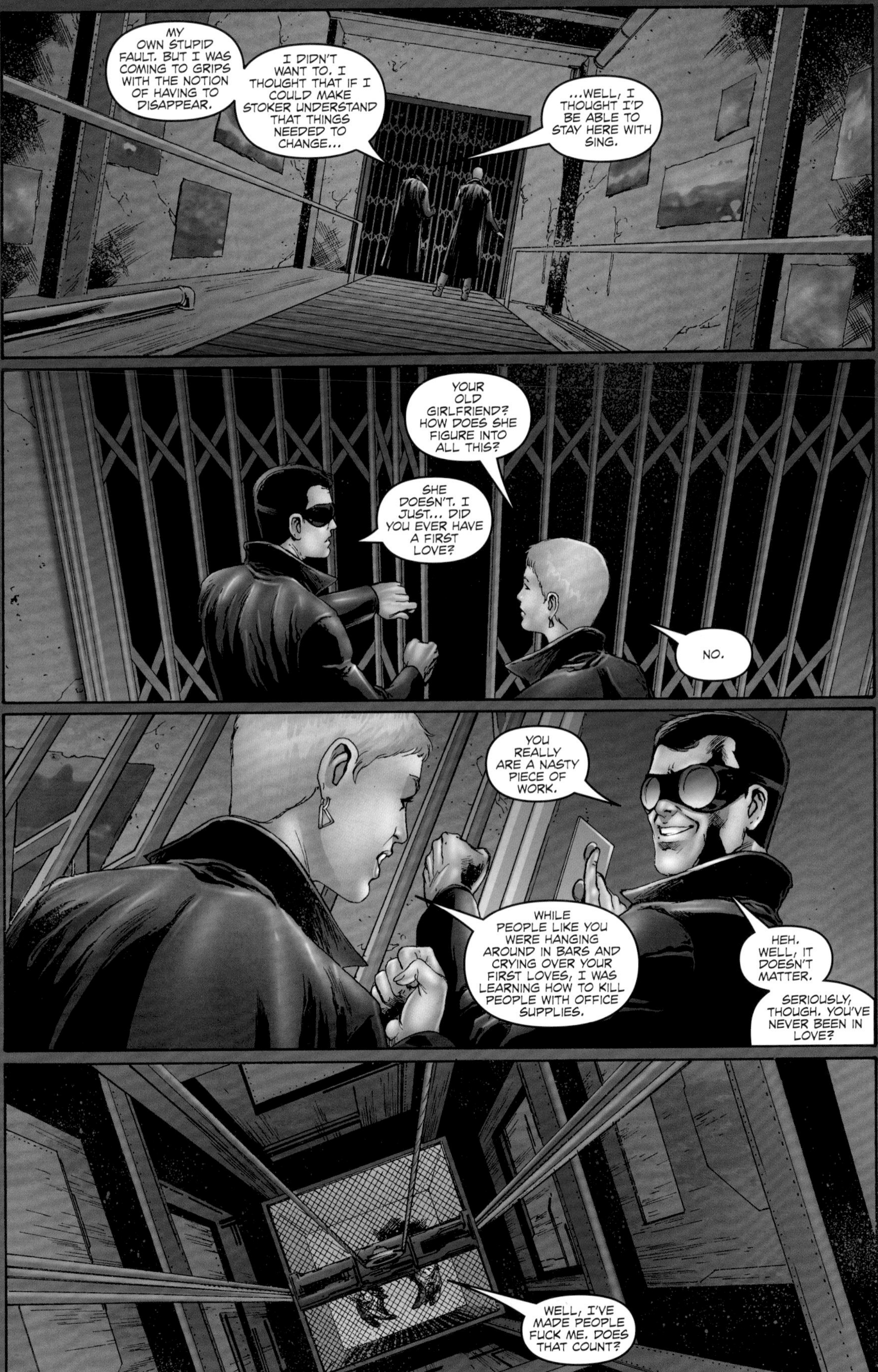
MY OWN STUPID FAULT. BUT I WAS COMING TO GRIPS WITH THE NOTION OF HAVING TO DISAPPEAR.
I DIDN'T WANT TO. I THOUGHT THAT IF I COULD MAKE STOKER UNDERSTAND THAT THINGS NEEDED TO CHANGE...
...WELL, I THOUGHT I'D BE ABLE TO STAY HERE WITH SING.
YOUR OLD GIRLFRIEND? HOW DOES SHE FIGURE INTO ALL THIS?
SHE DOESN'T. I JUST... DID YOU EVER HAVE A FIRST LOVE?
NO.
YOU REALLY ARE A NASTY PIECE OF WORK.
WHILE PEOPLE LIKE YOU WERE HANGING AROUND IN BARS AND CRYING OVER YOUR FIRST LOVES, I WAS LEARNING HOW TO KILL PEOPLE WITH OFFICE SUPPLIES.
HEH. WELL, IT DOESN'T MATTER.
SERIOUSLY, THOUGH. YOU'VE NEVER BEEN IN LOVE?
WELL, I'VE MADE PEOPLE FUCK ME. DOES THAT COUNT?

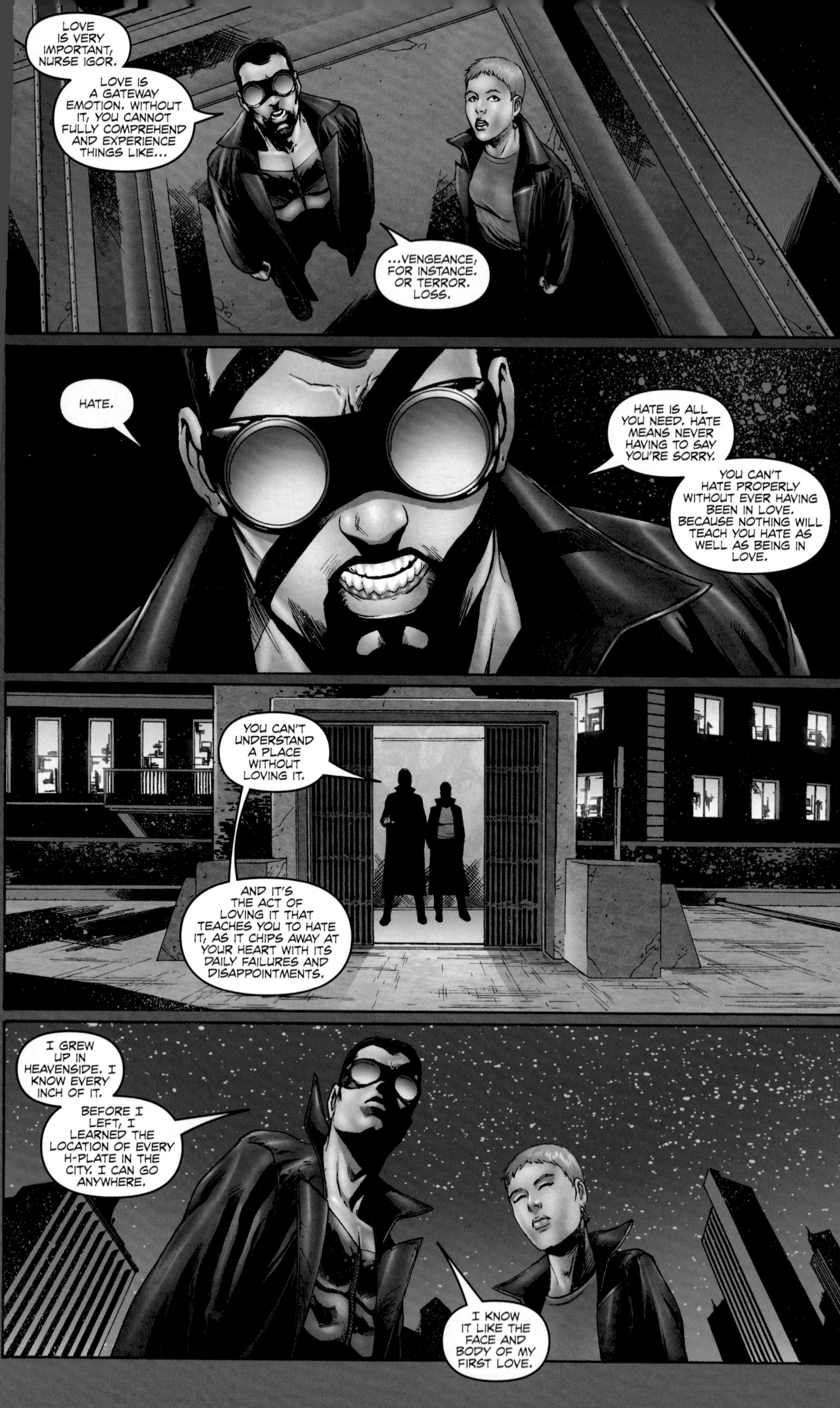

LOVE IS VERY IMPORTANT, NURSE IGOR.
LOVE IS A GATEWAY EMOTION. WITHOUT IT, YOU CANNOT FULLY COMPREHEND AND EXPERIENCE THINGS LIKE...
...VENGEANCE, FOR INSTANCE. OR TERROR. LOSS.
HATE.
HATE IS ALL YOU NEED. HATE MEANS NEVER HAVING TO SAY YOU'RE SORRY.
YOU CAN'T HATE PROPERLY WITHOUT EVER HAVING BEEN IN LOVE. BECAUSE NOTHING WILL TEACH YOU HATE AS WELL AS BEING IN LOVE.
YOU CAN'T UNDERSTAND A PLACE WITHOUT LOVING IT.
AND IT'S THE ACT OF LOVING IT THAT TEACHES YOU TO HATE IT, AS IT CHIPS AWAY AT YOUR HEART WITH ITS DAILY FAILURES AND DISAPPOINTMENTS.
I GREW UP IN HEAVENSIDE. I KNOW EVERY INCH OF IT.
BEFORE I LEFT, I LEARNED THE LOCATION OF EVERY H-PLATE IN THE CITY. I CAN GO ANYWHERE.
I KNOW IT LIKE THE FACE AND BODY OF MY FIRST LOVE.

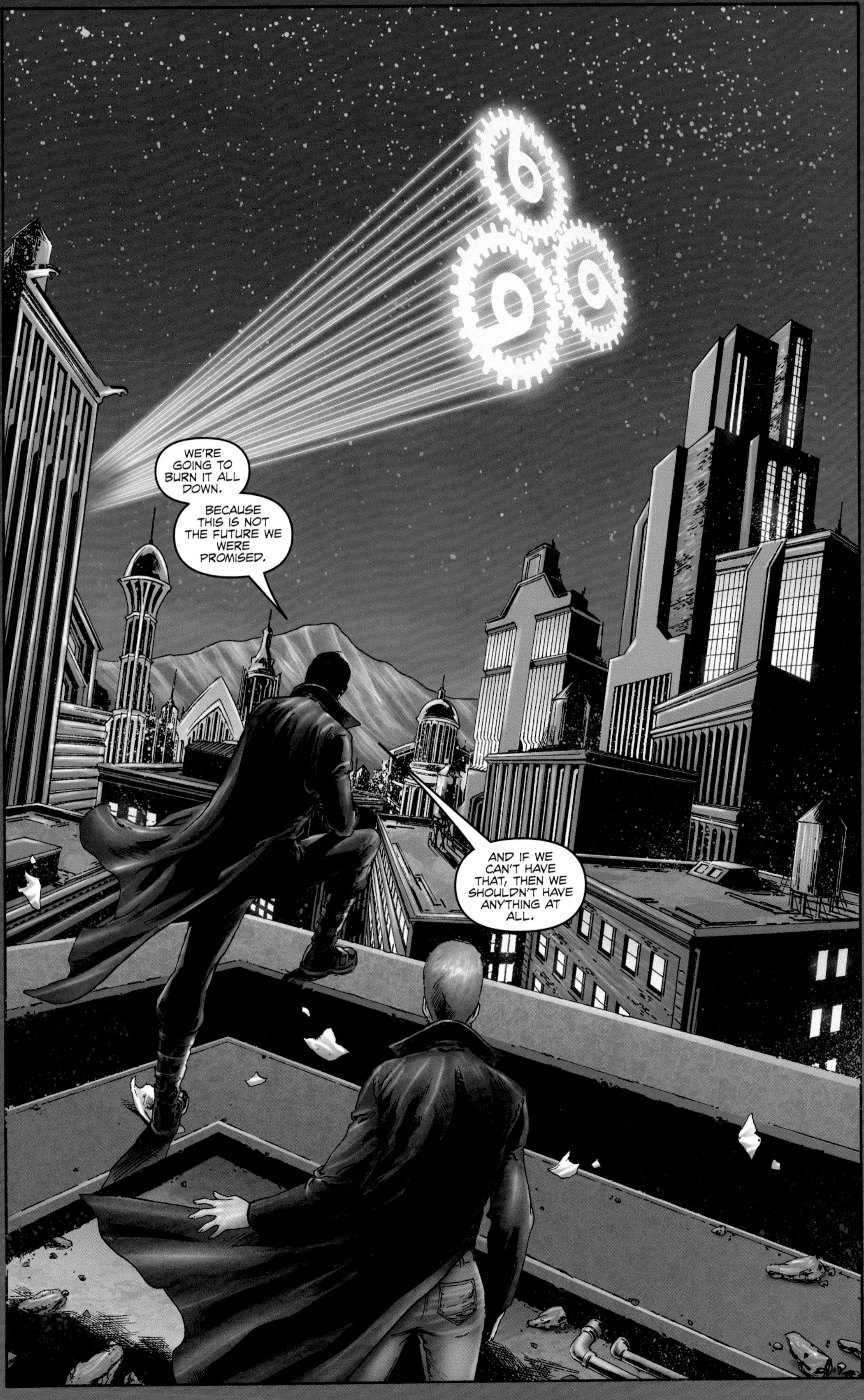
WE'RE GOING TO BURN IT ALL DOWN.
BECAUSE THIS IS NOT THE FUTURE WE WERE PROMISED.
AND IF WE CAN'T HAVE THAT, THEN WE SHOULDN'T HAVE ANYTHING AT ALL.

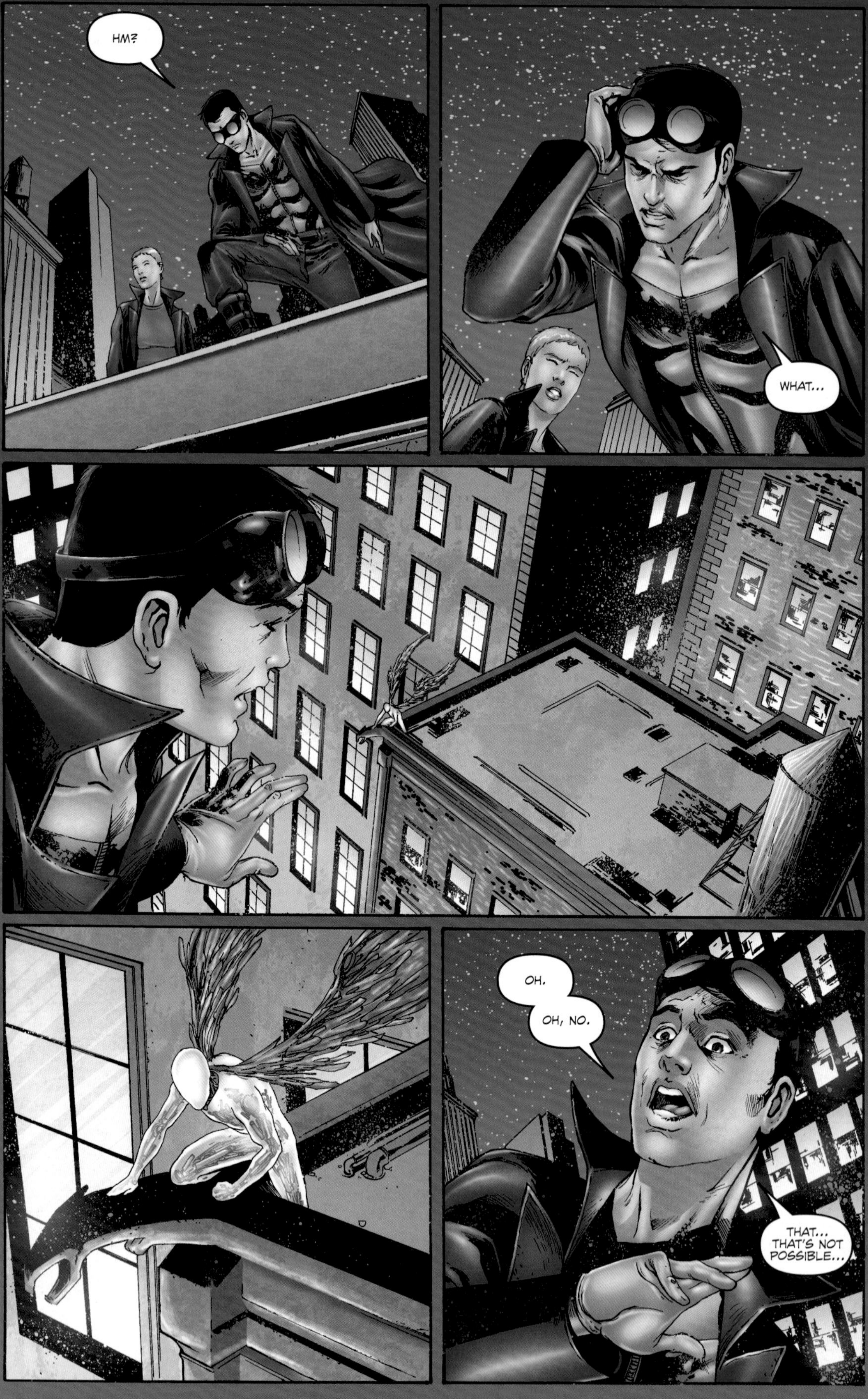
HM?
WHAT...
OH.
OH, NO.
THAT... THAT'S NOT POSSIBLE...

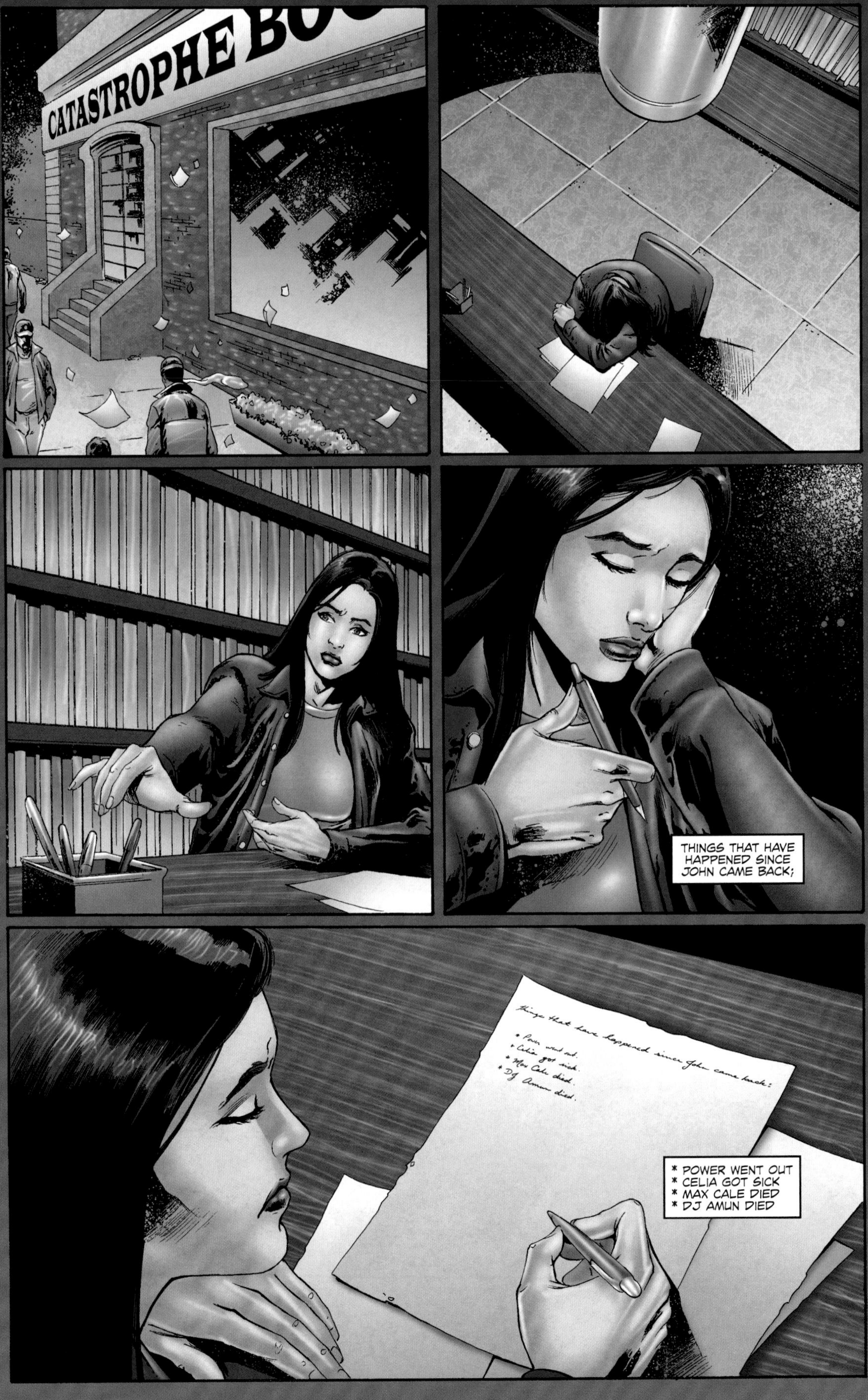

CATASTROPHE
THINGS THAT HAVE HAPPENED SINCE JOHN CAME BACK;
Things that have happened since John came back:
* Power went out.
* Celia got sick.
* Max Cale died.
* DJ Amun died.
* POWER WENT OUT
* CELIA GOT SICK
* MAX CALE DIED
* DJ AMUN DIED

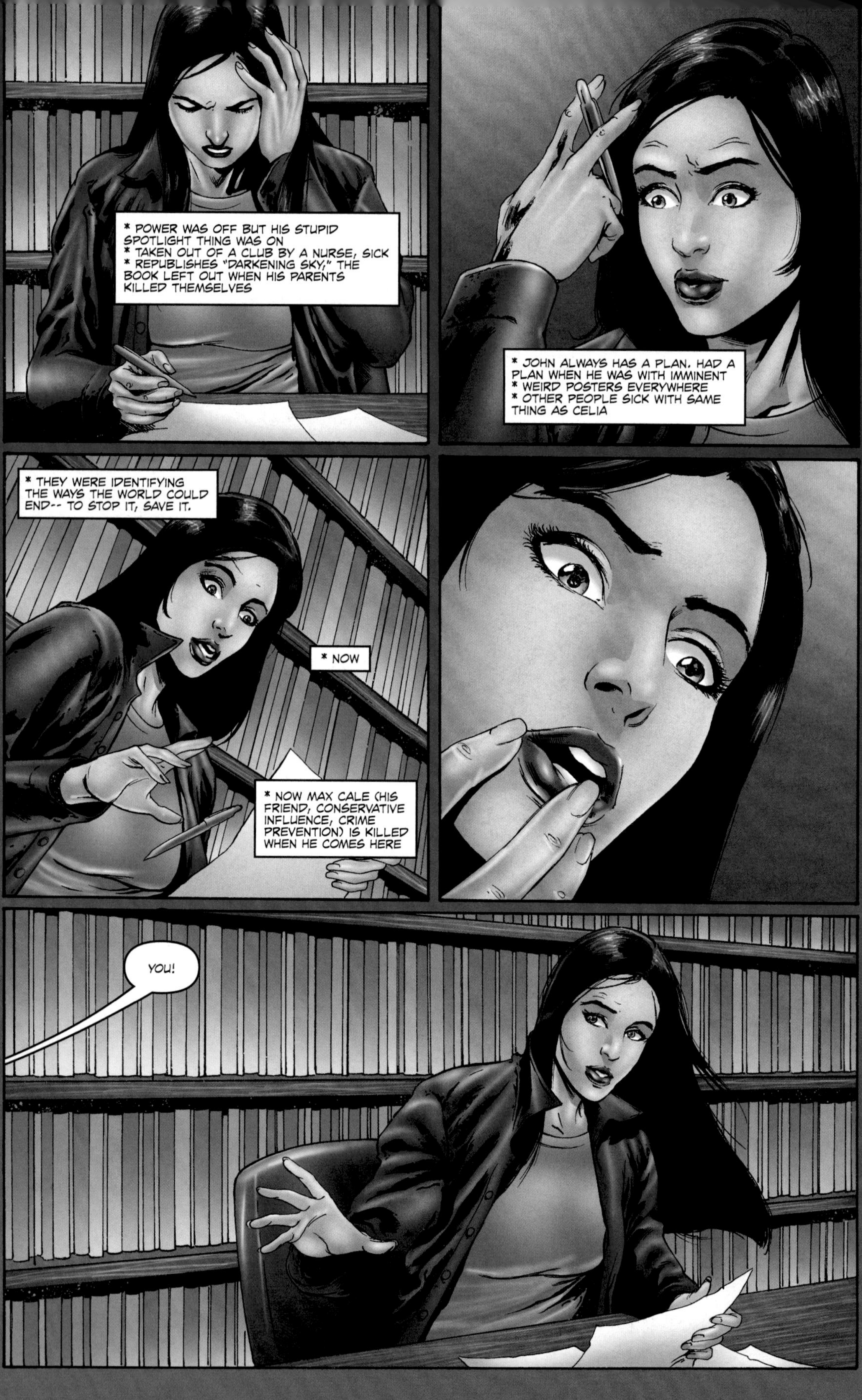

* POWER WAS OFF BUT HIS STUPID SPOTLIGHT THING WAS ON
* TAKEN OUT OF A CLUB BY A NURSE, SICK
* REPUBLISHES "DARKENING SKY," THE BOOK LEFT OUT WHEN HIS PARENTS KILLED THEMSELVES
* JOHN ALWAYS HAS A PLAN. HAD A PLAN WHEN HE WAS WITH IMMINENT
* WEIRD POSTERS EVERYWHERE
* OTHER PEOPLE SICK WITH SAME THING AS CELIA
* THEY WERE IDENTIFYING THE WAYS THE WORLD COULD END-- TO STOP IT, SAVE IT.
* NOW
* NOW MAX CALE (HIS FRIEND, CONSERVATIVE INFLUENCE, CRIME PREVENTION) IS KILLED WHEN HE COMES HERE
YOU!

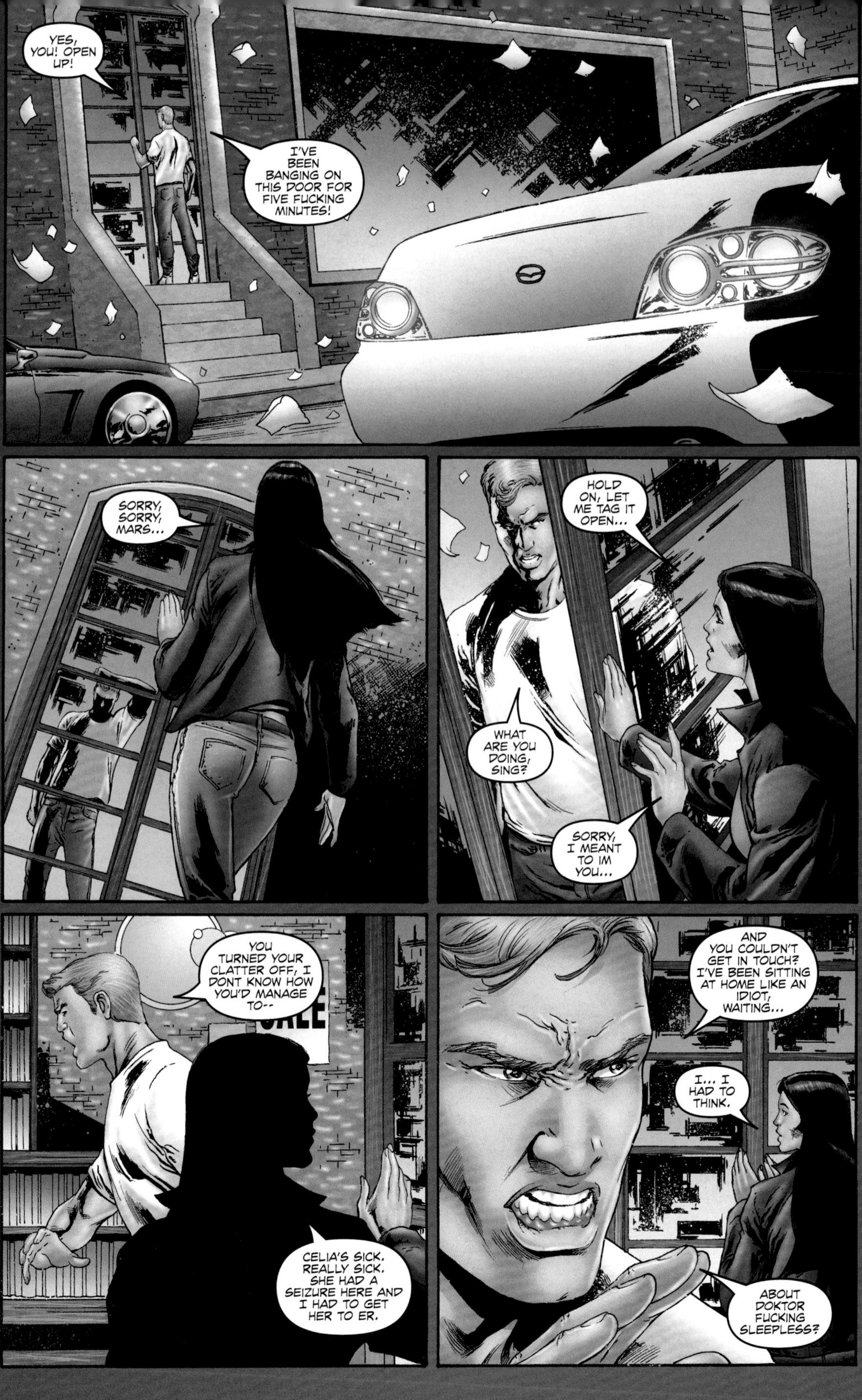
YES, YOU! OPEN UP!
I'VE BEEN BANGING ON THIS DOOR FOR FIVE FUCKING MINUTES!
SORRY, SORRY, MARS...
HOLD ON, LET ME TAG IT OPEN...
WHAT ARE YOU DOING, SING?
SORRY, I MEANT TO IM YOU...
YOU TURNED YOUR CLATTER OFF, I DONT KNOW HOW YOU'D MANAGE TO--
CELIA'S SICK. REALLY SICK. SHE HAD A SEIZURE HERE AND I HAD TO GET HER TO ER.
AND YOU COULDN'T GET IN TOUCH? I'VE BEEN SITTING AT HOME LIKE AN IDIOT, WAITING...
I... I HAD TO THINK.
ABOUT DOKTOR FUCKING SLEEPLESS?

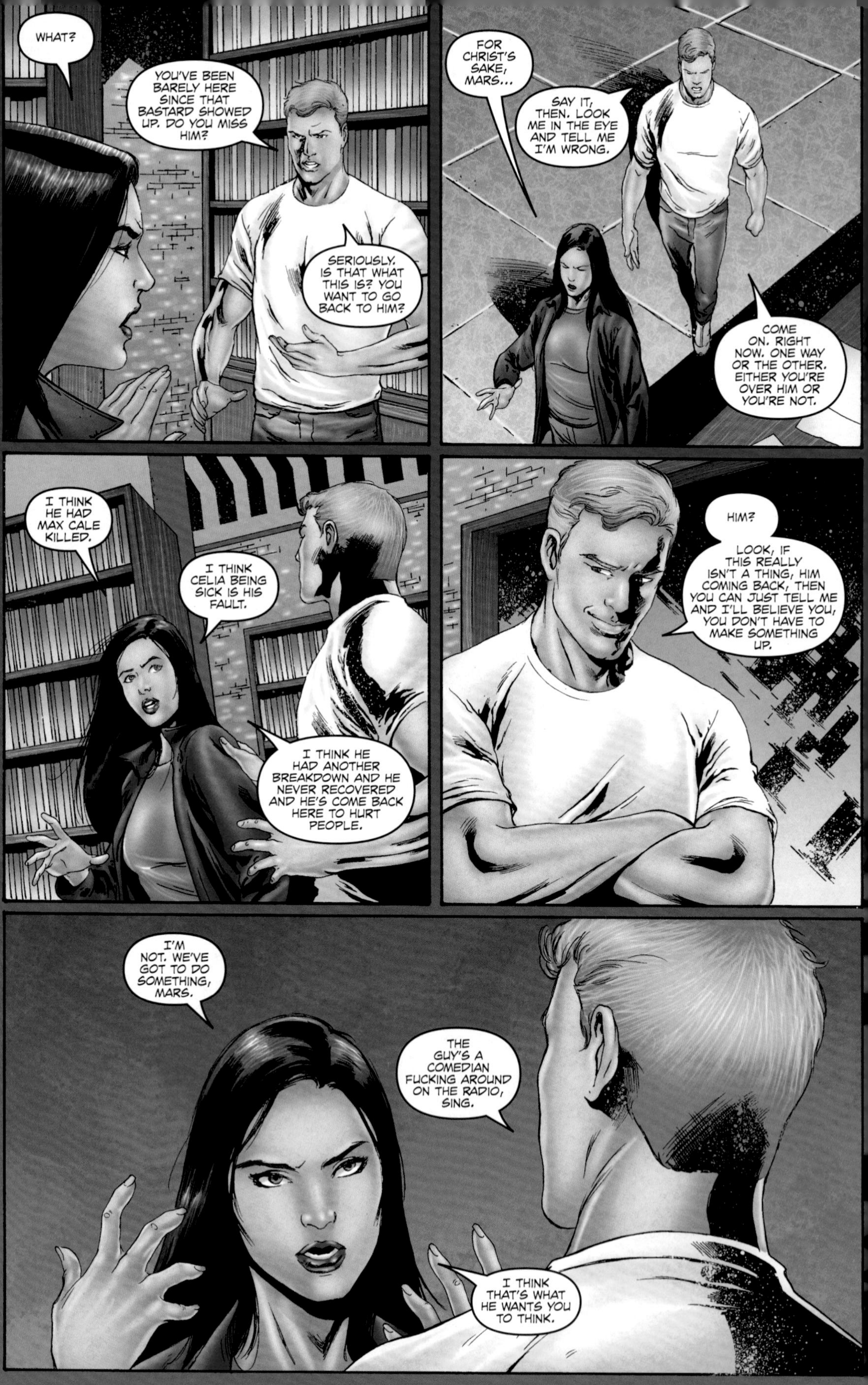
WHAT?
YOU'VE BEEN BARELY HERE SINCE THAT BASTARD SHOWED UP. DO YOU MISS HIM?
SERIOUSLY. IS THAT WHAT THIS IS? YOU WANT TO GO BACK TO HIM?
FOR CHRIST'S SAKE, MARS...
SAY IT, THEN. LOOK ME IN THE EYE AND TELL ME I'M WRONG.
COME ON. RIGHT NOW. ONE WAY OR THE OTHER. EITHER YOU'RE OVER HIM OR YOU'RE NOT.
I THINK HE HAD MAX CALE KILLED.
I THINK CELIA BEING SICK IS HIS FAULT.
I THINK HE HAD ANOTHER BREAKDOWN AND HE NEVER RECOVERED AND HE'S COME BACK HERE TO HURT PEOPLE.
HIM?
LOOK, IF THIS REALLY ISN'T A THING, HIM COMING BACK, THEN YOU CAN JUST TELL ME AND I'LL BELIEVE YOU, YOU DON'T HAVE TO MAKE SOMETHING UP.
I'M NOT. WE'VE GOT TO DO SOMETHING, MARS.
THE GUY'S A COMEDIAN FUCKING AROUND ON THE RADIO, SING.
I THINK THAT'S WHAT HE WANTS YOU TO THINK.

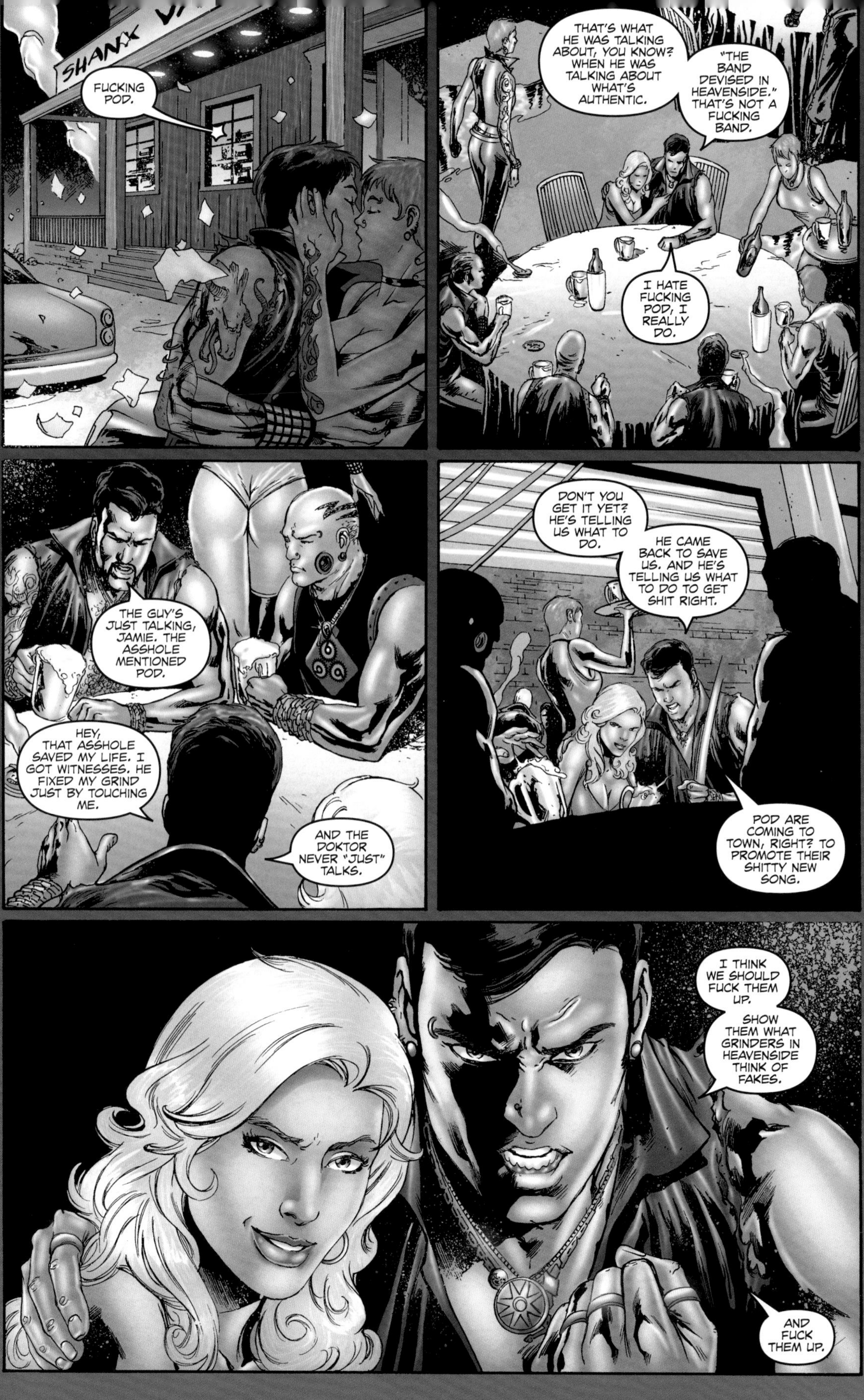
SHANX
FUCKING POD.
THAT'S WHAT HE WAS TALKING ABOUT, YOU KNOW? WHEN HE WAS TALKING ABOUT WHAT'S AUTHENTIC.
"THE BAND DEVISED IN HEAVENSIDE." THAT'S NOT A FUCKING BAND.
I HATE FUCKING POD, I REALLY DO.
THE GUY'S JUST TALKING, JAMIE. THE ASSHOLE MENTIONED POD.
HEY, THAT ASSHOLE SAVED MY LIFE. I GOT WITNESSES. HE FIXED MY GRIND JUST BY TOUCHING ME.
AND THE DOKTOR NEVER "JUST" TALKS.
DON'T YOU GET IT YET? HE'S TELLING US WHAT TO DO.
HE CAME BACK TO SAVE US. AND HE'S TELLING US WHAT TO DO TO GET SHIT RIGHT.
POD ARE COMING TO TOWN, RIGHT? TO PROMOTE THEIR SHITTY NEW SONG.
I THINK WE SHOULD FUCK THEM UP.
SHOW THEM WHAT GRINDERS IN HEAVENSIDE THINK OF FAKES.
AND FUCK THEM UP.

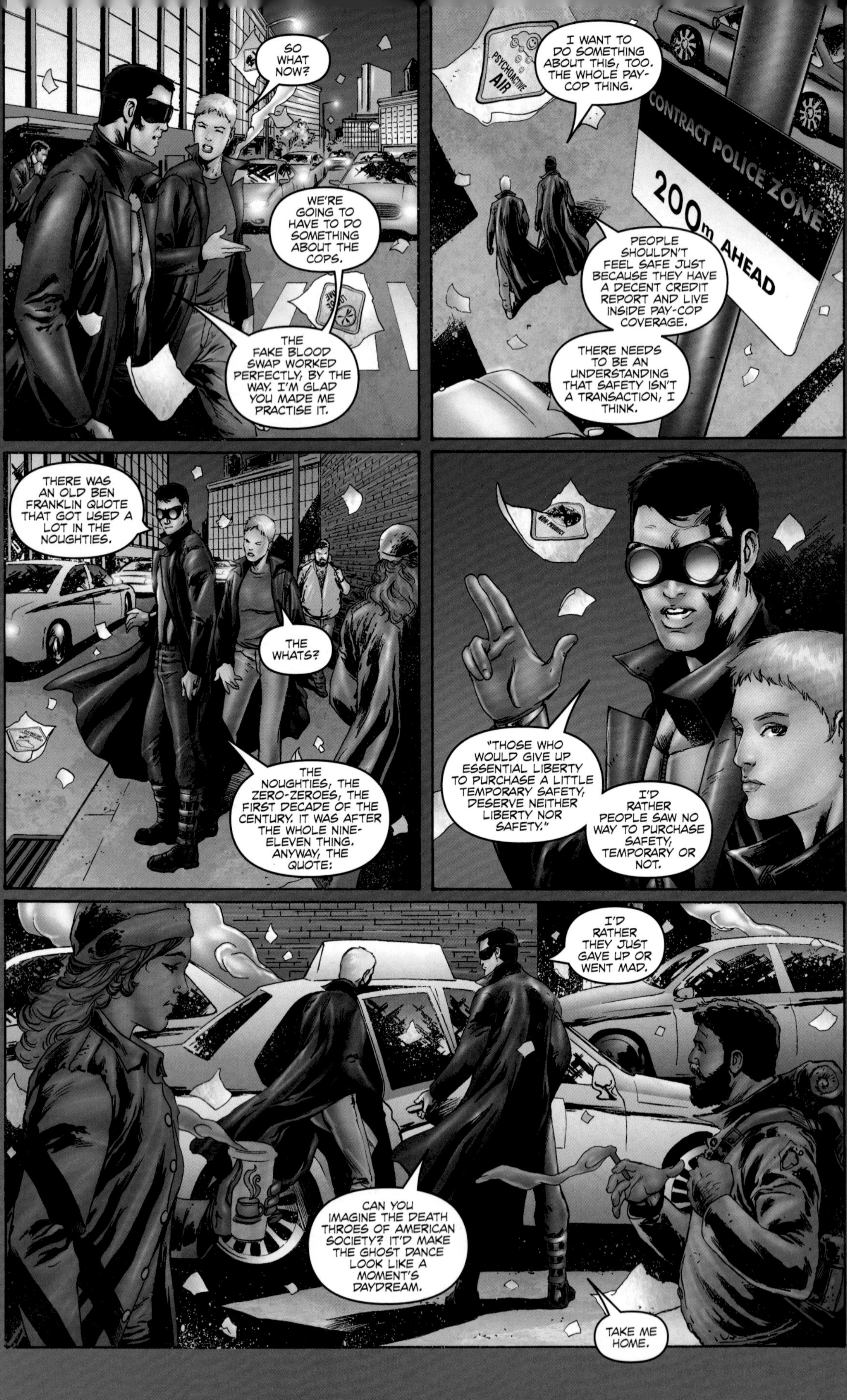
SO WHAT NOW?
WE'RE GOING TO HAVE TO DO SOMETHING ABOUT THE COPS.
THE FAKE BLOOD SWAP WORKED PERFECTLY, BY THE WAY. I'M GLAD YOU MADE ME PRACTISE IT.
PSYCHOACTIVE AIR
I WANT TO DO SOMETHING ABOUT THIS, TOO. THE WHOLE PAY-COP THING.
CONTRACT POLICE ZONE
200m AHEAD
PEOPLE SHOULDN'T FEEL SAFE JUST BECAUSE THEY HAVE A DECENT CREDIT REPORT AND LIVE INSIDE PAY-COP COVERAGE.
THERE NEEDS TO BE AN UNDERSTANDING THAT SAFETY ISN'T A TRANSACTION, I THINK.
THERE WAS AN OLD BEN FRANKLIN QUOTE THAT GOT USED A LOT IN THE NOUGHTIES.
THE WHATS?
THE NOUGHTIES, THE ZERO-ZEROES, THE FIRST DECADE OF THE CENTURY. IT WAS AFTER THE WHOLE NINE-ELEVEN THING. ANYWAY, THE QUOTE:
"THOSE WHO WOULD GIVE UP ESSENTIAL LIBERTY TO PURCHASE A LITTLE TEMPORARY SAFETY, DESERVE NEITHER LIBERTY NOR SAFETY."
I'D RATHER PEOPLE SAW NO WAY TO PURCHASE SAFETY, TEMPORARY OR NOT.
I'D RATHER THEY JUST GAVE UP OR WENT MAD.
CAN YOU IMAGINE THE DEATH THROES OF AMERICAN SOCIETY? IT'D MAKE THE GHOST DANCE LOOK LIKE A MOMENT'S DAYDREAM.
TAKE ME HOME.

PART SEVEN

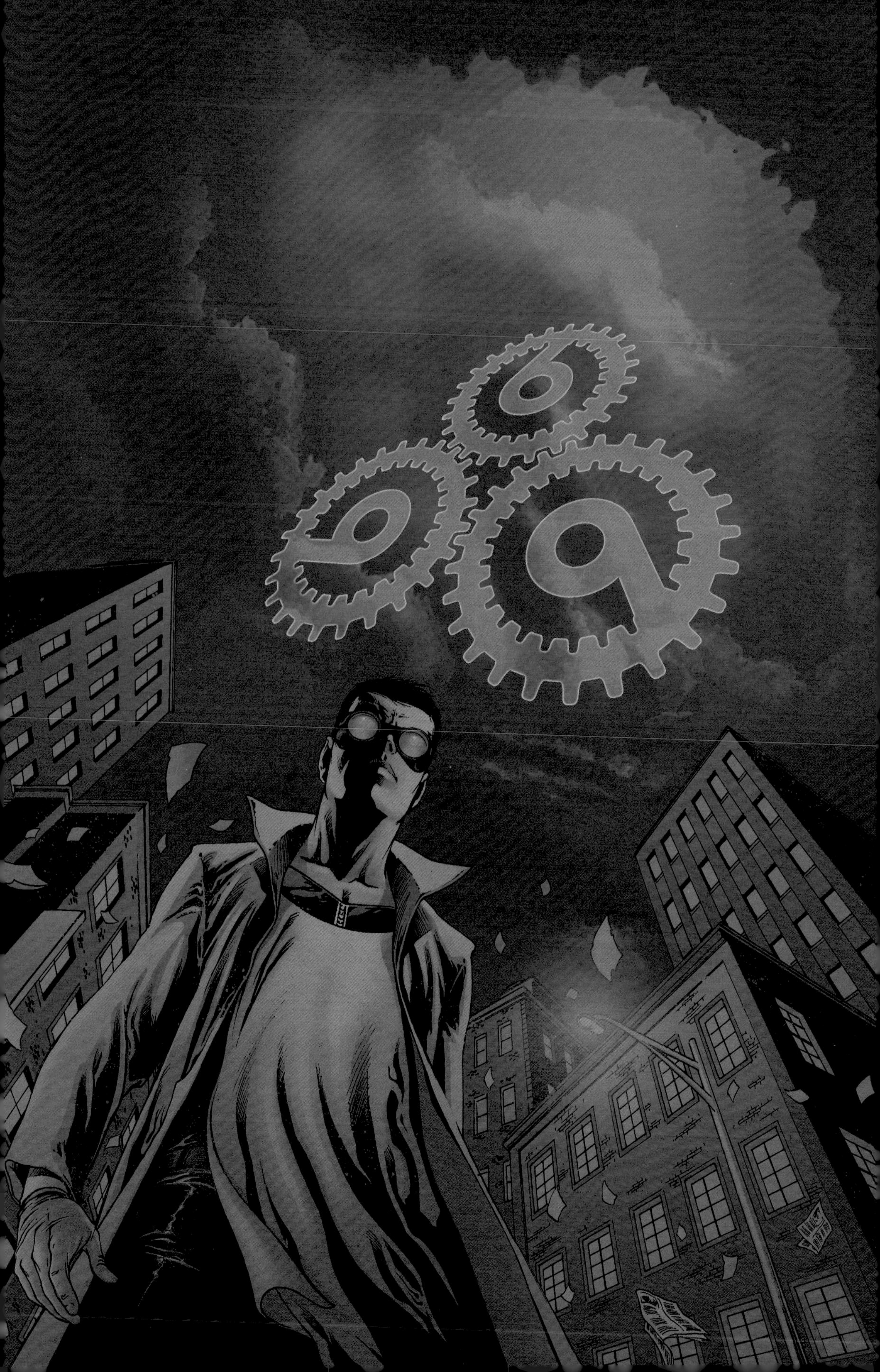

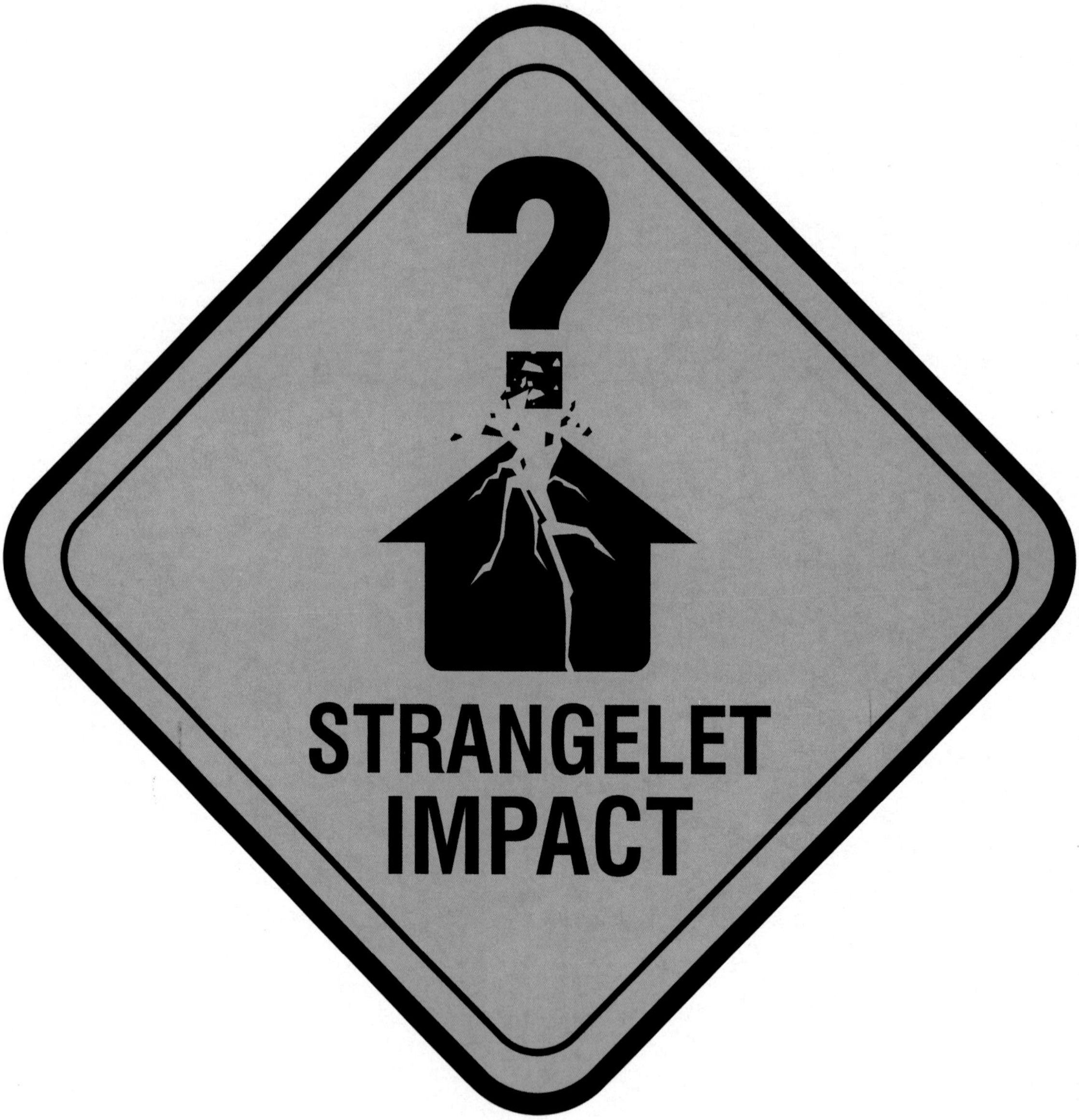
STRANGELET
IMPACT

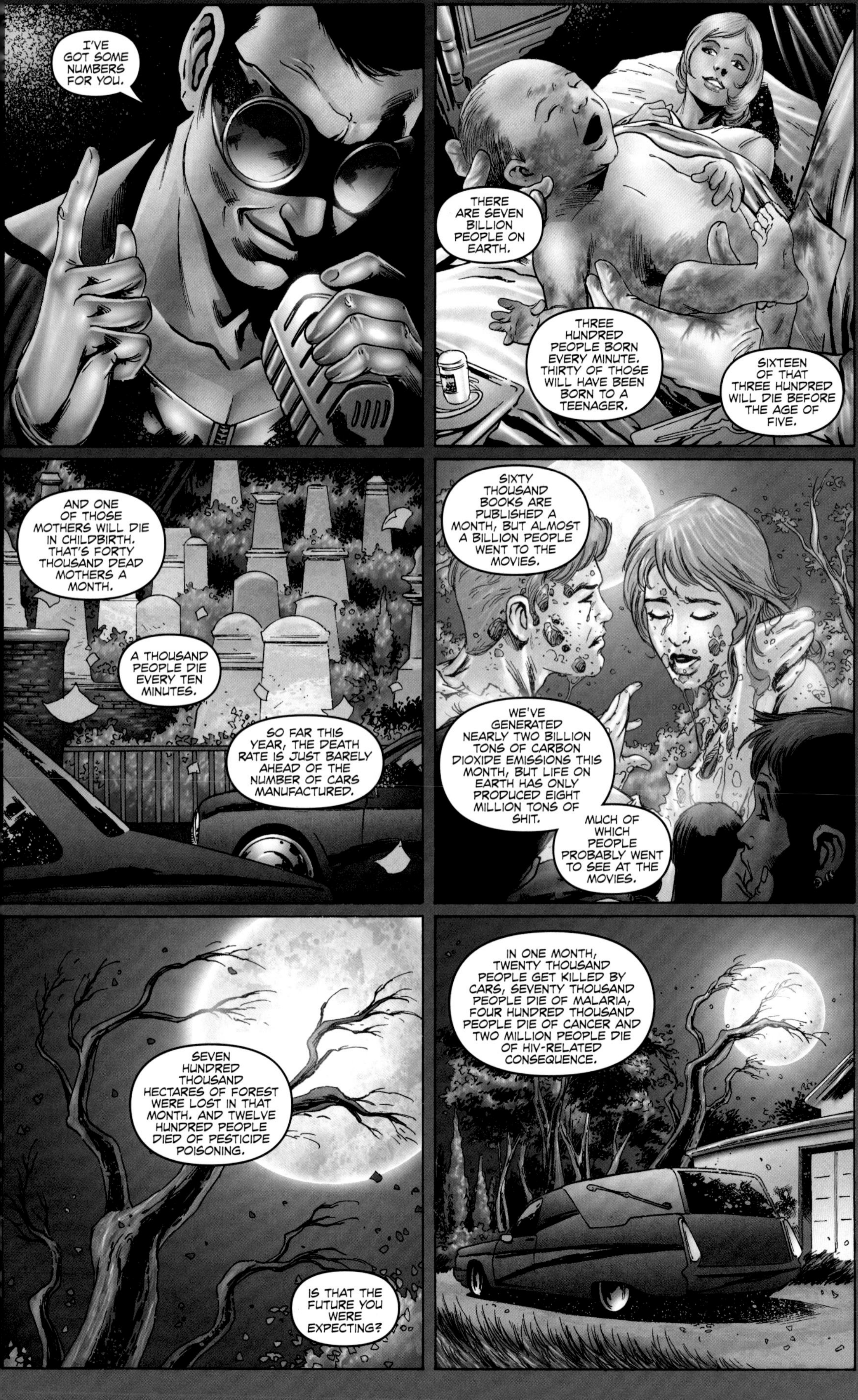
I'VE GOT SOME NUMBERS FOR YOU.
THERE ARE SEVEN BILLION PEOPLE ON EARTH.
THREE HUNDRED PEOPLE BORN EVERY MINUTE. THIRTY OF THOSE WILL HAVE BEEN BORN TO A TEENAGER.
SIXTEEN OF THAT THREE HUNDRED WILL DIE BEFORE THE AGE OF FIVE.
AND ONE OF THOSE MOTHERS WILL DIE IN CHILDBIRTH. THAT'S FORTY THOUSAND DEAD MOTHERS A MONTH.
A THOUSAND PEOPLE DIE EVERY TEN MINUTES.
SO FAR THIS YEAR, THE DEATH RATE IS JUST BARELY AHEAD OF THE NUMBER OF CARS MANUFACTURED.
SIXTY THOUSAND BOOKS ARE PUBLISHED A MONTH, BUT ALMOST A BILLION PEOPLE WENT TO THE MOVIES.
WE'VE GENERATED NEARLY TWO BILLION TONS OF CARBON DIOXIDE EMISSIONS THIS MONTH, BUT LIFE ON EARTH HAS ONLY PRODUCED EIGHT MILLION TONS OF SHIT.
MUCH OF WHICH PEOPLE PROBABLY WENT TO SEE AT THE MOVIES.
SEVEN HUNDRED THOUSAND HECTARES OF FOREST WERE LOST IN THAT MONTH. AND TWELVE HUNDRED PEOPLE DIED OF PESTICIDE POISONING.
IS THAT THE FUTURE YOU WERE EXPECTING?
IN ONE MONTH, TWENTY THOUSAND PEOPLE GET KILLED BY CARS, SEVENTY THOUSAND PEOPLE DIE OF MALARIA, FOUR HUNDRED THOUSAND PEOPLE DIE OF CANCER AND TWO MILLION PEOPLE DIE OF HIV-RELATED CONSEQUENCE.

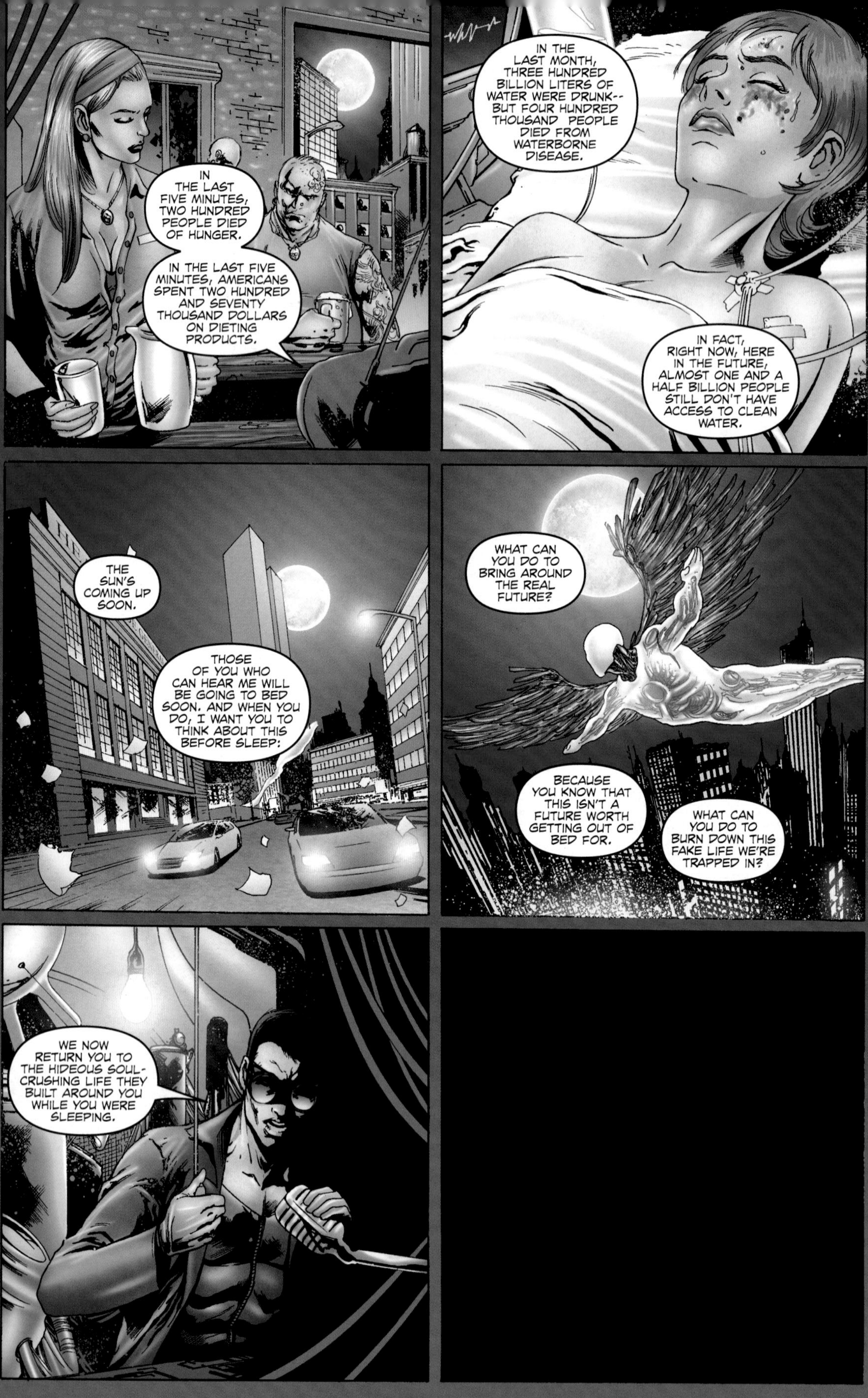
IN THE LAST FIVE MINUTES, TWO HUNDRED PEOPLE DIED OF HUNGER.
IN THE LAST FIVE MINUTES, AMERICANS SPENT TWO HUNDRED AND SEVENTY THOUSAND DOLLARS ON DIETING PRODUCTS.
IN THE LAST MONTH, THREE HUNDRED BILLION LITERS OF WATER WERE DRUNK-- BUT FOUR HUNDRED THOUSAND PEOPLE DIED FROM WATERBORNE DISEASE.
IN FACT, RIGHT NOW, HERE IN THE FUTURE, ALMOST ONE AND A HALF BILLION PEOPLE STILL DON'T HAVE ACCESS TO CLEAN WATER.
THE SUN'S COMING UP SOON.
THOSE OF YOU WHO CAN HEAR ME WILL BE GOING TO BED SOON. AND WHEN YOU DO, I WANT YOU TO THINK ABOUT THIS BEFORE SLEEP:
WHAT CAN YOU DO TO BRING AROUND THE REAL FUTURE?
BECAUSE YOU KNOW THAT THIS ISN'T A FUTURE WORTH GETTING OUT OF BED FOR.
WHAT CAN YOU DO TO BURN DOWN THIS FAKE LIFE WE'RE TRAPPED IN?
WE NOW RETURN YOU TO THE HIDEOUS SOUL-CRUSHING LIFE THEY BUILT AROUND YOU WHILE YOU WERE SLEEPING.

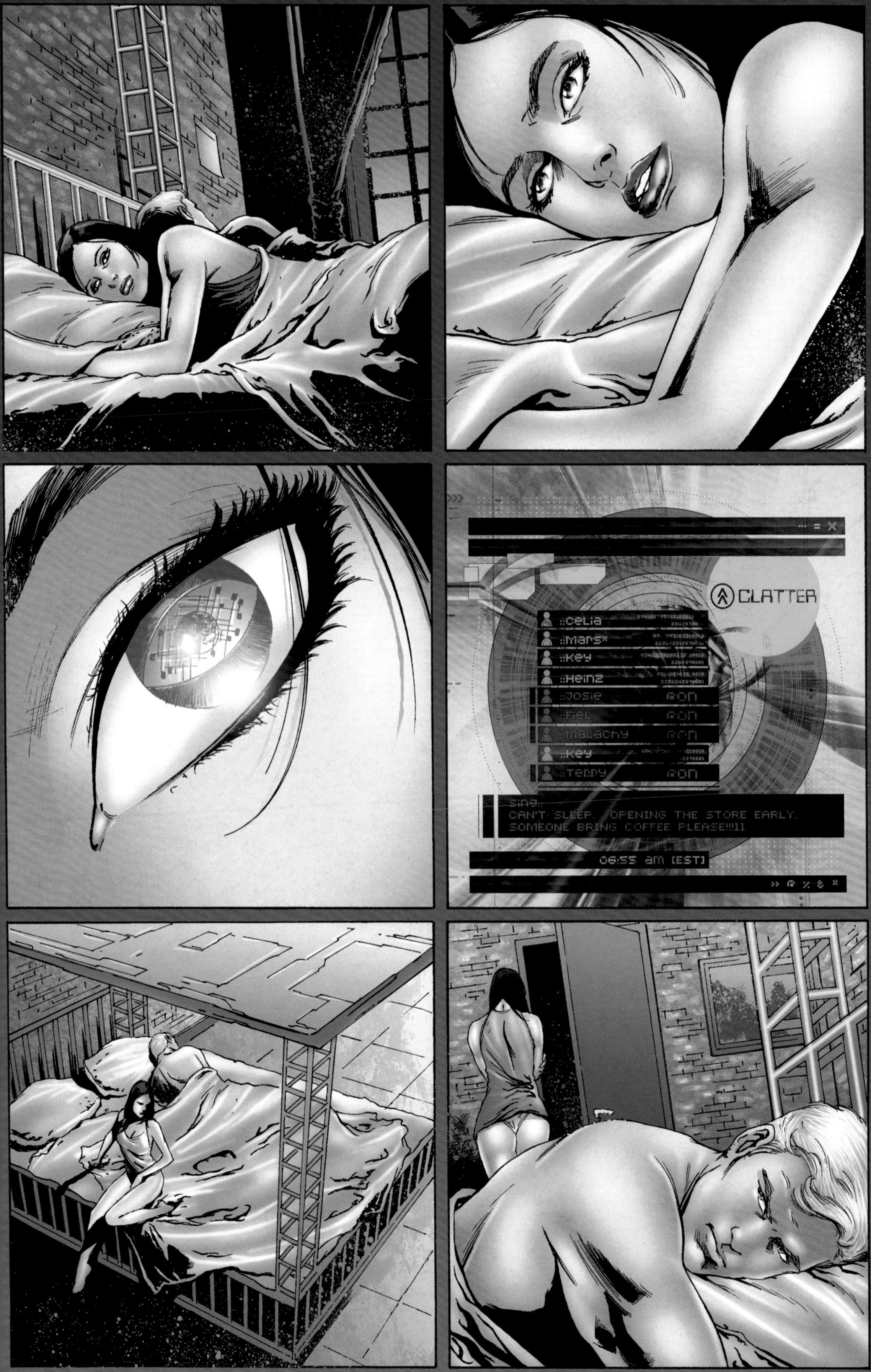
CLATTER
::Celia
::Mars*
::Key
::Heinz
::Josie on
::Fiel on
::Malachy on
::Key
::Terry on
Sing::
CAN'T SLEEP. OPENING THE STORE EARLY.
SOMEONE BRING COFFEE PLEASE!!!11
06:55 am [EST]

ESCHATON EVENT
INCOMING

LOOSE
TIME

STRANGELET
IMPACT

WAVY LINES
OV DETH

CULTURAL
FLUX

NON-PRODUCT

NO-NATURE
PARK
PLEASE ENJOY THE
LACK OF WILDLIFE

URBA...
ZO...

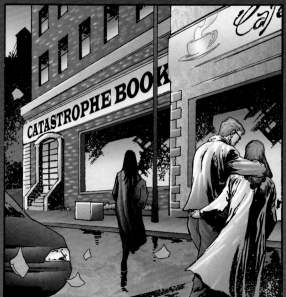

CATASTROPHE BOOK

...THE
HELL?

TOO EARLY
FOR THE
MAILMAN OR
THE PARCEL
SERVICES.

NO
ZINE KIDS
LEFT IN
TOWN.

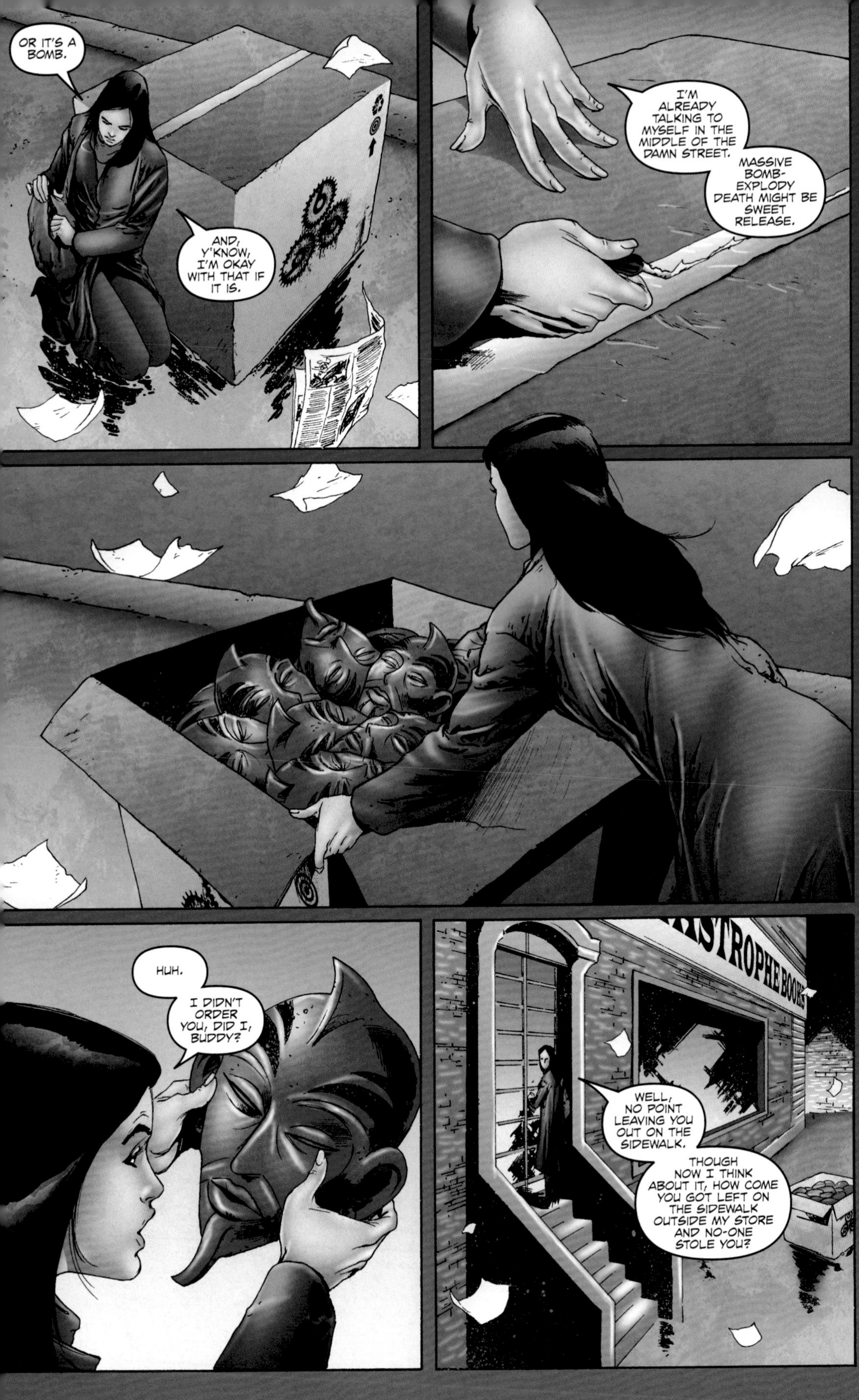
OR IT'S A BOMB.
AND, Y'KNOW, I'M OKAY WITH THAT IF IT IS.
I'M ALREADY TALKING TO MYSELF IN THE MIDDLE OF THE DAMN STREET.
MASSIVE BOMB-EXPLODY DEATH MIGHT BE SWEET RELEASE.
HUH.
I DIDN'T ORDER YOU, DID I, BUDDY?
STROPHE BOOKS
WELL, NO POINT LEAVING YOU OUT ON THE SIDEWALK.
THOUGH NOW I THINK ABOUT IT, HOW COME YOU GOT LEFT ON THE SIDEWALK OUTSIDE MY STORE AND NO-ONE STOLE YOU?

ARE ONE WEIRD GIFT HORSE.

LET'S GET YOU INSIDE; THERE'S GOT TO BE A PACKING NOTE OR SOMETHING INSIDE YOU.

THE PEOPLE IN THIS TOWN WOULDN'T GIVE AWAY A FRESH SHIT WITHOUT DEMANDING A RECEIPT.

YOU HEAR ME, YOU KIDS? I'M TAKING YOUR BOX NOW.

HUH.

SO WEIRD.

I NEVER THOUGHT I'D START DREADING SURPRISE DELIVERIES FROM NOWHERE...

...JESUS, HOW MANY OF THESE THINGS ARE IN HERE?

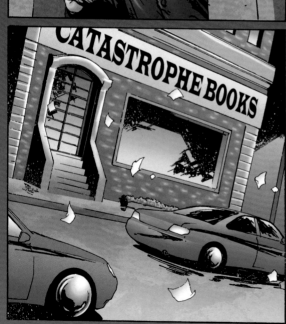

CATASTROPHE BOOKS

CATASTROPHE BOOKS

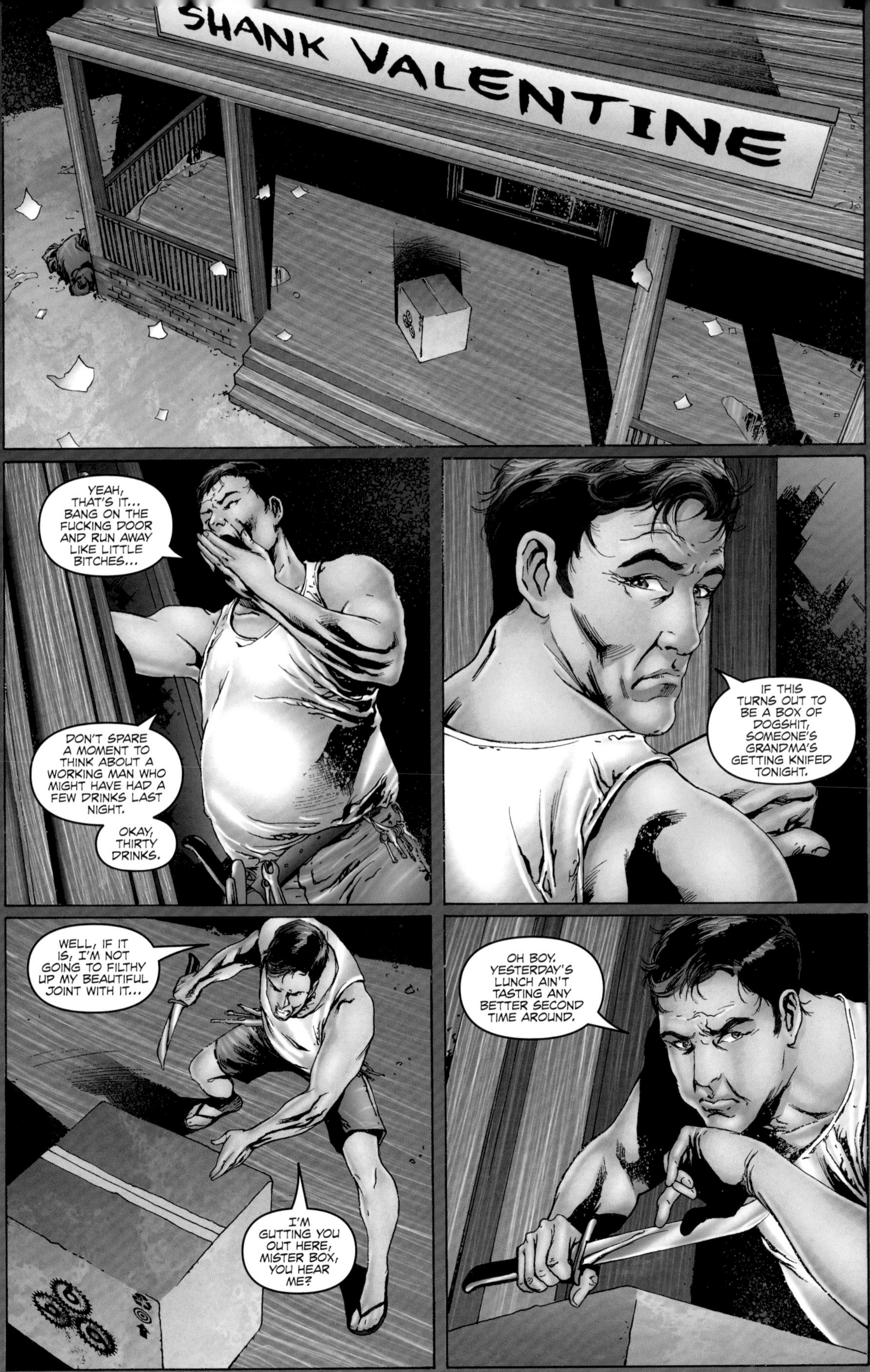
SHANK VALENTINE
YEAH, THAT'S IT... BANG ON THE FUCKING DOOR AND RUN AWAY LIKE LITTLE BITCHES...
DON'T SPARE A MOMENT TO THINK ABOUT A WORKING MAN WHO MIGHT HAVE HAD A FEW DRINKS LAST NIGHT.
OKAY, THIRTY DRINKS.
IF THIS TURNS OUT TO BE A BOX OF DOGSHIT, SOMEONE'S GRANDMA'S GETTING KNIFED TONIGHT.
WELL, IF IT IS, I'M NOT GOING TO FILTHY UP MY BEAUTIFUL JOINT WITH IT...
I'M GUTTING YOU OUT HERE, MISTER BOX, YOU HEAR ME?
OH BOY. YESTERDAY'S LUNCH AIN'T TASTING ANY BETTER SECOND TIME AROUND.

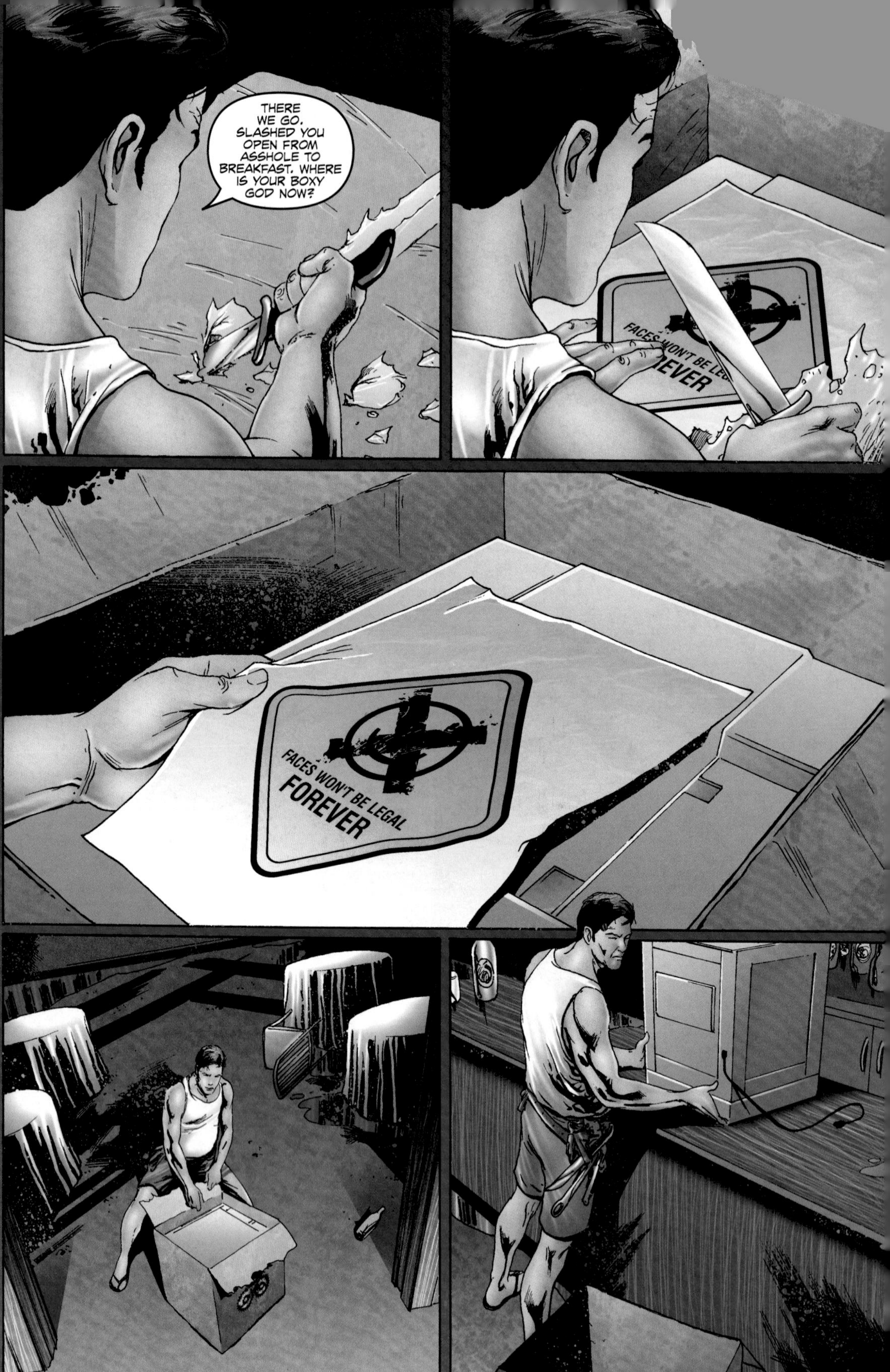
THERE WE GO. SLASHED YOU OPEN FROM ASSHOLE TO BREAKFAST. WHERE IS YOUR BOXY GOD NOW?
FACES WON'T BE LEGAL FOREVER
FACES WON'T BE LEGAL FOREVER

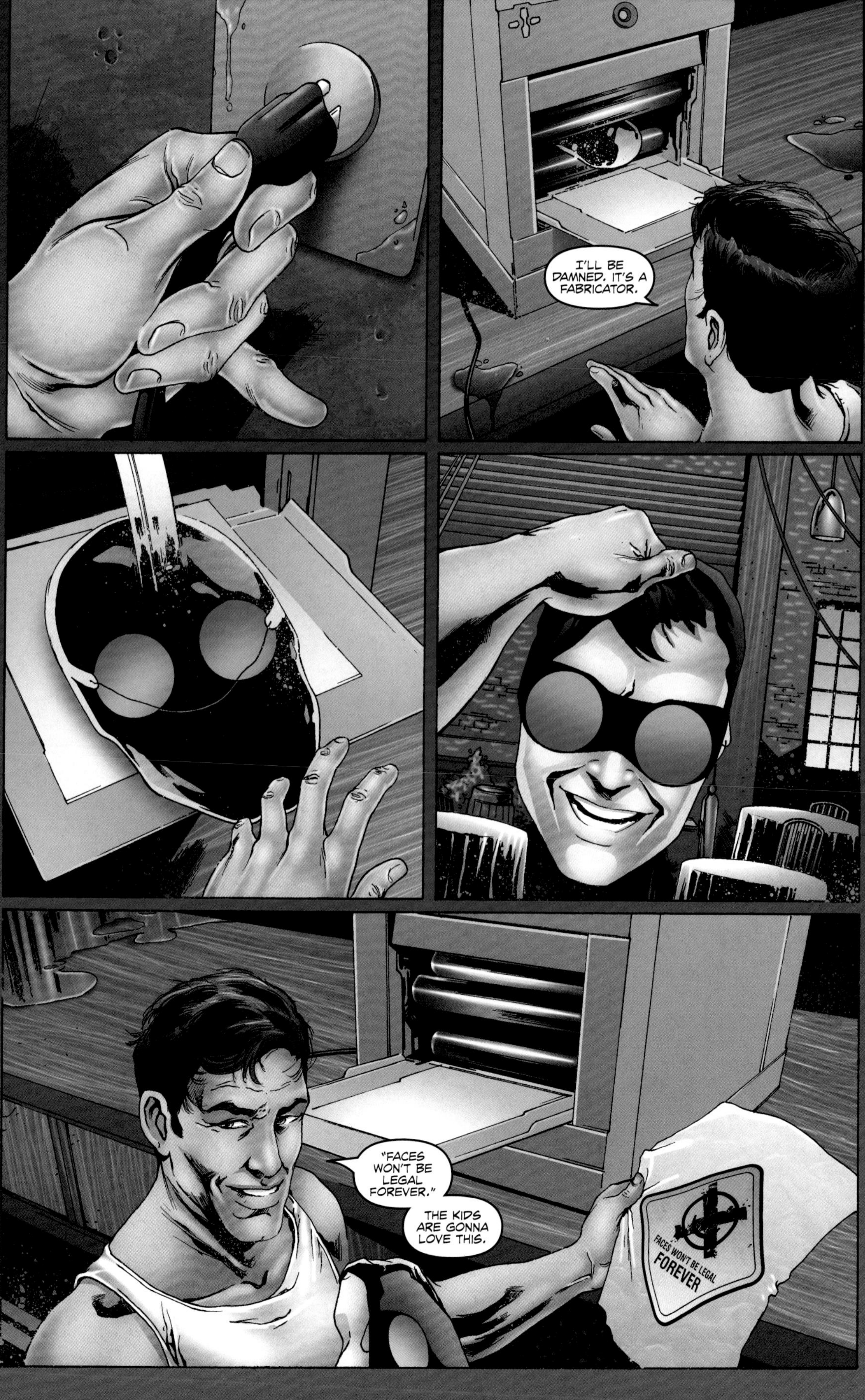
I'LL BE DAMNED. IT'S A FABRICATOR.
"FACES WON'T BE LEGAL FOREVER."
THE KIDS ARE GONNA LOVE THIS.
FACES WON'T BE LEGAL FOREVER

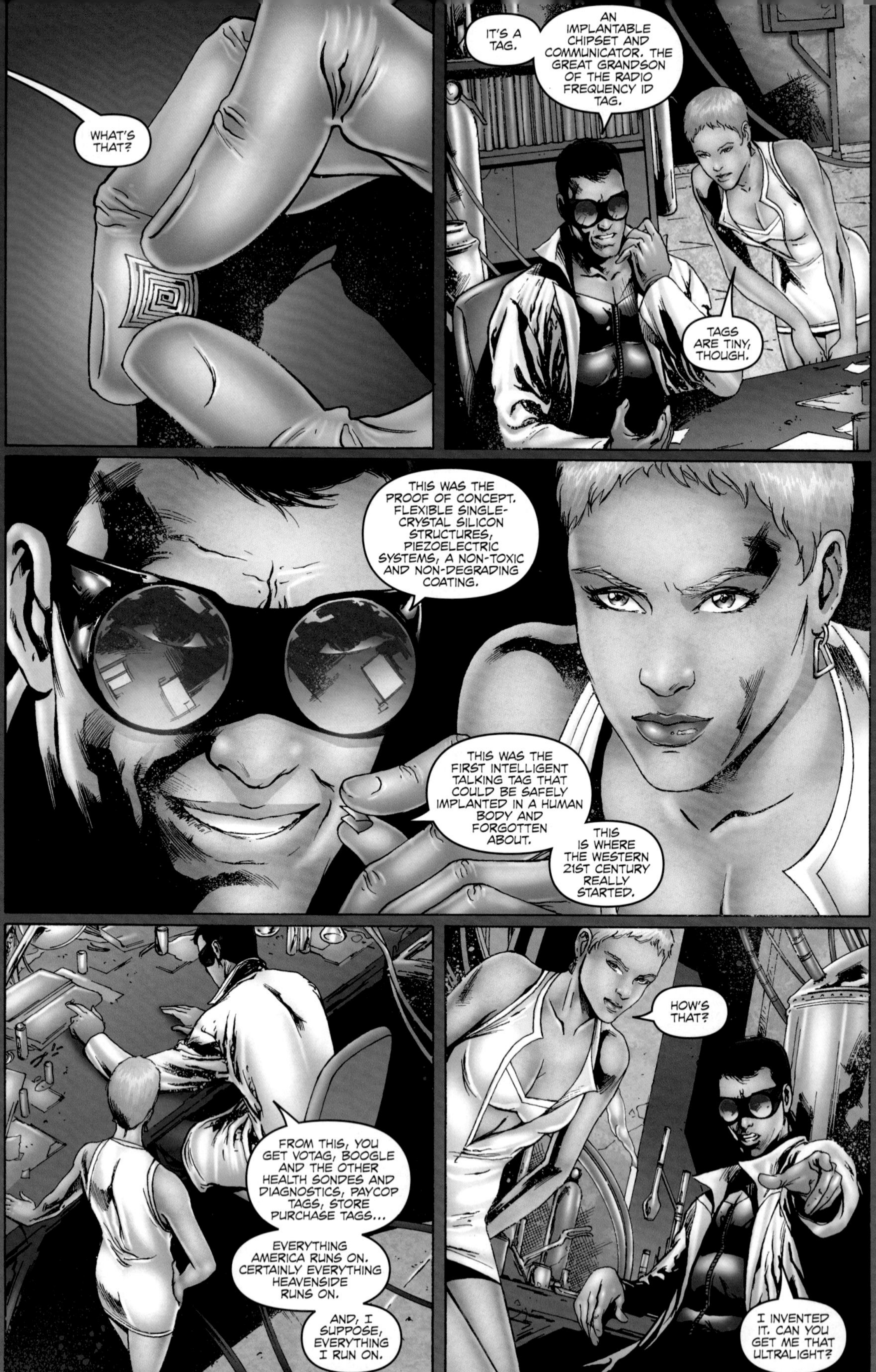
WHAT'S THAT?
IT'S A TAG.
AN IMPLANTABLE CHIPSET AND COMMUNICATOR. THE GREAT GRANDSON OF THE RADIO FREQUENCY ID TAG.
TAGS ARE TINY, THOUGH.
THIS WAS THE PROOF OF CONCEPT. FLEXIBLE SINGLE-CRYSTAL SILICON STRUCTURES, PIEZOELECTRIC SYSTEMS, A NON-TOXIC AND NON-DEGRADING COATING.
THIS WAS THE FIRST INTELLIGENT TALKING TAG THAT COULD BE SAFELY IMPLANTED IN A HUMAN BODY AND FORGOTTEN ABOUT.
THIS IS WHERE THE WESTERN 21ST CENTURY REALLY STARTED.
FROM THIS, YOU GET VOTAG, BOOGLE AND THE OTHER HEALTH SONDES AND DIAGNOSTICS, PAYCOP TAGS, STORE PURCHASE TAGS...
EVERYTHING AMERICA RUNS ON. CERTAINLY EVERYTHING HEAVENSIDE RUNS ON.
AND, I SUPPOSE, EVERYTHING I RUN ON.
HOW'S THAT?
I INVENTED IT. CAN YOU GET ME THAT ULTRALIGHT?

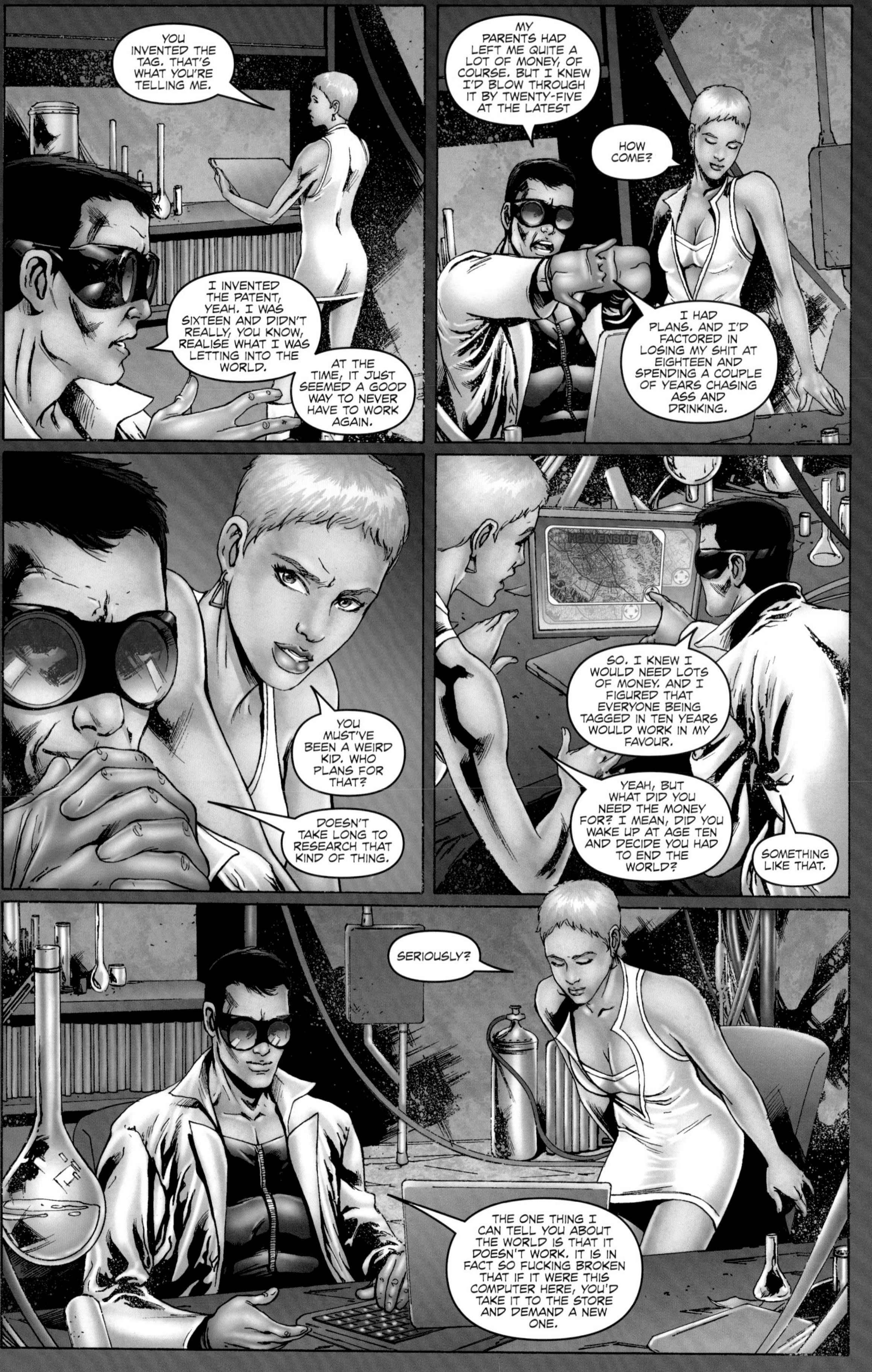
YOU INVENTED THE TAG. THAT'S WHAT YOU'RE TELLING ME.
I INVENTED THE PATENT, YEAH. I WAS SIXTEEN AND DIDN'T REALLY, YOU KNOW, REALISE WHAT I WAS LETTING INTO THE WORLD.
AT THE TIME, IT JUST SEEMED A GOOD WAY TO NEVER HAVE TO WORK AGAIN.
MY PARENTS HAD LEFT ME QUITE A LOT OF MONEY, OF COURSE. BUT I KNEW I'D BLOW THROUGH IT BY TWENTY-FIVE AT THE LATEST
HOW COME?
I HAD PLANS. AND I'D FACTORED IN LOSING MY SHIT AT EIGHTEEN AND SPENDING A COUPLE OF YEARS CHASING ASS AND DRINKING.
YOU MUST'VE BEEN A WEIRD KID. WHO PLANS FOR THAT?
DOESN'T TAKE LONG TO RESEARCH THAT KIND OF THING.
HEAVENSIDE
SO. I KNEW I WOULD NEED LOTS OF MONEY. AND I FIGURED THAT EVERYONE BEING TAGGED IN TEN YEARS WOULD WORK IN MY FAVOUR.
YEAH, BUT WHAT DID YOU NEED THE MONEY FOR? I MEAN, DID YOU WAKE UP AT AGE TEN AND DECIDE YOU HAD TO END THE WORLD?
SOMETHING LIKE THAT.
SERIOUSLY?
THE ONE THING I CAN TELL YOU ABOUT THE WORLD IS THAT IT DOESN'T WORK. IT IS IN FACT SO FUCKING BROKEN THAT IF IT WERE THIS COMPUTER HERE, YOU'D TAKE IT TO THE STORE AND DEMAND A NEW ONE.

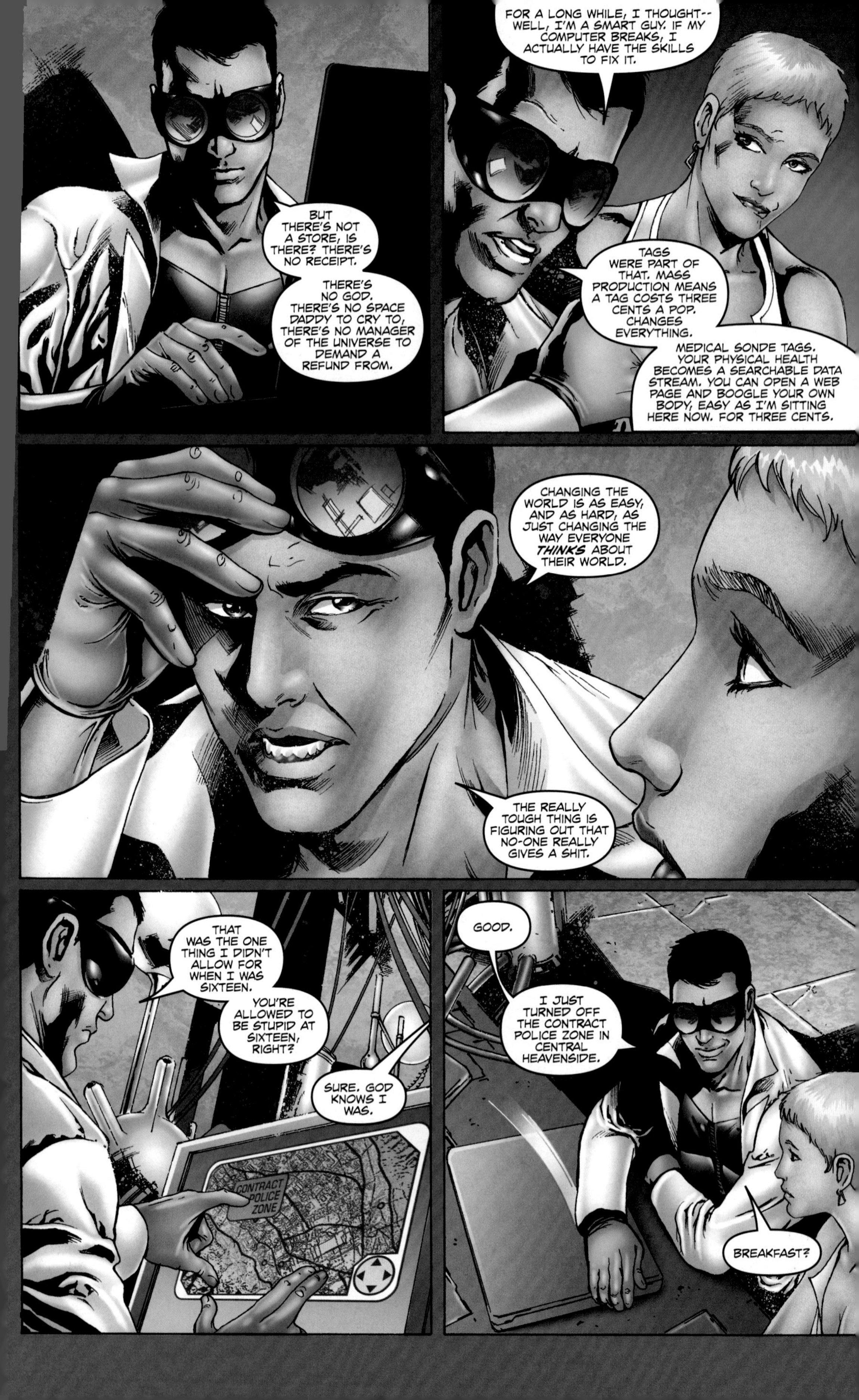
BUT THERE'S NOT A STORE, IS THERE? THERE'S NO RECEIPT.
THERE'S NO GOD. THERE'S NO SPACE DADDY TO CRY TO, THERE'S NO MANAGER OF THE UNIVERSE TO DEMAND A REFUND FROM.
FOR A LONG WHILE, I THOUGHT-- WELL, I'M A SMART GUY. IF MY COMPUTER BREAKS, I ACTUALLY HAVE THE SKILLS TO FIX IT.
TAGS WERE PART OF THAT. MASS PRODUCTION MEANS A TAG COSTS THREE CENTS A POP. CHANGES EVERYTHING.
MEDICAL SONDE TAGS. YOUR PHYSICAL HEALTH BECOMES A SEARCHABLE DATA STREAM. YOU CAN OPEN A WEB PAGE AND BOOGLE YOUR OWN BODY, EASY AS I'M SITTING HERE NOW. FOR THREE CENTS.
CHANGING THE WORLD IS AS EASY, AND AS HARD, AS JUST CHANGING THE WAY EVERYONE *THINKS* ABOUT THEIR WORLD.
THE REALLY TOUGH THING IS FIGURING OUT THAT NO-ONE REALLY GIVES A SHIT.
THAT WAS THE ONE THING I DIDN'T ALLOW FOR WHEN I WAS SIXTEEN.
YOU'RE ALLOWED TO BE STUPID AT SIXTEEN, RIGHT?
SURE. GOD KNOWS I WAS.
CONTRACT POLICE ZONE
GOOD.
I JUST TURNED OFF THE CONTRACT POLICE ZONE IN CENTRAL HEAVENSIDE.
BREAKFAST?

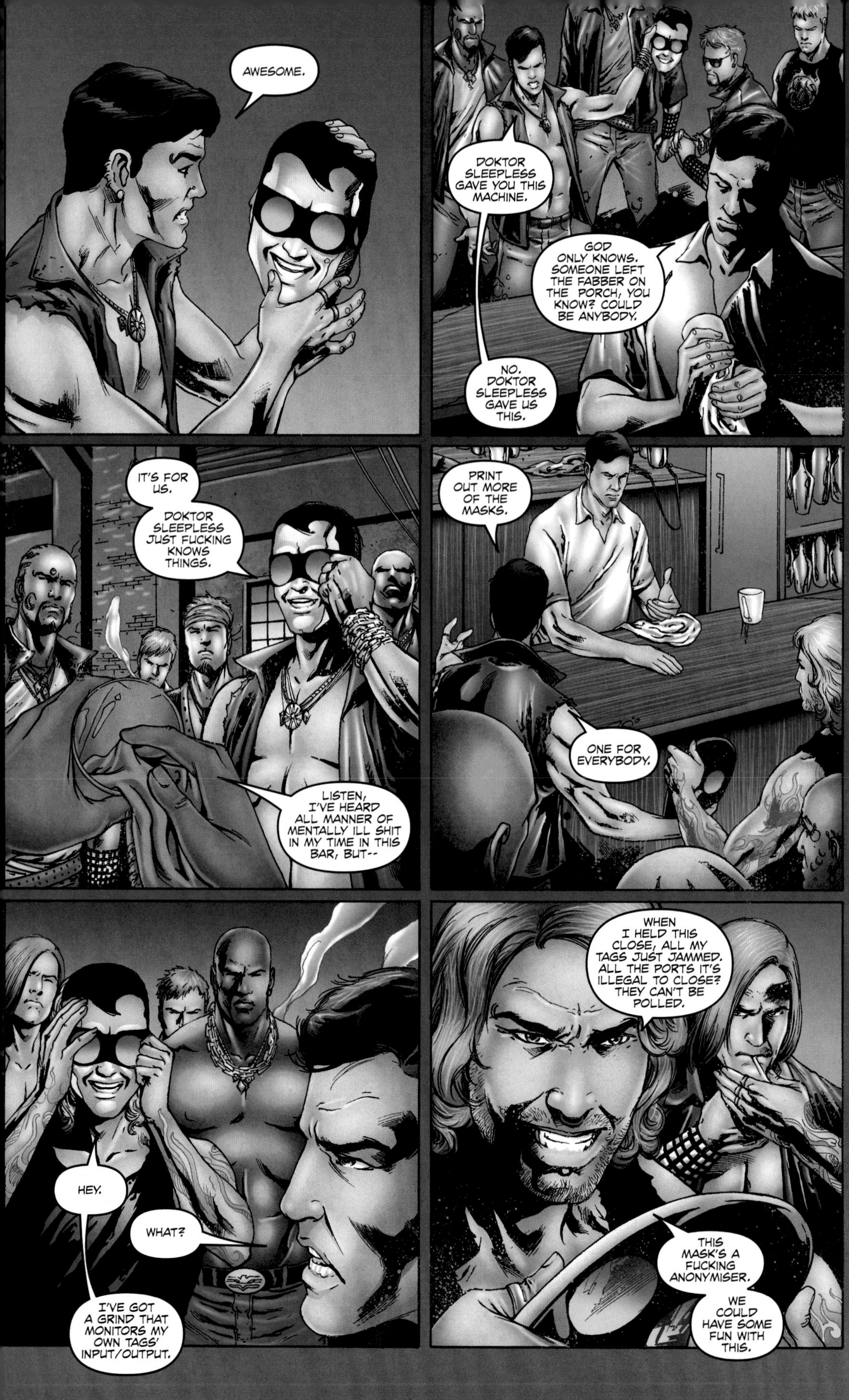
AWESOME.
DOKTOR SLEEPLESS GAVE YOU THIS MACHINE.
GOD ONLY KNOWS. SOMEONE LEFT THE FABBER ON THE PORCH, YOU KNOW? COULD BE ANYBODY.
NO. DOKTOR SLEEPLESS GAVE US THIS.
IT'S FOR US.
DOKTOR SLEEPLESS JUST FUCKING KNOWS THINGS.
LISTEN, I'VE HEARD ALL MANNER OF MENTALLY ILL SHIT IN MY TIME IN THIS BAR, BUT--
PRINT OUT MORE OF THE MASKS.
ONE FOR EVERYBODY.
HEY.
WHAT?
I'VE GOT A GRIND THAT MONITORS MY OWN TAGS' INPUT/OUTPUT.
WHEN I HELD THIS CLOSE, ALL MY TAGS JUST JAMMED. ALL THE PORTS IT'S ILLEGAL TO CLOSE? THEY CAN'T BE POLLED.
THIS MASK'S A FUCKING ANONYMISER.
WE COULD HAVE SOME FUN WITH THIS.

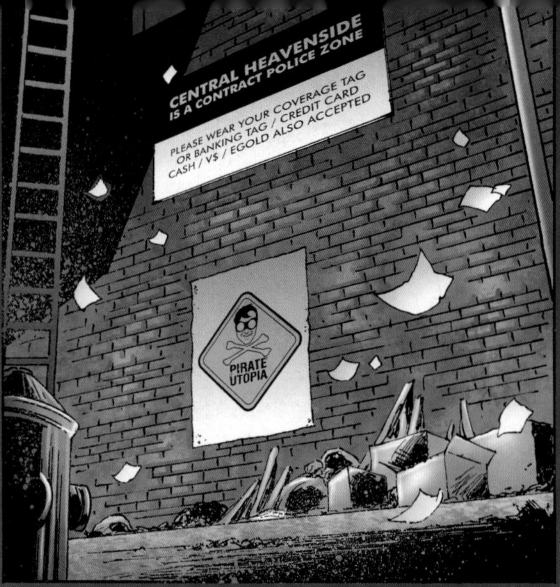
CENTRAL HEAVENSIDE
IS A CONTRACT POLICE ZONE
PLEASE WEAR YOUR COVERAGE TAG
OR BANKING TAG / CREDIT CARD
CASH / V$ / EGOLD ALSO ACCEPTED
PIRATE UTOPIA

Getting the Temporary Autonomous Zone started may involve tactics of violence and defense, but its greatest strength lies in its invisibility—the State cannot recognize it because history has no definition of it.

—Hakim Bey

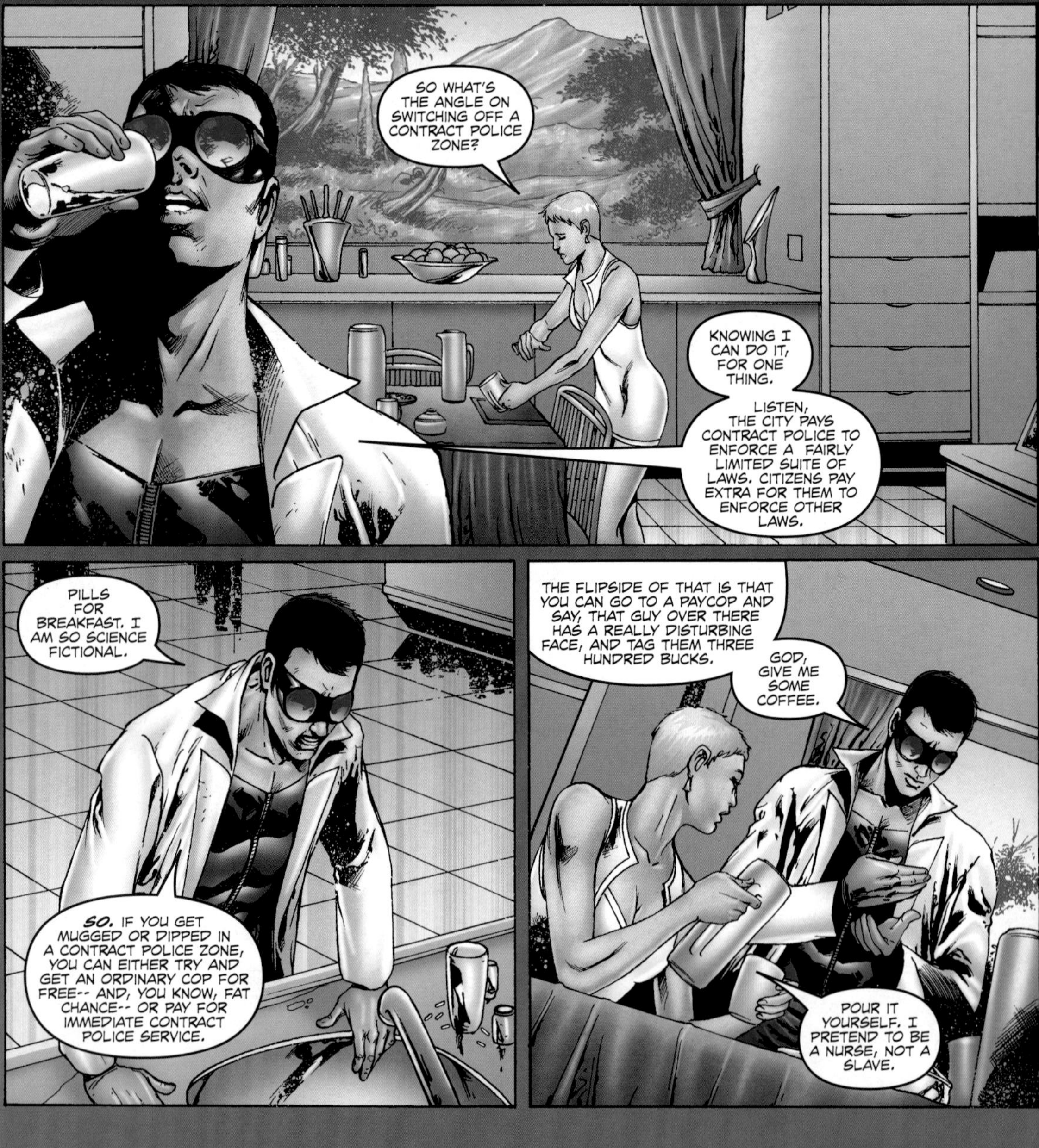
SO WHAT'S THE ANGLE ON SWITCHING OFF A CONTRACT POLICE ZONE?
KNOWING I CAN DO IT, FOR ONE THING.
LISTEN, THE CITY PAYS CONTRACT POLICE TO ENFORCE A FAIRLY LIMITED SUITE OF LAWS. CITIZENS PAY EXTRA FOR THEM TO ENFORCE OTHER LAWS.
PILLS FOR BREAKFAST. I AM SO SCIENCE FICTIONAL.
SO. IF YOU GET MUGGED OR DIPPED IN A CONTRACT POLICE ZONE, YOU CAN EITHER TRY AND GET AN ORDINARY COP FOR FREE-- AND, YOU KNOW, FAT CHANCE-- OR PAY FOR IMMEDIATE CONTRACT POLICE SERVICE.
THE FLIPSIDE OF THAT IS THAT YOU CAN GO TO A PAYCOP AND SAY, THAT GUY OVER THERE HAS A REALLY DISTURBING FACE, AND TAG THEM THREE HUNDRED BUCKS.
GOD, GIVE ME SOME COFFEE.
POUR IT YOURSELF. I PRETEND TO BE A NURSE, NOT A SLAVE.

THE PAYCOPS WILL BEAT THE LIVING SHIT OUT OF THE GUY AND FILE IT AS CAUSING A DISTURBANCE/RESISTING ARREST.

OH, FUCK THIS.

YOU'RE GETTING IT EVERYWHERE, JESUS CHRIST--

SEE? SCIENCE FICTION IS BAD FOR YOU.

NOT EATING OR SLEEPING IS BAD FOR YOU.

OH, SO *NOW* YOU'RE A REAL NURSE?

ANYWAY: YOU'LL NEVER SEE A GRINDER KID IN CENTRAL HEAVENSIDE BECAUSE A BUNCH OF STOREOWNERS PAY A WEEKLY FEE TO HAVE THE PAYCOPS BOUNCE THEM.

AND, OF COURSE, TAKE PHOTOS AND POLL THEIR TAGS FOR ID.

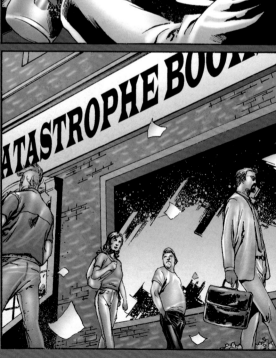

ATASTROPHE BOO

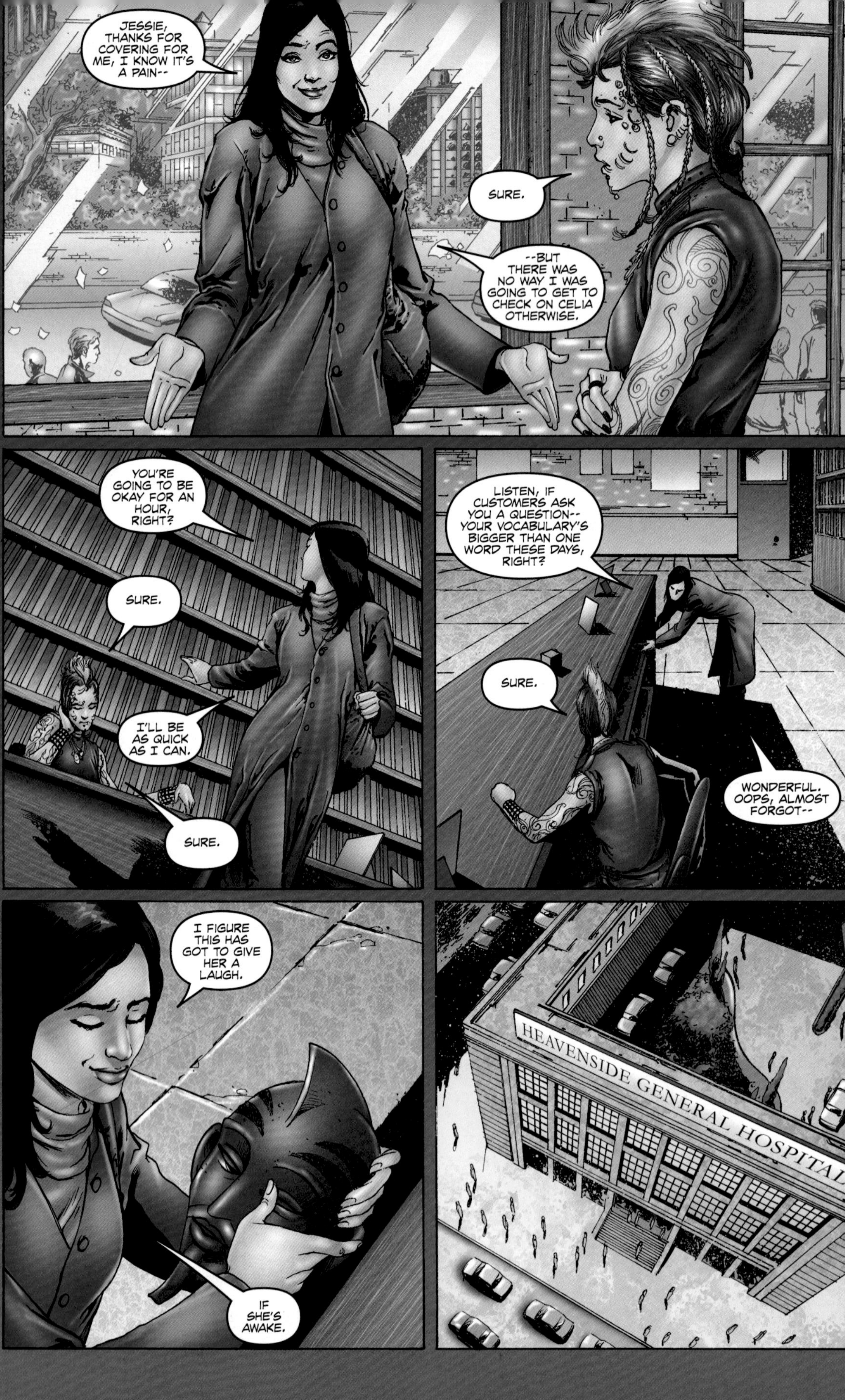
JESSIE, THANKS FOR COVERING FOR ME, I KNOW IT'S A PAIN--
SURE.
--BUT THERE WAS NO WAY I WAS GOING TO GET TO CHECK ON CELIA OTHERWISE.
YOU'RE GOING TO BE OKAY FOR AN HOUR, RIGHT?
SURE.
I'LL BE AS QUICK AS I CAN.
SURE.
LISTEN, IF CUSTOMERS ASK YOU A QUESTION-- YOUR VOCABULARY'S BIGGER THAN ONE WORD THESE DAYS, RIGHT?
SURE.
WONDERFUL. OOPS, ALMOST FORGOT--
I FIGURE THIS HAS GOT TO GIVE HER A LAUGH.
IF SHE'S AWAKE.
HEAVENSIDE GENERAL HOSPITAL

MS
WATSON?
YOU CAN SEE
CELIA NOW.

SHE'S
MUCH
IMPROVED
FROM
YESTERDAY,
BUT--

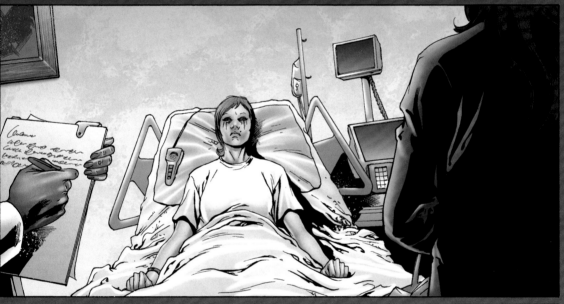

WHAT
HAPPENED?

THEY
DON'T
KNOW.

IS IT...
DOES IT
HURT?

NO.

AND THEY DON'T
KNOW IF IT'S
PERMANENT.

ONE OR TWO
DOCTORS GAVE
ME THEORIES THIS
MORNING. BUT
NOBODY KNOWS
ANYTHING.

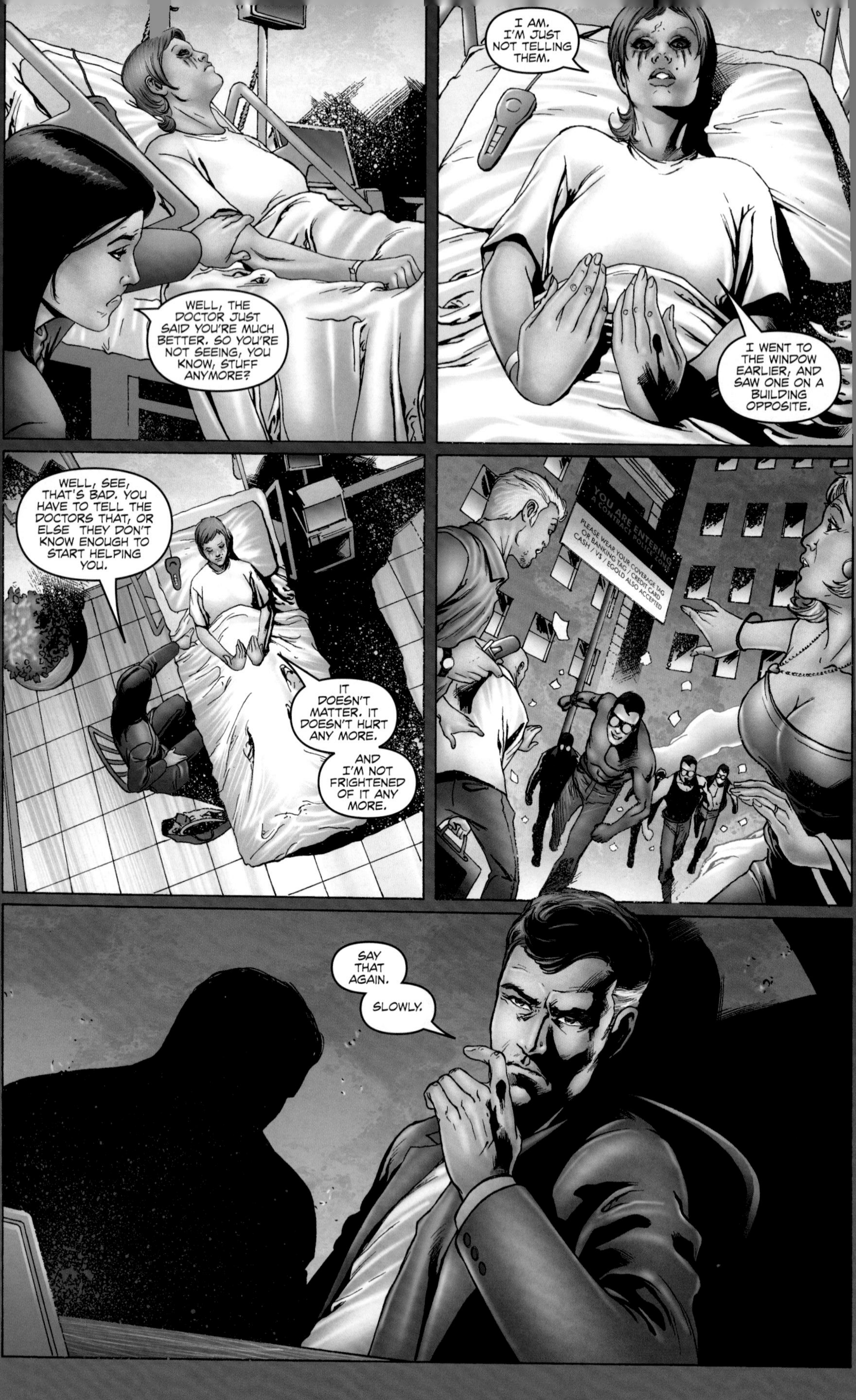
WELL, THE DOCTOR JUST SAID YOU'RE MUCH BETTER. SO YOU'RE NOT SEEING, YOU KNOW, STUFF ANYMORE?
I AM. I'M JUST NOT TELLING THEM.
I WENT TO THE WINDOW EARLIER, AND SAW ONE ON A BUILDING OPPOSITE.
WELL, SEE, THAT'S BAD. YOU HAVE TO TELL THE DOCTORS THAT, OR ELSE THEY DON'T KNOW ENOUGH TO START HELPING YOU.
IT DOESN'T MATTER. IT DOESN'T HURT ANY MORE.
AND I'M NOT FRIGHTENED OF IT ANY MORE.
YOU ARE ENTERING
A CONTRACT POLICE ZONE
PLEASE WEAR YOUR COVERAGE TAG
OR BANKING TAG / CREDIT CARD
CASH / VS / EGOLD ALSO ACCEPTED
SAY THAT AGAIN.
SLOWLY.

WE JUST GOT THE BLOODWORK BACK.

I DON'T KNOW WHO THAT IS, LIVING IN THAT HOUSE ON THE HILL.

BUT HE DOESN'T HAVE JOHN REINHARDT'S DNA.

I BROUGHT SOMETHING I WAS GOING TO SHOW YOU. I THOUGHT...

YOU KNOW HOW THE ZINE KIDS AND THE CRAFT KIDS JUST LEAVE STUFF ON THE DOORSTEP FOR US TO TRY AND SELL OR GIVE AWAY?

WELL, IT SEEMED FUNNY THIS MORNING, BUT...

IT DOESN'T SEEM SO FUNNY NOW.

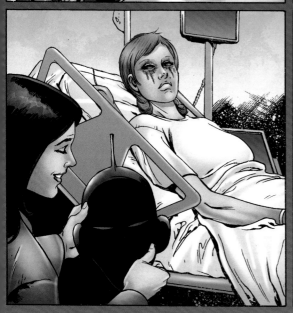

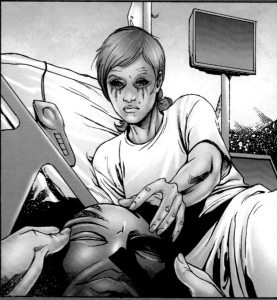

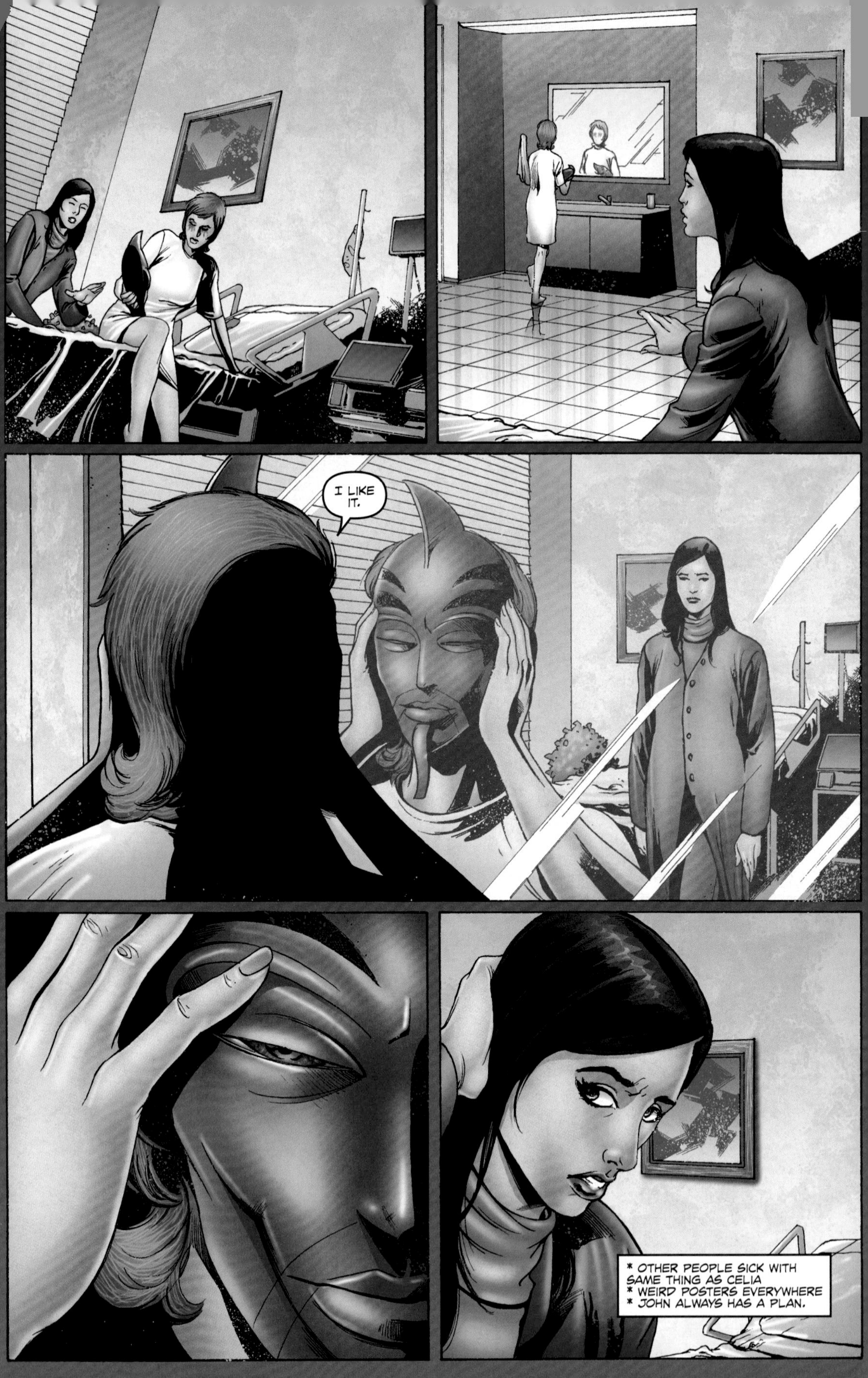
I LIKE IT.
* OTHER PEOPLE SICK WITH SAME THING AS CELIA
* WEIRD POSTERS EVERYWHERE
* JOHN ALWAYS HAS A PLAN.

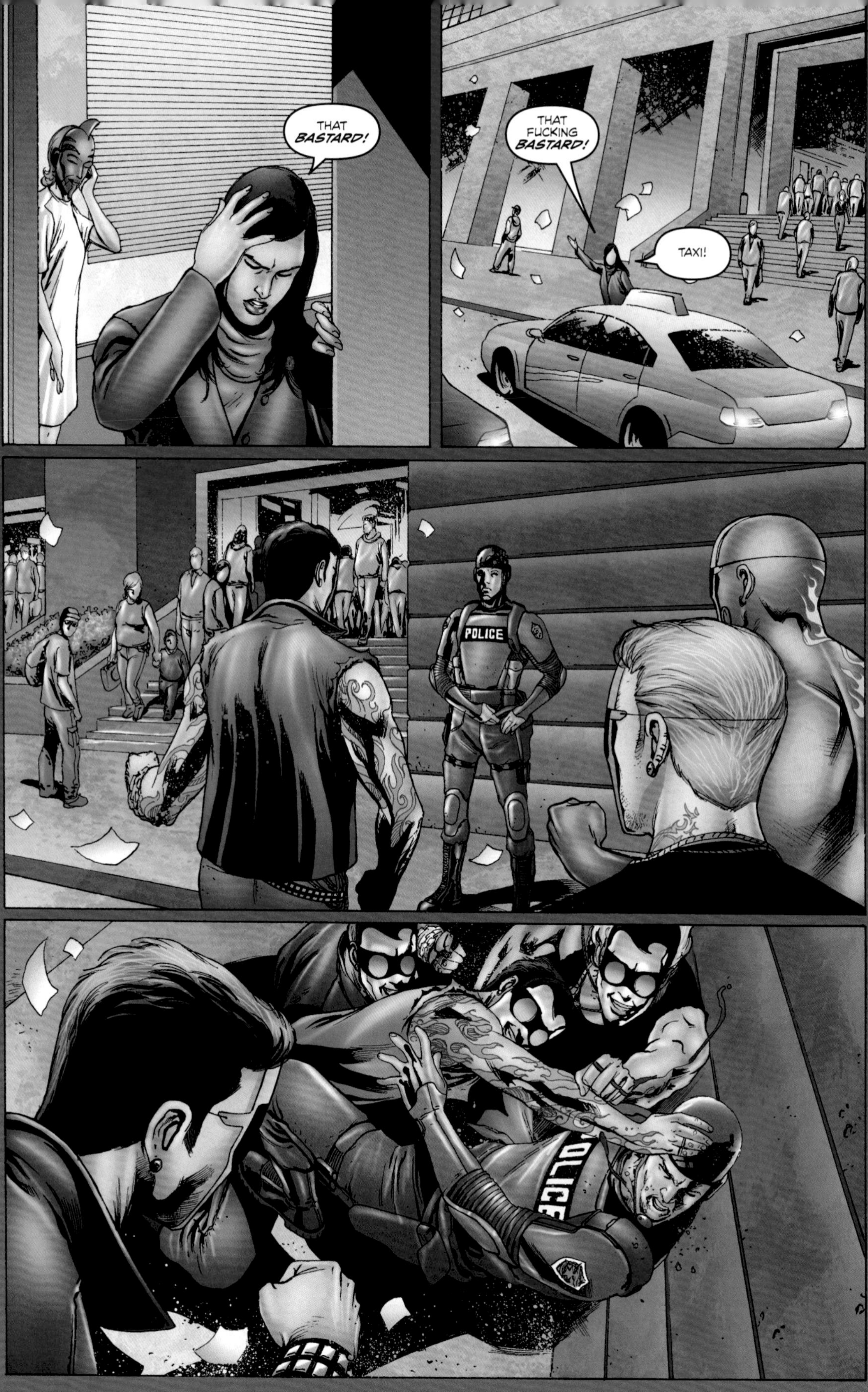
THAT BASTARD!
THAT FUCKING BASTARD!
TAXI!
POLICE
POLICE

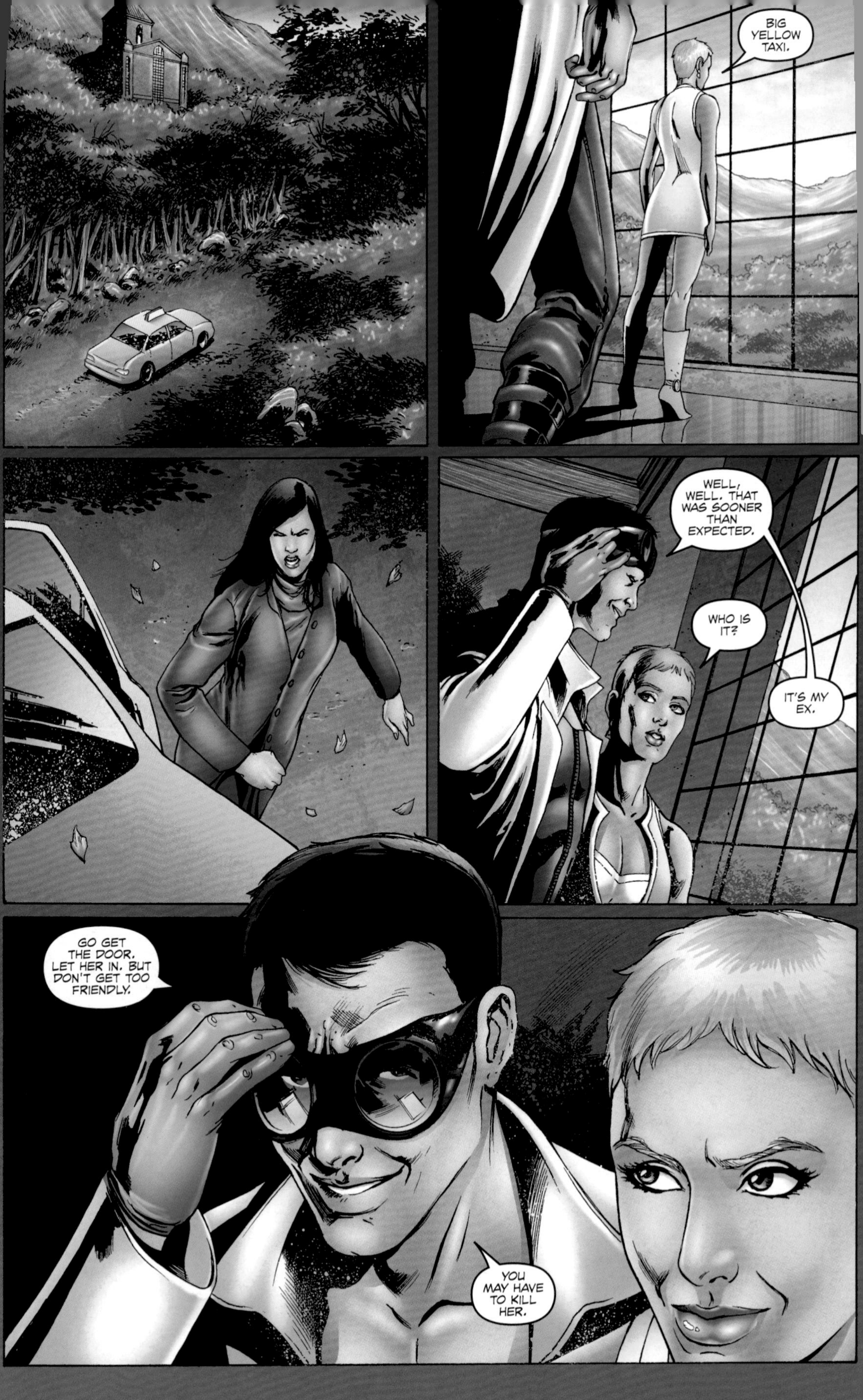
BIG YELLOW TAXI.
WELL, WELL. THAT WAS SOONER THAN EXPECTED.
WHO IS IT?
IT'S MY EX.
GO GET THE DOOR. LET HER IN. BUT DON'T GET TOO FRIENDLY.
YOU MAY HAVE TO KILL HER.

PART EIGHT

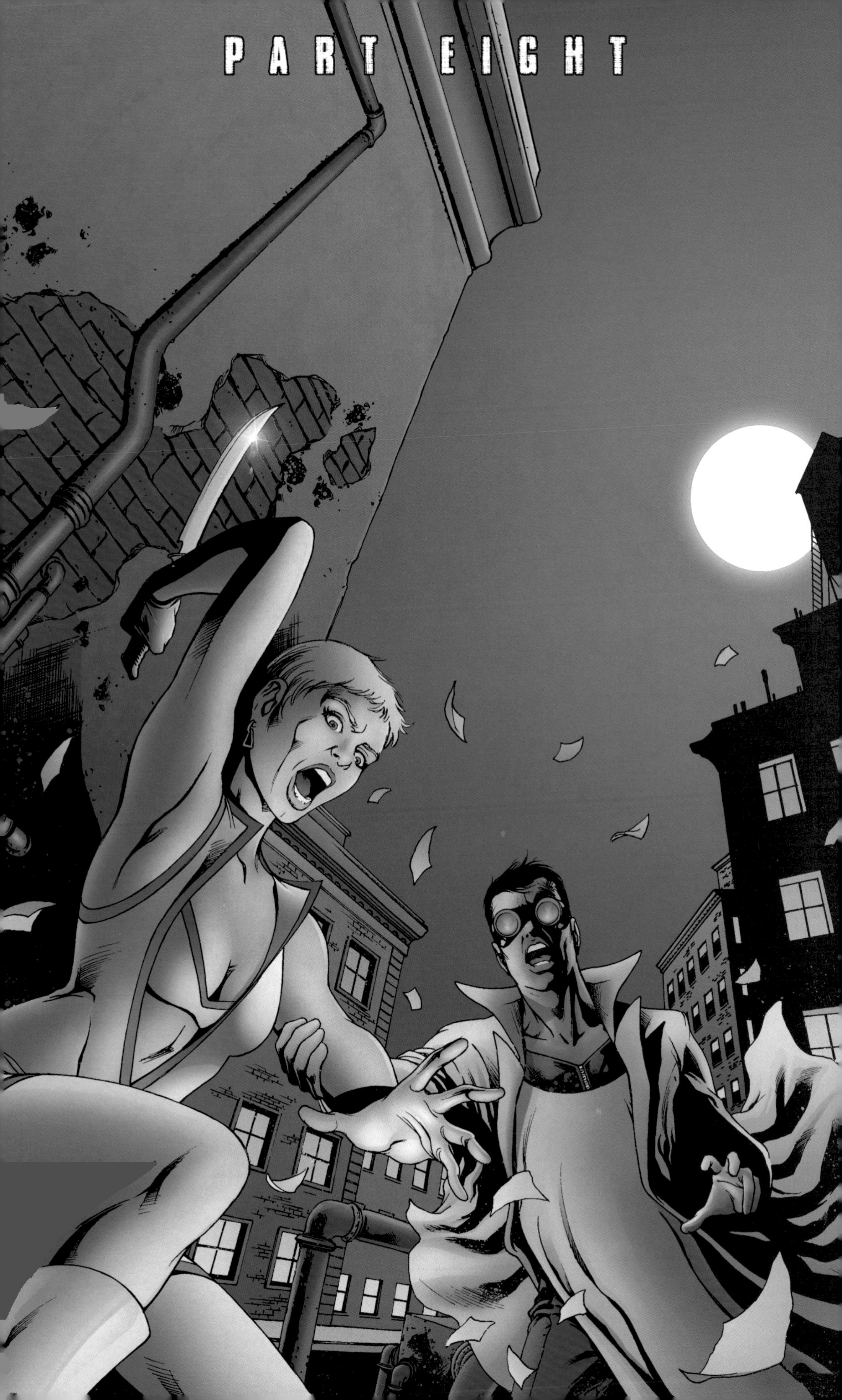

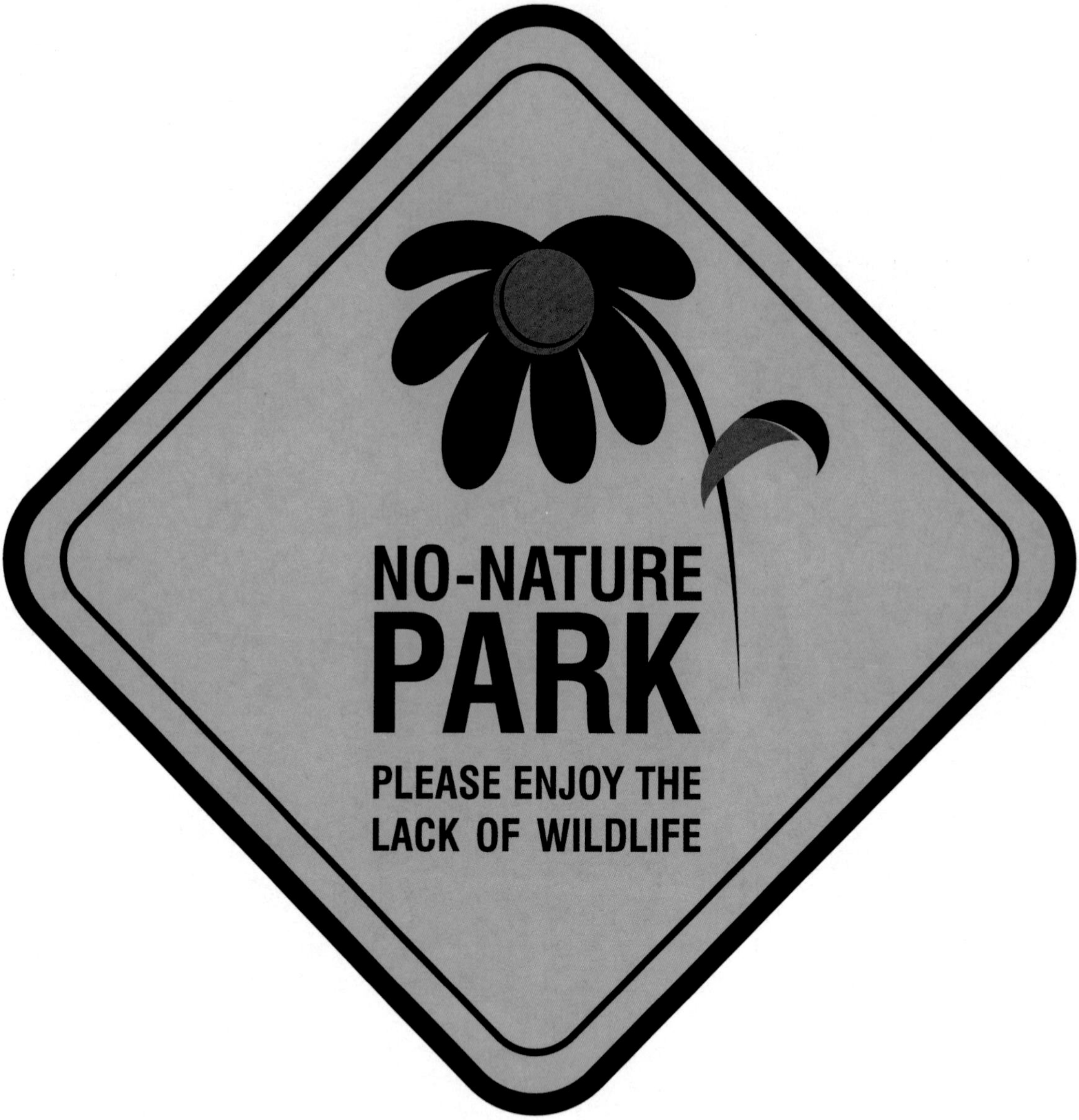
NO-NATURE
PARK
PLEASE ENJOY THE
LACK OF WILDLIFE

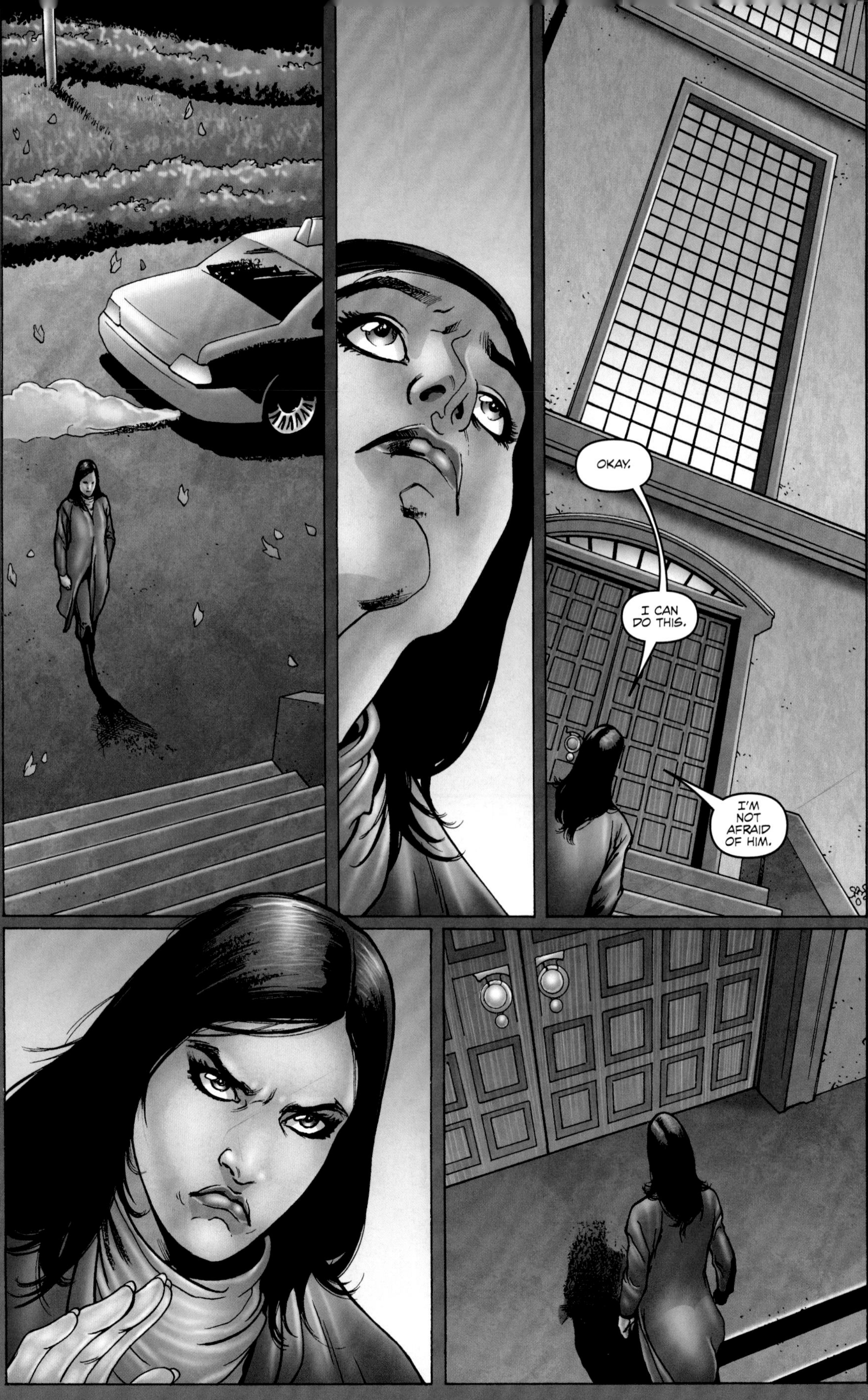
OKAY.
I CAN DO THIS.
I'M NOT AFRAID OF HIM.

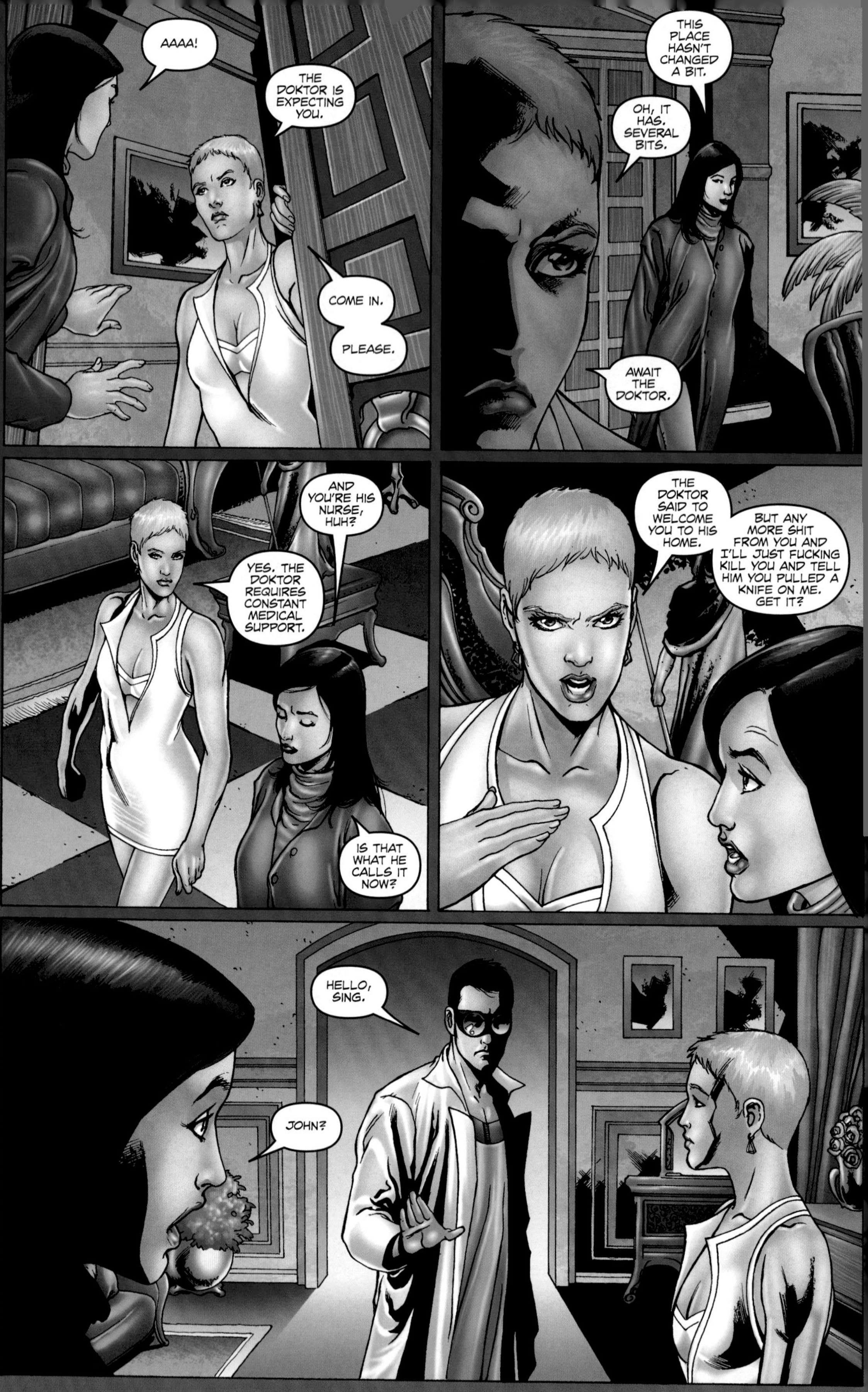
AAAA!
THE DOKTOR IS EXPECTING YOU.
COME IN.
PLEASE.
THIS PLACE HASN'T CHANGED A BIT.
OH, IT HAS. SEVERAL BITS.
AWAIT THE DOKTOR.
AND YOU'RE HIS NURSE, HUH?
YES. THE DOKTOR REQUIRES CONSTANT MEDICAL SUPPORT.
IS THAT WHAT HE CALLS IT NOW?
THE DOKTOR SAID TO WELCOME YOU TO HIS HOME.
BUT ANY MORE SHIT FROM YOU AND I'LL JUST FUCKING KILL YOU AND TELL HIM YOU PULLED A KNIFE ON ME. GET IT?
HELLO, SING.
JOHN?

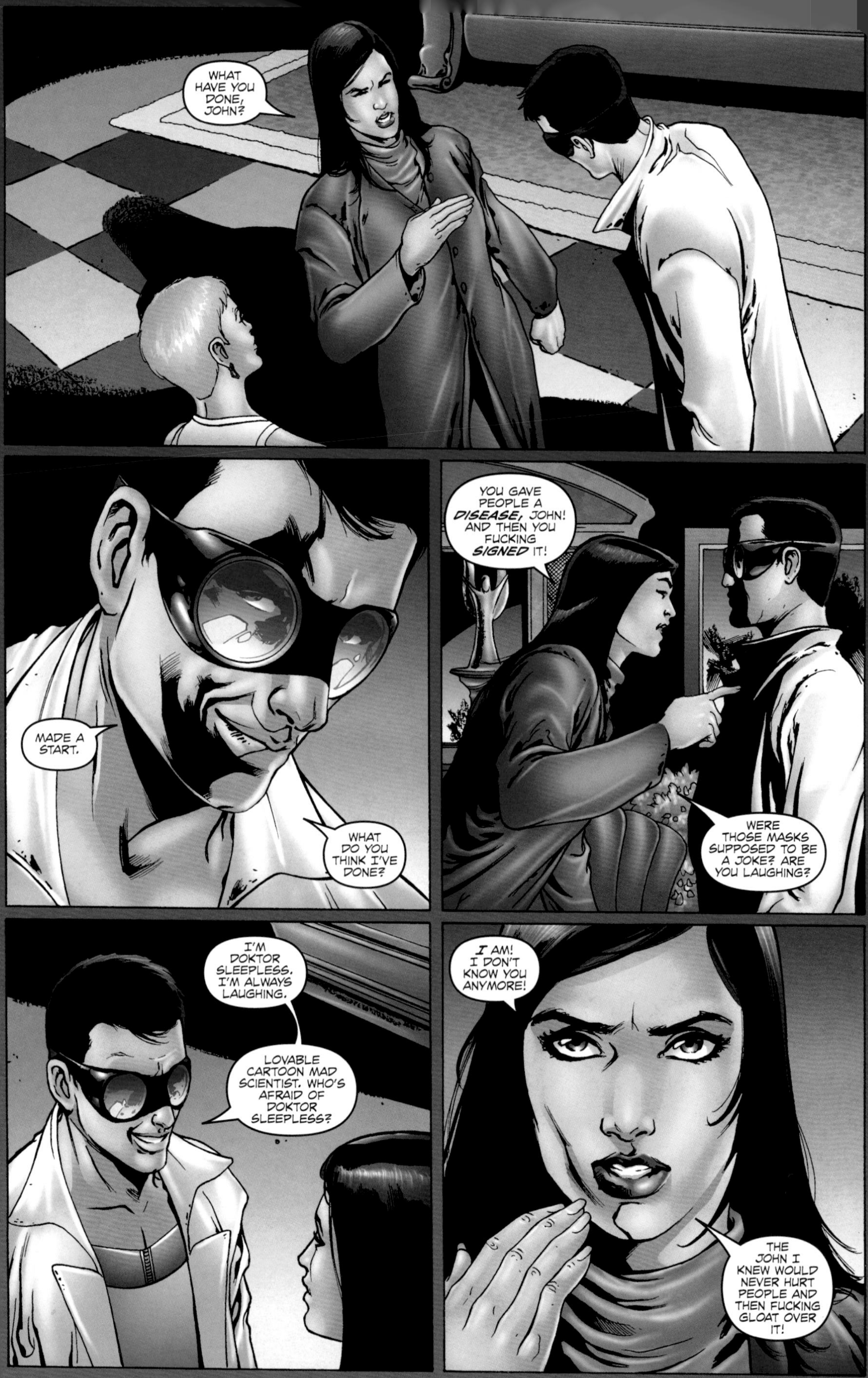
WHAT HAVE YOU DONE, JOHN?
MADE A START.
WHAT DO YOU THINK I'VE DONE?
YOU GAVE PEOPLE A *DISEASE,* JOHN! AND THEN YOU FUCKING *SIGNED* IT!
WERE THOSE MASKS SUPPOSED TO BE A JOKE? ARE YOU LAUGHING?
I'M DOKTOR SLEEPLESS. I'M ALWAYS LAUGHING.
LOVABLE CARTOON MAD SCIENTIST. WHO'S AFRAID OF DOKTOR SLEEPLESS?
I AM! I DON'T KNOW YOU ANYMORE!
THE JOHN I KNEW WOULD NEVER HURT PEOPLE AND THEN FUCKING GLOAT OVER IT!

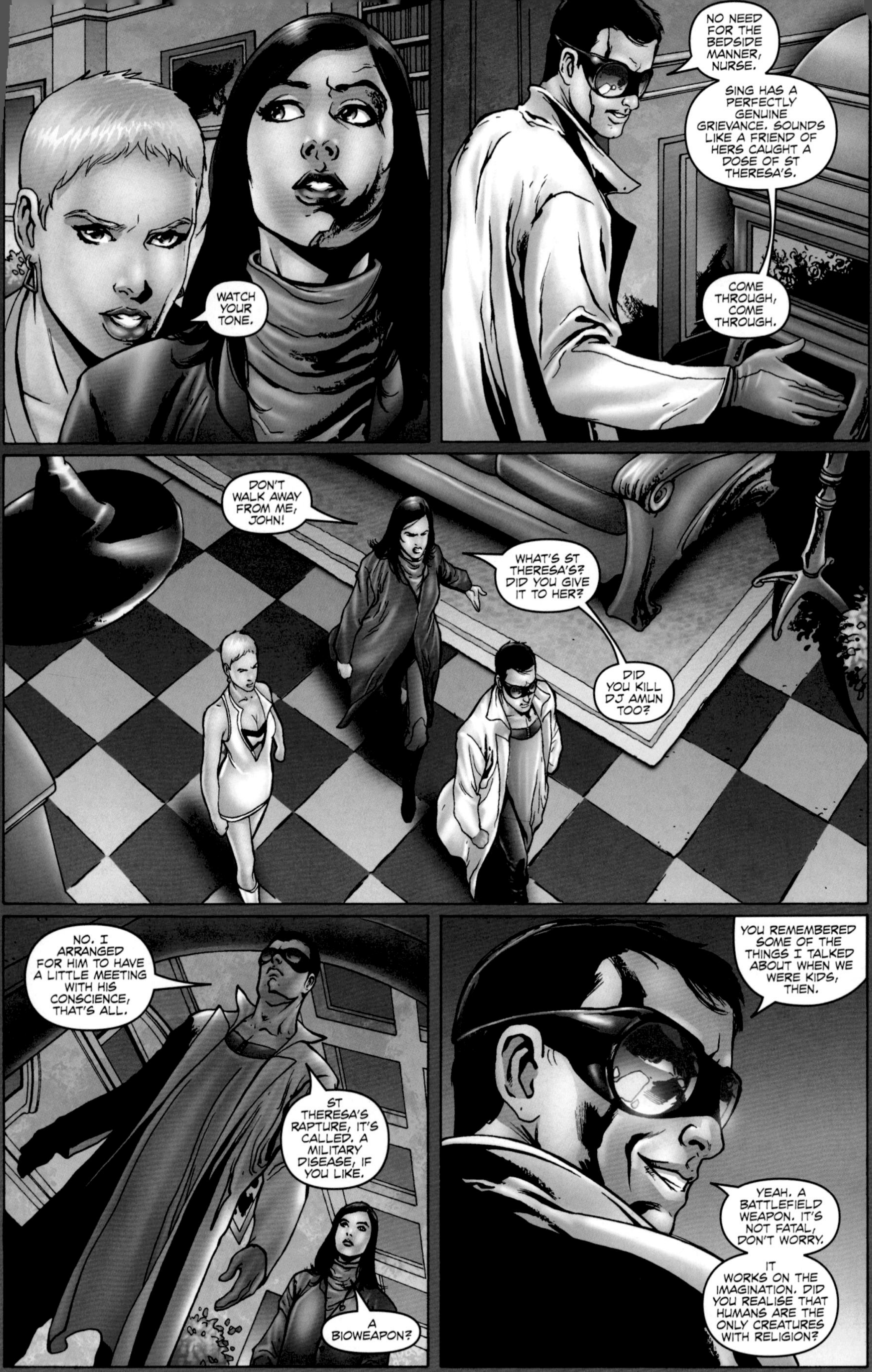
WATCH YOUR TONE.
NO NEED FOR THE BEDSIDE MANNER, NURSE.
SING HAS A PERFECTLY GENUINE GRIEVANCE. SOUNDS LIKE A FRIEND OF HERS CAUGHT A DOSE OF ST THERESA'S.
COME THROUGH, COME THROUGH.
DON'T WALK AWAY FROM ME, JOHN!
WHAT'S ST THERESA'S? DID YOU GIVE IT TO HER?
DID YOU KILL DJ AMUN TOO?
NO. I ARRANGED FOR HIM TO HAVE A LITTLE MEETING WITH HIS CONSCIENCE, THAT'S ALL.
ST THERESA'S RAPTURE, IT'S CALLED. A MILITARY DISEASE, IF YOU LIKE.
A BIOWEAPON?
YOU REMEMBERED SOME OF THE THINGS I TALKED ABOUT WHEN WE WERE KIDS, THEN.
YEAH. A BATTLEFIELD WEAPON. IT'S NOT FATAL, DON'T WORRY.
IT WORKS ON THE IMAGINATION. DID YOU REALISE THAT HUMANS ARE THE ONLY CREATURES WITH RELIGION?

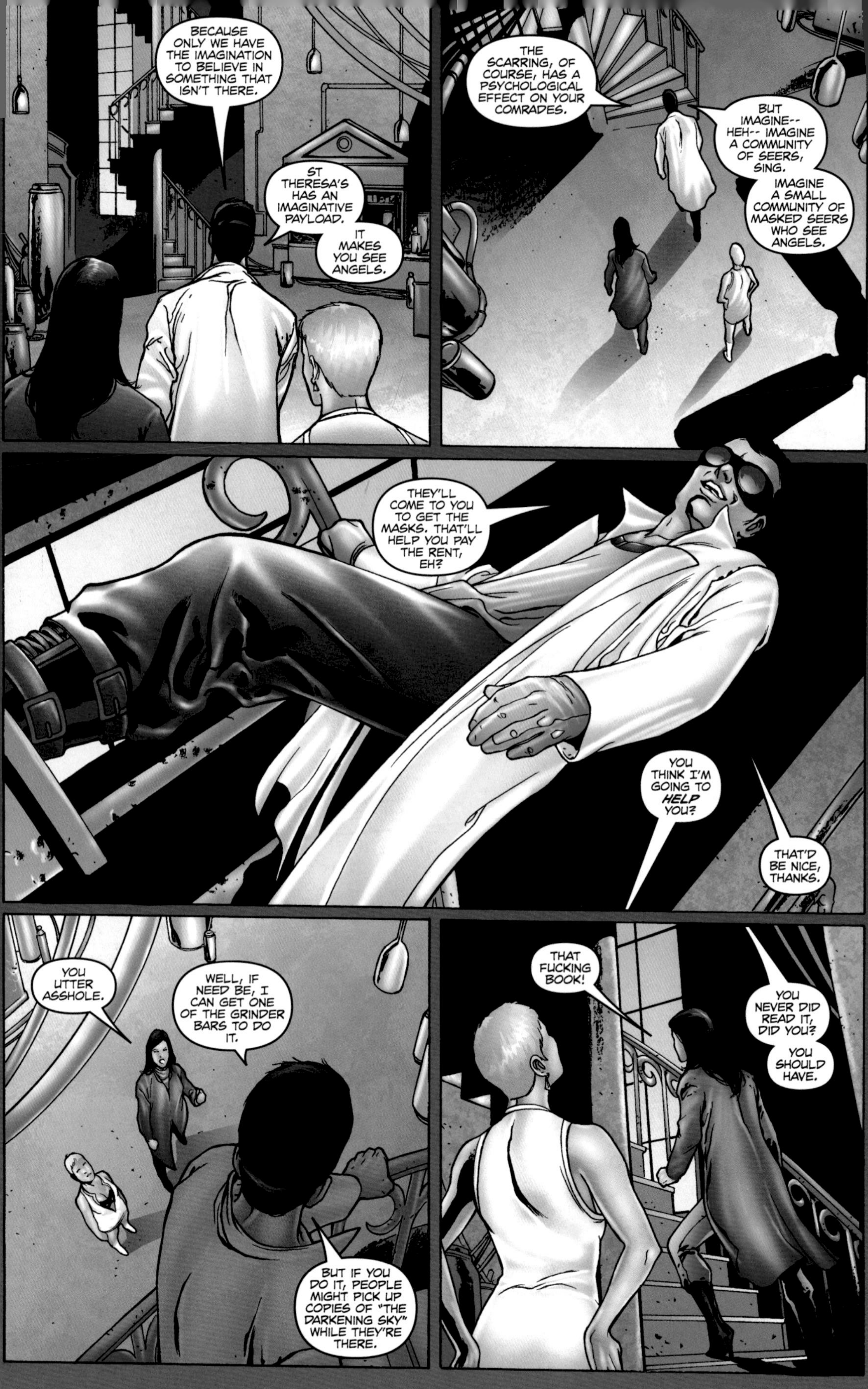
BECAUSE ONLY WE HAVE THE IMAGINATION TO BELIEVE IN SOMETHING THAT ISN'T THERE.
ST THERESA'S HAS AN IMAGINATIVE PAYLOAD.
IT MAKES YOU SEE ANGELS.
THE SCARRING, OF COURSE, HAS A PSYCHOLOGICAL EFFECT ON YOUR COMRADES.
BUT IMAGINE-- HEH-- IMAGINE A COMMUNITY OF SEERS, SING.
IMAGINE A SMALL COMMUNITY OF MASKED SEERS WHO SEE ANGELS.
THEY'LL COME TO YOU TO GET THE MASKS. THAT'LL HELP YOU PAY THE RENT, EH?
YOU THINK I'M GOING TO HELP YOU?
THAT'D BE NICE, THANKS.
YOU UTTER ASSHOLE.
WELL, IF NEED BE, I CAN GET ONE OF THE GRINDER BARS TO DO IT.
BUT IF YOU DO IT, PEOPLE MIGHT PICK UP COPIES OF "THE DARKENING SKY" WHILE THEY'RE THERE.
THAT FUCKING BOOK!
YOU NEVER DID READ IT, DID YOU?
YOU SHOULD HAVE.

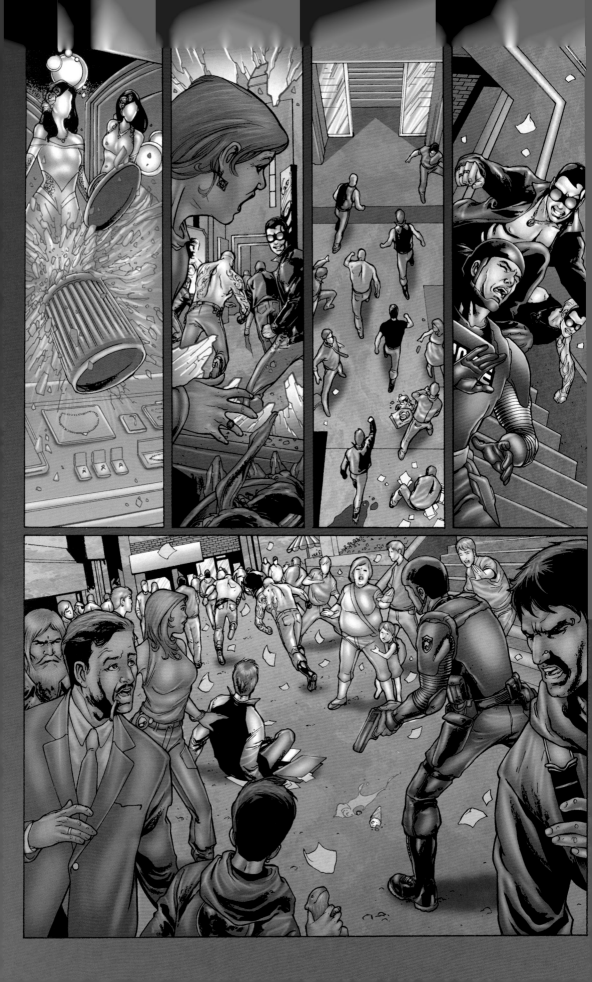

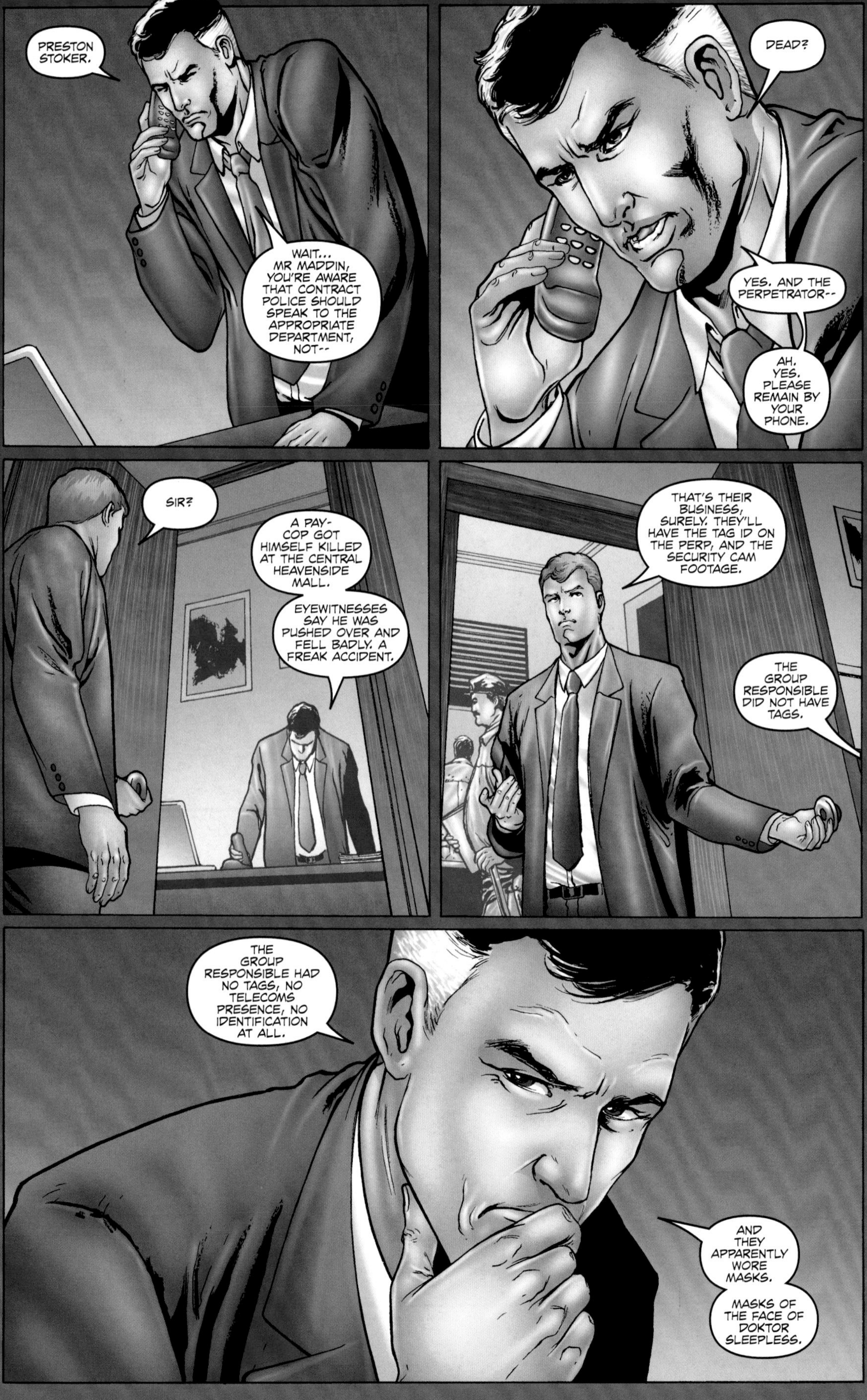
PRESTON STOKER.
WAIT... MR MADDIN, YOU'RE AWARE THAT CONTRACT POLICE SHOULD SPEAK TO THE APPROPRIATE DEPARTMENT, NOT--
DEAD?
YES. AND THE PERPETRATOR--
AH. YES. PLEASE REMAIN BY YOUR PHONE.
SIR?
A PAY-COP GOT HIMSELF KILLED AT THE CENTRAL HEAVENSIDE MALL.
EYEWITNESSES SAY HE WAS PUSHED OVER AND FELL BADLY. A FREAK ACCIDENT.
THAT'S THEIR BUSINESS, SURELY. THEY'LL HAVE THE TAG ID ON THE PERP, AND THE SECURITY CAM FOOTAGE.
THE GROUP RESPONSIBLE DID NOT HAVE TAGS.
THE GROUP RESPONSIBLE HAD NO TAGS, NO TELECOMS PRESENCE, NO IDENTIFICATION AT ALL.
AND THEY APPARENTLY WORE MASKS.
MASKS OF THE FACE OF DOKTOR SLEEPLESS.

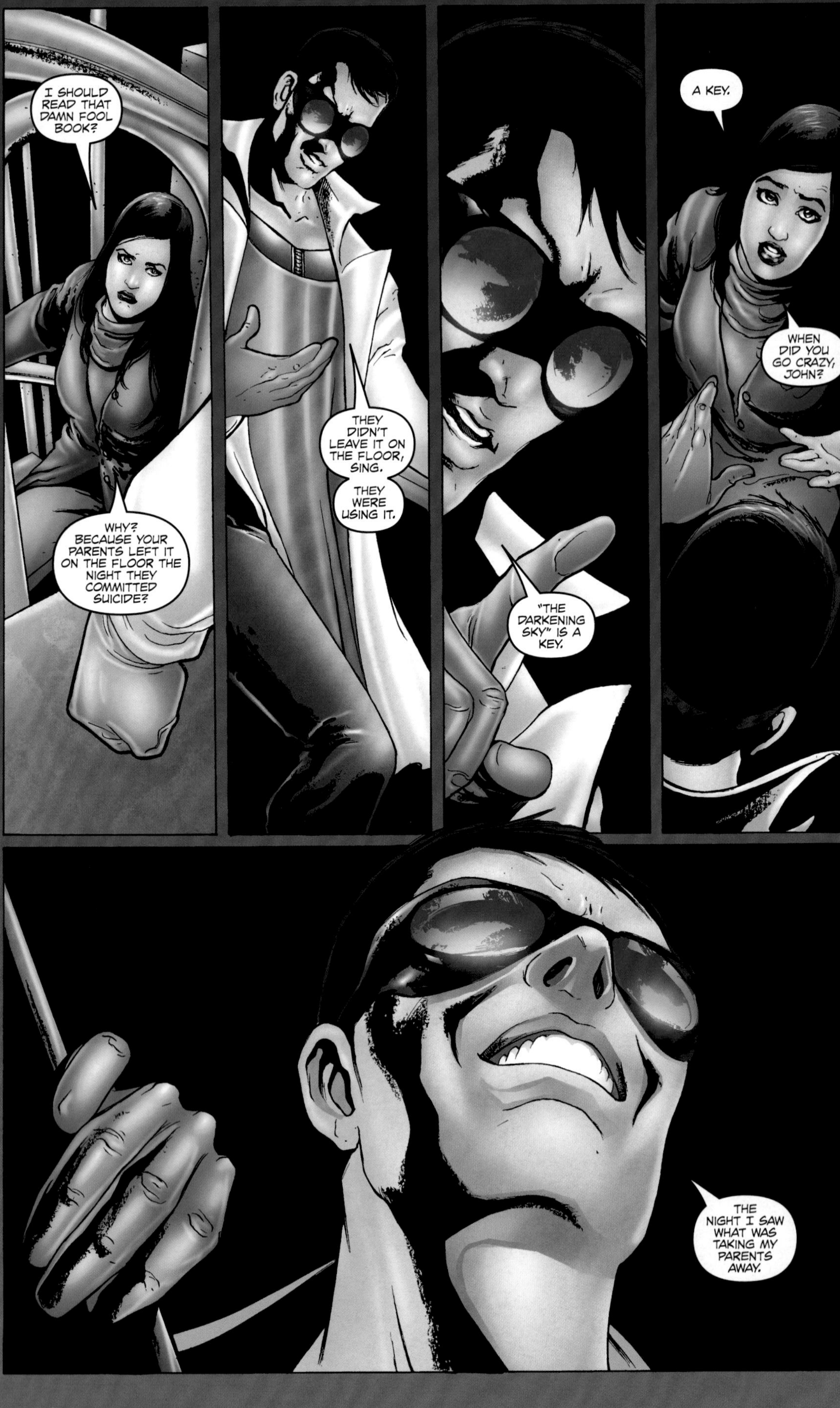
I SHOULD READ THAT DAMN FOOL BOOK?
WHY? BECAUSE YOUR PARENTS LEFT IT ON THE FLOOR THE NIGHT THEY COMMITTED SUICIDE?
THEY DIDN'T LEAVE IT ON THE FLOOR, SING.
THEY WERE USING IT.
"THE DARKENING SKY" IS A KEY.
A KEY.
WHEN DID YOU GO CRAZY, JOHN?
THE NIGHT I SAW WHAT WAS TAKING MY PARENTS AWAY.

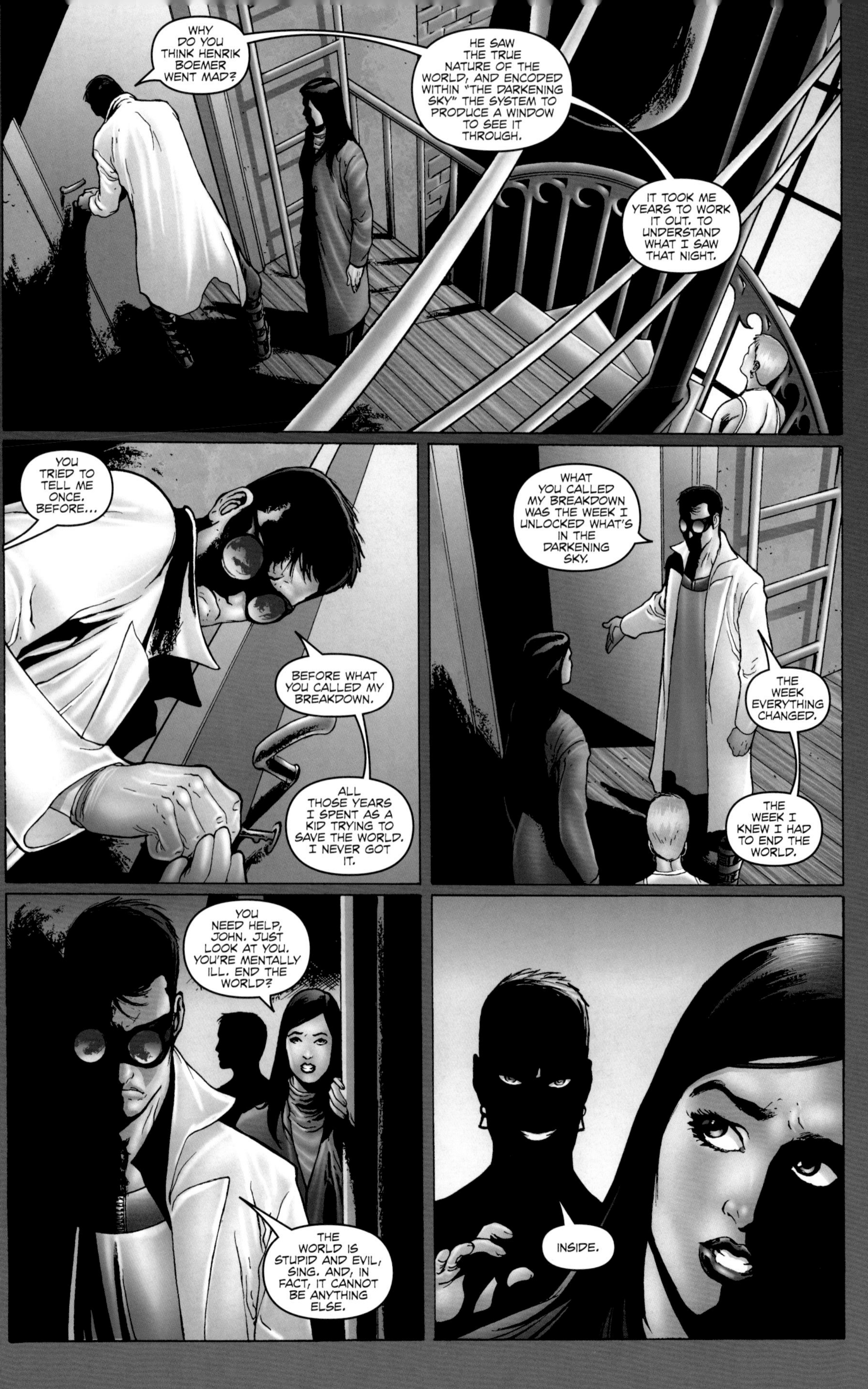
WHY DO YOU THINK HENRIK BOEMER WENT MAD?
HE SAW THE TRUE NATURE OF THE WORLD, AND ENCODED WITHIN "THE DARKENING SKY" THE SYSTEM TO PRODUCE A WINDOW TO SEE IT THROUGH.
IT TOOK ME YEARS TO WORK IT OUT. TO UNDERSTAND WHAT I SAW THAT NIGHT.
YOU TRIED TO TELL ME ONCE. BEFORE...
BEFORE WHAT YOU CALLED MY BREAKDOWN.
ALL THOSE YEARS I SPENT AS A KID TRYING TO SAVE THE WORLD. I NEVER GOT IT.
WHAT YOU CALLED MY BREAKDOWN WAS THE WEEK I UNLOCKED WHAT'S IN THE DARKENING SKY.
THE WEEK EVERYTHING CHANGED.
THE WEEK I KNEW I HAD TO END THE WORLD.
YOU NEED HELP, JOHN. JUST LOOK AT YOU. YOU'RE MENTALLY ILL. END THE WORLD?
THE WORLD IS STUPID AND EVIL, SING. AND, IN FACT, IT CANNOT BE ANYTHING ELSE.
INSIDE.

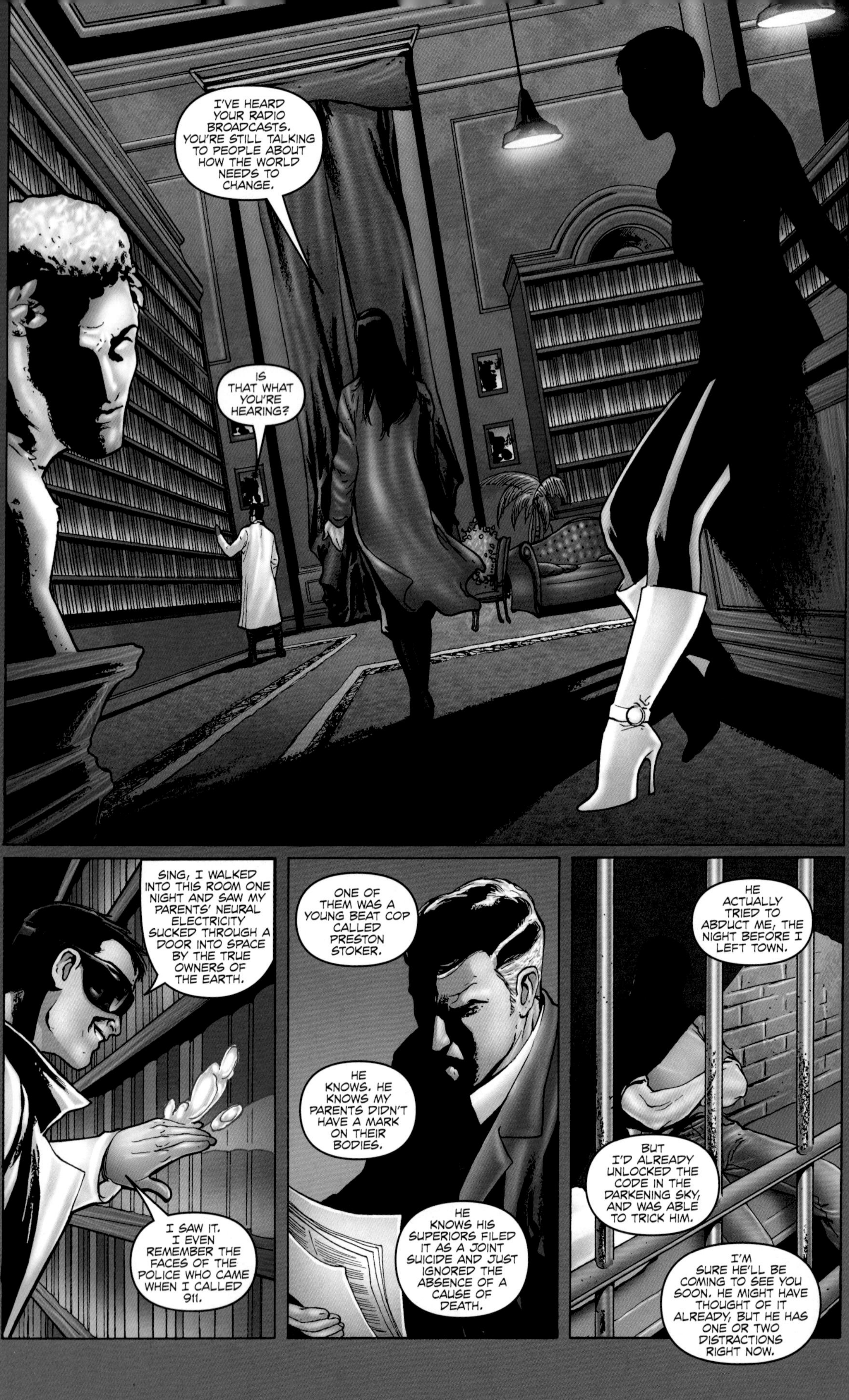
I'VE HEARD YOUR RADIO BROADCASTS. YOU'RE STILL TALKING TO PEOPLE ABOUT HOW THE WORLD NEEDS TO CHANGE.
IS THAT WHAT YOU'RE HEARING?
SING, I WALKED INTO THIS ROOM ONE NIGHT AND SAW MY PARENTS' NEURAL ELECTRICITY SUCKED THROUGH A DOOR INTO SPACE BY THE TRUE OWNERS OF THE EARTH.
I SAW IT. I EVEN REMEMBER THE FACES OF THE POLICE WHO CAME WHEN I CALLED 911.
ONE OF THEM WAS A YOUNG BEAT COP CALLED PRESTON STOKER.
HE KNOWS. HE KNOWS MY PARENTS DIDN'T HAVE A MARK ON THEIR BODIES.
HE KNOWS HIS SUPERIORS FILED IT AS A JOINT SUICIDE AND JUST IGNORED THE ABSENCE OF A CAUSE OF DEATH.
HE ACTUALLY TRIED TO ABDUCT ME, THE NIGHT BEFORE I LEFT TOWN.
BUT I'D ALREADY UNLOCKED THE CODE IN THE DARKENING SKY, AND WAS ABLE TO TRICK HIM.
I'M SURE HE'LL BE COMING TO SEE YOU SOON. HE MIGHT HAVE THOUGHT OF IT ALREADY, BUT HE HAS ONE OR TWO DISTRACTIONS RIGHT NOW.

WHAT THE DARKENING SKY TEACHES US, SING, IS THAT HUMANS ARE ANTS.

THE THING ABOUT ANTS IS THAT YOU CAN'T TELL THEM APART. PARTICULARLY WHEN THEY'RE MASSED IN A MARAUDING ARMY.

IT TEACHES US THE TRUE NATURE OF THE FOOD CHAIN.

I SWEAR, I THINK YOU'VE KEPT THIS ROOM THE SAME SINCE YOUR FOLKS DIED, YOU FUCKING FREAK...

ALL RIGHT. ALL RIGHT. SO WHY START IN HEAVENSIDE? IF YOU'RE REALLY BENT ON DESTROYING THE WORLD, WHATEVER THE HELL THAT MEANS. WHY HERE FIRST?

HEAVENSIDE ENJOYS CERTAIN ADVANTAGES, LET'S SAY.

THE GRINDERS, FOR ONE THING. THERE WERE ALWAYS MORE GRINDERS IN HEAVENSIDE THAN ANYWHERE ELSE.

ALSO-- WHY NOT? GOT TO START SOMEWHERE.

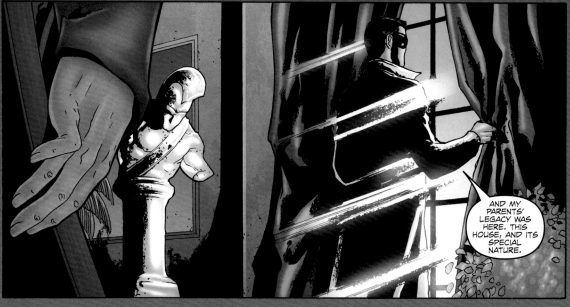

AND MY PARENTS' LEGACY WAS HERE. THIS HOUSE, AND ITS SPECIAL NATURE.

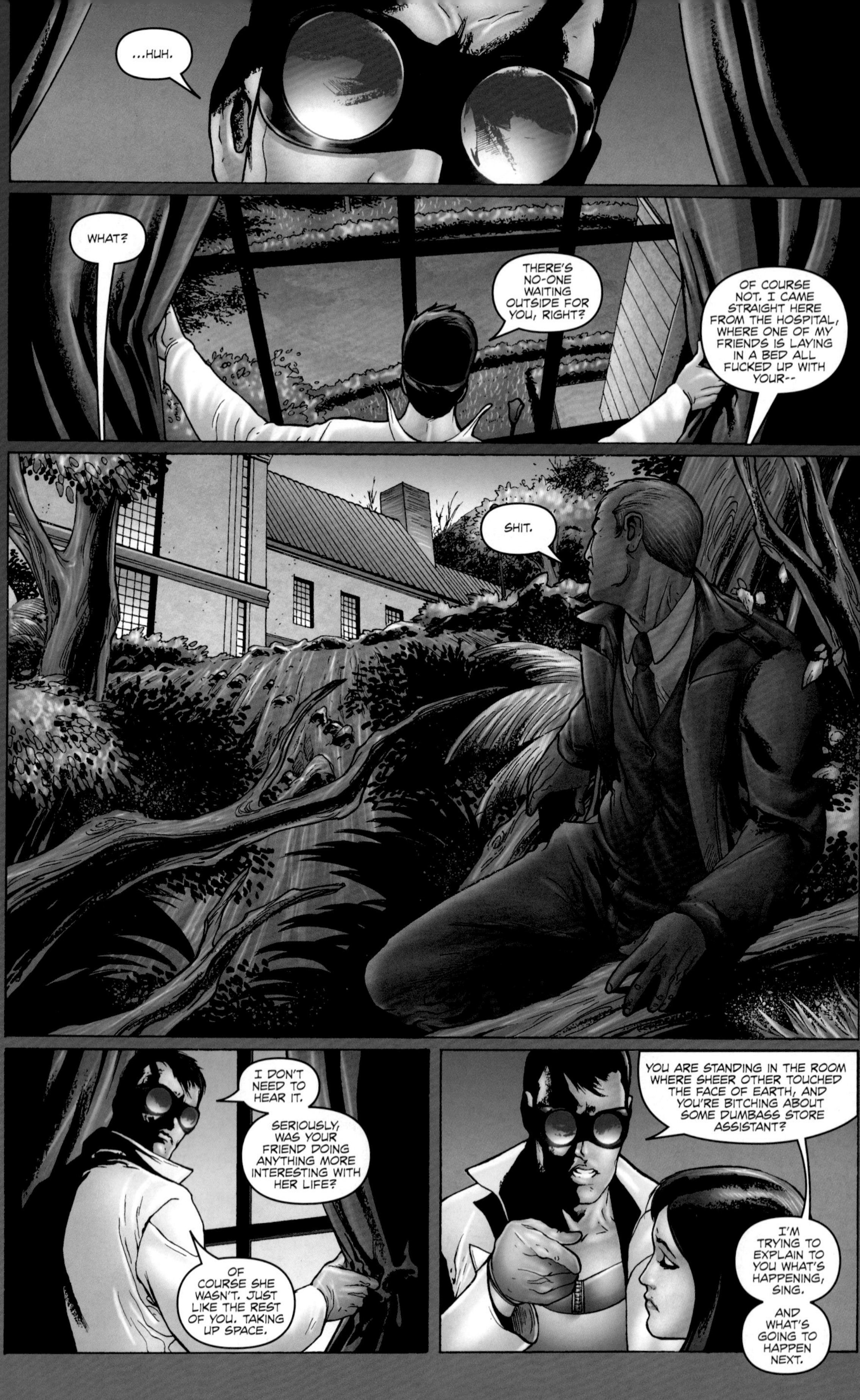
...HUH.
WHAT?
THERE'S NO-ONE WAITING OUTSIDE FOR YOU, RIGHT?
OF COURSE NOT. I CAME STRAIGHT HERE FROM THE HOSPITAL, WHERE ONE OF MY FRIENDS IS LAYING IN A BED ALL FUCKED UP WITH YOUR--
SHIT.
I DON'T NEED TO HEAR IT.
SERIOUSLY, WAS YOUR FRIEND DOING ANYTHING MORE INTERESTING WITH HER LIFE?
OF COURSE SHE WASN'T. JUST LIKE THE REST OF YOU. TAKING UP SPACE.
YOU ARE STANDING IN THE ROOM WHERE SHEER OTHER TOUCHED THE FACE OF EARTH, AND YOU'RE BITCHING ABOUT SOME DUMBASS STORE ASSISTANT?
I'M TRYING TO EXPLAIN TO YOU WHAT'S HAPPENING, SING.
AND WHAT'S GOING TO HAPPEN NEXT.

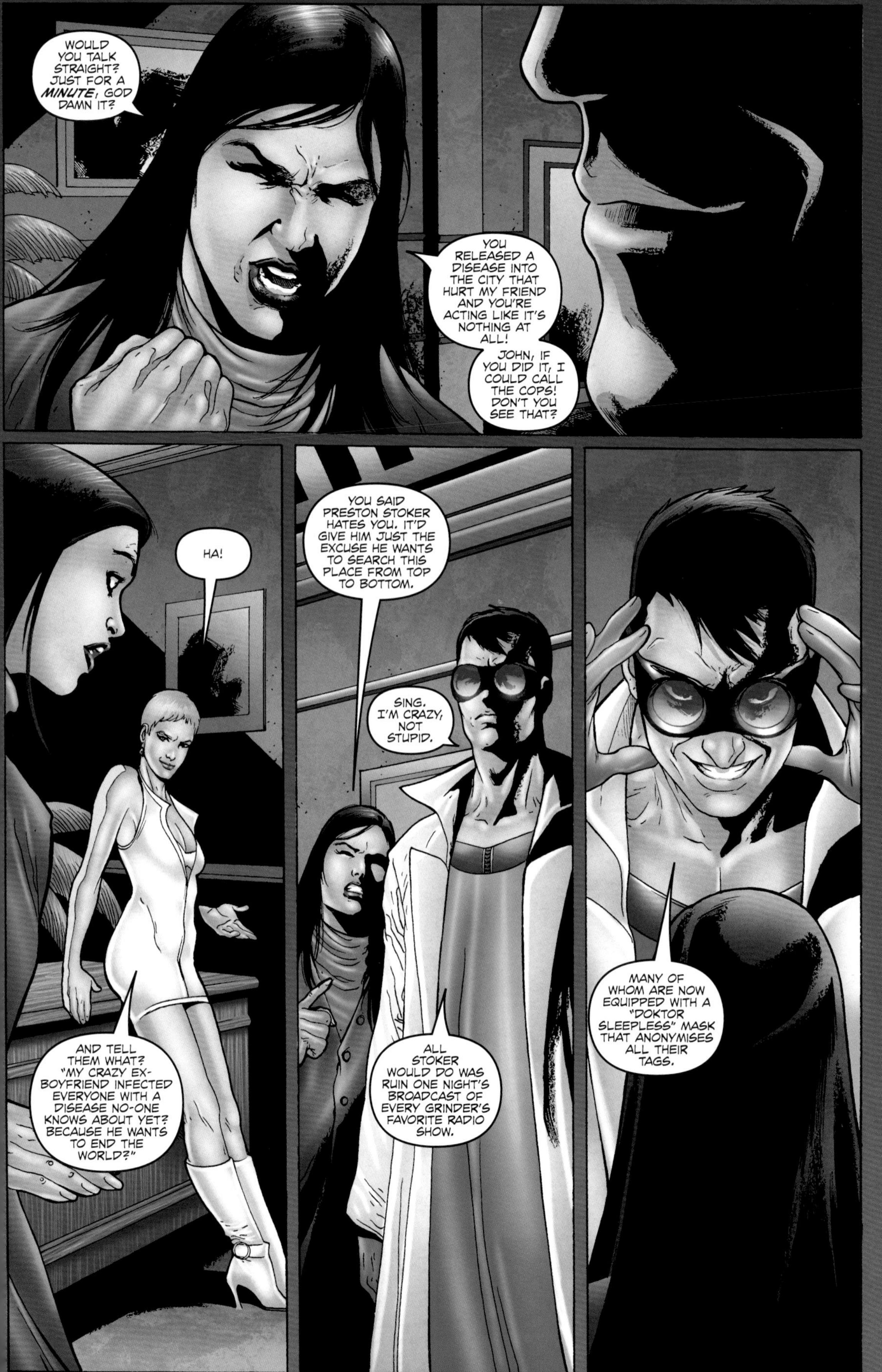

WOULD YOU TALK STRAIGHT? JUST FOR A *MINUTE*, GOD DAMN IT?
YOU RELEASED A DISEASE INTO THE CITY THAT HURT MY FRIEND AND YOU'RE ACTING LIKE IT'S NOTHING AT ALL!
JOHN, IF YOU DID IT, I COULD CALL THE COPS! DON'T YOU SEE THAT?
HA!
AND TELL THEM WHAT? "MY CRAZY EX-BOYFRIEND INFECTED EVERYONE WITH A DISEASE NO-ONE KNOWS ABOUT YET? BECAUSE HE WANTS TO END THE WORLD?"
YOU SAID PRESTON STOKER HATES YOU. IT'D GIVE HIM JUST THE EXCUSE HE WANTS TO SEARCH THIS PLACE FROM TOP TO BOTTOM.
SING. I'M CRAZY, NOT STUPID.
ALL STOKER WOULD DO WAS RUIN ONE NIGHT'S BROADCAST OF EVERY GRINDER'S FAVORITE RADIO SHOW.
MANY OF WHOM ARE NOW EQUIPPED WITH A "DOKTOR SLEEPLESS" MASK THAT ANONYMISES ALL THEIR TAGS.

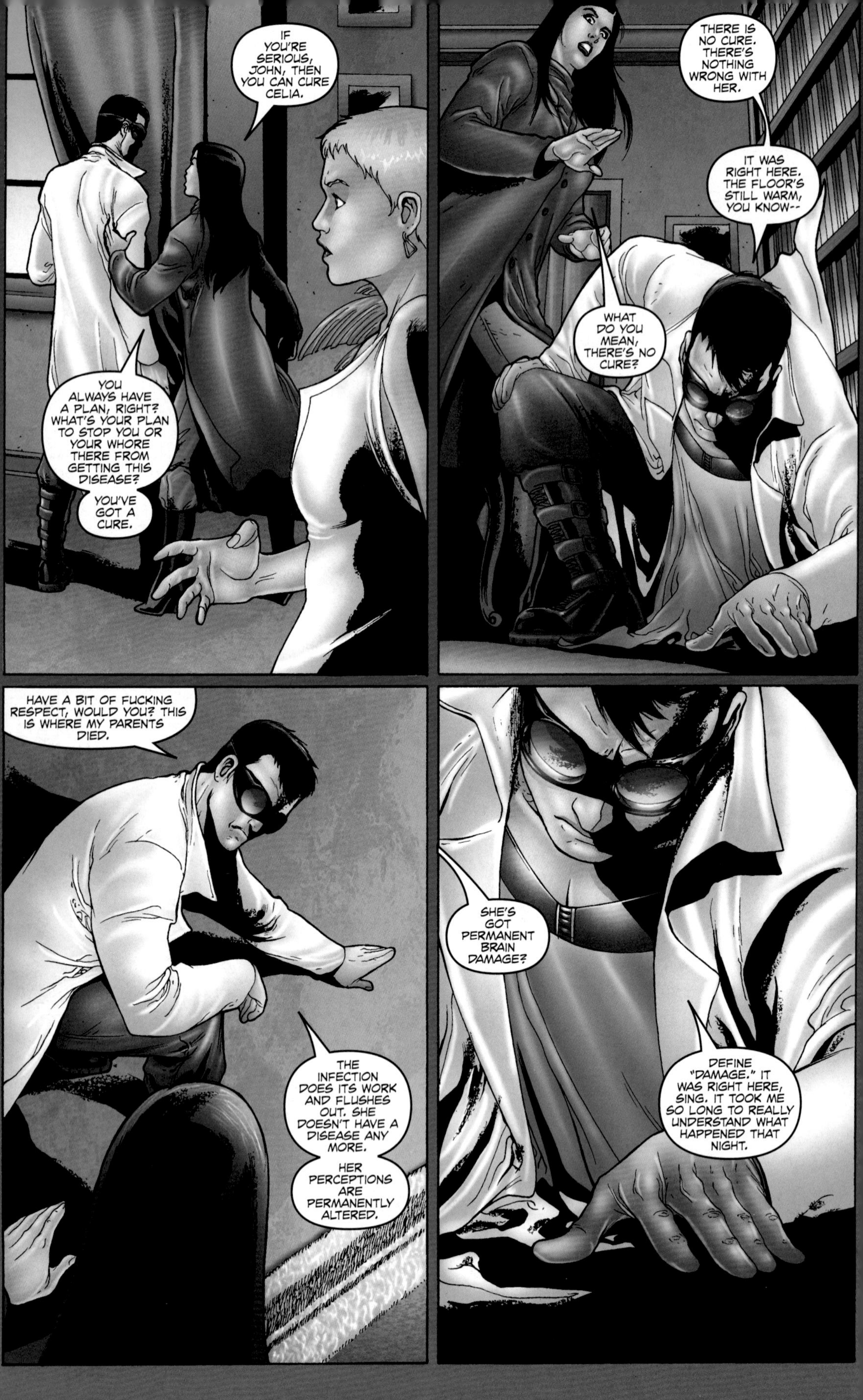
IF YOU'RE SERIOUS, JOHN, THEN YOU CAN CURE CELIA.
YOU ALWAYS HAVE A PLAN, RIGHT? WHAT'S YOUR PLAN TO STOP YOU OR YOUR WHORE THERE FROM GETTING THIS DISEASE?
YOU'VE GOT A CURE.
THERE IS NO CURE. THERE'S NOTHING WRONG WITH HER.
IT WAS RIGHT HERE. THE FLOOR'S STILL WARM, YOU KNOW--
WHAT DO YOU MEAN, THERE'S NO CURE?
HAVE A BIT OF FUCKING RESPECT, WOULD YOU? THIS IS WHERE MY PARENTS DIED.
THE INFECTION DOES ITS WORK AND FLUSHES OUT. SHE DOESN'T HAVE A DISEASE ANY MORE.
HER PERCEPTIONS ARE PERMANENTLY ALTERED.
SHE'S GOT PERMANENT BRAIN DAMAGE?
DEFINE "DAMAGE." IT WAS RIGHT HERE, SING. IT TOOK ME SO LONG TO REALLY UNDERSTAND WHAT HAPPENED THAT NIGHT.

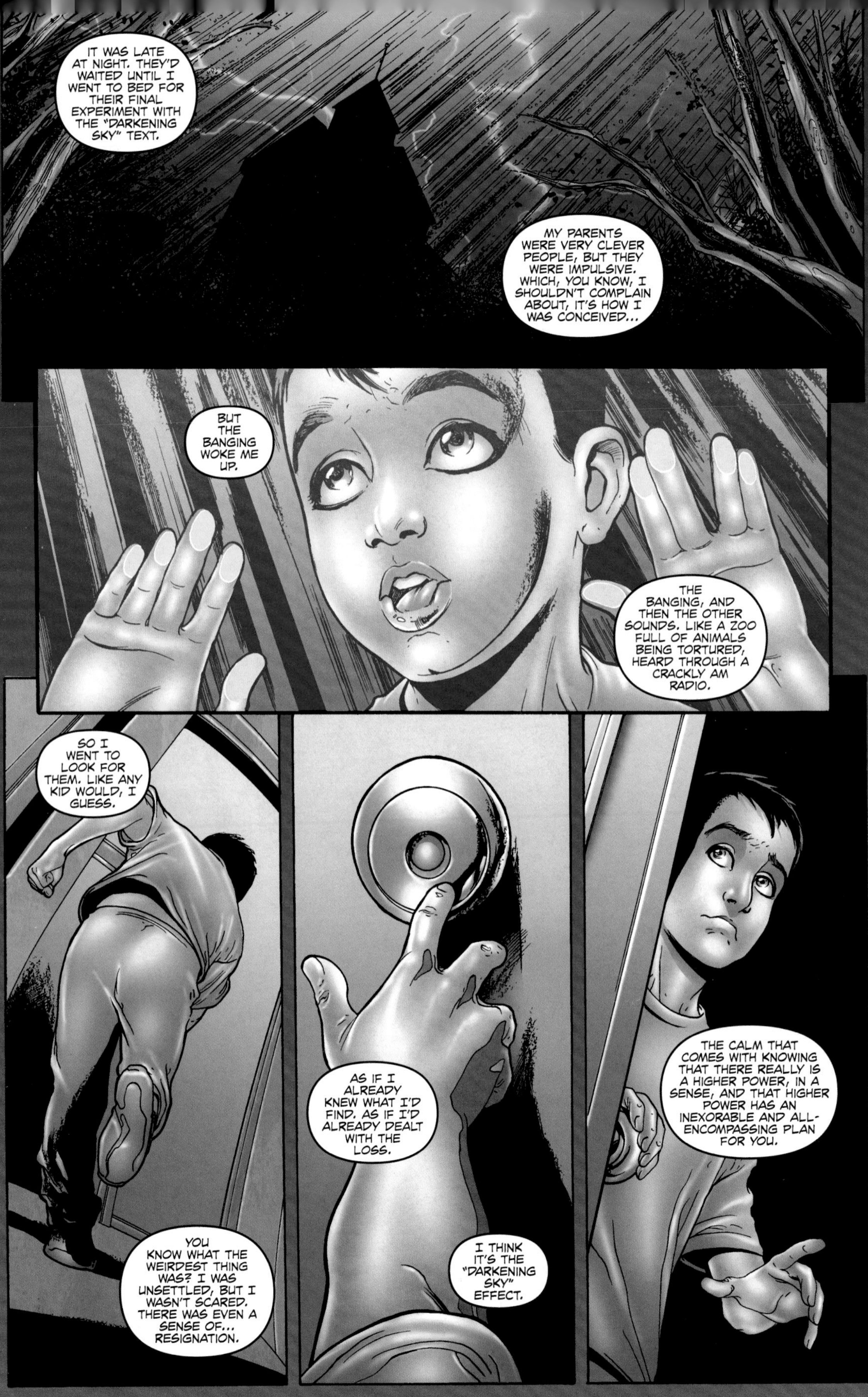
IT WAS LATE AT NIGHT. THEY'D WAITED UNTIL I WENT TO BED FOR THEIR FINAL EXPERIMENT WITH THE "DARKENING SKY" TEXT.
MY PARENTS WERE VERY CLEVER PEOPLE, BUT THEY WERE IMPULSIVE. WHICH, YOU KNOW, I SHOULDN'T COMPLAIN ABOUT, IT'S HOW I WAS CONCEIVED...
BUT THE BANGING WOKE ME UP.
THE BANGING, AND THEN THE OTHER SOUNDS. LIKE A ZOO FULL OF ANIMALS BEING TORTURED, HEARD THROUGH A CRACKLY AM RADIO.
SO I WENT TO LOOK FOR THEM. LIKE ANY KID WOULD, I GUESS.
YOU KNOW WHAT THE WEIRDEST THING WAS? I WAS UNSETTLED, BUT I WASN'T SCARED. THERE WAS EVEN A SENSE OF... RESIGNATION.
AS IF I ALREADY KNEW WHAT I'D FIND. AS IF I'D ALREADY DEALT WITH THE LOSS.
I THINK IT'S THE "DARKENING SKY" EFFECT.
THE CALM THAT COMES WITH KNOWING THAT THERE REALLY IS A HIGHER POWER, IN A SENSE, AND THAT HIGHER POWER HAS AN INEXORABLE AND ALL-ENCOMPASSING PLAN FOR YOU.

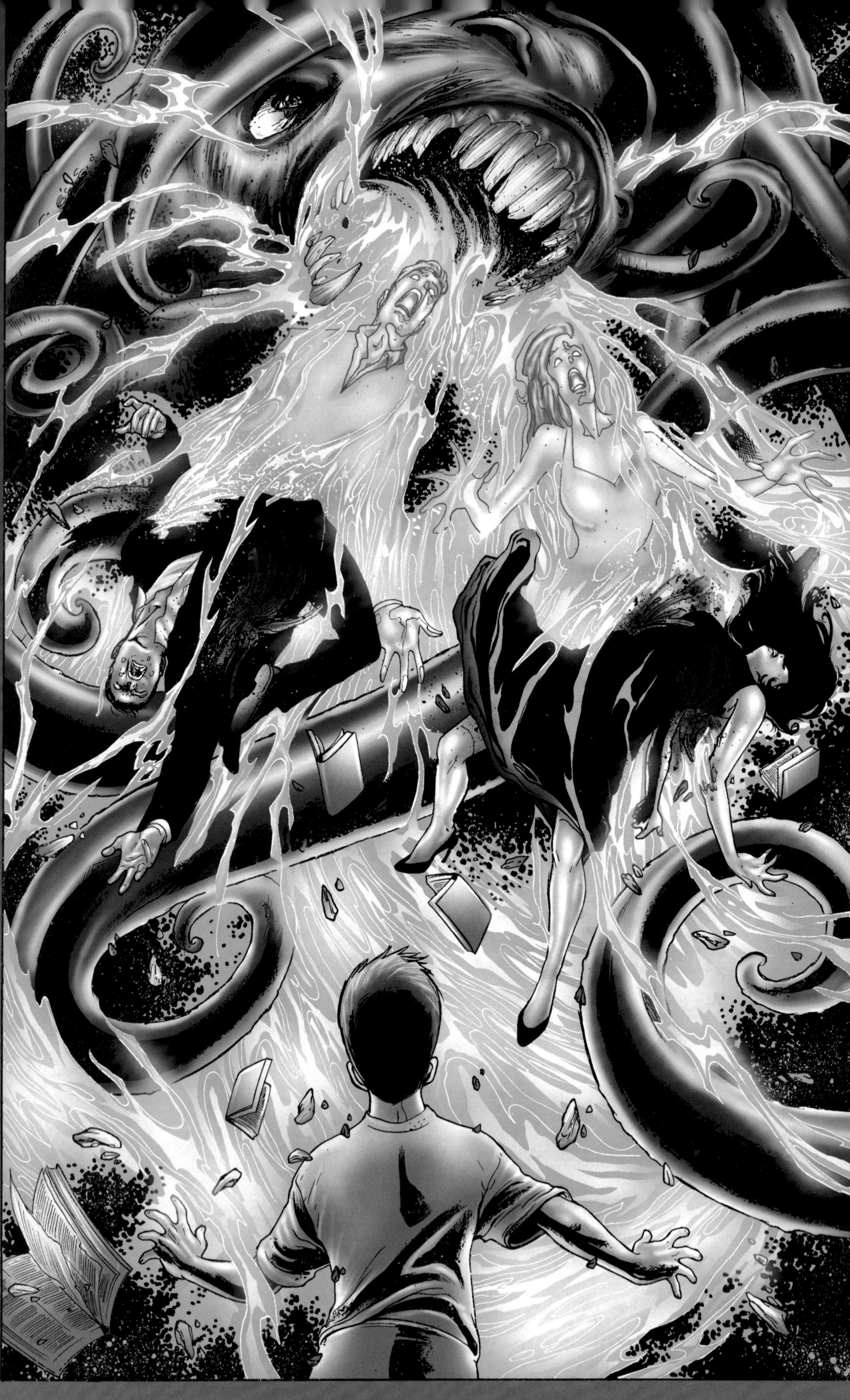

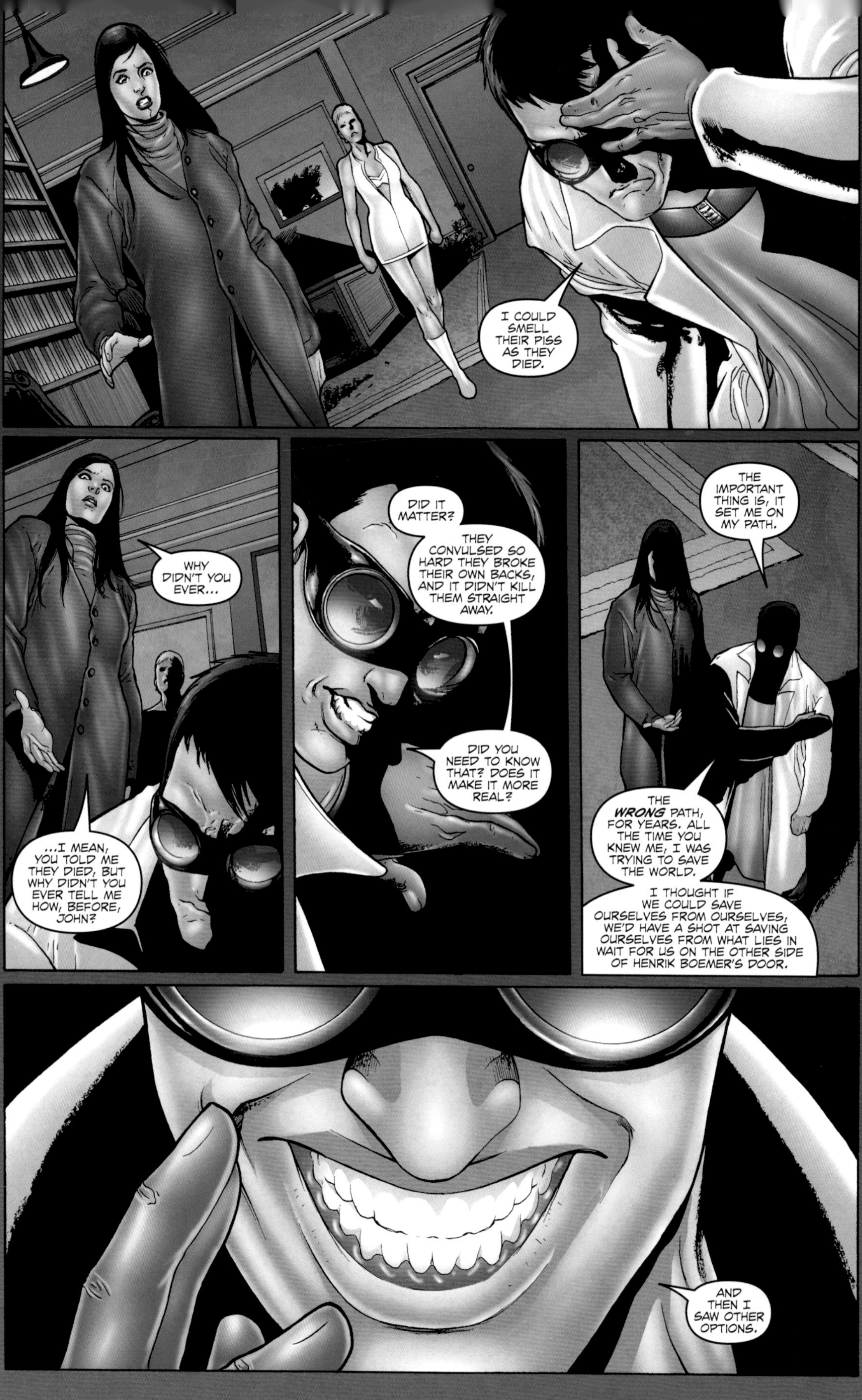
I COULD SMELL THEIR PISS AS THEY DIED.
WHY DIDN'T YOU EVER...
...I MEAN, YOU TOLD ME THEY DIED, BUT WHY DIDN'T YOU EVER TELL ME HOW, BEFORE, JOHN?
DID IT MATTER?
THEY CONVULSED SO HARD THEY BROKE THEIR OWN BACKS, AND IT DIDN'T KILL THEM STRAIGHT AWAY.
DID YOU NEED TO KNOW THAT? DOES IT MAKE IT MORE REAL?
THE IMPORTANT THING IS, IT SET ME ON MY PATH.
THE WRONG PATH, FOR YEARS. ALL THE TIME YOU KNEW ME, I WAS TRYING TO SAVE THE WORLD.
I THOUGHT IF WE COULD SAVE OURSELVES FROM OURSELVES, WE'D HAVE A SHOT AT SAVING OURSELVES FROM WHAT LIES IN WAIT FOR US ON THE OTHER SIDE OF HENRIK BOEMER'S DOOR.
AND THEN I SAW OTHER OPTIONS.

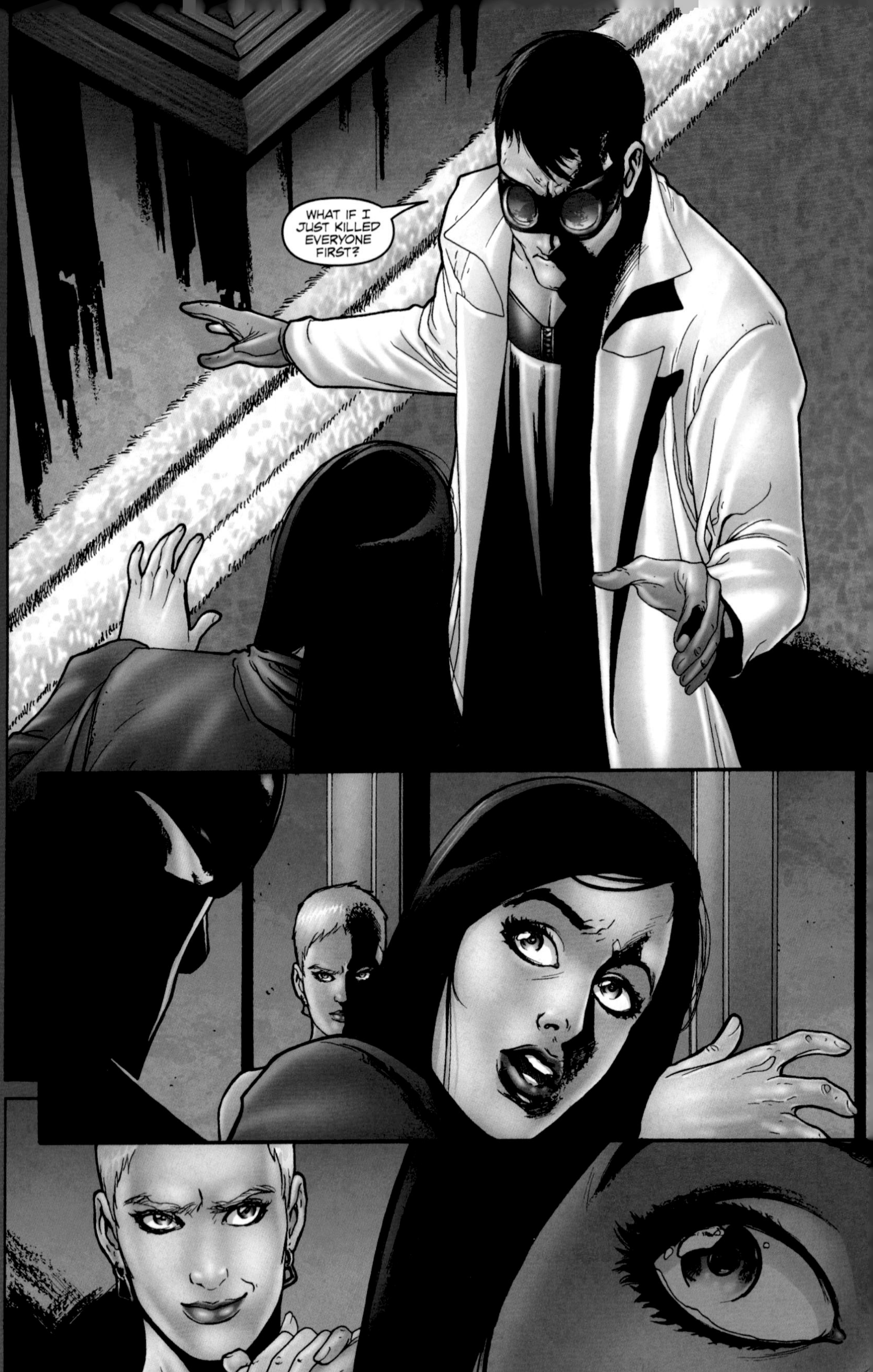
WHAT IF I JUST KILLED EVERYONE FIRST?

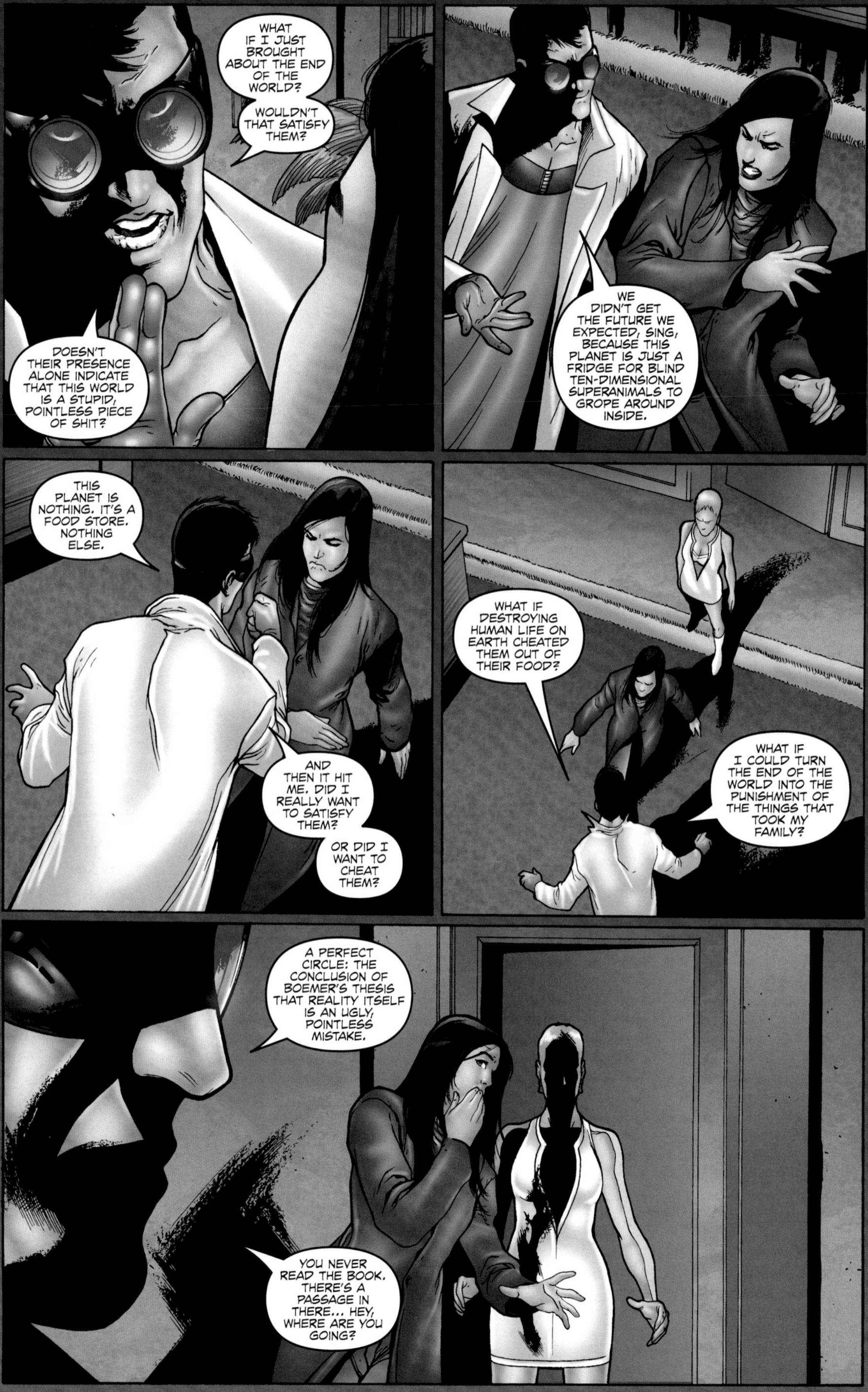
WHAT IF I JUST BROUGHT ABOUT THE END OF THE WORLD?
WOULDN'T THAT SATISFY THEM?
DOESN'T THEIR PRESENCE ALONE INDICATE THAT THIS WORLD IS A STUPID, POINTLESS PIECE OF SHIT?
WE DIDN'T GET THE FUTURE WE EXPECTED, SING, BECAUSE THIS PLANET IS JUST A FRIDGE FOR BLIND TEN-DIMENSIONAL SUPERANIMALS TO GROPE AROUND INSIDE.
THIS PLANET IS NOTHING. IT'S A FOOD STORE. NOTHING ELSE.
AND THEN IT HIT ME. DID I REALLY WANT TO SATISFY THEM?
OR DID I WANT TO CHEAT THEM?
WHAT IF DESTROYING HUMAN LIFE ON EARTH CHEATED THEM OUT OF THEIR FOOD?
WHAT IF I COULD TURN THE END OF THE WORLD INTO THE PUNISHMENT OF THE THINGS THAT TOOK MY FAMILY?
A PERFECT CIRCLE: THE CONCLUSION OF BOEMER'S THESIS THAT REALITY ITSELF IS AN UGLY, POINTLESS MISTAKE.
YOU NEVER READ THE BOOK. THERE'S A PASSAGE IN THERE... HEY, WHERE ARE YOU GOING?

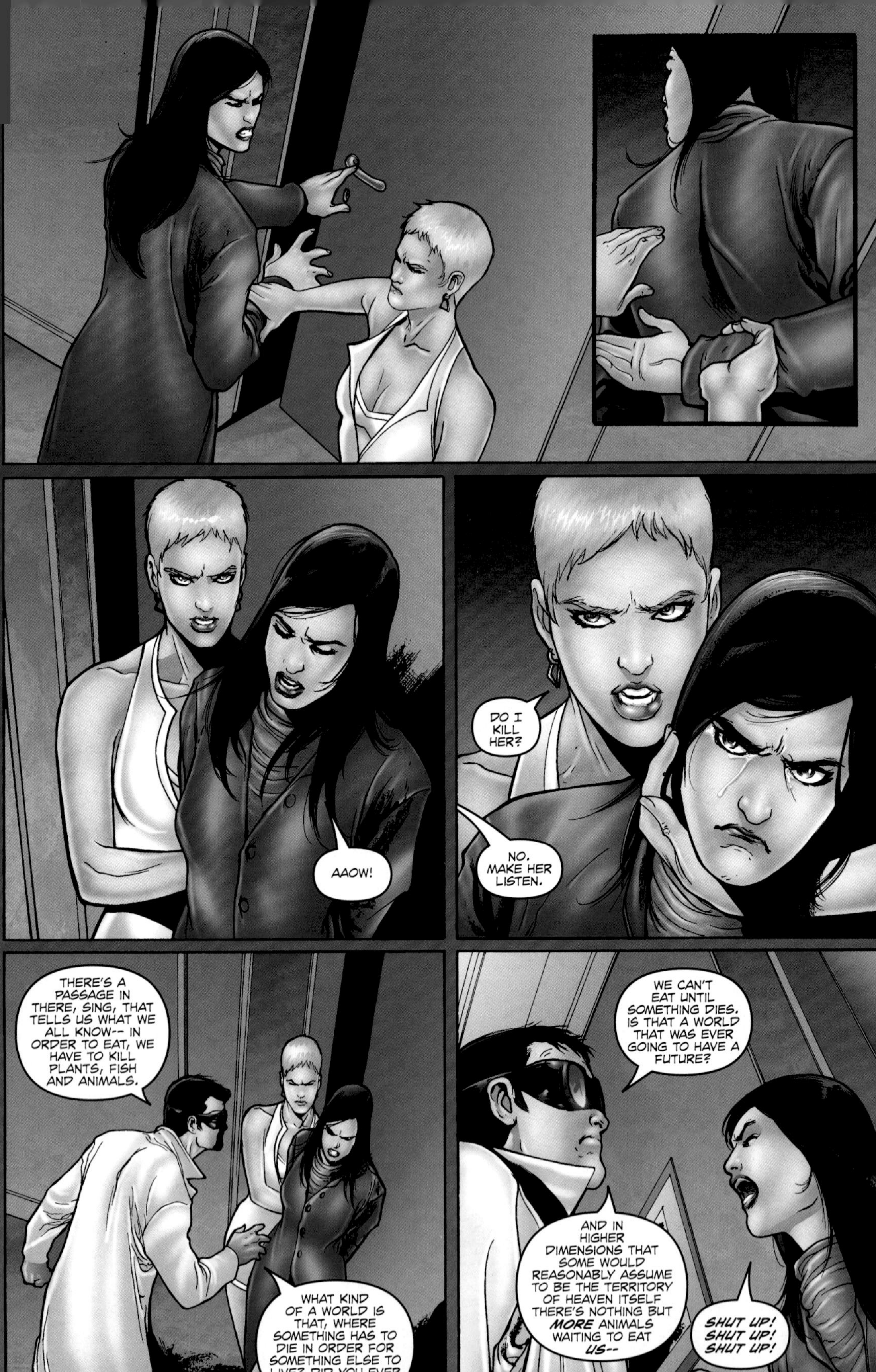

AAOW!
DO I KILL HER?
NO. MAKE HER LISTEN.
THERE'S A PASSAGE IN THERE, SING, THAT TELLS US WHAT WE ALL KNOW-- IN ORDER TO EAT, WE HAVE TO KILL PLANTS, FISH AND ANIMALS.
WHAT KIND OF A WORLD IS THAT, WHERE SOMETHING HAS TO DIE IN ORDER FOR SOMETHING ELSE TO LIVE? DID YOU EVER THINK ABOUT THAT?
WE CAN'T EAT UNTIL SOMETHING DIES. IS THAT A WORLD THAT WAS EVER GOING TO HAVE A FUTURE?
AND IN HIGHER DIMENSIONS THAT SOME WOULD REASONABLY ASSUME TO BE THE TERRITORY OF HEAVEN ITSELF THERE'S NOTHING BUT MORE ANIMALS WAITING TO EAT US--
SHUT UP! SHUT UP! SHUT UP!

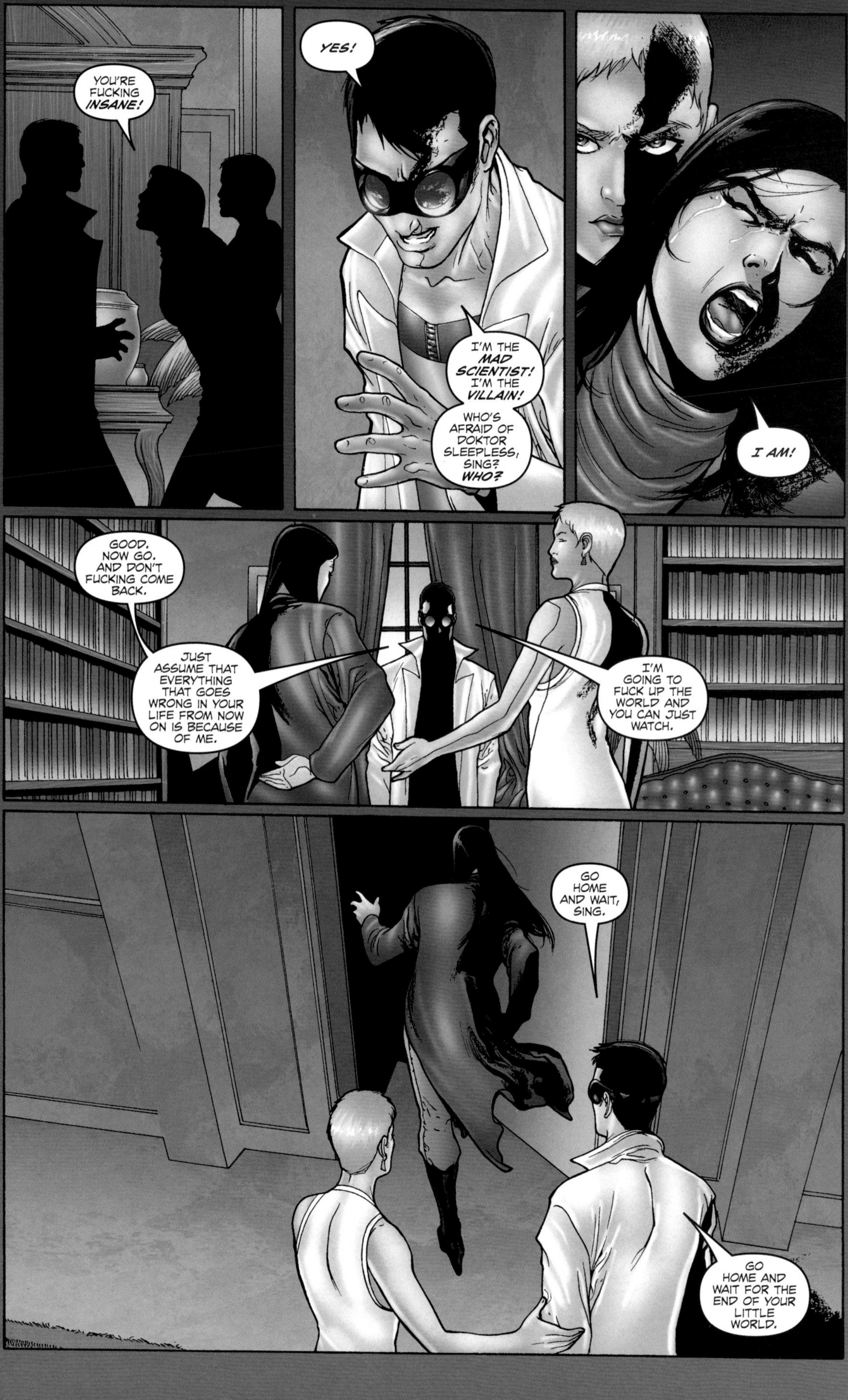
YOU'RE FUCKING INSANE!
YES!
I'M THE MAD SCIENTIST! I'M THE VILLAIN!
WHO'S AFRAID OF DOKTOR SLEEPLESS, SING? WHO?
I AM!
GOOD. NOW GO. AND DON'T FUCKING COME BACK.
JUST ASSUME THAT EVERYTHING THAT GOES WRONG IN YOUR LIFE FROM NOW ON IS BECAUSE OF ME.
I'M GOING TO FUCK UP THE WORLD AND YOU CAN JUST WATCH.
GO HOME AND WAIT, SING.
GO HOME AND WAIT FOR THE END OF YOUR LITTLE WORLD.

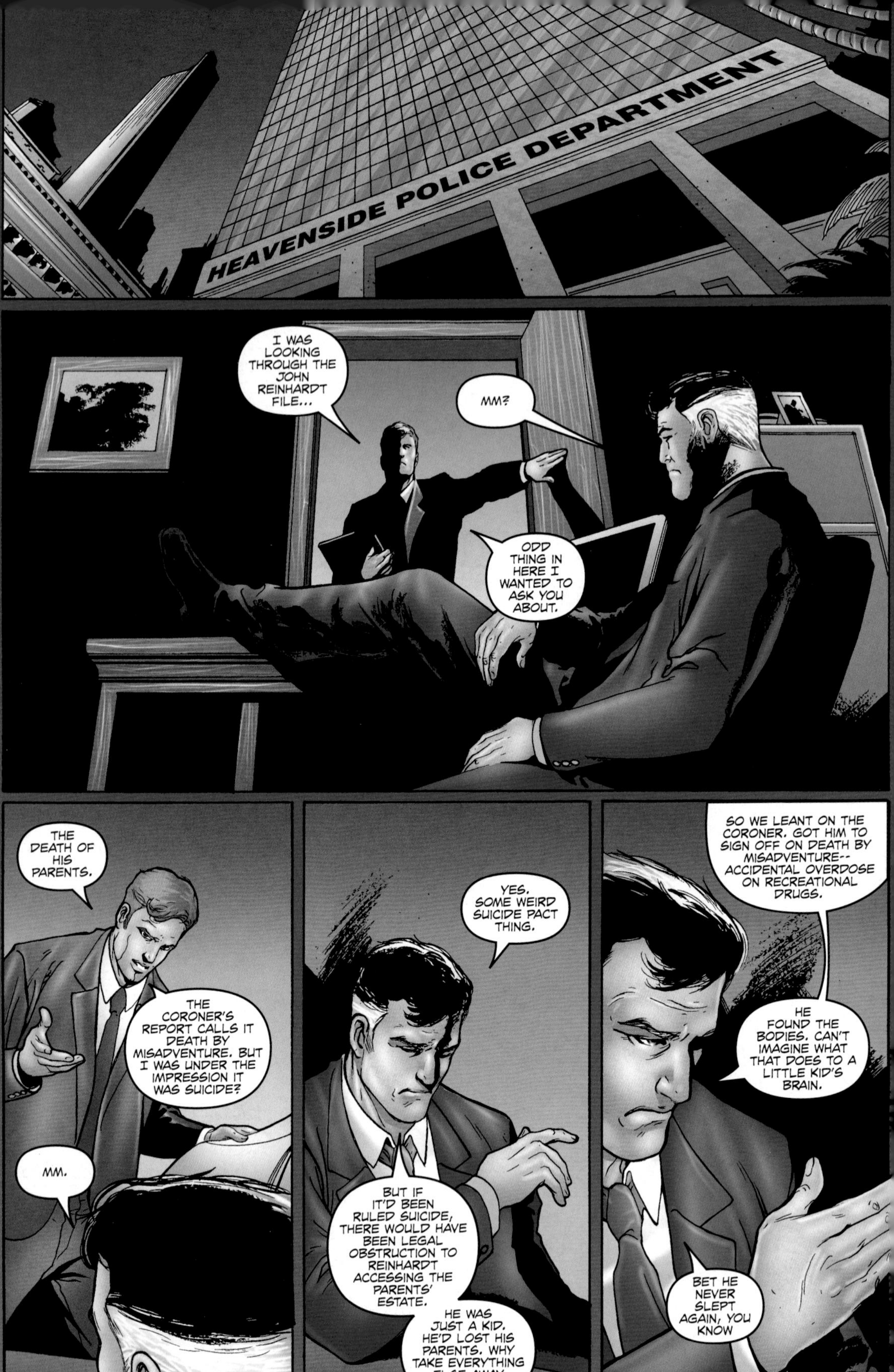
HEAVENSIDE POLICE DEPARTMENT
I WAS LOOKING THROUGH THE JOHN REINHARDT FILE...
MM?
ODD THING IN HERE I WANTED TO ASK YOU ABOUT.
THE DEATH OF HIS PARENTS.
THE CORONER'S REPORT CALLS IT DEATH BY MISADVENTURE. BUT I WAS UNDER THE IMPRESSION IT WAS SUICIDE?
MM.
YES. SOME WEIRD SUICIDE PACT THING.
BUT IF IT'D BEEN RULED SUICIDE, THERE WOULD HAVE BEEN LEGAL OBSTRUCTION TO REINHARDT ACCESSING THE PARENTS' ESTATE.
HE WAS JUST A KID. HE'D LOST HIS PARENTS. WHY TAKE EVERYTHING ELSE AWAY FROM HIM?
SO WE LEANT ON THE CORONER. GOT HIM TO SIGN OFF ON DEATH BY MISADVENTURE-- ACCIDENTAL OVERDOSE ON RECREATIONAL DRUGS.
HE FOUND THE BODIES. CAN'T IMAGINE WHAT THAT DOES TO A LITTLE KID'S BRAIN.
BET HE NEVER SLEPT AGAIN, YOU KNOW
END OF BOOK ONE

H

00-00-669

HENRIK BOEMER

THE DARKENING SKY by Henrik Boemer, a Dutch art professor (1918 - 1976), published by The Fourth International Press 1966. Described as "a new exploration of the philosophy of Fatalism" on its back cover, this short-run paperback combines treatise and fiction in its discussion of cyclical history and its notion that humanity can combine into a perceptual-reality "machine" that can overthrow the tyranny of "time" itself. It's a frequently bizarre, self-sabotaging work that often conflates inevitable, almost Creationist cycles of rise and fall with the Elder Gods of HP Lovecraft, whom Boemer had something of an obsession with. One chapter simply lists the more frightening events in world history that occurred in 1925, the year he estimated that Lovecraft first conceived of his main sequence of horror tales.

Samizdat copies of THE DARKENING SKY have existed into the 21st Century, the few remaining original copies often jealously guarded in private libraries: far outliving Boemer himself, who, after a series of psychotic breaks following the publication of his final book in 1971 (THE EUROPEAN LLOIGOR (Weisen Books), an attack on what he saw as an usurpation of the occult traditions by middle-class European intellectuals like Colin Wilson), hanged himself in a jail cell in Amsterdam on June 6, 1976 following an arrest for public indecency.

The Fourth International was an international organisation of Trotskyist communists, founded in 1938 with Trotsky's backing and informed by his theory and program of "permanent revolution" . The Fourth International suffered two serious splits in the 40s and 50s, and a partial reunification in 1963. It's believed that the short-lived Fourth International Press was a small esoteric-minded splinter group that fell away from the main direction of The United Secretariat of the Fourth International sometime in 1964. They published spottily until late 1966, when they reconfigured as the San Francisco publishing house International Echo.

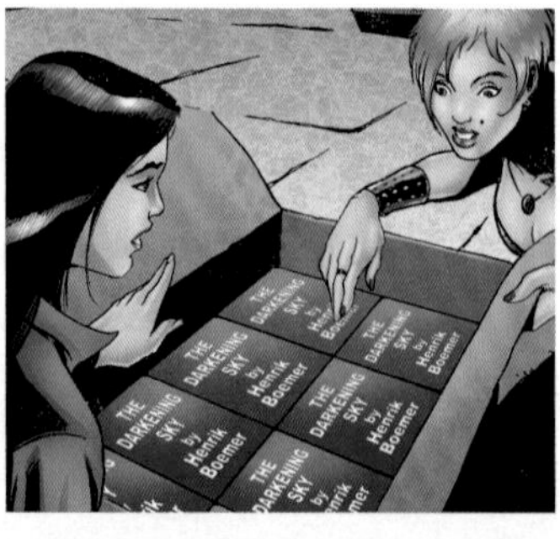
THE DARKENING SKY by Henrik Boemer

article | discussion | view source | history

SHRIEKYWARE

Used almost exclusively by the "Shrieky Girl" subculture, Shriekyware consists of a set of networked receivers and transmitters -- usually two false fingernails or rings, a tongue-ring or false tooth, neckwear and an IM lens (most often a Clatter system). Put together, they form a crude motion-capture unit and haptic interface that allows transmission of simulated touch between wearers. If one Shrieky Girl is taken by the hand, for example, every other Shrieky Girl on the net experiences the same sensation of their hand being held.

CLATTER

Clatter is a wireless IM Lens instant messaging system built on to a soft contact lens. Clatter differs from other, commercial lens services by being open source and "riding" other services to create free cross-platform access.

CLATTER
::Celia
::Mars*
::Key
::Heinz
::DJ AMUN @OFF
::Echo*
08:18am [EST]

Log In / Create Account

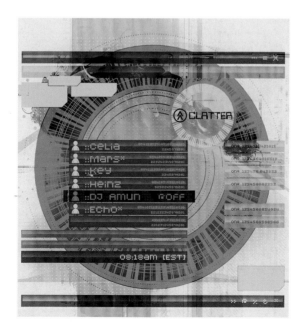

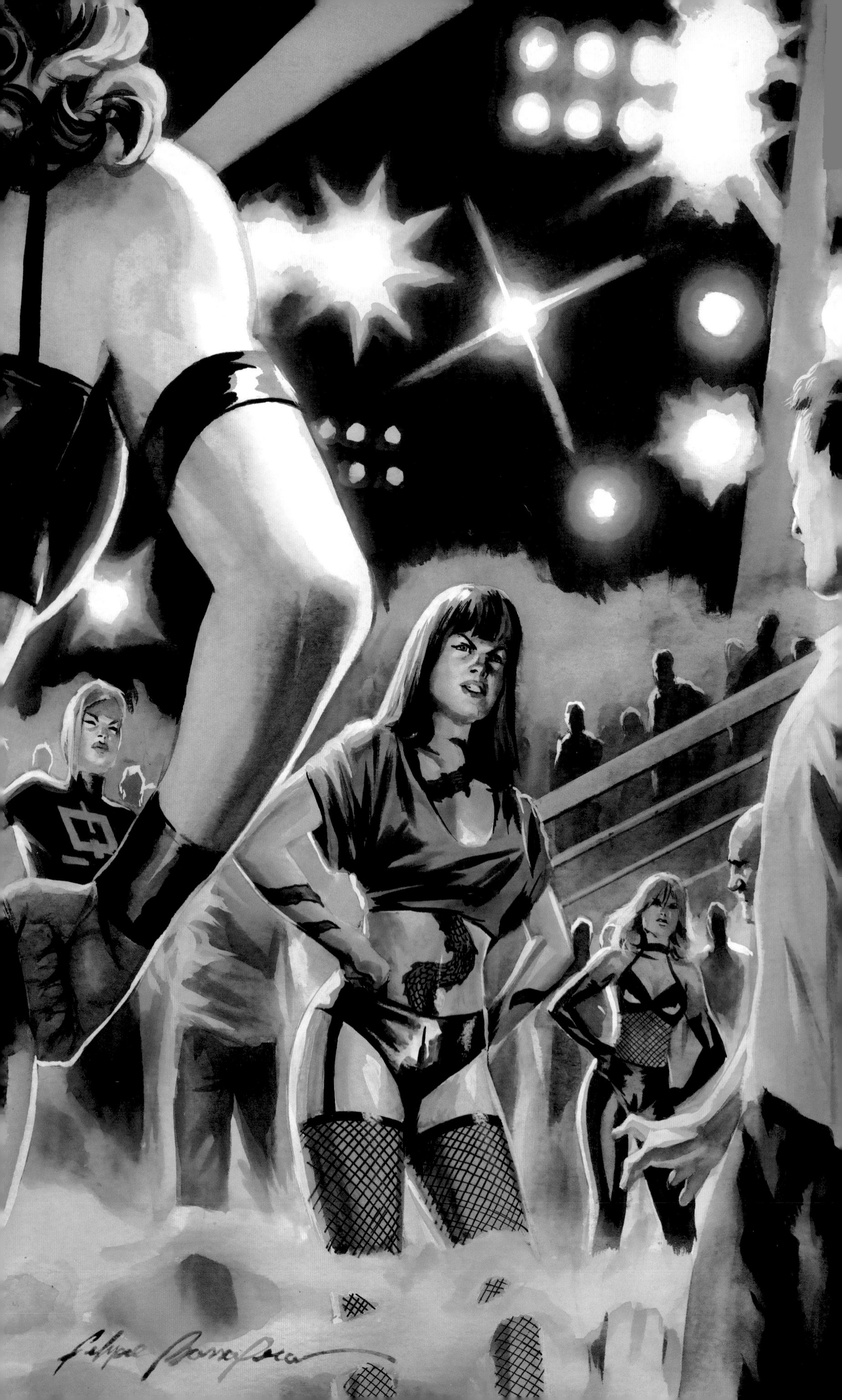

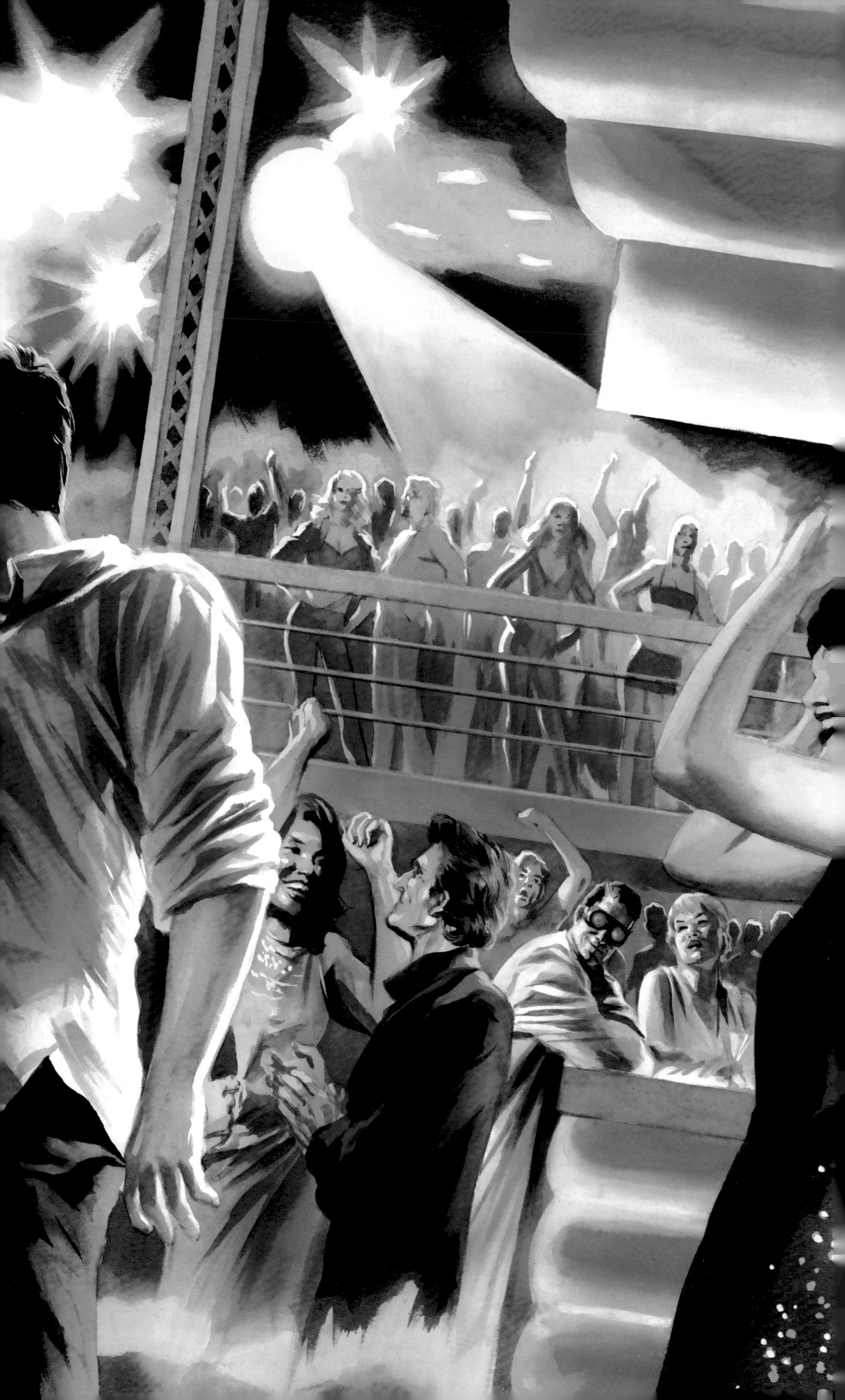

WWW.IMMINENT.SEA

www.imminent.sea was a groupblog -- a magazine-style journalling website created and written by a team of participants -- addressing the state of futurism in this first quarter of the 21st Century. Each writer came from a different discipline or field of interest, creating what was an unusually well-rounded and wide-ranging view of new trends and possible future conditions. In all, thirteen writers contributed to Imminent over its four-year run, with seven people on the groupblog at any one time.   Contributors included criminologist Max Cale, environmentalist Gabrielle Pichette and three pseudonymous writers (sex futurist "Irene Adler," security specialist "Captain Swing" and the human-computer interface expert "Professor Zero").

As suggested above, the site was usually referred to as Imminent. However, the purchase of the .sea domain name, created for the "independent state" of Sealand, was intended to lend the site the name "imminentcy". The site's "about" page says that the idea came from a repeated phrase in Robert Shea & Robert Anton Wilson's ILLUMINATUS! novels -- "immanentising the Eschaton." The page indicated that this was Professor Zero's idea. It means, loosely, "bringing on the end of the world."

Blog metric sites record that Imminent was one of the one hundred most-read and authoritative websites in the world for much of its run. The site went static six months after Professor Zero ceased writing for it, the remaining six authors claiming that he had disappeared and that he'd left software management and other services locked behind encryptions they couldn't break.

Many similar groupblogs sprang up in its wake, but none had the impact of Imminent. In the last few weeks, it has been noted that Imminent-style sites are emerging from the Grinder culture, emanating particularly from the subculture's home in the American city of Heavenside. These sites include Darkening and grinding.be.

CAPTAIN SWING

Captain Swing was one of the earliest examples of a multiple identity or multiple-use name, as later popularised in the 20th Century by the Dadists, Neoists and the Diggers (see "Karen Eliot," "Monty Cantsin," "Luther Blissett," "Emmett Grogan."   Captain Swing was the name signed on many letters and documents during the Swing Riots of 1830 England. These were a series of post-Luddite protests against the industrialisation of agriculture in the rural South and East. The multiple-use name was intended to protect the more violent wing of the protest movement, which was unusually organised. More than a thousand people eventually met some form of punishment in regard to Swing, a number including 19 executions.

 Log In / Create Account

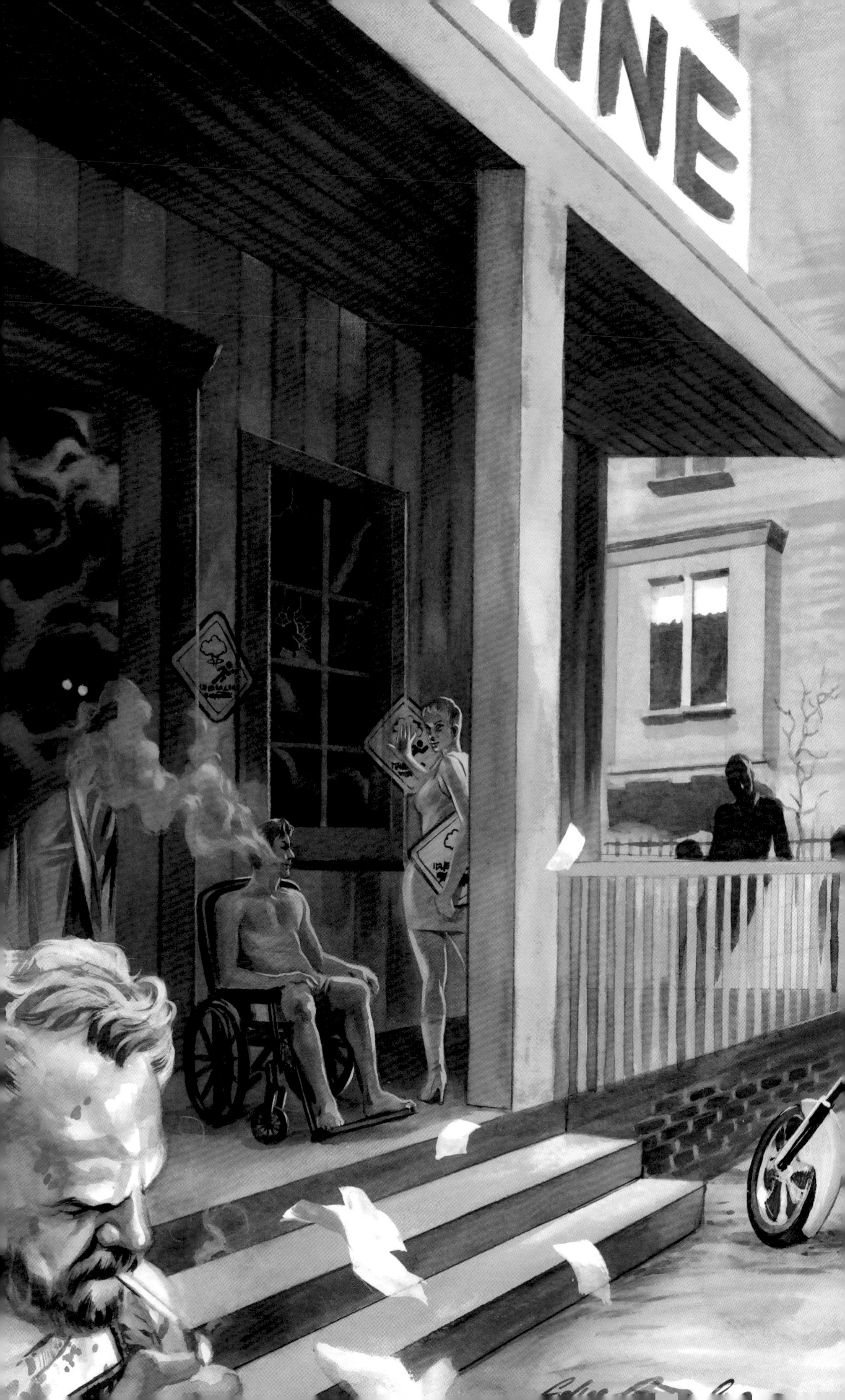
INE

CATASTROPHE BOOKS

Catastrophe Books was founded five years ago by [John Reinhardt](#) and [Sing Watson](#) as a source for alternative culture. Reinhardt bought the building and provided a standing fund for utilities and other bills, and Watson, whose vision the store was, is the legal owner.

Today, Watson is the sole proprietor. A fraction of the original fund remains, and Watson pays the bills and draws a wage from the store's thin profits in order to keep that fraction as a buffer.

Catastrophe Books serves today as both bookstore and a focal point for what remains of alternative culture in Heavenside. It and its attached coffee shop are a meeting point and salon of sorts, although a pale echo of what the place was five years ago.

(What street is it located on? Who have you seen there?)

ST. THERESA

St. Theresa of Avila was an important Christian mystic of the 1500s. Intensely devout from a young age, she attempted to martyr herself at the hands of the Moors at age seven. Theresa became a nun at age nineteen, and soon after fell ill. This sickness commenced a lifetime of experiencing spiritual ecstasies and divine visions, including but not limited to an angel repeatedly penetrating her heart with a flaming lance. This was the inspiration for Gian Lorenzo Bernini's famed sculpture "The Ecstacy Of St. Theresa."

She died on the cusp of the shift from the Julian to the Gregorian Calendar in Spain in 1582 – hence, her time of death may be said to not exist in Catholic chronology, falling as it may within the several days excised from the calendar in order to correct the shift.

 Log In / Create Account

of use for doktorsleepless.com   This page has been accessed 75,447 times.   This page was last modified 19:24, 6 J

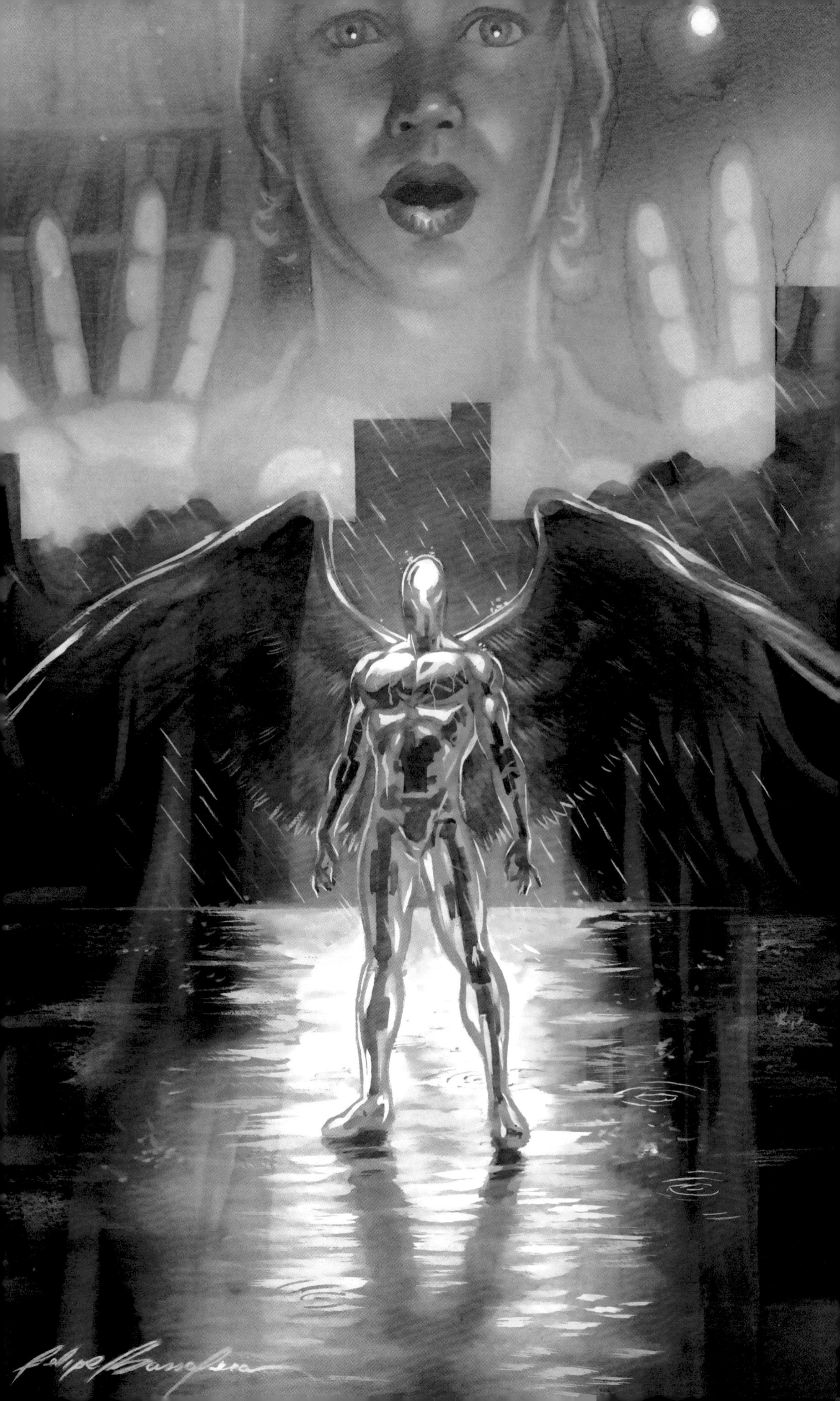

ENDTRODUCTION

Listen, I don't have a hell of a lot of time here, because we go to press in less than 24 hours – as I write this, it's July 5, George Melly just died and scientists in Cambridge just announced human trials of an artificial pancreas – so I'm going to have to make this quick.

What preceded this piece was the Datashadow for DOKTOR SLEEPLESS. It lives both here, in the back of each episode, and on http://www.doktorsleepless.com. I'm adding to the website – which is built on something called a wiki, an editable hyperlinked collaborative encyclopedia emulator – as I go. Entries will appear here, and more entries will appear at the wiki. And you can add to them too. Everything in DOKTOR SLEEPLESS is connected. Feel free to add entries for anything you see in the book that isn't already up there. Update entries as more information becomes available. If you want to just read, that's fine too. Once you get home from your local comics pusher, check out the Datashadow – you'll find a fair old chunk of stuff on there already.

The Datashadow isn't the only place on the web where content is hidden, by the way.

You can find a message board at http://www.freakangels.com/whitechapel. You can find me at warrenellis@gmail.com, an address I check once a week for DOKTOR SLEEPLESS email. This "backmatter" area will expand next issue with more Datashadow material and… things. Yes. Many things.

The playlist for this issue was mostly Nic Endo, Mephistosystem, Panda Bear, Burial and the Besnard Lakes.

-- Warren Ellis

 Log In / Create Account

COVER GALLERY

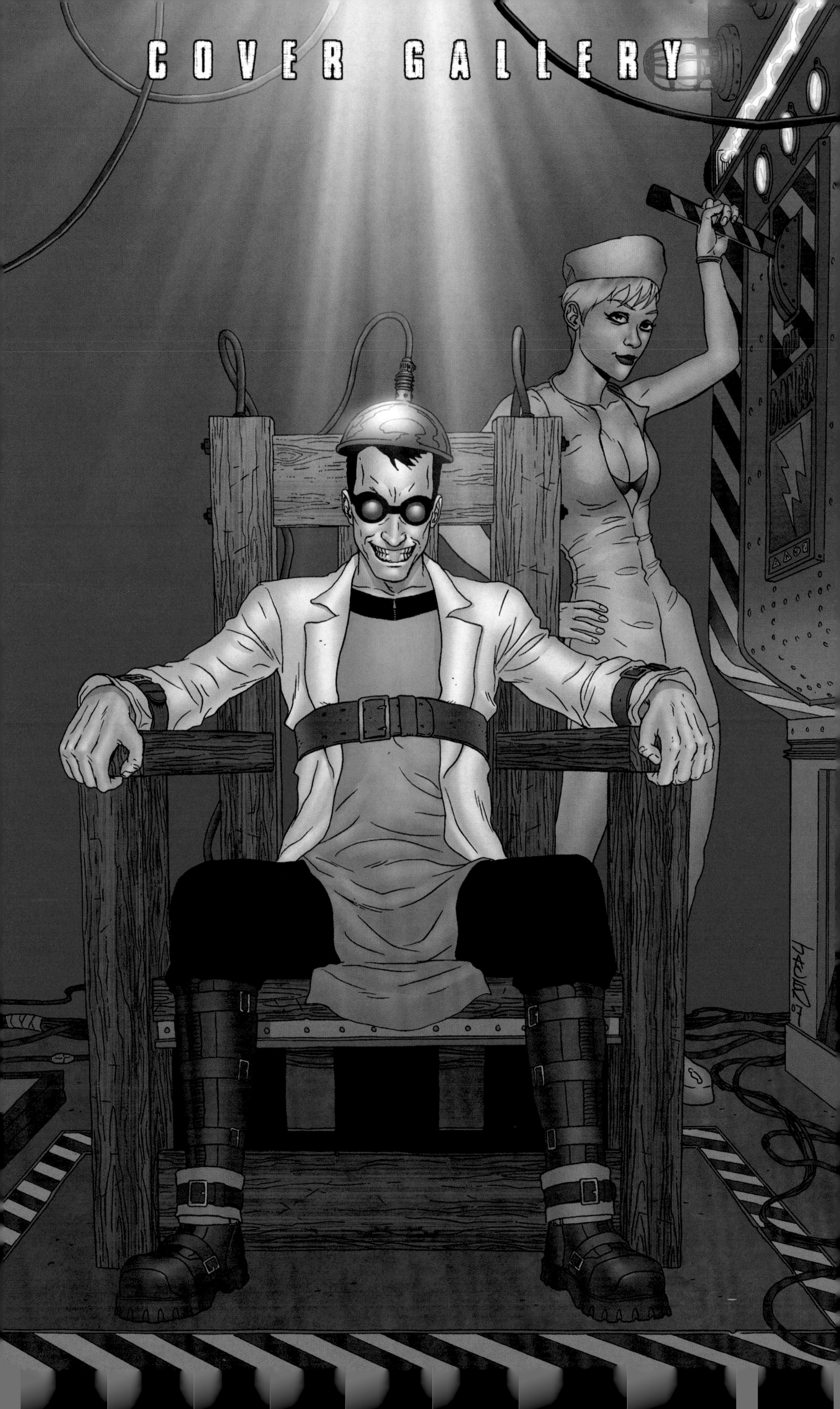

DANGER

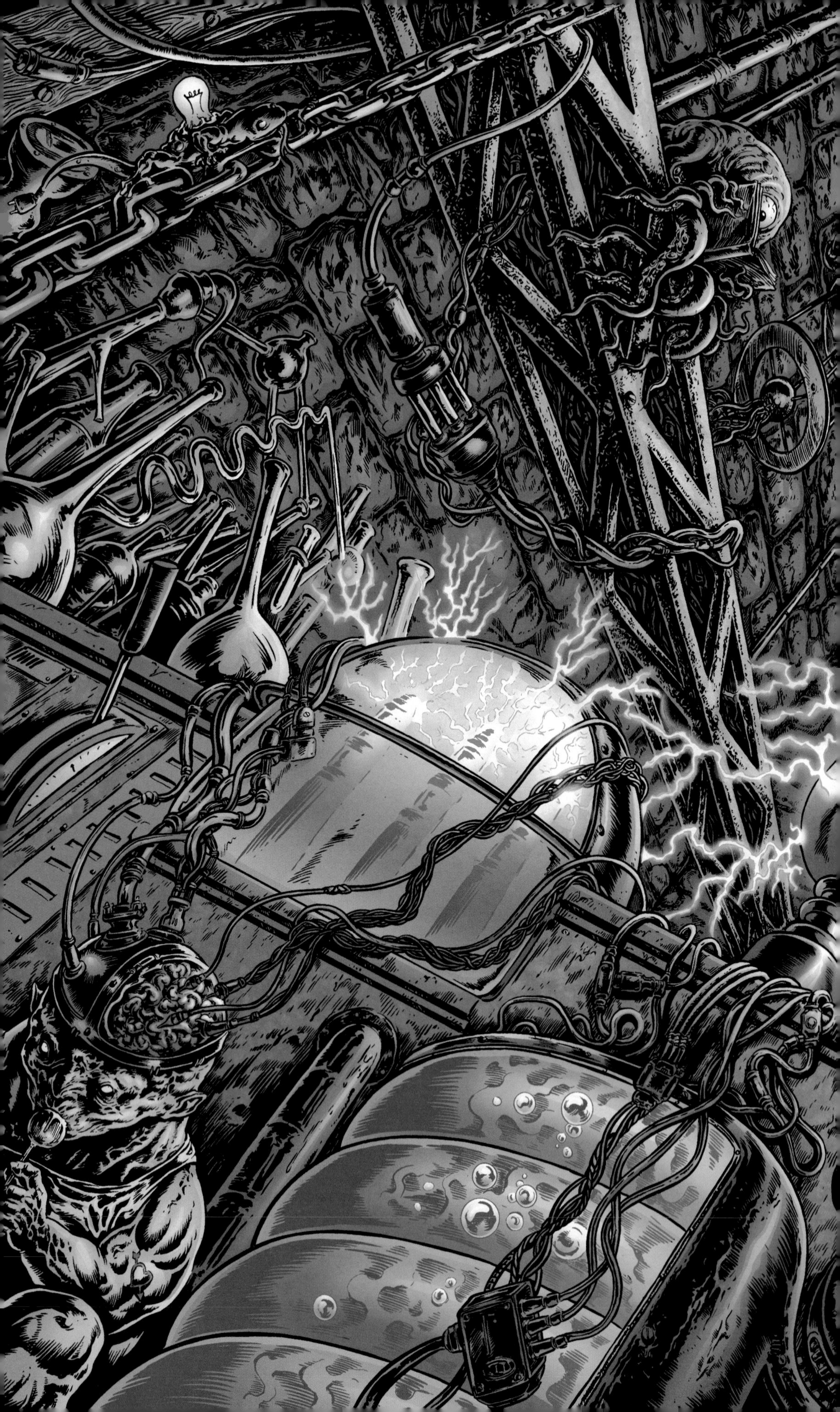

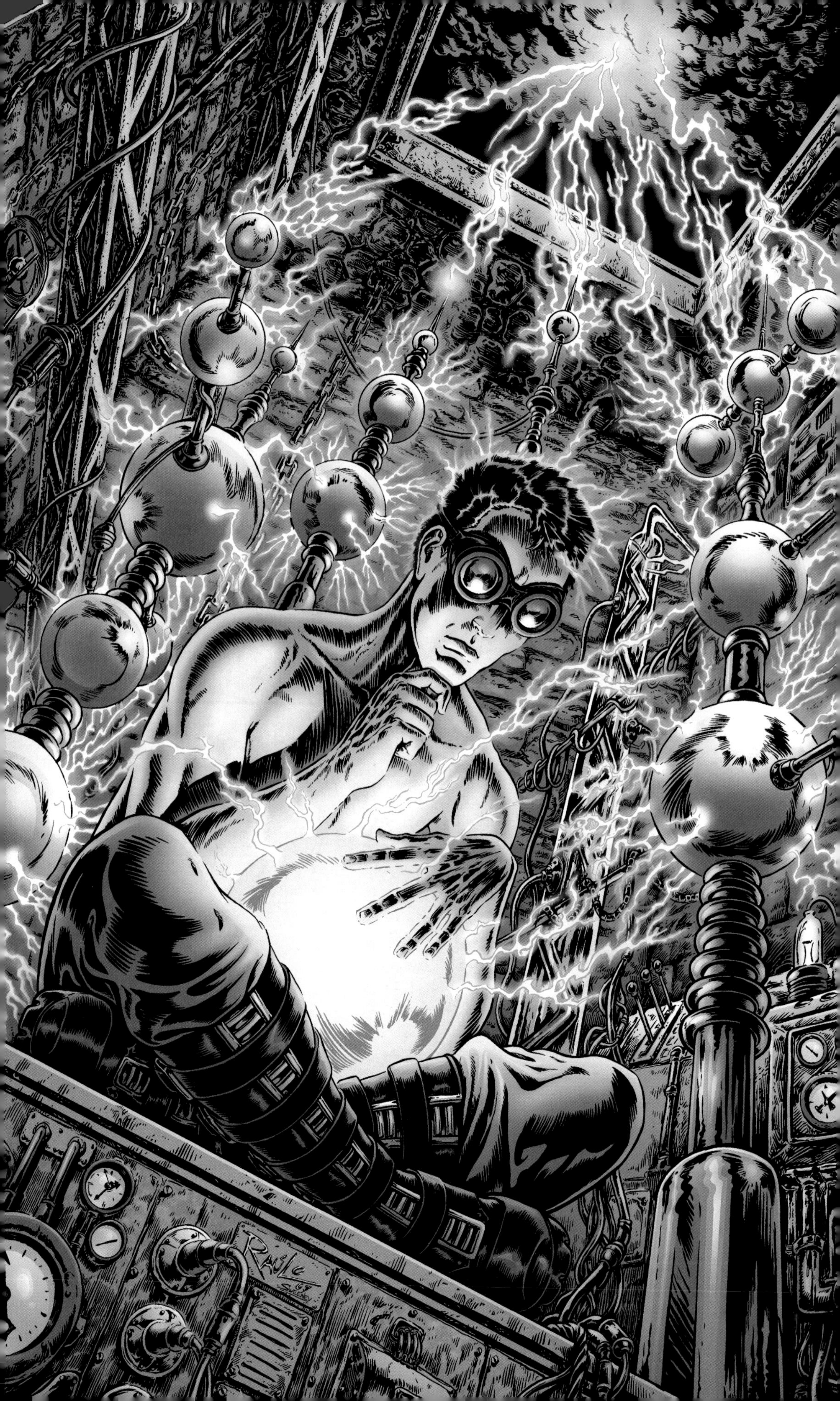

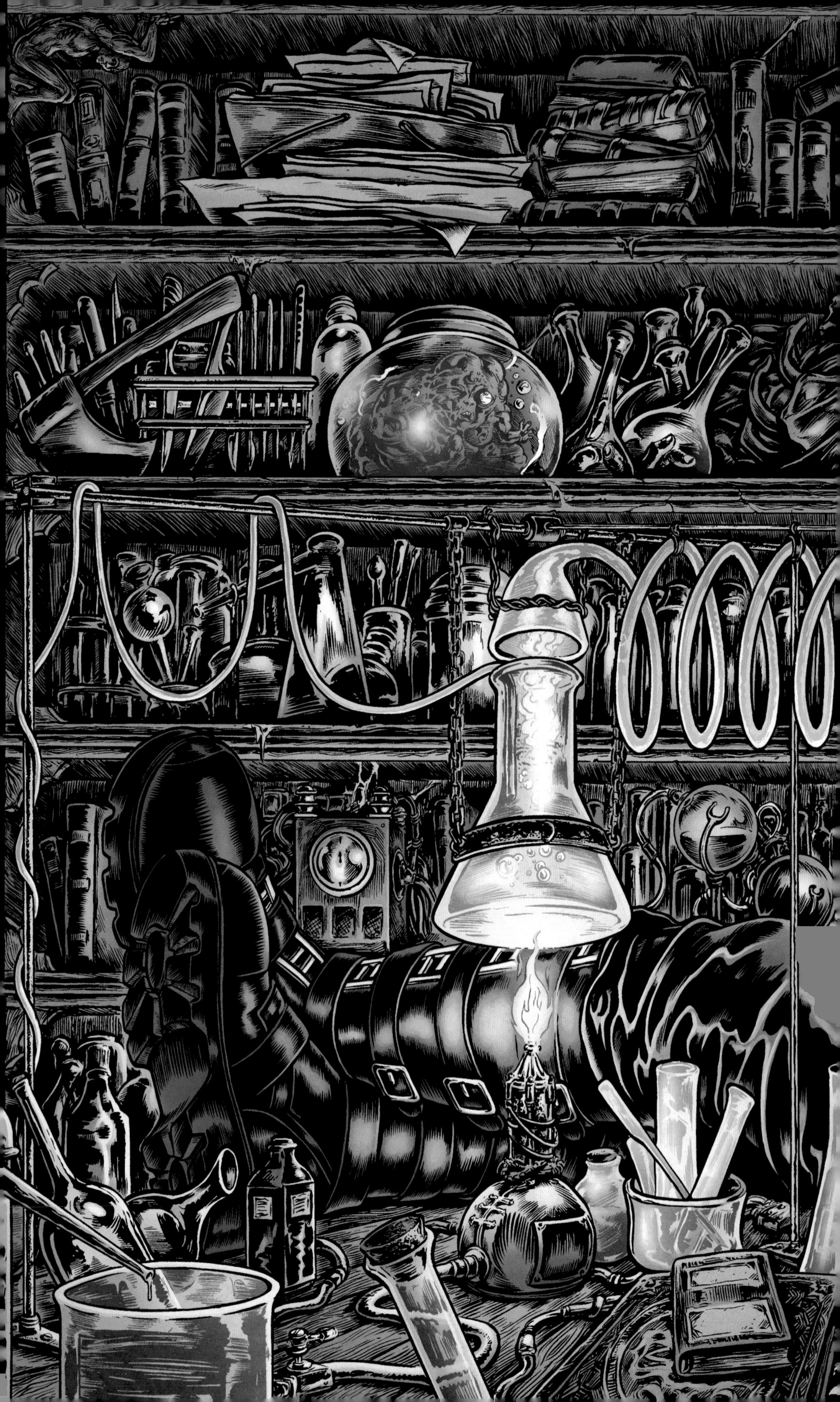

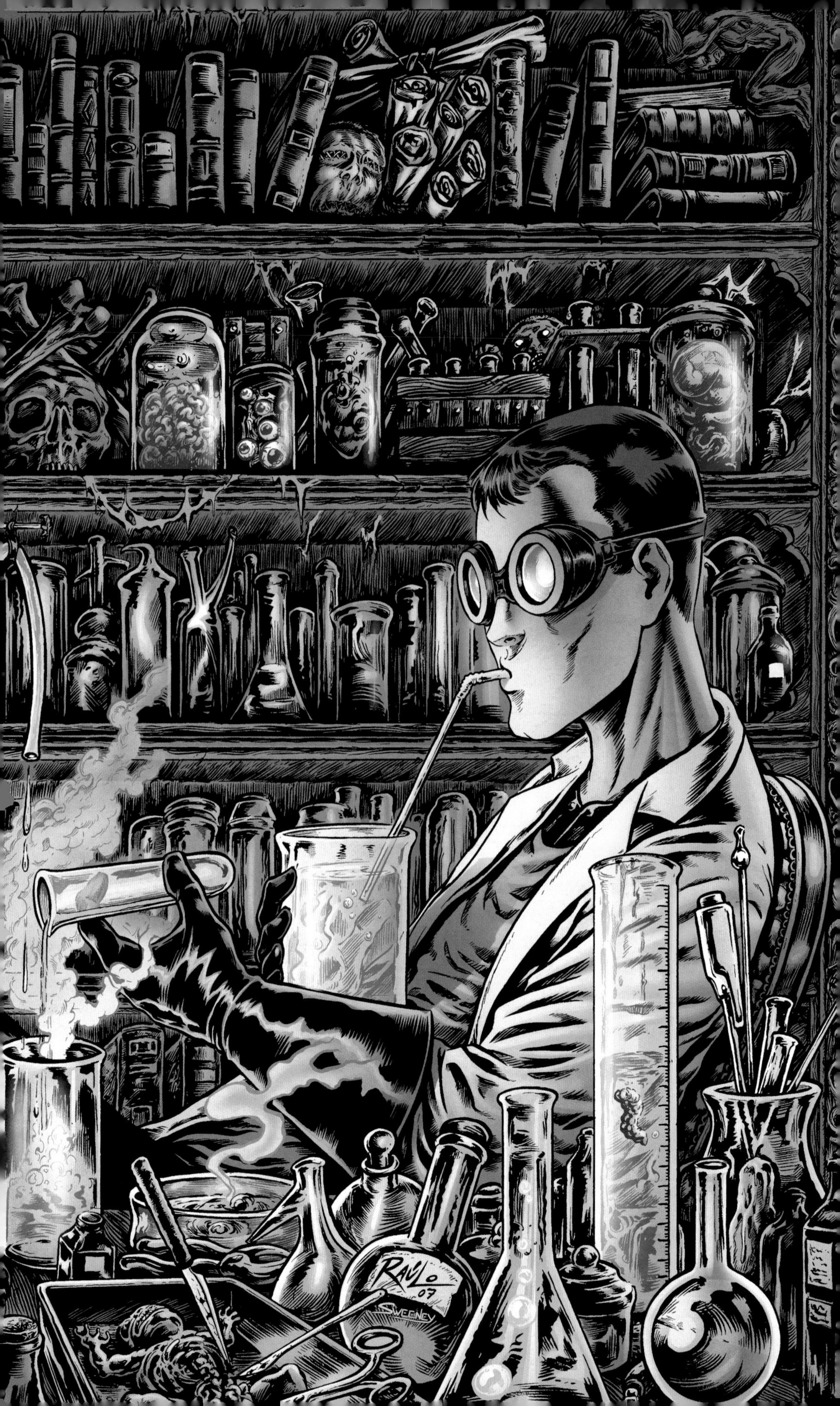
RAULO 07
SWEENEY

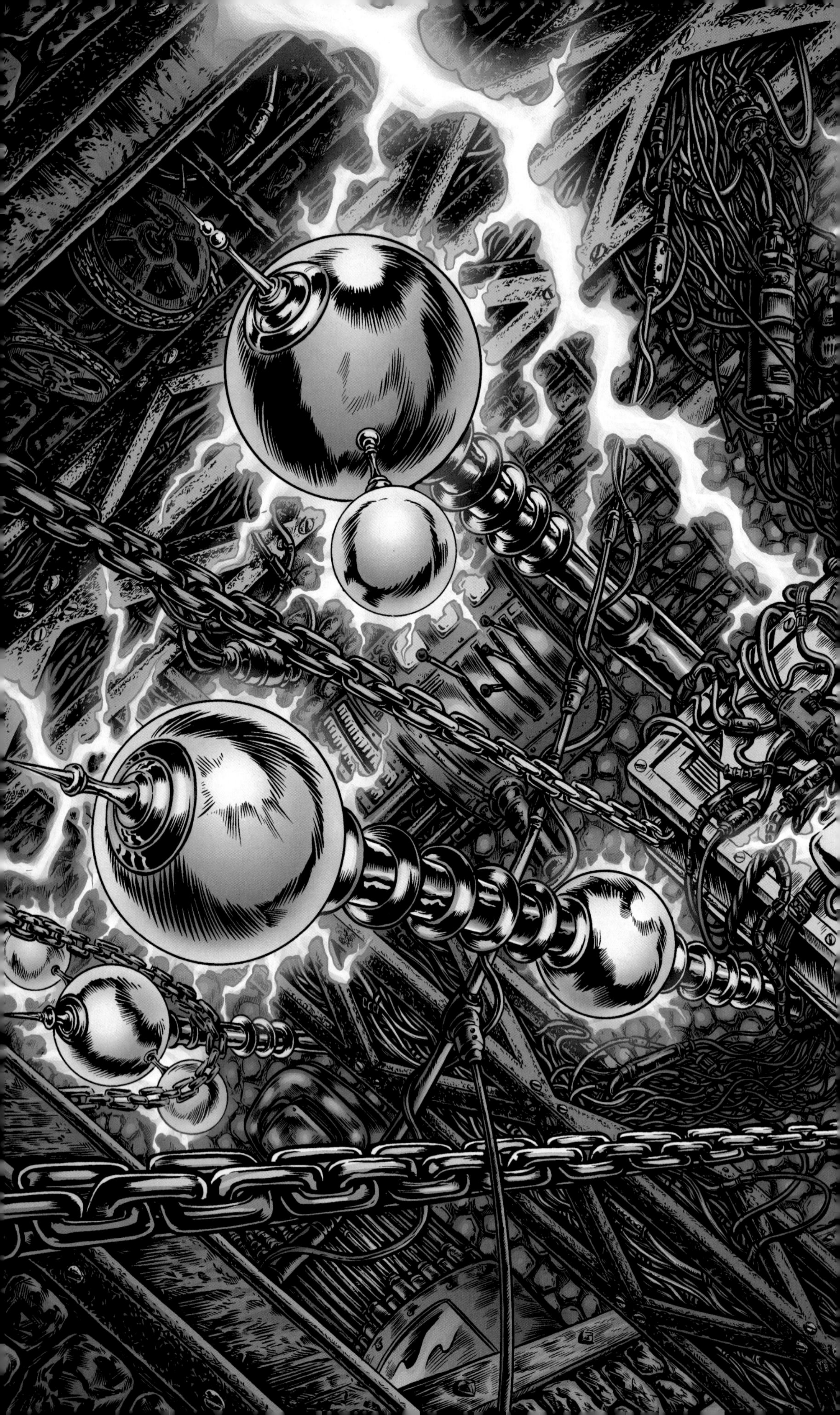

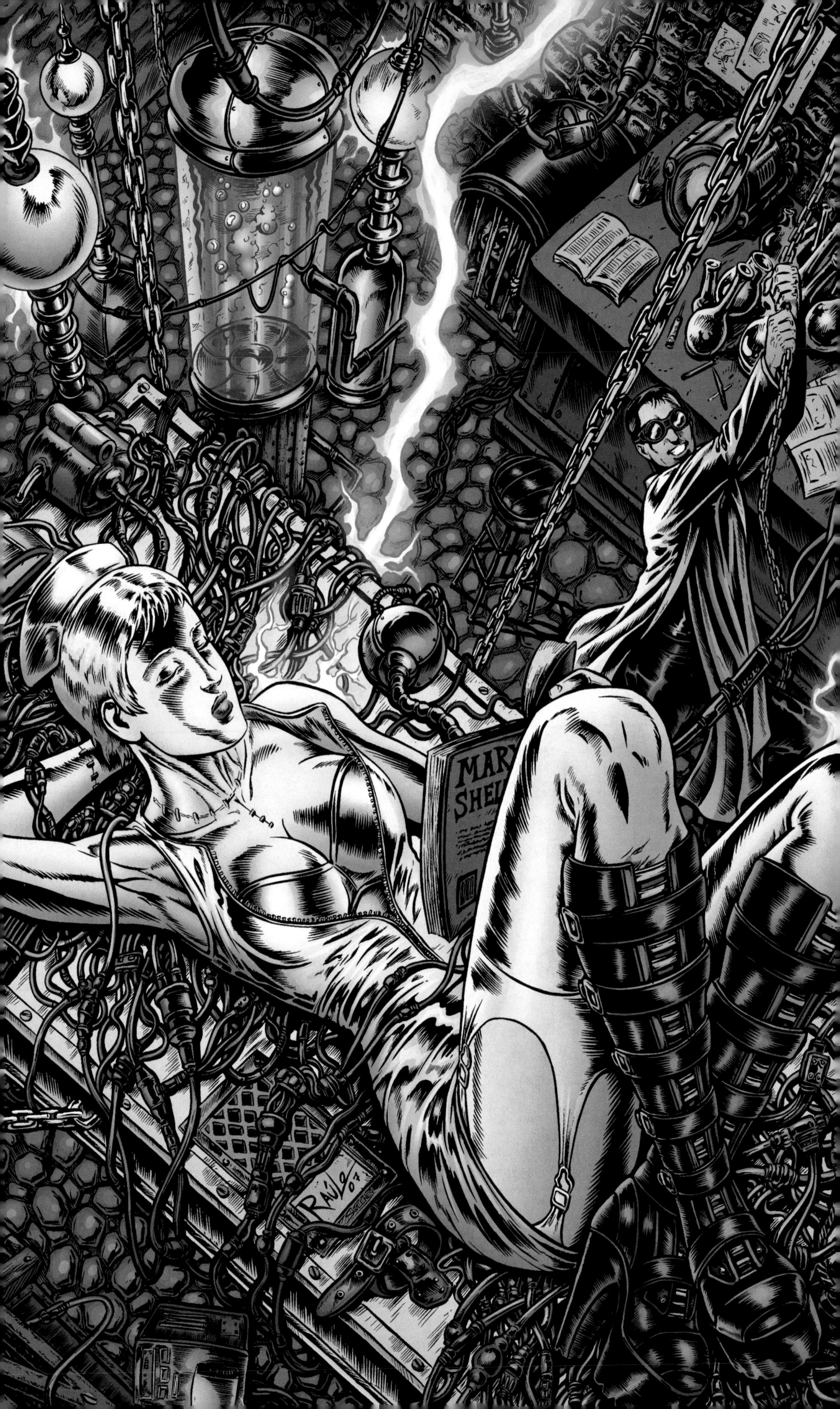

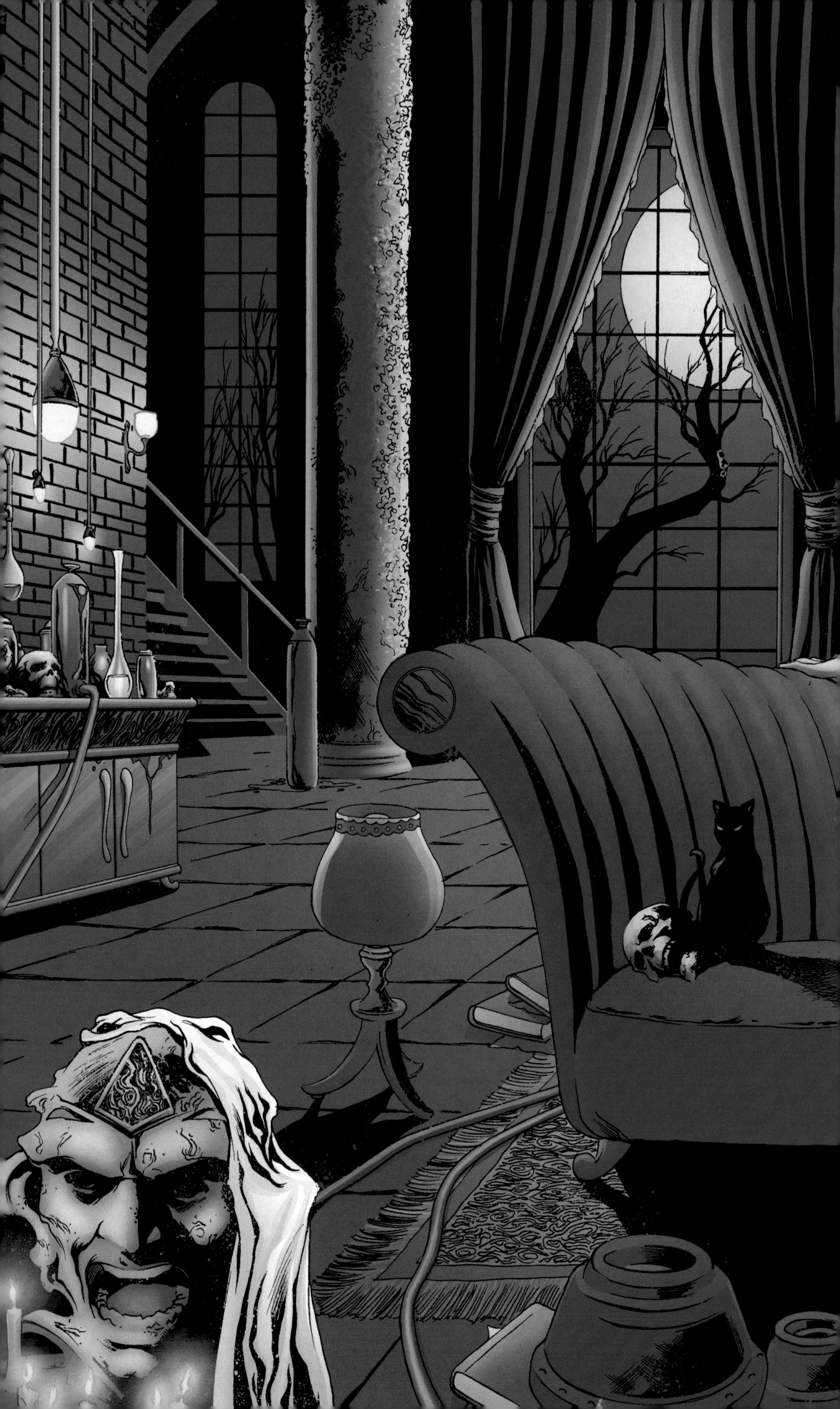

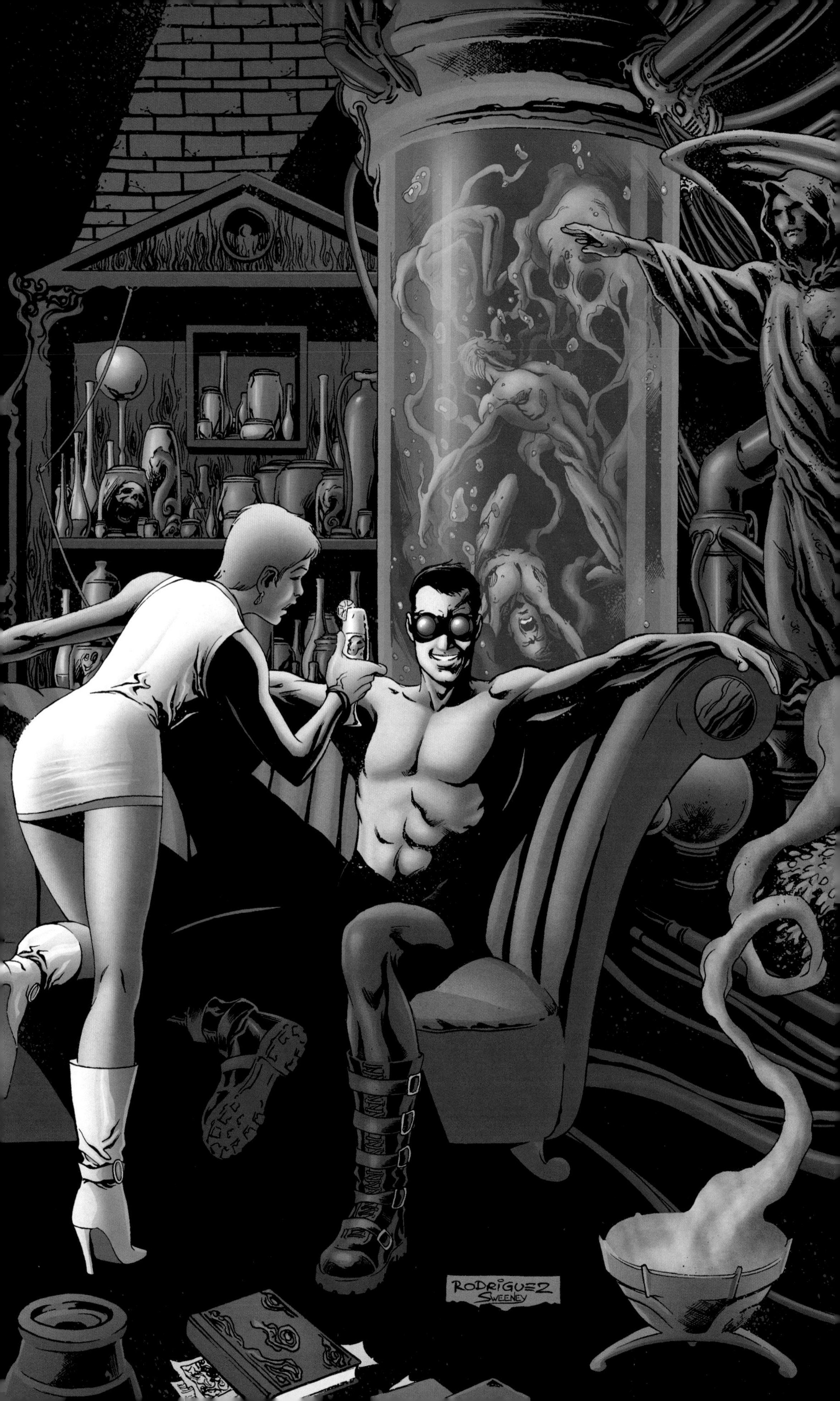
RODRIGUEZ
SWEENEY

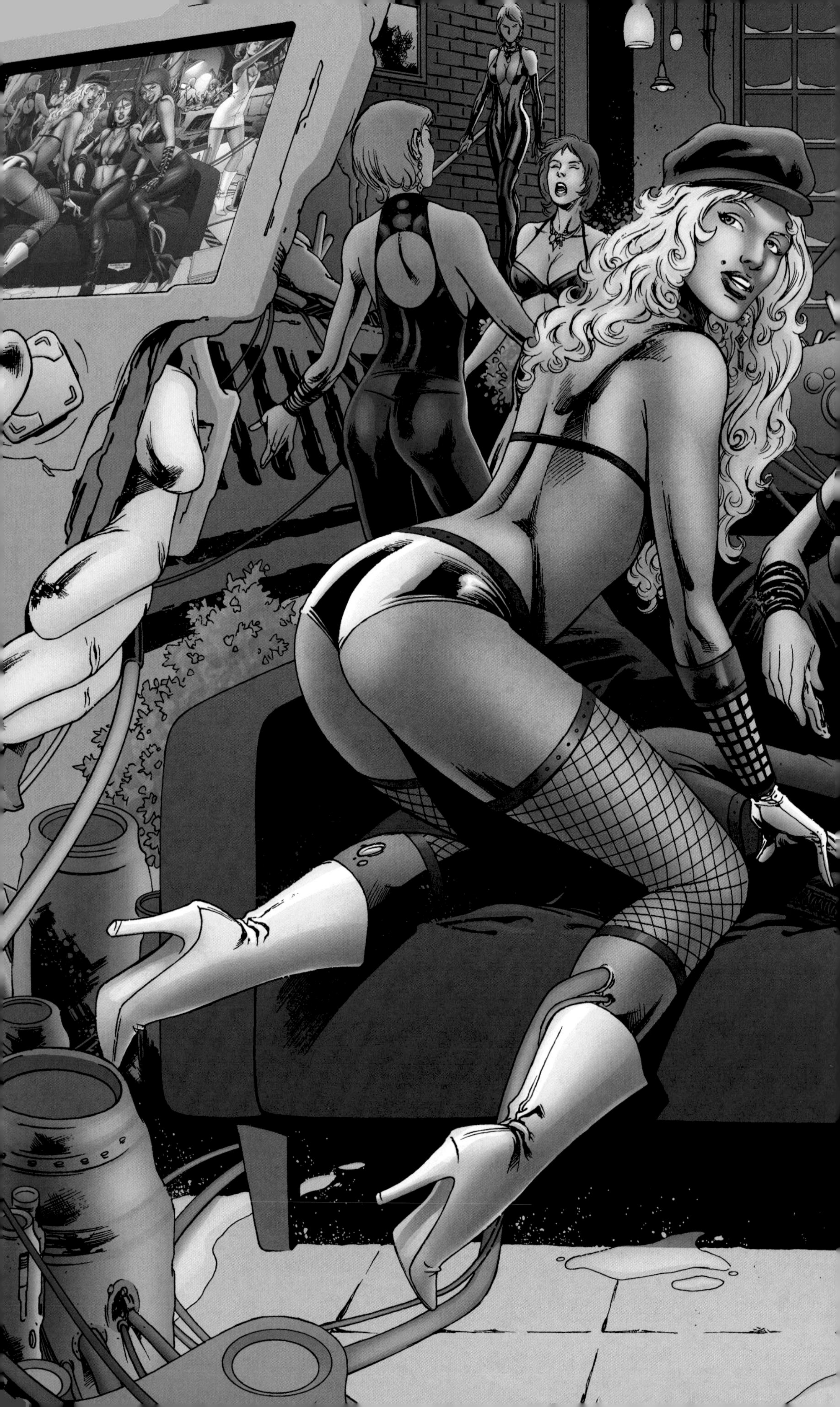

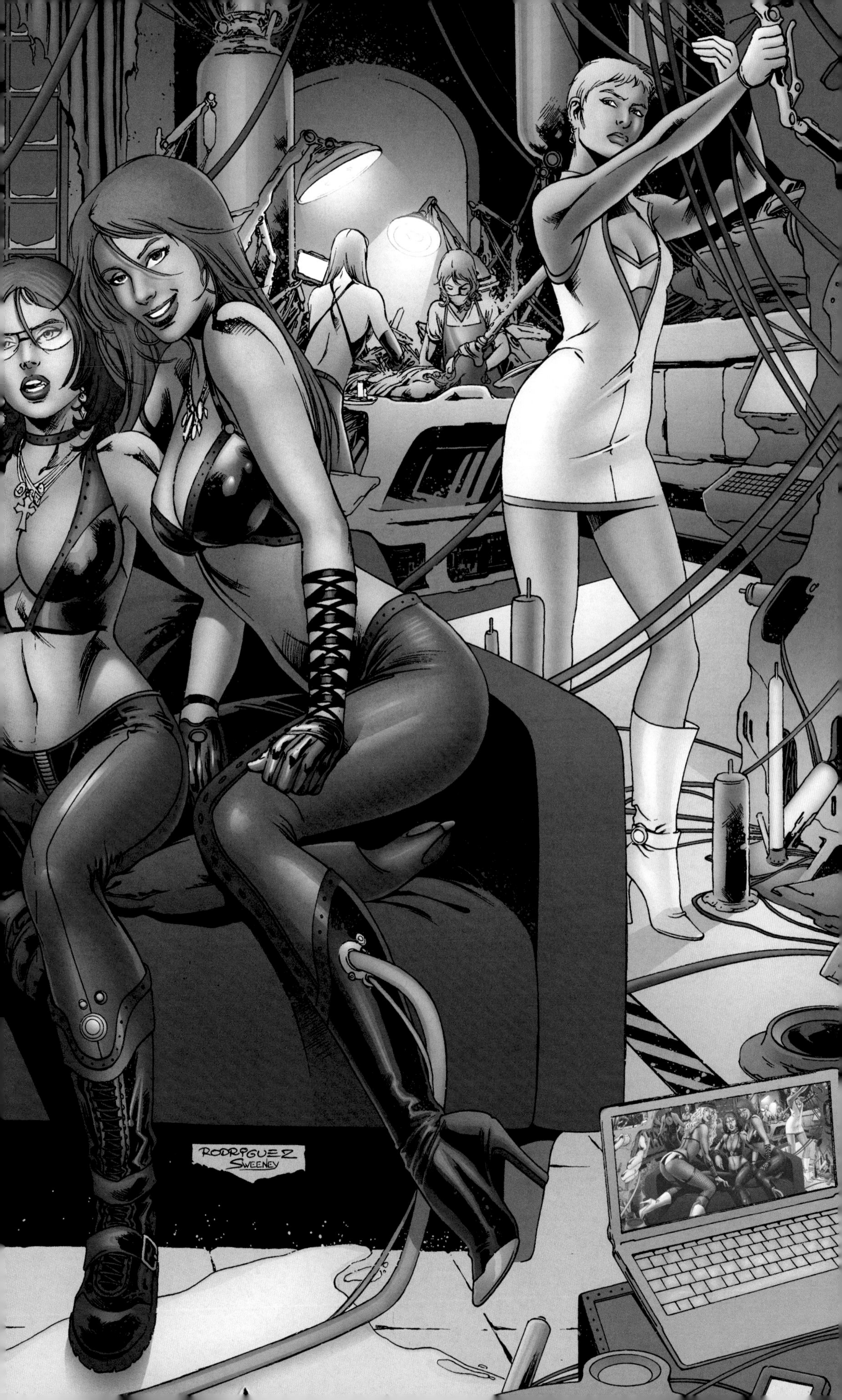
RODRIGUEZ
SWEENEY

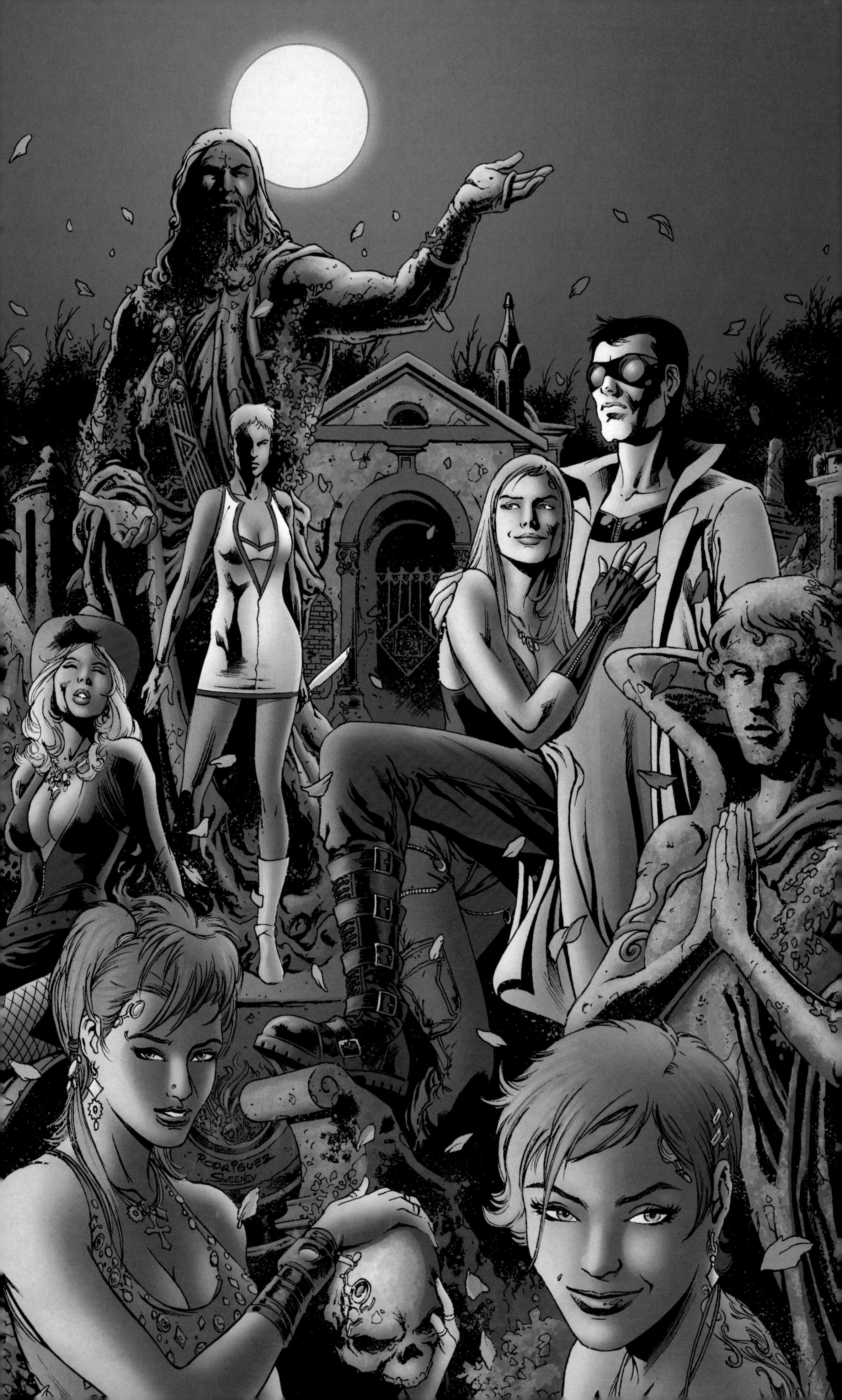
RODRIGUEZ
SWEENEY

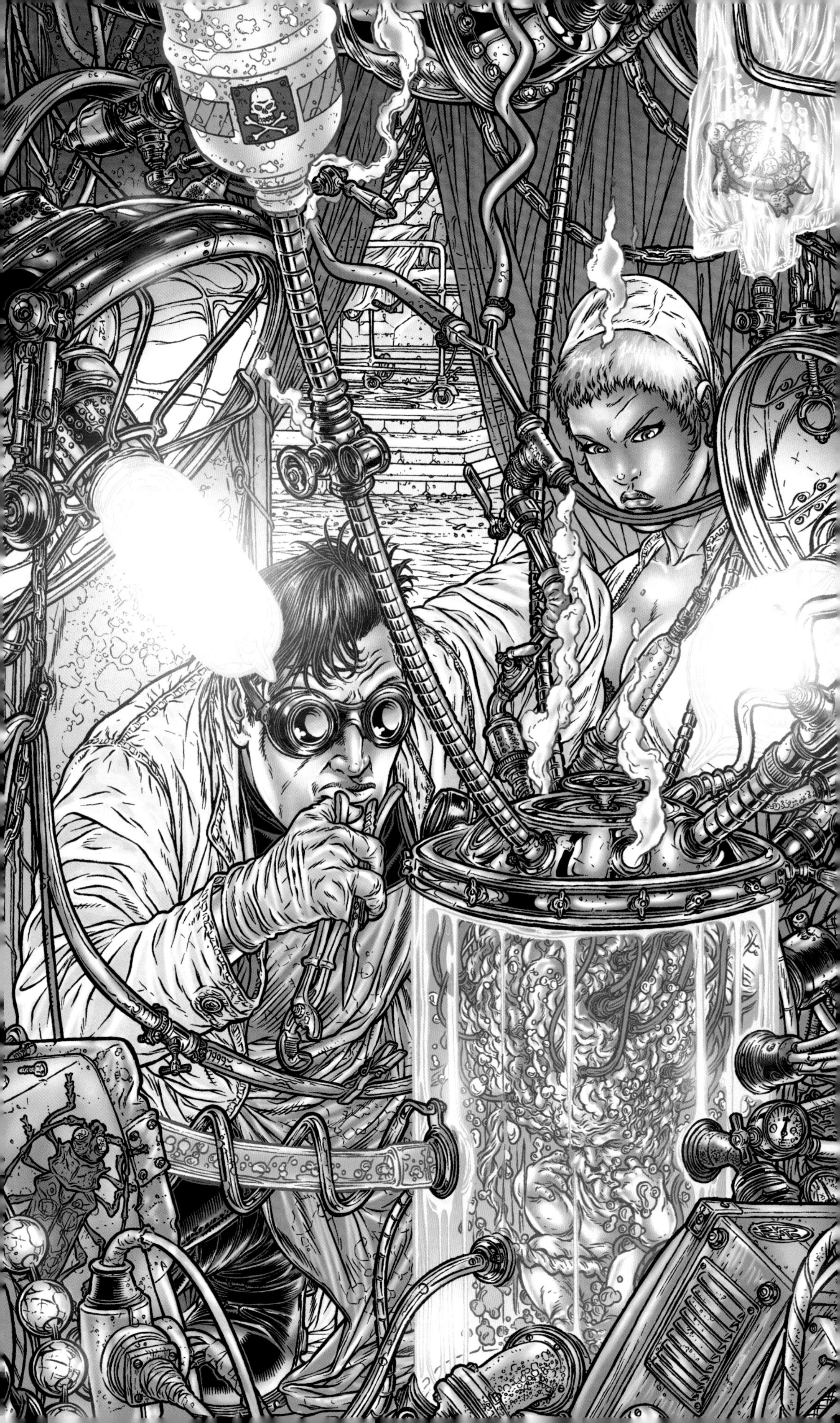

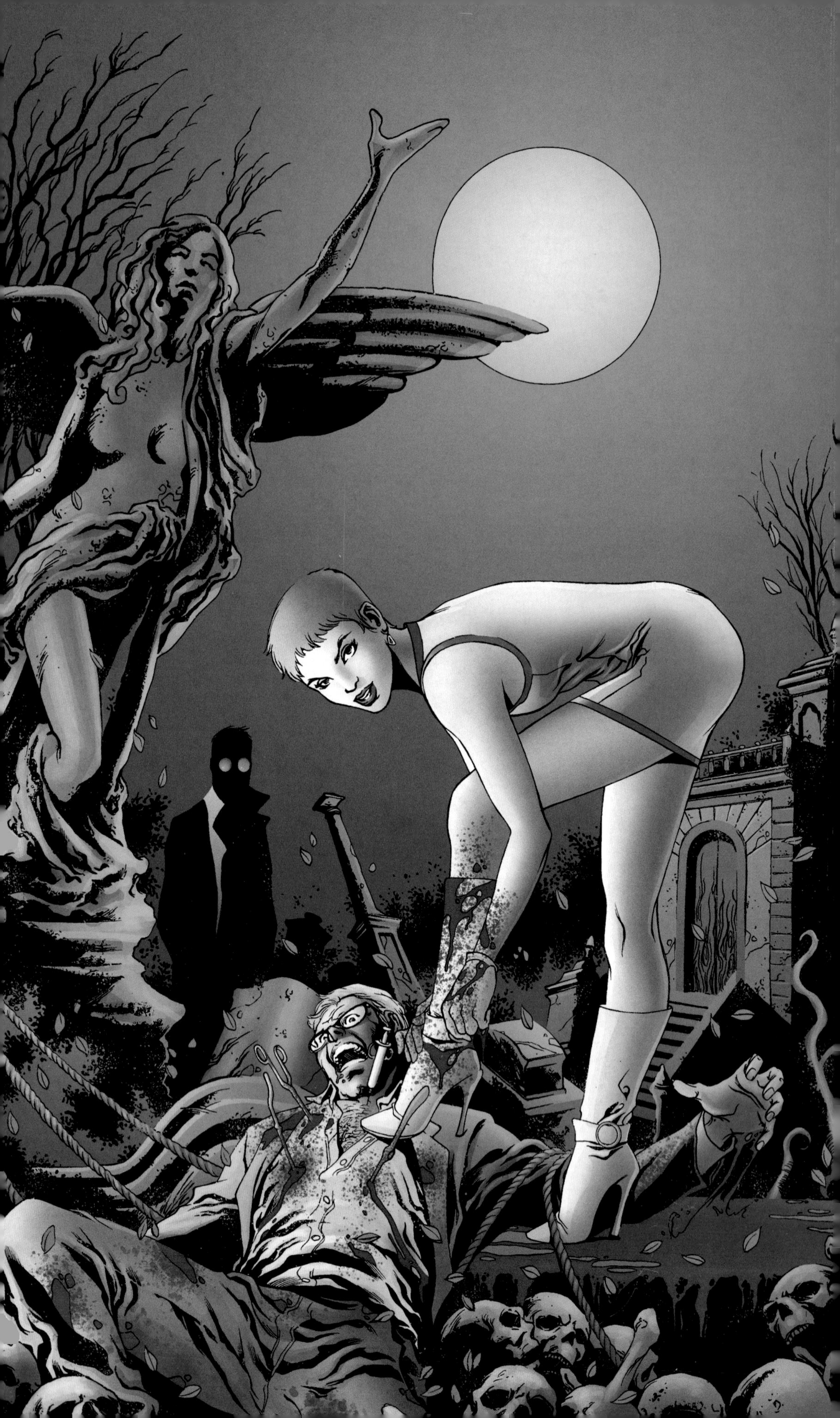